Detroit's
Hidden
Channels

Detroit's Hidden Channels

The Power of French-Indigenous
Families in the Eighteenth Century

Karen L. Marrero

MICHIGAN STATE UNIVERSITY PRESS | *East Lansing*

Michigan State University Press
East Lansing, Michigan 48823-5245

LIBRARY OF CONGRESS CATALOGING-IN-PUBLICATION DATA
Names: Marrero, Karen L., author.
Title: Detroit's hidden channels : the power of French-Indigenous families
in the eighteenth century / Karen L. Marrero.
Description: East Lansing : Michigan State University Press, [2020]
| Includes bibliographical references and index.
Identifiers: LCCN 2019028370 | ISBN 978-1-61186-359-8 (cloth) | ISBN 978-1-60917-634-1 (PDF)
| ISBN 978-1-62895-396-1 (ePub) | ISBN 978-1-62896-397-7 (Kindle)
Subjects: LCSH: French—Michigan—Detroit—History—18th century.
| Indians of North America—Mixed descent—Michigan—Detroit—History—19th century.
| Families—Michigan—Detroit—History—18th century.
| Kinship—Michigan—Detroit—History—18th century.
| Social networks—Michigan—Detroit—History—18th century.
| Detroit (Mich.)—History—18th century. | Detroit (Mich.)—Ethnic relations—18th century.
Classification: LCC F574.D49 F863 2020 | DDC 305.8009774/3409033—dc23
LC record available at https://lccn.loc.gov/2019028370

Book design by Charlie Sharp, Sharp Designs, East Lansing, Michigan
Cover design by Erin Kirk New
Cover art: Map of the western end of Lake Erie, Lake St. Clair, and the St. Clair River, 1813.
William L. Clements Library, University of Michigan, Map Division, 5-K-1813-Ma.

Visit Michigan State University Press at *www.msupress.org*

Contents

.

For my mother
Diana LaBute Marrero—
I miss you with
une nostalgie incomparable

.

Acknowledgments

I don't think I was fully aware until very recently that this book has two histories. The first and most obvious is what can be read in its pages—an examination of French and Indigenous families of eighteenth-century Detroit. The second history, however, is more subterranean and invisible to the reader. It is embedded in every word and is testimony to the process by which this book came together and to pivotal people, events, and locations in my life. It has altered me in ways I could never have imagined but which now seem preordained. I honor this process, but most importantly, I honor the people who have made it possible.

After its completion in an earlier iteration as a dissertation, there was a period during which it seemed that this project and my momentum in general had stalled. It was a time of profound challenges in my life, including the passing of my beloved mother. But there were people who may not have realized then or fully realize now how important they were in keeping me engaged with this work and my life-of-the-mind in general. They cheered and encouraged me, provided opportunities to speak and write, and listened. For this I thank Ginny Bales, Catherine Cangany, Jay Gitlin, Adriana Greci-Green, and Susan Sleeper-Smith. Tracy Steen coached me to the completion of the dissertation and this book and shared in my trials and tribulations through the years. She knows what it means to me to be closing this chapter and to be eagerly anticipating what comes next.

Once fully reengaged with my scholarship, I continued to benefit from opportunities that kept me moving forward. I was awarded the Earhart Foundation on American History Post-Doctoral Fellowship from the William L. Clements Library at the University of Michigan, which made it possible for me and my husband (and our two new kittens) to spend a glorious summer in Ann Arbor. I had been lucky to have received a Jacob M. Price visiting fellowship at the Clements early in my days as a doctoral student, and I was thrilled to be returning to my favorite research library. My thanks to Terese Austin, Anne Bennington-Helber, Shneen Coldiron, Brian Dunnigan, Clayton Lewis, and Valerie Proehl for making my experience there uplifting on many levels.

The Clements opportunity had brought me tantalizingly closer to my home on the Windsor/Detroit, Canada/U.S. border. Just a few years later, a life-affirming event would take me the rest of the way. Against all the odds of a tough job market and with the support of Ginny Bales, Catherine Cangany, John Demos, Johnny Faragher, Jay Gitlin, Adriana Greci-Green, and Nancy Shoemaker, I crossed my fingers and prepared myself for an interview for a tenure-track position in the Department of History at Wayne State University. I felt instantly comfortable with committee members Marc Kruman, Jennifer Hart, Janine Lanza, and Sandra Van Burkleo and even more convinced that I wanted to become part of the community of historians at WSU. My subsequent visit to campus and interactions with gracious faculty and graduate students sealed the deal for me. I am grateful to Marc for making my transition to Wayne possible and to the faculty for inviting me to join them. My thanks to Eric Ash, John Bukowczyk, Jorge Chinea, Liz Faue, Jennifer Hart, Hans Hummer, Paul Kershaw, Tracy Neumann, Andrew Port, Aaron Retish, Sylvia Taschka, and Sandra Van Burkleo, who went out of their way to make me and my husband Michael feel welcome.

A strong community of exceptional women scholars and administrators in the Departments of History and Anthropology have cheered and encouraged me and helped me in many ways. I'm proud to be among their number. I am grateful to Liz Faue, Liette Gidlow, Jennifer Hart, Yuson Jung, Janine Lanza, Betsy Lublin, Tracy Neumann, Jessica Robbins, Marsha Richmond, Krysta Ryzewski, Sylvia Taschka, Sandra Van Burkleo, and Kidada Williams for this support and their good example. I could not have negotiated all there has been to learn about our department and students without the guidance and good humor of Gayle McCreedy, another multitalented woman. I am also thankful to Marilyn Vaughn, who helped me navigate departmental procedures.

I am immensely appreciative of our department's current chair, Liz Faue, who has been unceasingly and unfailingly generous in her encouragement and validation. Janine Lanza became a mentor before I had met her in person and has continued to offer advice and support while providing a kind and understanding listening ear. Tracy Neumann has dedicated large chunks of her time to advise me on a myriad of matters pertaining to the University and our profession that I have thoroughly enjoyed. Knowing full well I was loath to ask for help, she anticipated my needs and unstintingly shared materials and insights that have been essential to my progress. Kidada Williams offered sage advice and encouragement and devoted time to helping me navigate the complexities of departmental and university systems which was especially crucial in my first few years.

My scholarly community has been the greatest benefit of my life as a professional academic. I have learned from, exchanged ideas with, and been uplifted by exceptional thinkers, including Daryl Baldwin, Ned Blackhawk, Catherine Cangany, Sara Chapman Williams, Leslie Choquette, Christian Crouch, Katherine Grandjean, Paul Grant-Costa, Allan Greer, Adriana Greci-Green, Rob Harper, Lawrence Hatter, Eric Hemenway, George Ironstrack, Benjamin Johnson, Ann Keating, Tom Killion, Kathryn Labelle, the late Pierre Lebeau, Jacob Lee, Emily MacGillivray, Kyle Mays, Ann McGrath, Marlene Medrano, Tiya Miles, Lucy Murphy, Michael Nassaney, James Nichols, Sharon Person, Angela Pulley-Hudson, Brett Rushforth, Eric Schelereth, Nancy Shoemaker, Susan Sleeper-Smith, Christina Snyder, Taylor Spence, Cristina Stanciu, Melissa Stuckey, Andrew Sturtevant, Coll Thrush, and Benn Williams.

Bob Morrissey has been very generous as a fellow scholar over time and as I navigated my first few years as a teacher. I can't thank him enough for his support. Robert Englebert has become a good friend and colleague with whom I've had many edifying and interesting conversations. Guillaume Teasdale and I share an interest in and commitment to the history of Detroit, Windsor, and the Detroit River borderlands. An accomplished historian of early Detroit history, he has been unstinting in his efforts to work with me and my students in the establishment of a critical borderlands research partnership between the University of Windsor and Wayne State University. Suzanne Boivin Sommerville, Gail Moreau-DesHarnais, and Diane Wolford Sheppard generously shared their resources and extensive experience working on French Detroit and its early settlers. I have also benefited from discussions about the historic French communities of the Illinois Country with Cece Boyer Myers and Emily Horton.

All of these scholars and many more at conferences, colloquia, and informal meetings through the years have helped shape my thinking about this book and my scholarship in general. Catherine Desbarats, Michael McDonnell, and Sophie White went above and beyond in taking precious time to read all or parts of the book manuscript and offer insight and advice as to how it could be made better. I am also grateful to the anonymous reviewers who provided helpful feedback. In any way this book comes up short, I am entirely responsible. In another of a series of events that now seem preordained, Michigan State University Press editor-extraordinaire Julie Loehr enthusiastically took on this project at a critical moment. I will forever be grateful to her for her belief in this book's viability and her support, guidance, and patience. Bonnie Cobb and Amanda Frost lent their editorial eagle-eyes to the manuscript in its final stages which has made the it better in many ways. Tim Pearson created a wonderfully comprehensive and inclusive index that is crucial to my vision for this book. My sincerest thanks go to cartographer Ellen White, who created an excellent map that captures the geography of the French-Indigenous family networks. My artist brother Craig suggested the compelling design for the cover of the book utilizing a map from the William L. Clements collection and Kristine Blakeslee and her staff at Michigan State University Press executed that design beautifully.

I am grateful for the funding I received to conduct research for this book from the American Philosophical Society, Beinecke Rare Book and Manuscript Library, Howard R. Lamar Center for the Study of Frontiers and Borders, National Endowment for the Humanities, Newberry Library, Social Sciences and Humanities Research Council of Canada, Wayne State University, William L. Clements Library, and Yale University. I thank John Demos, Johnny Faragher, Jay Gitlin, original members of my dissertation committee, and Nancy Shoemaker, the fourth unofficial member, for persevering with me and my work and for the myriad of things I have learned from them.

No matter where I have lived, my friends and family have been the touchstones that have maintained me. Now that I have come home, I have the privilege of seeing some of them on a regular basis but each of them, whether near or far, has made it possible for me to complete this book. My love and deepest thanks go to Monique Bontront, Angie Cecile, the late Delores LaBute Cecile, Leslie Edwards, Lynda Ellis, Beth Gignac, Darlene House, Janet LaBute Karcz, Denis LaBute, Maria

Perry, Paula Rawlinson, Joel Trotter, Gwen Wagner, and Natasha Wiebe. Monique provided added support, lending her expertise to help me think through meanings of Windsor-Detroit French-language terminology. I could not have imagined the happy circumstances that would have made it possible for me to live close to my brother Craig, my sister-in-law Robin, and nephew Dylan. Craig and Robin made that arrangement possible and have cheered me on in everything I have undertaken, especially this book. My dad, Lou, has been a constant and steadfast source of support throughout my life and as I worked to finish this book. I love him for all he has done to help me create my wonderful life. Michael Kral, my husband and soulmate, has lovingly sustained me mind, body, and soul and has been the most essential person in my journey from the challenging times to the realization of many of my hopes and dreams. We have had many adventures and many more await us. There are not enough words, or words entirely appropriate enough, to fully express how much my mother, Diana LaBute Marrero, is a part of this book. Her stories, which have been the foundation of my life and this work, continue to bind us to each other, even though she passed away ten years ago.

Early drafts of portions of chapters 5, 6, and 7 appeared in the following publications:

"Women at the Crossroads: Trade, Mobility, and Power in Early French America and Detroit." In *Women in Early America: Transnational Histories, Rethinking Master Narratives*, edited by Thomas Foster. New York: New York University Press, 2015.

"On the Edge of the West: The Roots and Routes of Detroit's Urban Eighteenth Century." In *Frontier Cities: Encounters at the Crossroads of Empire*, edited by Jay Gitlin, Barbara Berglund, and Adam Arenson. Philadelphia: University of Pennsylvania Press, 2013.

"'She is Capable of Doing a Good Deal of Mischief': A Miami Woman's Threat to Empire in the Eighteenth-Century Ohio Valley." *Journal of Colonialism and Colonial History*, 6, no. 3 (2005).

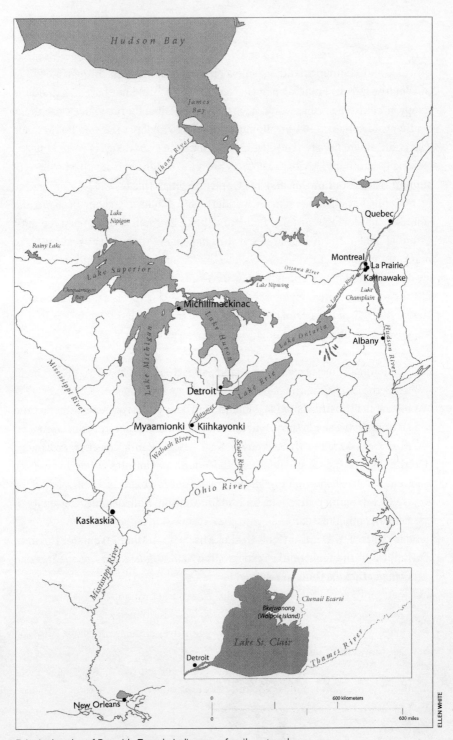

Principal nodes of Detroit's French-Indigenous family networks

Speaking Silences and Divulging Secrets

Toward a Recovery of Detroit's French-Indigenous History

I t was the only time the genealogist who had assembled the LaBute family history in 1977 interrupted her recitation of people, places, and dates. Her bold statement was an attempt to explain away the appearance of a woman named Marie Magdelene Roy, daughter of Pierre Roy and Marguerite Ouabankikoué, the latter listed as being "of Indian descent." Marie Magdelene had been born May 25, 1710, in Detroit, married to Pierre Labutte in 1728 at Fort Miamis, and buried November 20, 1732, in Detroit. The genealogist came out from behind familial details to deliver her opinion clearly and with conviction: "Marie Madeleine was of French descent, you are what your father is, not what your mother is or was, her father Pierre Roy was French."[1] In one bold stroke, Marie Magdelene had been changed from being of mixed Indigenous and European blood and culture, to French, and had been shorn of half her ethnic identity. Her mother Marguerite's presence had been revealed, only to be erased. Both women were "hidden in plain view" beneath a "facade of whiteness" within a genealogy, where lives circulate outside traditional histories of wars and nations.[2]

The women were also doubly subjugated, or buried twice, by a society bent on submerging an Indigenous past and recording only those lines drawn between fathers across time.[3] It was a racialized and gendered forgetting, because Indigenous bloodlines that intertwined with those of Europeans could be traced back in almost every instance to an Indigenous woman. In many of these cases, there had never been a marriage according to Christian rites, which further disturbed or introduced the possibility of dispute into genealogies.[4] By literally "rooting out" these women, genealogies preserved the illusion of an endless and unbroken chain that linked a dynasty of white men. The only reason Marguerite and Magdelene had appeared in this genealogy was because Magdelene had been married in the Roman Catholic Church. An integral part of this erasure also involved the tendency to romanticize cross-cultural sexual encounters, rather than exploring the full range of experiences of Indigenous and mixed-blood women, including the violence they could suffer at the hands of Euro-American men.

But for whose supposed greater good or collective well-being was the keeping of this secret demanded? Had the rough edge of Magdelene's and Marguerite's indigeneity been chiseled away for the construction of a seamless national history of Canada or of the United States, or of an Anglo-Canadian or French-Canadian ethnic identity? These exclusions in historical narratives, or "acts of oblivion" involve deliberate suppression of memories of people, places, and events in the interest of "social cohesion."[5] Each of these types of narratives, according to historian Michel-Rolph Trouillot, are unique in being "a particular bundle of silences" that "crisscross or accumulate over time to produce a unique mixture."[6] I wanted to look closely enough to find the almost invisible seams or scars in the complex narrative of Detroit's French-Indigenous community and discover a method by which I could open those seams, pulling the whole apart and revealing the distinct and messy collection of secrets inside.

If family history had been the mechanism for the creation of silences, perhaps now it could be the means of restoring those who had been marginalized and resituating them in the larger context of European and Indigenous relations at Detroit and in the Great Lakes in the eighteenth century. Familial narratives could be viewed as "community talk" used as a protective mechanism to counter the force of a "supposedly universal history" or national narrative that threatens to engulf individuals and localities.[7] Geographer Nicholas Entrikin proposes that "place is best viewed from points in between" the local and the universal. Otherwise, either the significance of historical subjects becomes lost in "generic relations," or too close a focus on those subjects makes it difficult to connect them to the larger meaning-making systems of which they were a part.[8]

Reintegrating marginalized historical agents also means reintegrating geneal-ogies into standard histories and, in the case of French-Indigenous family history, turning those genealogies inside out by connecting the dots between women across time. It was in the "gendered and racialized intimacies of the everyday" that European empires sought to turn individuals into colonial subjects even as the same sites of intimacy provided cover from these efforts, frustrating imperial agents.[9] As historian Ann McGrath has pointed out, marriages across colonizing boundaries created family histories and "expansive diasporic connections" that remain outside the parameters of traditional historical narratives.[10] In her research on mixed-blood communities, historian Heather Devine found that because "kin obligations generally superseded other commitments," genealogical materials reveal sociopolitical alliances, migrations of individuals and their families across regions, and socioeconomic status of families.[11]

There has been another layer of secrecy that has obscured the historic roles of French-Indigenous families of the Great Lakes and of southwestern Ontario and southeastern Michigan in particular. Indigenous and mixed-blood histories are predominantly oral, which, according to historian Carolyn Podruchny, have left few records and makes the study of their cultures a challenge.[12] Scholars working on reintegrating these peoples have adopted alternative methodologies, including the study of folksongs combining French and Indigenous (Anishinaabowin and Iroquoian) lyrics, because their historical agents are often missing from traditional sources.[13] These auditory artifacts document cultural change over time.[14] Also, the stories they tell, "like good theories, make connections that may not at first glance seem straightforward."[15]

Charting the history of Detroit's French-Indigenous kinship networks requires an understanding of how community knowledge developed relative to empire. The complexities of this relationship are readily apparent when we compare the dueling narrative trajectories generated at the level of the state on one hand and at the local level on the other. Local knowledge is comprised of what James Scott describes as a "wide array of practical skills and acquired intelligence in responding to a constantly changing natural and human environment." The state is constantly attempting to destroy, control, or appropriate this highly adaptive knowledge in an effort to exert "administrative order."[16] The state's account minimizes, sometimes deliberately and sometimes out of ignorance, the power and authority of local persons and networks. The local, often frustrated imperial agents who served time-limited terms in their administrative positions were bent on quickly maximizing their career and earning opportunities, and therefore sought to read and exploit local resources as quickly and easily as possible.

There are numerous examples of this tendency in the French and British imperial records of eighteenth-century Detroit. One such case appears in the voluminous correspondence of Antoine de la Mothe Cadillac, Detroit's first French commandant. By focusing on the name of one fur trader named Pierre Roy, who we met briefly at the beginning of this chapter, it becomes clear that Cadillac either misunderstood the culture of French-Indigenous family networks he lived among at Detroit, or knowingly misrepresented this man's role in order to elicit sympathy in the eyes of Cadillac's superiors and better his chances at monetary compensation. Whether the distortion was deliberate or not, it constitutes a form of erasure perpetrated by Cadillac that has a profound effect on the way we read those records and contextualize the history of local persons and events in Detroit.

By following Pierre Roy through the correspondence of Cadillac and other imperial agents, it is possible to recover a trail that stretched across New England, New York, Montreal, New Orleans, and Indigenous nations, including the Myaamia, Mascouten, Meskwaki, Haudenosaunee, Wendat, and Odawa/Anishinaabe. The extended Roy family appears consistently in French and British records and in the correspondence of imperial agents such as Cadillac and British superintendent of Northern Indian Affairs Sir William Johnson. A Monsieur Roy also appears in oral testimony, in a song about the Mascouten—a western Great Lakes Algonquian nation that figured in Detroit's early eighteenth-century history—still sung in the twentieth century by local French residents of the Detroit and Windsor area.[17] Scholars have largely ignored these seemingly "peripheral" persons and their connections to Detroit's history.

In addition to recovering instances of tension between local peoples and the empires attempting to control them, it is also necessary to understand if, when, and how these tensions were resolved. The intricacies of the relationship between the two could be complicated depending on whether they sought to work, if even temporarily, toward a shared purpose and successfully managed antagonisms. Historic moments at which the two were in opposition, both in their purpose and the manner in which this purpose was perceived to be best attained, are equally telling. Historian Sheldon Pollock points out that the state can practice "coercive cosmopolitanism" and the local community a "vernacularism of necessity." Thus, individuals can be compelled to participate in the larger world of the state while an equal level of participation can be demanded, based on family ties, in the smaller world of the local community. Conversely, there are other times at which the state practices a "voluntaristic cosmopolitanism" and the local community a "vernacularism of accommodation," in each case inviting, rather than compelling, "affiliation to these cultural-political orders."[18] The implications are that the loyalty of an individual or family in the eighteenth century could be engaged by both an imperial power and the local community in a variety of ways that sometimes worked at cross-purposes.

The description of local peoples in imperial archives reflected whether they were cooperating with or challenging imperial (be this Indigenous or Euro-American polities) strictures. The French imperial state, for example, marginalized French traders or designated them as other with the moniker "coureurs de bois" if these individuals were perceived to be operating illegally or in opposition to the state. This same French state distinguished Indigenous nations based on whether or not they were in alliance with the French king. Add to this the fact that in the early modern period, when regionally based concepts of collective identity prevailed over an incipient sense of French nationhood, it is as anachronistic to insist on a single, global French identity for persons residing in and moving across the North American continent as it is to posit a generic Indigenous nationhood.

Writing the Chenail Écarté: Hidden Histories and Half Told Truths of Detroit

If the mixed communities between nations and cultures increasingly became "backwater" or hidden locations set apart from the "overbearing forces" of universal history, how do we write more inclusive narratives? We can use the lens of family and community and follow one such peripheral path to construct a different history that crosses the boundaries of nation and reconfigures our notions of region, gender, race, and class. The Chenail Écarté—meaning diverted, remote, obscure, lost, or hidden channel—is to this day a narrow and navigable water route through the landscape of southwestern Ontario and southeastern Michigan. Its name appears on eighteenth-century maps and in eighteenth- and nineteenth-century records of treaty negotiations between British imperial agents and Anishinaabe nations whose homelands stretched from present-day southwestern Ontario to the northern reaches of the Great Lakes and into the heart of the American Midwest.[19] Its very name is locally circumscribed—it is an alternative form of the word "chenal," which is the word for "channel" used universally today by French speakers. Historical linguist Peter Halford traced use of the word *chenail* (pronounced *shen-I*) to a Jesuit priest living at Detroit in the mid-eighteenth century, and earlier to the accounts published by Baron Lahontan of his travels in the area of Detroit and the upper country or *pays d'en haut* in the late seventeenth and early eighteenth centuries.[20] Both the word and place remain in use today in local Anishinaabe communities.

Other terminology used in reference to local geography guides in recovering alternative histories. La Rivière à la Tranche, which is today the Thames River, is a major waterway through southwestern Ontario. The French term translates into "the river that cuts through" (the English "trench" is recognizable in the French "tranche"). The English name Thames was adopted from the well-known river of the same name in England and applied locally in the 1790s. It took some years for the English word to replace the French, because local English-speaking inhabitants merely anglicized the French name into Tranch or Trench River before the name Thames took hold. Indeed, the French had laid their French name for the river over that used by local Indigenous groups. The river was called Askunessippi, meaning "the antlered river," by the Odawa and Ojibwe living in its vicinity. Whereas the English word Thames says nothing about the river's physicality, the French and Odawa/Ojibwe terms make reference to the river's shape and course.

The much larger, heart-shaped Lake St. Clair to which the Chenail flows like a vein is known as Wabasajonkasskapawa.[21] Lake St. Clair borders both the state of Michigan and the province of Ontario, and is part of the Great Lakes water system as it empties into the Detroit River, which in turn flows into Lake Erie. Ironically, its status as an aquatic line of demarcation had been viewed in the late eighteenth and early nineteenth centuries in multiple ways by various groups negotiating over land rights. Indigenous nations never intended waterways or their resources to be part of land surrenders.[22] Discussions over aquatic territory therefore warranted special consideration. In the nineteenth century, for example, the same Ojibwe collective held talks with both the American and British Canadian governments for land in what is now southeastern Michigan and southwestern Ontario. Unlike their Canadian counterparts, however, American representatives pressed for and obtained rights to the water and its resources.[23] In the twenty-first century, knowledge of the Chenail has become more locally circumscribed. Many non-Indigenous peoples have erroneously considered it a virtually uninhabited expanse of land and water dotted with makeshift lodges catering to seasonal hunting activity and histories celebrating the establishment of Anglo-Canadian communities continue to marginalize Indigenous presence.[24] But the Chenail is part of Bkejwanong and Anishinaabe territory, where residents participate in seasonal hunting, fishing, trapping and gathering while also taking part in local commerce and industry.[25]

The linguistic history of the word *chenail* also sheds light on the significance of varying types of "Frenchness." Historian Yvan Lamonde uses the Chenal du Moine, a waterway that is part of the topography of central Quebec, as a metaphor for the trajectory he follows in writing the history of eighteenth- and nineteenth-century political ideas in Quebec.[26] Like the Chenail Écarté, Lamonde's Chenal du Moine bends this way and that. It has many tentative and rarely traveled ("pointillés discontinues") or unknown and forgotten ("lambeaux d'inconnu et d'oubli") branches. But Lamonde's path through Quebec's history is a *chenal,* not a *chenail,* its local Detroit-area counterpart. For the most part, Quebec-based historians of the French and Indigenous experience have not adequately constructed inclusive histories that take into consideration the experience of French and Indigenous communities outside of Quebec where French is spoken.[27] As Christophe Horguelin points out, this has resulted in an ethnically, culturally, and linguistically homogeneous origin story of French identity tied to the St. Lawrence valley that is overly simplistic and historically inaccurate.[28] Nor have these historians consistently ventured outside the physical boundaries of the St. Lawrence valley to understand the history of what Jay Gitlin has labeled the Creole Corridor and Robert Englebert describes as the French River World, an early transcultural and transnational milieu that linked Montreal to the Great Lakes, Illinois Country, and the northwest.[29] The fact that linguists have found other *chenails* in portions of present-day Missouri located along the Mississippi River attests to the prevalence of this river world and its unique cultural and linguistic history.[30]

The Chenail Écarté is a fitting symbol to portray the process by which notions of community were constructed and reconstructed by the state and by local contingents at Detroit. Knowledge of the Chenail, perceptions of what nation or group it belonged to, what it bordered or separated, and its historic importance have changed shape and meaning over time. Through the use of church registers, records generated by French and British imperial agents, accounts of French and British traders, Indigenous/tribal histories, nineteenth-century Anglo-American ethnographic materials, and local stories and songs, this book is a critical examination of the channels traveled by early Detroit's French-Indigenous family networks. Family members traversed the extensive network of interior waterways that functioned as lines of communication between communities and made trade possible and profitable. Their activities were often carefully hidden from imperial authorities who sought to control them, and as a result, their history has remained largely hidden and absent from mainstream scholarly narratives.

Until fairly recently, there had been few scholarly monographs that examined Detroit's early history, but a spate of new books over the last five years has offered fresh critical insight. Catherine Cangany's *Frontier Seaport: Detroit's Transformation into an Atlantic Entrepôt* places Detroit within the larger context of its role as a transatlantic hub in the fur trade and manufacturing center through the eighteenth century and into the American era. Lawrence Hatter's *Citizens of Convenience: The Imperial Origins of American Nationhood on the U.S.-Canadian Border* explores the ability of merchants on Detroit's British/American border to utilize fluid British and American identities to further trade, frustrating the new American government's efforts to solidify a sense of nationhood in the years following the American Revolution. Tiya Miles's *Dawn of Detroit: A Chronicle of Slavery and Freedom in the City of the Straits* sheds new light on the extent and effect of slavery by French, British, and Americans of Indigenous people and African Americans and the pervasive effects of this institution on Detroit's development. Guillaume Teasdale's *Fruits of Perseverance: The French Presence in the Detroit River Region, 1701–1815* charts the establishment and growth of a French colonial presence amidst Indigenous settlements on both sides of the river, aided by a French government eager to replicate the agriculturally based society of the St. Lawrence. My work has been shaped by these books and by conversations with their authors.

Very little has been known about how the French-Indigenous networks operated on the ground and in ways unique to particular geographic locations such as Detroit, or how they managed to create multinational conglomerates combining trade and diplomacy that allowed them to influence the course of European imperial power throughout the eighteenth century. Members of the French-Indigenous networks hailed predominantly from the Great Lakes, Montreal, and the St. Lawrence valley, but their commercial activities took them to Boston, New York, Louisiana, Hudson Bay, and in some cases, England, France, and Holland. At Detroit, they capitalized on their role as imperial representatives and emissaries to amass considerable prestige and personal fortune. As part of Myaamia, Anishinaabe, Wendat, and Haudenosaunee homelands and with an imperial French presence that had been established just weeks after the close of the momentous Great Peace of Montreal in 1701, Detroit became the apex of French-Indigenous relations.

Through the activities of the kinship networks, Detroit became a bustling thoroughfare and a location of enhanced political and economic importance in the continental interior. Exploring these contextualized intimacies allows for a fresh interpretation of key events of the eighteenth century, such as the Fox Wars, placing the French-Indigenous kinship networks at the political and economic center of the hostilities, and as the reason for their outbreak at Detroit. Some of these same individuals and their close relations were also at the center of Pontiac's War, which forty years later also erupted at Detroit. In both instances, European imperial efforts to regulate trade and diplomacy ran up against well-established French-Indigenous cultural and commercial practices. By the mid-eighteenth century, members of the networks had become so powerful, incoming British traders and imperial officials courted their favor and influence among Indigenous nations. They would maintain that power as British imperial presence splintered on the eve of the American Revolution.

A pivotal means by which they constructed their surreptitious political and economic empires was their skill at utilizing metaphors of gendered hybridity in diplomacy and transecting gender norms in trade. Men pressed their political agendas by adopting or demanding enactment of the role of father-nurturer who offered both martial support and symbolic breasts that provided spiritual and economic sustenance. Women furthered trade by navigating a multitude of gender norms of their nations (Myaamia, Odawa, Haudenosaunee, and French), allowing them to defy the state that sought to hold them to European ideals of womanhood. These women operated in opposition to imperial strictures that were ultimately ineffectual in curbing their agency because the women were perceived as a scarce "commodity" in a colony where they were vastly outnumbered by marriageable men.

At mid-century, British merchants and imperial officials viewed marriage to French women of the kinship networks much as French men had viewed marriage to Indigenous women earlier in the eighteenth century—as a means for greater access to and success in trade. In this way, the British gendered French women of the kinship networks differently from British women, seeing them as "Indian-like." These men would eventually attempt to control their wives' expressions of indigeneity. But members of the family networks would ultimately thwart these efforts. The Myaamia woman civil chief Tahkamwa, granddaughter of Marguerite Ouabankikoué and Pierre Roy and wife of two French men, would force these same British officials to recognize her efforts to maintain her family's commercial empire.

Chapter 1, "Creating the Place Between: Building Indigenous and French Communities in Early Detroit," considers the gendered configurations of settlement and family for the French and Indigenous nations resident at Detroit. It also explores the shifting reactions to and support of marriage between French men and Indigenous women by French imperial authorities. These representatives of state used the parent-child metaphor predominantly in their negotiations with Indigenous groups, but within Indigenous communities, other symbols of kinship were equally powerful. The French-Indigenous family networks had access to a much larger variety of metaphoric kinship relationships to develop and solidify their connections to each other and to tie imperial European representatives to an expanding series of economic and political obligations.

Chapter 2, "Corn Mothers, *Commandantes,* and Nurturing Fathers: Negotiating Place at Detroit," looks at how men and women of the French-Indigenous family networks understood and utilized Detroit's liminal status for resident Indigenous nations. Their burgeoning cultural and economic agency made them so powerful, their activities were often deemed illegal by the state because they defied rules and regulations that attempted to control access to Indigenous communities and to the complex and highly lucrative trade based on furs. Like the state, these networks attempted to control the flow of goods and persons in order to maximize economic and political gain as a hedge against imperial intrusions. They also used their resources to build their own corporate identity through the elaboration of and performance of a distinct culture.

Chapter 3, "War, Slavery, Baptism: The Formation of the French-Indigenous Networks at Detroit," examines the initial conflagration at Detroit that would launch a decades-long French campaign against the Meskawaki. Leading up to the outbreak of hostilities in 1712, members of the French-Indigenous family networks, as speakers and interpreters had benefitted by helping to steer the course of diplomacy. But French imperial authorities increasingly balked at the costs associated with maintaining Detroit. As they dismantled the settlement, dismissing its soldiers and constricting its physical dimensions, however, the strength and influence of the local networks continued to grow as members diverted resources to bolster an alternative configuration of political agency that crossed European and Indigenous nations. It was this conflict between imperial and local sources of power in the second decade of the eighteenth-century that caused war to break out at Detroit.

Chapter 4, *"Ils s'en allaient tous:* Roots and Routes of the French-Indigenous Family Networks," looks closely at the nature and extent of influence of French-Indigenous families by focusing on two kinship networks. Both the Bizaillon and Cuillerier family networks utilized Detroit's status as a center of mobility to conduct trade and expand power and influence in both French and Indigenous worlds. Both families anchored themselves at Detroit with landholdings while also extending their economic reach in every direction. The Bizaillons' tenure at and through Detroit would reach its apex during the early Fox Wars and the pivotal second decade of Detroit's French-provisioned fort. The Cuillerier dit Beaubien family would operate in the vicinity of Detroit during this same period, strengthening their economic base in the years leading up to the Seven Years' War.[31] Both families maintained power by linking their activities at Detroit to Myaamionki (the Myaamia homelands) and the Illinois Country. The path between these locations would grow in importance just as the families who expertly traversed it strengthened their economic and political presence.

Chapter 5, "On Such Does the Fate of Empires Depend: Women of the French-Indigenous Family Networks," considers the multiple roles of women of the families who were crucial to navigating trade between the French and Indigenous nations and who linked the needs of their home communities to the demands of the state. Their economic control extended from the St. Lawrence valley to the Illinois Country and made them so powerful, they were consistently seen as a threat by European imperial agents. This was especially evident at mid-century, when the British attempted to gain control of preexisting trade networks. As a result, French and Indigenous women were the targets of distrust and were maligned and sometimes harassed as imperial agents attempted to control their activities.

Chapter 6, "Unveiling the Conspiracy: Women at the Heart of Pontiac's War," examines the multiple narratives that have been generated about two women variously conjectured to have been the reason for the failure of Pontiac's efforts to expel the British from the upper country. Like the crucial first battle at Detroit that launched the Fox Wars, Pontiac's attack was believed to have been the linchpin in Indigenous plans to reestablish Indigenous sovereignty. The two women, one Indigenous and one French, were held up as the reason Pontiac failed because they divulged his plans in advance of his attack. An examination of multiple narratives generated by British and French sources at the time, and in the decades and century afterwards, exposes both the integral role of women in a historic series of events from which scholars have continued to exclude them, as well as their pivotal position as agents who continued to control trade and diplomacy.

Chapter 7, "Bastards and Bastions: Domestic Disorder and the Changing Status of the French-Indigenous Family Networks," looks at the troubled marriage of the Myaamia leader Tahkamwa and her first French husband, which became the basis for British imperial efforts to maintain a political and economic toehold in the Ohio Valley on the eve of the American Revolution. Imperial efforts at maintaining a presence at Kiihkayonki (Fort Miami) were contingent on navigating the complex networks of kin, as well as recognizing and responding to cues for proper behavior in the ritualized world of Indigenous and British political negotiation. By examining concepts of family held by both the British and the Myaamia, it is possible to reconstruct the complexity of multiple and competing claims to marital and familial legitimacy, and to see how these claims came up against British legal concepts. British, French, and Indigenous men placed this Myaamia woman at the center of a political and economic groundswell that threatened the foundations of European-Indigenous relations.

In 1774, the year in which the marriage of the Myaamia woman and French man prompted imperial concern, the winds of change from rebellious American colonists meeting in the First Continental Congress in the east threatened British hegemony and caused British imperial agents to lean more heavily on Great Lakes Indigenous groups for support. This is also the year the Quebec Act was passed, which constituted, among other things, a concession by the British, fifteen years after the Seven Years' War, to some aspects of the culture of French-Indigenous populations. The book's afterword jumps ahead to the closing decade of the eighteenth century, when Detroit and the upper country were at the center of increasingly contentious relations between the United States, Britain, and Great Lakes Indigenous nations. Members of the French-Indigenous family networks continued to shape political and economic events at Detroit and along a well-worn route into the continental interior that they had shaped for nearly a century. In 1793, visiting Quakers who were new to Detroit and to the history and agency of the French-Indigenous family networks provided an intriguing portrait of the resiliency of the networks at a time just before war would break out between the United States and Britain in 1812.

At Detroit, members of the kinship groups had grown in economic, political, and cultural influence in the course of the eighteenth century, producing individuals with varying levels of allegiance to community and nation. Although Anglo-American power ebbed and flowed, the influence of Indigenous-French intermediaries remained intact. Well into the nineteenth century, the families would maintain an identity independent of any particular nation. When we examine the influence of these kin-based networks, we complicate traditional histories that focus solely or mostly on military conflict between English- and French-allied Indigenous nations. Without understanding the dynamics of the familial relationships, it is impossible to hypothesize fully the motives behind these power struggles. In discovering places in the imperial record where French-Indigenous family members grappled with the machinations of empire, scholars become mindful of their own positions in relation to empire, and participate, as Jodi Byrd describes, in making visible what imperial settler colonialisms and their diasporas attempted to obscure.[32] The hidden channels of Detroit's French-Indigenous history run backward and forward through time, cutting through and becoming visible in the expanse of the imperial record only to disappear into local story and song. These are seams in Detroit's history that reveals the contingent and "messy" nature of national borders and local identities.

CHAPTER 1

Creating the Place Between

Building Indigenous and French Communities in Early Detroit

I t was one death, its description buried in a myriad of details in a lengthy report composed less than a year into Cadillac's tenure as commandant at the newly established Fort Pontchartrain at Detroit. According to Cadillac, a newborn infant had starved as its mother stood helplessly by. It was a death that need not have occurred, but nonetheless, it was described as inevitable under the circumstances. The deaths of newborns were not unusual at this time, with infant mortality among Europeans both in Europe and North America a matter of course for virtually every family.[1] The loss of this particular child, however, was something different and more ominous, and not just because the child's mother seemingly could not manage to feed it from her own breasts. In all likelihood, she had never fed any of her other infants with her own milk. The woman with whom she had traveled to Detroit in September 1701—only weeks after the elaborate peace negotiations conducted in Montreal between French, Haudenosaunee, and Algonquian groups had come to a close—could not be expected to assist or instruct her either because she had probably also never suckled her own children. Under the circumstances, it would seem, neither woman could have prevented the death of this baby.

The death had occurred at a pivotal moment in the development of the French settlement at Detroit—only one year into its life and at a point at which it was completely reliant for its continued existence on the flow of resources from Quebec. There was blame to be laid for the death of this baby—if there hadn't been, the event would have gone unnoticed and unrecorded in the imperial record—but not at the feet of the infant's mother or father.[2] In his letter written to French imperial authorities describing the progress he had made as commandant at Detroit in the settlement's first year, Antoine de la Mothe Cadillac subtly placed the blame for the death on the state—represented by the men to whom he addressed his letters and reports—which controlled the necessary resources. According to Cadillac, the death of this baby of his co-commandant Tonty and concerns for the welfare of Cadillac's own soon-to-be-born child underscored the potential threat to both the future of the settlement and French economic and political dominance in the upper country:

> It is not possible that our families could live in a place that would be inhabited by natives only. Their distress would be extreme, for they would be without any relief, as happened to Madame Tonty, who saw her infant die for want of milk, which she had not anticipated. I fear the same may happen to my wife who was just about to be confined when I left. That is not extraordinary because these ladies have wet nurses for their children. Hence there can be no hesitation in sending them down next year, unless a few families are permitted to go and settle there, so that they can find some assistance in these grievous conjunctures.[3]

Despite the apparent urgency of the situation, by the end of his report Cadillac put aside the death of the Tonty infant in order to emphasize what he had accomplished. He proudly reported that he had had no one sick nor any deaths in the first year of the fort's existence, a rare event, he added, in distant locations such as Detroit.[4] Cadillac thus claimed no responsibility for the infant's death, transferring this loss to the "account" of the king of France, the funder and father of colonial subjects and projects. The two very different perspectives presented by Cadillac in his report on the death of the infant—as both insignificant "nonevent" and the tragic result of imperial politicking—reflect conflicting French views of the purpose behind its North American colonial project and, more specifically, its attitude toward French-Indigenous interactions. In the end, Cadillac would not take any chances with his king's largesse. He made certain to procure a French wet nurse for the child his wife was about to deliver, using beaver skins that were probably taken illegally from the supply kept at Detroit by the Compagnie de la Colonie, the agency that had funded the establishment of the fort.[5]

Ultimately, Governor General Callière agreed to send six French families to Detroit. The Compagnie concurred that these six families should pay one third less than Indigenous peoples for goods. This would allow the families to trade these materials in Indigenous communities and make a profit in skins, which would subsequently be returned to the coffers of the Compagnie and ultimately, the king. The greater objective of sending families was to further trade, and to realize an economic advantage at the fort and in the upper country. The plight of the Tonty infant served as a symbol of European imperial shortsightedness, jeopardizing the development of productive Indigenous-European relations and the survival of posts in the continental interior.

But there were other expressions of the parental relationship, as well as other familial arrangements that resonated within Indigenous communities. Those who hoped to maintain good relations between Indigenous peoples and Europeans were required to understand and navigate multiple notions of family, parenthood, and settlement. This chapter explores how concepts of family relation were used to direct French imperial resources and manage imperial expectations for settlement and the interaction with Indigenous peoples at Detroit. Cadillac and other French imperial agents used kinship metaphors to express important issues at Detroit, a location that would become a pivotal political, economic, and military meeting point between Indigenous and European worlds throughout the eighteenth century. By understanding concepts of Indigenous and European parenthood and related-ness leading up to the moment of Detroit's "birth" as a European settlement, it is possible to understand how French-Indigenous families took root and how their formation impacted Detroit's development.

In Ancien Regime France and early modern Europe, the best interests of chil-dren were the state's concern and not a private matter. Infant mortality, particularly in areas like New France that were sparsely populated by Europeans, decreased the European population and therefore threatened the continued existence of the state.[6] The care and feeding of infants and the metaphorical significance of these activities had direct bearing on the political and economic growth of colonial populations.[7] In addition, in French society, the symbolic significance of milk and the practice of wet-nursing delineated socioeconomic, racial, and gender categories. The majority of seventeenth- and early eighteenth-century women of the political and military elite and merchant classes in New France mimicked the manners and habits of upper-class women of France, choosing to employ a wet nurse for their children drawn from the lower ranks of the socioeconomic ladder.[8] Also, as was the case in France, genteel women of the metropole (Quebec and Montreal) sent their babies to the hinterland/country to be nursed.[9]

A concurrent belief that physical characteristics and moral virtues could be transmitted through blood explains Cadillac's inference that Madame Tonty would not have enlisted the services of an Indigenous wet nurse.[10] In 1660, a group of French men and a woman and her children, along with their Wendat companions, were captured by the Haudenosaunee. Expecting she would perish, the French mother worried that after her death, her children would "imbibe the Iroquois nature with their milk, and lose every trace of Christianity."[11] Early modern Europeans believed that breast milk, like blood, carried one's essential nature. Church leaders warned parents that handing their newborns to heretical or immoral wet nurses would cause the infants to imbibe "the gross humours and qualities of the nurse."[12] The French mother's fear that her children would lose their Frenchness at the breast of a Haudenosaunee woman also suggests European awareness of the power of Indigenous women to shape cultural identity. According to Oneida scholar Bob Antone, it is women who "pass on the inner desire" to be Haudenosaunee.[13] As the eighteenth century unfolded, realization of the power of lactating women to determine identity would be reflected in the shift from hiring wet nurses to the feeding of infants at a mother's own breast, transforming a "class-stratified to a strictly gendered activity."[14]

The event of the Tonty infant's death presented other challenges for Cadillac and the French state. The Tonty family symbolized French imperial power and the ability of its elites to establish this power in new locations by enacting particular cultural practices. Imperial funds and families were pivotal to this project. But paradoxically, on the ground in the upper country, building and maintaining this power periodically required a usurpation of the state and, at times, a repudiation of these same cultural practices. With so much at stake, it is possible that the Tonty infant did not die because its mother could not feed it and Cadillac fabricated the reason for the death.

Cadillac had a habit of dramatizing events and drowning officials at Quebec and Versailles in thousands of pages of reports and letters. Minister of the Navy and Cadillac's patron at court, Jérôme Phélypeaux had asked Cadillac to send a more exact account of the complete circumstances of the country around Detroit that did not read like fiction; otherwise, he warned, Cadillac would not be taken seriously by the king.[15] But Cadillac crafted his prose for maximum effect to elicit sympathy and support for his endeavors at Detroit and was less concerned with presenting an accurate picture of what was happening on the ground. A skilled storyteller and what historian Richard Weyhing characterizes a "misinformation elite," Cadillac was in a good position to impact French colonial policy and was well aware that "honesty was not always the best policy for extracting power from Versailles."[16] He shared his literary abilities with a transatlantic network of mid-level colonial officials who, according to historian Sara Chapman, borrowed from a carefully honed language of colonial description. Indeed, for his Detroit narrative, Cadillac had appropriated tropes and images used by his colleague Henri Tonty to describe Louisiana.[17]

With the veracity of Cadillac's report in question, the particularities of the Tonty infant case also demonstrate the relationship between the crown and Indigenous communities. We can view alternative models of European-Indigenous relations that functioned alongside or sometimes in spite of the state and how this empowered French-Indigenous family networks. The Tonty infant had been born into a family whose members traveled extensively in the continental interior and engaged in trade with Indigenous nations. The mother of the doomed infant was Marie-Anne Picoté de Belestre, daughter of a France-born and Montreal-based officer and successful merchant who had begun his career as a fur trader at the annual fairs held in seventeenth-century Montreal.[18] Her traveling companion in 1701 had been Marie-Thérèse Guyon, wife of Antoine de la Mothe Cadillac. The father of the baby was Marie-Anne's husband Alphonse Tonty, a captain in the French navy who was second in command of Detroit. Tonty had spent many years engaged in the fur trade at Montreal and in the upper country, capitalizing on his brother Henri's extensive activities with René-Robert Cavelier de La Salle in the Illinois Country.[19]

Older brother Henri Tonty, a trader on the Mississippi with La Salle and commandant of Fort St. Louis (Pimitou), spent significant time living among the Illinois nations and in Louisiana.[20] As a result of their activities in the Illinois Country, members of the Tonty family had come to the attention of imperial authorities well before the turn of the eighteenth century. Henri Tonty and François Dauphin de La Forest, the latter of whom would later serve a term as commandant at Detroit, had been granted exclusive rights to trade in the Illinois Country by Governor General Frontenac. Intendant Jean Bochart de Champigny attempted to revoke this monopoly, complaining to imperial authorities in France that Henri

Tonty and La Forest should not be the only ones allowed to conduct business in the west.[21] Champigny was closely allied to Governor General Jacques-René de Brisay de Denonville in a shared view that the settlement of New France should be concentrated in the St. Lawrence valley. They felt that a scattered French presence put the entire colony at risk of military attack, and that the men who traveled to the interior depleted the labor force needed to maintain agricultural output and to protect the colony. But they also felt that trade in the Illinois Country threatened trade in the St. Lawrence valley.[22] To this end, in 1686, Denonville and Champigny had instituted a different system of awarding "congés" or permits for travel to the upper country, limiting the number in any year to twenty-five, and the number of men per canoe to three, and requiring them to register their names and travel plans. Under the previous governor, Louis de Buade de Frontenac, there had been no such limits.[23]

In 1697, Alphonse Tonty had assumed the command of Fort de Buade at Michilimackinac vacated by Cadillac. Situated at the juncture of Lakes Michigan and Huron and with easy access to Lake Superior, this post was located in Anishi-naabewaki, the "social formation" of the Anishinaabe (People of the Three Fires: Odawa, Ojibwe, Bodéwadmi [Potawatomi]).[24] At this place, the Odawa controlled trade relations between the French and Indigenous nations of the lakes further north and west.[25] Tonty and Cadillac knew each other well because the network of officers who conducted trade with Indigenous groups was small, stretching west from Montreal to the Great Lakes and the Ohio Valley, north to Hudson Bay, and south to Louisiana. It was an especially intimate group because many of its members were related by blood and marriage. Cadillac was an exception to this culture of relatedness. In the ten years he would command at Detroit, he would take many opportunities to complain to imperial authorities investigating his activities about how he had been victimized by enemies arranged against him by their multiple and intersecting ties of family.

Tonty's tenure at Michilimackinac had been short—only one year—because French imperial authorities had made the momentous decision to close all of their posts in the upper country to address the overabundance of beaver fur that sat rotting in Montreal warehouses. All trading and concourse with Indigenous groups was supposed to stop in order to stem the tide of skins that flowed into the St. Lawrence valley, which required, in turn, the recall of all voyageurs, coureurs de bois, and officers from the great expanse of the upper country. The Great Peace negotiated in Montreal that summer of 1701 had coincided with the French imperial decision to establish a post at "le détroit," the strait that connected Lake Erie to Lake Huron. The strait was a crucial shortcut through the extensive lakes that had been made safe for travel by the 1701 cessation of hostilities between the Haudenosaunee and the French and their Algonquian allies. There had been much at stake for European and Indigenous empires with the establishment of Fort Pontchartrain at Detroit.

Cadillac portrayed Detroit as an undeveloped space, brimming with unlimited natural resources, but far removed from and lacking the essential elements of French culture that existed in the St. Lawrence valley. It required the king's investment to develop the raw materials of what Cadillac called this "earthly paradise of North America." In turn, this would attract inhabitants, who would then transform Detroit into a settlement that was immune to the usual challenges faced by other posts that were mere garrisons (places with a military presence but no families).[26] In 1702, there were three Indigenous villages established at Detroit. According to Cadillac, the rest of the neighboring groups were waiting to see whether the French would hold true to their promise to make a permanent settlement. Sending the families and allowing inhabitants to settle at Detroit would prove this intention. These remaining Indigenous nations and a robust trading center would follow.[27]

But despite potential economic advantages that could be realized by their presence, maintaining families was an expensive proposition for the state. In 1703, an official criticized the drain on resources made by the officers and their families at Detroit. If the post was allowed to continue, the official concluded, the officers and the entire garrison should be removed. Such a move, however, would effectively expose residents to the threat of war, making it impossible for the fort to continue its operations. Cadillac countered that the removal of the garrison would be a mistake because more trade could be conducted at Detroit than in the entire upper country.[28] But the French state equivocated not only in the fiscal responsibility it felt it owed families, but in what types of families it chose to support, whether those of its elite classes or Indigenous allies.

In the same letter in which he begged for wet nurses and French families, Cadillac distinguished these desired settlers from the four hundred Abenaki, Odawa, and Wendat men capable of bearing arms, and their families.[29] Seeing them as warriors who would fight for the French king, Cadillac initially described them as men, but later in his missive, Cadillac rescinded their manhood, insisting in a complex discussion of cause and effect that these individuals could not become men without the investment of the king in the development of the fort:

How can we make these barbarians Christian if one hasn't made them men first? How to make them men, if one doesn't humanize them, and if one doesn't render them docile? How can one humanize and tame them except by the society that they would have from a civilized people? How to bind them and make them serve the King, if they don't have docility or religion, nor sociable commerce?[30]

By conflating manhood with French identity, Cadillac created gender-based parameters within which settlement would unfold at Detroit. Christianity was supposed to "domesticate" Indigenous males by making them men according to European standards and, ostensibly, trustworthy allies of Europeans. Indeed, Cadillac would advocate that Indigenous men at Detroit who had been "Frenchified" ("francisé") be organized into military companies and provided with salaries, arms, and designations similar to their European counterparts.[31] As historian Joyce Chaplin points out, however, "converted" Indigenous men were potentially stripped of their warrior status—the quality that impressed Europeans—and thus of their manhood if they did not perform their gender within the parameters established by their nations.[32] In acknowledging the need to provide for the families of Indigenous men who had fought on behalf of France, Cadillac demonstrated that the French state sought to control and even eradicate Indigenous masculinity, but also benefited from and rewarded its performance.[33] In this double-bind of European notions of gender, Indigenous men and women who were perceived as "bowing" to the influence of European religion and culture could never be, in European imperial eyes, equals to their French counterparts. These categorizations of race and gender worked together to "cast nonsedentary native peoples as . . . lacking virtue and, therefore, as proper targets of military assault/containment."[34]

French authorities were equally uncomfortable with the behavior of Frenchmen who participated in the fur trade and who, in spending extended periods with Indigenous peoples, learned to model the behaviors of Indigenous peoples. These men exhibited a hybrid masculinity combining European and Indigenous gender norms that played itself out in a multitude of ways impossible for imperial agents to understand and control. From the early seventeenth century, French imperial agents categorized men who participated in the fur trade based on their propensity to remain mobile.[35] They also delineated these men as culturally distinct, by classifying them according to their "moeurs" (customs, habits and morals) and setting them apart as potential risks to imperial aims.[36]

Coureurs de bois, who plied their trade without legal permits and whose movements could therefore not be tracked and controlled, were deemed especially dangerous. By refusing to remain yoked to the land and to an agricultural lifestyle, they were labeled by the state as morally corrupt men who possessed an "independent spirit." At one time imperial authorities in France suggested that the governor general and intendant require them to carry "certificats de bonnes moeurs" or certificates of good morals that would be issued once Catholic Church representatives had judged them suitable Frenchmen.[37] Such certificates would have generated funds for the state (income lost when coureurs de bois traded without government permits) and provided the state with another avenue for controlling the traders. In response, these Frenchmen would learn to negotiate imperially mandated expressions of masculinity and legality by adapting their behavior to these norms when necessary.

There was something distinctly different in the eyes of the state between Indigenous and French families; between New France's elite/officer class and its voyageurs, coureurs de bois, and habitants; and between Indigenous males designated as men and those who were not. Such distinctions were the means by which the state sorted its settled spaces from areas that remained outside its control. As historian Rony Blum has noted, letters and reports such as those generated by Cadillac "guaranteed that a continual comparison of metropolis/settlement penetrated the French/ Native dialogue." The Canadian elite set the parameters, rules, and definitions of settler identity, with an aim of placing themselves as the ultimate example.[38] In addition to the significance of the bodies of real children, French and other European nations utilized the father-child relationship within the greater context of symbolic family relations in their negotiations and diplomatic relations with Indigenous groups in North America. This was a relational arrangement carried over from European courts, where the symbol of political fatherhood resided in the person of the monarch and was reenacted at various locales by his representatives.[39]

A Father with Many Children and a Child with Many Fathers: European and Indigenous Concepts of Relatedness

Both early modern European and Indigenous worlds operated according to clearly defined notions of kinship. When they came into contact, these systems needed to expand upon and reinvent traditional motifs in order to incorporate the other. Such efforts at inclusion required a greater emphasis on the affinal—what historian Sylvia van Kirk distinguishes as "marrying-in"—than consanguineal kin connections.[40] As historian Susan Sleeper-Smith has detailed, affinal ties between Europeans and Indigenous peoples created extensive kin networks that controlled trade from the St. Lawrence valley to the Mississippi River.[41] European and Indigenous communities attempted this affinal adaptation or adoption in different ways, based on preexisting concepts of relatedness.

In France, one area in which the Catholic Church placed greater importance on affinal ties was through marriage. The church increased the number of degrees of blood-relatedness allowed between two people before they could marry, thereby tightening restrictions on and limiting consanguineal marriages. The only way to bypass this prohibition was to apply to the bishop for a dispensation, which could be acquired for a donation to the church.[42] Those who could afford to make such a donation had a vested interest in skirting these church restrictions. Consanguineal marriages, whether at or closer than proscribed degrees of relatedness, were most often practiced by families at the top of the socioeconomic hierarchy, in order to keep their daughters' property in the family.[43]

In Indigenous North America, people interacted with one another first and most importantly as kin, in a system that designated the performance of roles depending on the specific relationship in a particular nation. Acting according to these rules grounded in the larger concept of family, individuals then took on other social, political, economic, or religious roles.[44] Every level of connection was infused with the notion of the familial. The terms "mother," "father," "son," and "daughter" were not only used to designate biologically related individuals. A "mother" and "father" could also designate the same-sex siblings and parallel cousins of one's biological parents. As kinship scholar Raymond DeMallie makes clear, the sisters of one's mother were not *like* mothers; they *were* mothers. The status of "mother" was not limited to the act of giving birth, but referred as well to the "patterns of relationship" that represented and expressed this act. In most Indigenous societies, a given person had many fathers and mothers.[45]

Exchange of goods and services flowed along the lines of family. Among the Wendat, politics, sexuality, and the social interaction that facilitated economic production were all tied to matters of kinship.[46] Among the Anishinaabe, kinship structured spiritual, economic, and political aspects of society. Each person with whom they engaged in any type of exchange had to be made "kin-like," so that the activity in question could be properly conducted and understood.[47] The Myaamia and Inoka (Illinois) for example, who spoke dialects of the same language, sometimes referred to each other as siblings to couch the terms of peace between their two nations.[48] They would have also used kinship terminology to refer to Meehtikoošia (French) and would have provided corresponding opportunities to integrate them into Myaamia families and society.[49] If a French man married to a Myaamia woman became a good provider, for example, he could then forge relationships with the sisters of his wife, and his children would have more than one mother.[50]

In contrast, there were fewer kinship metaphors utilized by Europeans and they were less successful in integrating Indigenous peoples into prevailing systems of relatedness. The relationship of parent to child became the dominant motif around which European male imperial agents and elites organized political relations with Indigenous peoples.[51] It was an arrangement that recognized the power of the father-patriarch to determine what was best for his children and to act on this knowledge, sometimes gently and sometimes forcefully. A prevailing contemporary opinion held by Europeans emphasizing this relation of inequality, depicted ancient ancestors of Indigenous peoples as willful children who had wandered away from God, the quintessential patriarch, and as a result had become ensnared in superstition.[52]

In countries such as England that were struggling with the maintenance of a monarchy and the development of parliamentary government, the figure of the father-king was in considerable dispute. In what sociologist Julia Adams terms the "patrimonial" tendency of early modern European nations—governments modeled and based on the rulers' familial households—power diffused downward as kings handed out "bits of monopolistic resource-bearing political privilege." Early modern empires faced many challenges: their existence over huge geographical distances, the gaps of time between the issuance of orders and their receipt, and the need—in order to counter some of these challenges—to "recruit large numbers of Indigenous elites as agents to accommodate at least some of their demands and desires." Interestingly, as Adams points out, state power grew as empires were able to aggregate these previously autonomous agents. It was essential that early-modern states have the trust, allegiance, and obedience that characterized kinship ties to balance forces that threatened empire. The father-king spent much time attempting to dissolve "competing family solidarities" that manifested themselves as instances of "creole nationalism" in the colonies, and to instead "nourish" the king's version of the expression of proper family ties among his agents at home and abroad.[53]

The father-king was continually forced to switch between the metaphorical and the metonymic to express the relationship between the state and colonial subjects.[54]

Indeed, this issue was not confined solely to European nations debating or casting off their monarchs. In the colonies of every European state, the notion of king as symbolic father was stretched to its geographic, linguistic, and political limit. The metaphorical monarch could not always operate as a sufficiently authoritative parent to ensure the obedience and loyalty of children/subjects, because a metaphoric monarch was merely an echo of the genuine article. In the colonies, there was need for a metonymic father—an individual who embodied the king's imperial person, or, in the case of France, was a shining piece of the Sun King, Louis XIV. This was particularly essential when the presence of the king, represented in North America by the governor general as Onontio, was required to settle disputes and engage in diplomacy with Indigenous nations. Onontio was a person of real power based less on military might and more on his role as a father who was ally, protector, supplier, and mediator.[55] These meetings required carefully planned and elaborately staged performances. As historian Kenneth Banks points out, "lavish state ceremonies" meant to "awe the king's subjects" were not easily reproduced in the colonies, requiring instead "public celebrations and ritualized announcements" on the part of colonial authorities who used these events to augment their own prestige.[56]

Cornering the Market: Establishing Onontio at Detroit

Cadillac's letters indicate that he was attempting to represent the king in this manner by bypassing the governor general. He did this by exploiting the division of the king's power in New France into economic (centered at Montreal) and political (centered at Quebec) channels. The merchants at Montreal controlled the flow of imperial resources into trade networks, which was essential for the colony's survival and continued good relations with Indigenous groups, while the politicians at Quebec directed the application of the king's laws and policies. Along with his request for wet nurses, Cadillac had complained to minister of the marine Jérôme Phélypeaux, comte de Pontchartrain, that a handful of Montreal-based merchants were opposed to his plans for Detroit because trade at that location would interfere with their long-standing networks among the Odawa. A settlement at Detroit would make it an entrepôt or center of trade for posts further west, which would cut into the profits of these merchants.[57]

Cadillac sought to renegotiate the terms of relationship with local Indigenous groups and become their father-king. In so doing, he seized the opportunity to act as his own metonymic piece of the king of France, bypassing Quebec and the governor general much as he was seeking to have Detroit bypass Montreal as a center of commerce in the upper country. Such a maneuver required the alliance and support of Detroit's powerful local Indigenous nations. For their part, leaders of these nations were as adept at playing local European imperial authorities such as Cadillac against those at Quebec and Montreal as they were at playing the French against the English for political and economic gain.

In 1705, the Compagnie de la Colonie had discontinued its funding of the fledgling settlement at Detroit, and Cadillac, no longer in the Compagnie's employ, answered directly to the king and governor general. In 1706, Cadillac requested wampum belts from Governor General Louis-Philippe de Rigaud de Vaudreuil that would be kept at Detroit in the event that Cadillac needed to settle troubles arising between the nations in Detroit's vicinity. Governor General Vaudreuil grudgingly granted his request, allowing a few belts to be sent to Cadillac for use only when the king's service required it, but he did not want Cadillac to profit from communicating with Indigenous groups.[58] In 1707, Vaudreuil complained to his superiors that Cadillac was operating with the Detroit nations as if he and Vaudreuil were on equal footing in the colonial hierarchy. According to Vaudreuil, Cadillac was declaring in his meetings with Indigenous leaders that he and Onontio, the symbolic representative of the king in New France residing in the person of the governor general, were one. In declaring himself Onontio, Cadillac declared himself the supreme power at Detroit.[59] There were two symbolic fathers operating—a situation that caused crisis from a French point of view, but that Indigenous leaders would have viewed in an entirely different manner.

Vaudreuil wished to strengthen his hold on the role of Onontio, and he may also have attempted to subsume the particularities of local Indigenous-French politics at Detroit under the mantle of the father-king centered at Quebec.[60] During a meeting with the Odawa held to address Odawa/Myaamia/French tensions at Detroit, an Odawa leader offered Vaudreuil wampum from his personal/private supply, rather than the stash maintained by his nation. Vaudreuil refused to accept the wampum and the perceived offer to speak privately. Vaudreuil could have interpreted this gesture as working against his efforts to concentrate his fatherly power and prevent Detroit from becoming a center for diplomacy with Cadillac as its de facto Onontio. For his part, the Odawa leader may not have had the backing of his nation, or he may have been attempting to bypass normal diplomatic channels and gain a more favorable position for his nation. Finally, the Odawa leader could have recognized two personifications of Onontio—Cadillac and Vaudreuil—requiring him to utilize a different message to speak with Vaudreuil than that which he would have used with Cadillac.

The continual creation of entrepôts in New France further splintered the power of the father-king by diffusing his image and authority over time and space. The state grappled with provisioning Detroit either as a center for trade in the upper country or as a spoke emanating from an alternative hub. Three months after Detroit's formal establishment as a French post, the directors of the Compagnie de la Colonie complained to Versailles of the steep expenses they were incurring in underwriting the fort. They suggested that other posts be established on the Wabash River, at the Ouiscousing (Wisconsin), and among the Sioux in order to prevent Frenchmen and Indigenous peoples from going to trade with the English at Carolina and on the lower Mississippi. According to this model, Detroit could then act as a center to which Indigenous peoples from all of these posts would carry furs.[61] A few years later, however, the French state was considering relegating Detroit to the periphery through the establishment of a fort at Niagara that would act as a center for the trade at Detroit.[62]

As this was happening, imperial agents operating in these hubs on behalf of the father-king had to mediate between embodying his person in interactions with local people, and adapting or shaping their own basis of power, which meant working together with local groups as brothers and equals, and recognizing and enacting other versions of family. The "creole nationalisms" referred to by Julia Adams were the result of these efforts at the local level. French-Indigenous family networks at Detroit became increasingly powerful because they successfully navigated multiple versions of French and Indigenous kinship, including those of matrilineal and matrilocal nations such as the Wendat and Haudenosaunee, transforming Detroit into an entrepôt. By recognizing the symbolic power of the mother that was the cornerstone of these nations, the French-Indigenous networks empowered their women as much as they did their men, as the situation demanded. They also had a larger variety of metaphoric kin relationships to choose from in their displays of power. The networks therefore represented a threat to the authority of the European father-king.

When imperial representative Michel Bizaillon spoke to the Illinois, Ouiatenon, and Myaamia to convince them to cease any alliance with the English and remain loyal to the French, he stated that a father could have many children, but a child could not have many true fathers. His statement, however, might have resonated on a different level for his listeners. These three nations already considered themselves siblings and they may have understood that their loyalty could be divided equally between an English and a French father, and that both would be "true" fathers.[63] As will be discussed in greater depth later in this book, Michel Bizaillon was a member of Detroit's French-Indigenous family networks and played an integral and complex role as at times a proponent of and at other times an opponent of French imperial aims. His statement, therefore, hints that he too understood and operated according to Indigenous concepts of fatherhood even as he urged the use of a French model at official meetings.

If we follow the structure of Indigenous concepts of parenthood, in order to have both an English and a French father, Indigenous nations could have perceived the kings to be brothers. According to Indigenous kinship terminology, brotherhood was often a more powerful determinant of relationship than that of parent to child. As historian Heidi Bohaker points out, "in a patrilineal system, brothers would live together for life, raising their children together who would regard each other as siblings and would share the same nindoodem or clan."[64] Brotherhood was a powerful metaphor for ordering Indigenous-European relations at the diplomatic level and was usually invoked by Indigenous representatives to describe a state of equality between two groups.[65] For Europeans, it would be "bands of brothers" that fanned out across the North American interior and operated within Indigenous nations. In all these cases, as familial ties were established, they rendered the spaces of the upper country places of settlement.

Regulating Sex and Manipulating French and Indigenous Bodies

All matters of family were the basis for government opinion and legal intrusion with the ultimate purpose of increasing the profitability of the colony. Indeed, sex was "intimately linked to the formation of the colonial state."[66] Imperial officials were constantly attempting to control how the colony was populated by legislating who could marry and when marriage could take place, which often meant overriding the authority of priests and parents. Jean Talon, New France's first intendant, had sought to encourage the burgeoning of the colonial population through laws and government sanctions. A decree of 1669 honored fathers who were heads of large families by rewarding them monies and civil offices. Talon was also frustrated that Indigenous women were unable to bear many children because they did too much heavy work and nursed their babies too long. He spoke of addressing this impediment to the peopling of the colony through legislation that would control the length of time these women would breastfeed.[67]

Governors general at times sought to prevent soldiers from marrying during their years of service (a term that could last eight to ten years) and at other times proposed enacting laws requiring priests to obtain permission of the governor general before performing marriages for officers or soldiers.[68] Religious officials resisted these efforts, claiming that these strictures left these men free to "continue taking liberties and engage in disorderly behavior," which gave the colony an infinite number of illegitimate children. Alternatively, many officers and inhabitants circumvented Vaudreuil's control and risked excommunication from the Church by marrying à la gaumine, or clandestinely.[69]

The penalty for infraction of government legislation that sought to define the parameters of marriage was to deprive the men of the right to hunt, fish, or engage in the fur trade. The biggest challenge to these carefully crafted decrees and ordinances had been the increasing incidence of young men who were taking to the woods to engage in the fur trade and live in Indigenous communities. Imperial officials had hoped to stem the tide by enacting an ordinance that forbade men from leaving the colony without a license from the intendant or governor. Vaudreuil would outlaw marriages between French and Indigenous peoples, claiming that the children of these unions were "libertins" and lazy.[70] In seventeenth- and eighteenth-century French, "libertin" was used to describe individuals who flouted the strictures of their socioeconomic class by refusing to perform the duties expected of them and who hated any type of constraint or subjugation. They also eschewed religious convention by failing to observe the Commandments, the rules of the church, or the authority of the clergy and refusing to live a pious lifestyle.[71]

Antipathy at the top levels of government to the mingling of Indigenous and French blood continued, reflecting a shift in attitude of the role Indigenous peoples could play in entrenching a French presence in New France. The seventeenth-century belief that Indigenous peoples would submit to French culture was giving way to the reality that Indigenous peoples had no need or desire to adopt French lifeways. The blending of Indigenous and French blood was becoming more a marker of the failure of assimilation by the French than an indicator of the triumph of French culture over that of Indigenous peoples. French civil authorities in the seventeenth century had adopted a policy of "francisation" or Frenchifying of Indigenous peoples, hoping interaction would strengthen a French presence in the colony. Although they were vastly outnumbered by Indigenous peoples, they felt overwhelmingly confident nonetheless that their society was economically, politically, and culturally superior to Indigenous societies and that Indigenous peoples would realize this.[72]

Cadillac seems to have entertained both views, depending on which position benefited his interests. In a 1700 letter touting the benefits of a fort at Detroit, Cadillac had been a proponent of the marriage between French soldiers and Indigenous women, suggesting that it would be an advantageous arrangement, as long as these women had been instructed in Catholicism and could speak French. The women would then act as agents who would assure the goodwill of their nations toward the French.[73] Eight years later, Cadillac had never received official approval of his plan because Governor General Vaudreuil continually refused to sanction this type of marriage.

As Detroit became established, Cadillac further delineated his official position regarding French-Indigenous interaction. In his request for wet nurses and French families, Cadillac promised that by allowing them to settle at Detroit, there would be no sexual debauchery because French men with French wives present would not seek out Indigenous women. Indeed, he may have implicitly included himself and Tonty among the men who would eschew these extramarital relations. It was a common belief throughout Europe that sexual activity while a woman was lactating endangered the baby because sex drew blood away from the breasts.[74] By employing wet nurses, Cadillac and Tonty could remain faithful to their wives and maintain the sanctity of elite French bloodlines. The two perspectives on relations between French men and Indigenous women rested on the definition of sexual debauchery that described relations outside of marriage or between single French men and Indigenous women who had not been converted to Christianity.

French men traveling to Indigenous communities, and the officers and soldiers who were sent to establish garrisons among them, did choose to marry Indigenous women they perceived as being of superior rank in their societies. The sisters and daughters of Indigenous men who acted as speakers in council or were civil or war chiefs, or women who were themselves civil chiefs or empowered as part of matrilineal and matrilocal societies provided an important bridge into the community that could translate into greater success in trade. These men were indeed "marrying in" and marrying up, something with which they would have been familiar in French society. In the French upper echelons, "matrilineal kin patronage was as important to careers as patrilineal kin patronage" and French officers had been engaging in this practice in France for generations in order to advance their career prospects.[75] If there were marriages that would take place between French and Indigenous men and women, it behooved imperial authorities to regulate such marriages in a way that would maximize all of their possibilities, which included the augmentation of the colonial French population in general and the development of important alliances with Indigenous nations in the upper country.

There were three reasons it did not serve Cadillac to reveal in his correspondence with imperial authorities these kin networks that some of his French associates had established with Indigenous peoples at Detroit. He would have communicated that Detroit possessed the means of sustaining itself with minimal imperial contribution. Secondly, this would have required that imperial authorities acknowledge the existence and prominence of Indigenous nations with complex kinship arrangements that ordered the upper country in other political and economic configurations. Last, but certainly not the least of the state's concerns was the power of these alternative networks to engage French men. These tightly woven and well-established Indigenous kinship networks altered and ordered nascent Euro-American political and commercial formations to produce an "attenuated arena of domestic provisioning."[76] European and Indigenous concepts of settlement can be seen as clashing in Cadillac's description of the needs of the unfortunate Tonty/French infant and of the fort at Detroit, and in imperial notions of hub and hinterland that fueled the state's anxiety over control of vast areas of North American interior space. Cadillac played on these preoccupations and fears in order to gain the resources he needed.

New settlements in the upper country, like the newborn French infant of Cadillac's report, were invested with considerable significance as manifestations of European cultural and commercial clout. But their well-being rested precariously on French ideals of class and was weakened by imperial confusion over the type of intimate coexistence and cooperation with Indigenous groups that was required to help them flourish. Those who understood the complexities of this interaction would gain power and authority at Detroit as the eighteenth century progressed. As historian Saliha Belmessous points out, the establishment of the colony at Detroit marked an important turning point in imperial attitudes about the way in which French and Indigenous cultures could exist. The seventeenth-century belief that French society was superior and would attract Indigenous converts to French belief systems and lifestyles gave way to a cynical vision based on the truth that Indigenous peoples did not desire or feel they needed to make such a conversion. The eighteenth century would thus feature a growing belief on the part of French imperial agents that nothing good could come of mixing French and Indigenous blood, and that such a combination, playing out in the growing number of mixed-blood children, brought out the worst in both races. Belmessous suggests that Cadillac was operating on the basis of the seventeenth-century belief that marriage between French and Indigenous individuals was a way to bring about the conversion of Indigenous peoples to French ways, and that his private aim was to use this to bring about peace and strengthen alliances.[77]

It may be that the concern Cadillac felt imperial authorities would have over the death of an elite French baby marked the turning point between the two centuries and the two ways the state viewed the marriages and liaisons of French and Indigenous peoples. Cadillac had expertly manipulated the importance of the death in order to gain greater resources. A newly established fort, like a newborn infant, would not survive if it was deprived of that which was essential for its existence. It was not the first time, nor would it be the last in his massive volume of correspondence to imperial authorities that he would conflate the needs of his immediate family and those of the families of Detroit's upper classes with the larger needs of the settlement. The loss of an elite French baby represented the loss of the dream that Indigenous peoples would convert themselves into French men and women. If this belief had somehow become a reality, the loss of one French child would not matter—a French life could be exchanged for that of an Indigenous life, or an Indigenous mother easily substituted for a French mother to nurse an infant. There would be no need to import French wet nurses or French families because local Indigenous men and women, desiring Frenchness and becoming, for all intents and purposes, French, would fill these roles.

Cadillac's private aim was more likely to empower select French-Indigenous marriages and the networks of which they were part in order to strengthen his authority at Detroit. Unlike Henri Tonty, he did not have brothers or other kin connections among the larger group of officers who were making inroads in the upper country. He sought to create these affinal connections through his designates, including Pierre Roy, a French man married into the Myaamia nation. Cadillac seems to have periodically allowed designates such as Roy to function as Cadillac's designate as a local rendition of Onontio/governor general. Even though the commandant resident at Detroit had been given a monopoly on trade, that trade was restricted to the fort. Through partnership with Pierre Roy, who had married into the Myaamia nation, Cadillac could extend his trade to Kiihkayonki (Fort Miami) and beyond to the Illinois Country.[78] This partnership, which skirted the perimeters of legality, undercut imperial aims for Detroit's development.

Although ultimately unsuccessful, Cadillac sought to install himself as a seigneur or lord and came to see himself as Onontio as he envisioned Detroit becoming its own diplomatic, economic, and political hub for forts and posts located further west. As historian Guillaume Teasdale has demonstrated, Cadillac's notion of the powers of a seigneur more closely resembled the system in effect in France and not the more limited parameters of seigneurialism of the St. Lawrence valley.[79] As was the case at Quebec, diplomatic and political operations at Detroit required the display of ceremonial power. Detroit would therefore require its own father or Onontio who represented or embodied the father-king of France. Governor General Vaudreuil furiously fought this parceling out of his power and authority. The settlement at Detroit thus became a potential threat not only to the Montreal merchants who may have feared their profits would slip away if Detroit became an entrepôt for the posts of the *pays d'en haut,* but also to imperial authorities who feared their authority among Indigenous nations of the *pays d'en haut* would be similarly undermined. These authorities would attempt to regulate, control, and at times destroy the French-Indigenous family networks through a variety of means, including diminishing the size of the fort, withdrawing the garrison, and attempting to force residents to work the mines in the Illinois Country. Ultimately, these attempts would fail because the families had access to resources in a multitude of Indigenous communities and in the English colonies.

Cadillac's use of the symbolic construct of the family and metaphors of relatedness to gain the trust of Detroit's Indigenous peoples were often at odds with his actions, which would eventually cost him the favor of both imperial agents in Quebec and some Indigenous communities at Detroit. Cadillac presented elite French families as a bellwether of the intention of the French state to invest resources in Detroit's development. Where the families of Cadillac and Tonty would fail, however, French-Indigenous families would flourish.

CHAPTER 2

Corn Mothers, *Commandantes,* and Nurturing Fathers

Negotiating Place at Detroit

n the same letter in which he had begged for wet nurses and warned of the implications for French imperial designs if these women were not forthcoming, Cadillac launched into another dramatic description that placed his wife at the center of French-Indigenous relations at Detroit. Marie-Thérèse Guyon (Madame Cadillac) and Marie-Anne Picoté de Belestre (Madame Tonty) had set out for Detroit six weeks after their husbands, fifty soldiers, fifty traders, artisans, and farmers had traveled there to build a fort in July 1701.[1] According to Cadillac, the arrival of the women had had a profound effect on resident Indigenous nations. Haudenosaunee women had been astonished to see the wives and had kissed their hands, knowing that women of the French elite rarely accompanied their husbands to the upper country. The Haudenosaunee had expressed their satisfaction that the presence of women of such rank was proof that Governor General Callière had been sincere in treating for peace at Montreal in the summer of 1701.[2] The Algonquian nations allied to the French had been equally enthusiastic, firing their muskets to salute the women and commenting that they now knew that the French intended to establish a settlement and were committed to seeing it flourish.

Three years later, Madame Cadillac would again tie French imperial plans to her husband's activities. When Cadillac traveled to Quebec to answer allegations

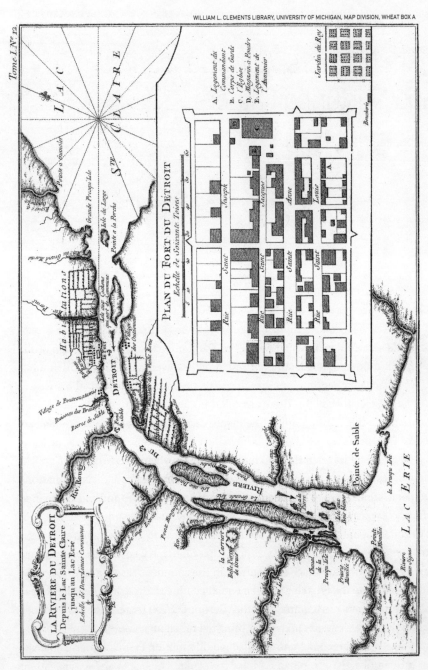

La rivière du Détroit depuis le Lac Sainte Claire jusqu'au Lac Érie, 1764

he had engaged in illegal trade, he faced the possibility of dismissal from his post by the Compagnie de la Colonie. Indigenous representatives from Detroit would demand of the governor general that Madame Cadillac remain at Detroit as proof that Cadillac intended to return. Governor General Philippe de Rigaud de Vaudreuil and Intendant François de Beauharnois de la Chaussaye were convinced Cadillac had received advance warning that his position was in jeopardy and had encouraged the Indigenous speakers to travel to Quebec to make their ultimatum.[3] Whether or not Cadillac had planned these events to buttress his position at Detroit, Indigenous insistence on Madame Cadillac's presence illustrates that French imperial agents knew the symbolic power of women to translate inchoate imperial dreams into French settlements.

Cadillac's description of Indigenous women's reaction to the arrival of his wife suggests he was also aware of the importance of these women to the growth of the Detroit community. The Haudenosaunee matrons had remarked that they had never seen French women come willingly to *their* country, meaning they regarded Detroit as part of their homelands and therefore under their control. "Critical identity holders" of their nation who played a central role in allowing the French to settle, the women also called out a European system different from their own, one dominated by men that discouraged the presence and willing participation of French women.[4] Included in Cadillac's report, this event communicated to the governor general that the Great Peace hammered out in 1701 between the French and Haudenosaunee remained in force.

The meeting of the French and Haudenosaunee women at Detroit was a recapitulation of the rituals of peace enacted in Montreal in 1701. This second diplomatic ceremony held in a region already considered part of the territories of Indigenous peoples (Iroquoian and Algonquian, as evidenced by the greeting of the French women with Algonquian musket fire) created a new and alternative space where multiple symbolic concepts of feminine agency converged. French-allied Algonquian nations would have also conducted peace negotiations with each other and with the French, and these ceremonies would have been led by designated women who walked ahead of male negotiators.[5] Anishinaabe men and women who took part in these rituals would have called the earth Aki on which the Detroit settlement was established, and would have understood it to be gendered female.[6] All of the women present in the first years of French presence—Haudenosaunee, Wendat, Anishinaabe, Myaamia, Wabanaki, and French—exercised gendered power in ways specific to their nations and enacted ritualized demonstrations of womanly behavior as part of state-sponsored projects.

The significance of these representations was augmented by the perceived scarcity of women by the French imperial state. In a colony that was consistently anxious over the lack of sufficient bodies needed to defend it and produce its crops, women, and particularly mothers, were of utmost importance. Indigenous women not only helped to people the colony (whether or not official imperial policy sanctioned it), they also provided pivotal kin access to their nations for many French men. Algonquian and Iroquoian women exhibited political, economic, and spiritual power that was not evident in European nations. As a consistent threat to French dominance in both the St. Lawrence valley and the upper country, the Haudenosaunee commanded a level of wary respect that necessitated the observance of and understanding by the French of Haudenosaunee policies and customs, including women's ceremonial roles.

In this chapter, I examine the basis for the symbolic status of French and Indigenous women at Detroit, a unique location where converging cultural norms allowed for the performance of a range of gendered behaviors by both men and women. Many European state agents not only misunderstood Detroit's distinctive position, they also attempted to enforce their models of settlement and associated gender roles. Some were savvier and sought to negotiate with Indigenous communities using the hybridized or transgender metaphors operating at Detroit. French-Indigenous families would succeed where these agents failed or fumbled, however, because they would make best use of the knowledge that as part of Haudenosaunee and Algonquian hunting territories, Detroit acted as a "transitional location" in Indigenous concepts of settlement. French, Iroquoian, and Algonquian nations would negotiate new ways to access Detroit's innovative cultural landscape in order to gain the necessary resources to launch successful commercial enterprises.

Naming and Claiming Detroit

Naming Detroit has always reflected its dual nature as both place and path. Detroit was called "Karantouan" by Wendat, meaning "coast of the straits." It was designated as "Waweatonong" by the Anishinaabe, meaning "crooked way." Its French moniker also expressed a topographic duality. At the time of its use by the French to name this region, the meaning of the word *detroit* was in flux. A sixteenth-century definition of *destroit* referred to a land-based location, translated as "district" or "locale." An eighteenth-century meaning of *detroit* referenced its nature as a strait or narrow water passage between two lands.[7] For the French, Detroit's natural geographic feature of being the narrowest point or strait on the waterway between Montreal in the east and the Mississippi River in the west made it both a boon and a threat to state security and economic development.

French official correspondence would consistently tout the unique benefits of Detroit's geography. In the late 1740s, New France's governor general stressed Detroit's strategic importance: "It is to [this] post that we must cling. If there were once a thousand farmer inhabitants in that region, it would feed and defend all the others. In all the whole interior of Canada, it is the fittest site for a city where all the commerce of the lakes would center, and which . . . would overawe all the Indians of the continent. To see its position on the map is enough to perceive its usefulness."[8] As historian Catherine Cangany has demonstrated, there would be regular and often apathetic imperial schemes to turn Detroit into an economic entrepôt.[9] These efforts had the potential to turn the region into a "bottleneck," where the flow of goods and information across great distances would narrow and possibly come to a halt. But, as was the case in many state-backed trade ventures that combined pecuniary accumulation with the "projection of sovereign power," these bottlenecks also often concentrated a disproportionate share of colonial profits.[10]

A decade later, as the British were assessing the limits of their newly acquired colony of Canada, Colonel John Bradstreet had dreams of becoming governor at Detroit and controlling the vast North American interior, an ambition held fifty years before by Cadillac. In a letter to his superiors, he touted Detroit's benefits: "This will secure the Frontier of our colonies, give us the whole of the Indian Trade in safety, effectually put a stop to the great and dangerous French plan of surrounding us with Inland Colonies and enable us to execute that Plan ourselves."[11] Detroit's location was its primary resource. Looked at through French and British eyes, it would become a launching point for imperial settlement schemes that would organize the trade with western Indigenous nations, while regulating and controlling the people who operated it.

Shaped by these dreams of empire, Detroit became a polyglot community and a highly charged space where the rituals of political negotiation grew in importance throughout the eighteenth century alongside the constant threat of violence. As historian Richard White has pointed out, these conflicts, which at times boiled over into open warfare, made it the most volatile of what White has identified as the five zones of Indigenous-French interaction in the upper country.[12] By the mid-eighteenth century, Detroit acted as "a thoroughfare between North and South for Indians" where communities of multiple Indigenous nations "were seen there, going and coming, the year round." While for Europeans it became a central point between northwestern and eastern regions, more than one Indigenous nation would depict Detroit as ground zero in tribal origin histories of the eighteenth and nineteenth centuries.[13]

In 1795, Myaamia leader Mihšihkinaahkwa (Little Turtle) declared to General Anthony Wayne at Fort Greenville: "It is well known to all my brothers present that my forefathers kindled the first fire at Detroit." Little Turtle used this primary geographic location to indicate the parameters of Myaamionki (Myaamia territory), as it stretched west and south to the headwaters of the Scioto, down the Ohio River, to the mouth of the Wabash River, and to Lake Michigan. "I have now informed you of the boundaries of the Miami nation where the Great Spirit placed my forefathers a long time ago and charged him not to sell or part with his lands but to preserve them to his posterity. This charge has now been handed down to me."[14]

In 1796, during negotiations to ascertain the limits of his nation's reserve on the Canadian side of the Detroit River, Wendat leader Dayenty reminded Sir John Johnson (son of former British superintendent of Northern Indian Affairs Sir William Johnson) that the Wendat had long been in residence at Detroit. In his claim, he made reference to specific features of the landscape (River Canard) and people (Wendat Deer clan leader Sasteresti):

> When our fore fathers were living they were always at war and fighting with different Nations of Indians and were drove from place to place until at last they came to the River Kannard and other places about it where the Sastereche fixed his seat, and said this Ground I appoint for the Present Generation and the Posterity that is to come after them, I have made it known to all Nations around me that this Ground I intend to stand upon—and here we must Perish before any other power dispossesses us of it.

At the same meeting, Odawa leader Egouchaway, representing a combined group of his nation and a Wendat community in their land negotiations with the British, drew out the bounds of a territory radiating west from Detroit to Bois Blanc Island in the middle of the river, and then east and south from Detroit, encompassing a sugar camp.[15] The speeches of Mihšihkinaahkwa, Egouchaway, and Dayenty occurred almost simultaneously. With Detroit at the center, their respective territories overlapped, the westernmost section of the Wendat/Odawa lands encompassing some of the easternmost portion of Myaamionki.

A century later, Indigenous historians published their nations' chronicles of Detroit. Wendat annalist Peter Dooyentate Clarke claimed a prominent place for his people who predated the arrival of Europeans. What the French had identified as the Huron, and the British referred to as the Wyandot, referred both more generally to the Wendat and also to the Tionontati (Tobacco band, also known as Petun), the latter of which was a large constituency of the greater Wendat nation. Clarke noted that "the first colony of Europeans pitched their tents on the bank of Detroit river, where the city of Detroit now stands, and they were the first French colony the Wyandotts ever met with in this part of the country."[16] Ojibwe historian William Warren similarly described how the French in the upper country first met his nation at Detroit. From the earliest years of the seventeenth century, the Ojibwe had made an annual trip from their home in the upper Great Lakes to Quebec and then Montreal to trade their furs. The length of the journey gradually lessened "as the whites advanced toward them step by step, locating their trading posts, first at Detroit, then at Mackinaw, then at Sault Ste. Marie."[17] In his book *History of the Ottawa and Chippewa Indians of Michigan,* Odawa historian Andrew Blackbird explained how his ancestors had extended their settlements south along the shore of Lake Michigan, eventually settling at Detroit, a location they considered was the "extent of their possessions."[18]

The Common Bowl: Detroit as Place Between

As Blackbird's history demonstrated, ties of family across time defined space, creating various levels of settlement as their members traveled.[19] Forts, cultivated fields, and hunting areas all constituted places of settlement. Hunting regions were transitional places situated on the edges of agricultural fields and houses, often overlapping areas designated in a similar fashion by bordering nations.[20] Located within such a space of intersecting territories, Detroit was claimed by Anishinaabe and was located in Bkejwanong ("where the waters divide"), at the southern periphery of Anishinaabewaki. It "held a special place in the spiritual world of the peoples of Lake Huron."[21] For other Algonquian nations including the Myaamia, Detroit was the easternmost point to which they had traveled during a period of widespread war with the Haudenosaunee in the seventeenth century. Detroit was also at the western edges of Haudenosaunee territory, contiguous to Seneca lands, the nation at the western door of the confederacy. In the early seventeenth century, the Haudenosaunee had forcibly absorbed large numbers of Neutrals, an Iroquoian group already resident in the Detroit region.[22] Haudenosaunee war parties made their way to Detroit later in the seventeenth century, as they launched large-scale offensives against Algonquian nations of the upper country. In 1700, the year before the Great Peace of Montreal, a skirmish had ensued when Odawa and Haudenosaunee contingents encountered each other while they were hunting at Detroit.

At Montreal in 1701, Haudenosaunee representatives had expressed their concern over the French plan to build a fort at Detroit that year. The territory around Detroit was referred to as a "common bowl" by negotiators because it was acknowledged as a territory shared by the Haudenosaunee and Algonquians. As Mohawk scholar Susan M. Hill points out, for the Haudenosaunee, the "dish with one spoon" entailed that "the bounty of the shared hunting grounds is meant to be enjoyed by all; land and the benefits of land belong to everyone."[23] The Haudenosaunee at first resisted the implications of French settlement, claiming that Detroit was the only place they had had for hunting. But in the decades immediately preceding 1701, they had been driven from the area when the tide had turned in their war with Algonquian nations.[24] The French, and Europeans in general, had different ideas about the notion of shared terrain. According to historian Allan Greer, there was a growing effort to "reinforce control over the land and its revenues" that involved "encroaching on village commons."[25] With these competing visions of settlement, it is not surprising that communal lands required special consideration at Montreal in 1701. Detroit was one of only two such territories discussed at the meeting.[26]

Dekanitsore, chief sachem of the Onondaga, reported to New York's governor that he had protested the presence of the fort at Detroit to the French governor general and that the Haudenosaunee hadn't been notified of its construction in advance.[27] The Haudenosaunee complained of the French encroaching on territory "where the Beaver hunting is which wee won with the sword eighty years ago" without Haudenosaunee consent, and requested that the king of England take steps to prevent it. They expressed their desire to "let the covenant chain reach from New York to Sinnondowanne [Seneca territory] . . . that all the people that live under itt may be secure from all attempts of an enemy—We would remove the end of the chain to Tiochsaghrondie [Detroit], the end of the Covenant Chain."[28] After their negotiations with the French at the Great Peace, with Cadillac en route to Detroit, the Haudenosaunee composed a deed. Signed by twenty sachems, it granted to the king of England a tract of land stretching from western Pennsylvania through Detroit, Chicago, and north to Michilimackinac.[29] As Daniel Richter points out, these transactions over Detroit marked a shift to a "reinterpreted Covenant Chain" that put the Haudenosaunee under the "protection" of the English in any dispute with the French.[30]

Haudenosaunee understanding of Detroit's unique status allowed them to treat with both the French and English over their continued presence in the region. The concept of the common bowl provided the means by which Haudenosaunee acknowledged Detroit as a shared space with the French and Algonquian nations of the upper country, which in turn promoted peace and the resumption of unrestricted travel and trade from Montreal to the Illinois Country. Whereas for the Haudenosaunee, the common bowl provided the context for the renegotiation of their alliance with the English through the lengthening of the metaphoric Covenant Chain, the English would stake their claim to Detroit based on past wartime successes of their Haudenosaunee allies.

The English had made their own voyages to the Great Lakes as early as 1685, in an effort to engage western Indigenous nations in commerce. That year, Arnout Cornelissen Viele, interpreter of Indigenous languages for the colony of New York, traveled to the lands of the Seneca. With the help of a French deserter, he continued west to Lakes Erie and Huron. The English were not satisfied with merely engaging the western Algonquian nations in trade. Secretary of Indian Affairs Robert Livingston believed the only way to induce the Odawa (Ottowawaes), Myaamia (Twichtwicks), and other western Algonquian nations (Dowaganhaes) to cease their attacks on the Haudenosaunee and allow hunting and trade to resume was to establish a presence at Detroit.

Livingston suggested Detroit as an ideal location at which to acquire beaver, and a place that rightfully belonged to the English. Livingston called for two hundred English Christians, joined by four hundred Haudenosaunee and their Algonquian prisoners to construct a fort at Wawijachtenok (Waweatonong). The Christians would establish a settlement, which they and the Haudenosaunee would use as a launching point for negotiations with Great Lakes nations, keeping the path open by introducing these new trading partners to cheaper English goods.[31] He described "De Troett" as "the most pleasant and plentiful inland place in America by all relation, where there is arable land for thousands of people, and the only place for beaver hunting for which our Indians have fought so long."[32] Livingston's description presents Detroit as a central point between two concepts of development in North America—stationary settlement attending concentrated agricultural activity and mobility required to hunt furs. The peace negotiated between the Haudenosaunee, French, and western Algonquian nations would prevent the English from testing the viability of this model at Detroit.

French imperial effort was devoted to ensuring that furs and French goods flowed between Montreal and certain carefully maintained and strategic posts in the upper country. The official intent of a cessation of permits to voyageurs traveling to the *pays d'en haut* before 1701 had been to redress a surplus that was driving the price of furs down and the price of goods up. Left unchecked, this situation could send Indigenous traders into the hands of the English, who provided them with less expensive goods. The threat of two encroachments always remained—war brought on by Indigenous nations not allied to the French, and the partnership of British and Haudenosaunee traders who sought to establish trade relations with the Algonquian nations of the upper country. After 1701, with the establishment of Detroit and the end of the suspension of *congés* (trade permits), these threats became of paramount concern to French imperial agents in the St. Lawrence valley. It was hoped that agricultural settlement would anchor the French community, but it would become increasingly more urgent to maintain alliances with Detroit's Indigenous nations. This would include honoring the ties that continued to be forged between the French and Indigenous communities through marriage and trade.

Clearing the Way: Gendering Settlement at Detroit

Detroit's first census would demonstrate the state's determination to differentiate those who were tethered to the land through the yielding of crops, and those who moved across it to secure furs and trading relations with Indigenous groups. This tally did not enumerate women, but the way in which it was organized nonetheless communicated two things: the continued symbolic importance of marriage and wives as markers of their families' lifestyle, and the virtual invisibility in imperial records of women who were mobile through participation in the fur trade.

The census was arranged with separate categories: single Canadian men; Canadian men who lived with their wives at Detroit; widowers; Frenchmen whose wives refused to move to Detroit; soldiers who had their wives at Detroit; and men who had wives and children at Detroit. Of thirty-four men enumerated, only eight had wives with them. The census also separated those who cultivated land from those who did not. All those listed as holding land were married with children. These categories are evidence of the importance placed on French women as indicators of a man's potential willingness to adopt an agrarian lifestyle and settle at Detroit. Of the men who did not engage in farming, 90 percent were single or had wives who did not live with them at Detroit, suggesting two things: their wives were equally mobile as their husbands, and/or these men were living with Indigenous women to whom they were not married according to Catholic rites. These women would have been doubly invisible in imperial eyes: their relationships with white men were illegitimate, and because Indigenous peoples were not enumerated in the census, their presence was not a viable predictor of potential success of the state's plans for settlement.[33]

Despite this invisibility, Indigenous nations continued to maintain and adapt their own methods of occupying their territories. As the wars between the Haudeno-saunee and Algonquian nations broke out and subsided in the seventeenth century, vast areas of the Great Lakes and Ohio Valley had been cleared of agriculture. At times during this period of political, cultural, and economic unrest, Indigenous col-lectives moved to different locations within their extended territories or relocated to new places, turning the upper country into a swath of mutable communities. War upset the balance of the cycle of mobility, which in the winter called for hunting and occupation of winter territories, followed by settlement in summer villages, where crops could be planted and harvests gathered. Indigenous nations couched the cycle of mobility/war/hunting and sedentariness/agriculture in different ways, but in all cases, the relationship between the two ways of living on the land was rooted in notions of gender.

Detroit's terrain and what it produced was gendered differently by each resident Indigenous community. The three sisters—corn, beans, and squash—formed the cornerstone of Indigenous diets and were manifestations of sacred beings. Their planting and harvesting was marked with appropriate ceremony. Of these three, corn was regarded as the most important and an essential source of sustenance across a multitude of North American Indigenous nations.[34] It is therefore not surprising that corn played a decisive role in Indigenous religious ceremonies and creation stories. Each nation at Detroit produced its own corn and its own gendered version of corn's origins. The Mississippian culture, which sprang from the earlier Mound Builder societies of the upper and lower Mississippi and Great Lakes, saw corn as sacred and experimented with developing different varieties. Corn was grown primarily by women and knowledge of its cultivation was orally transmitted. It provided the bulk of essential nutrients—far greater than meat or fish.[35]

To Iroquoian and Algonquian nations, including the Wabanaki who settled briefly at Detroit, corn was female, as was the earth from which it and every other crop sprang. Tekawerahkwa, known as "the Lynx" to the Haudenosaunee and as Nigawes (meaning "our mother") to the Wabanaki, was part of the creation narrative of the Corn Mother story.[36] In the Haudenosaunee version, Tekawerahkwa was the daughter of Sky Woman, who had created the earth. Tekawerahkwa became pregnant with twin boys by Great Turtle, who visited her one night disguised as a middle-aged man. Tekawerahkwa's two boys were named Teharonghyawago ("Holder of Heaven" or "Skyholder"), who was born first from Tekawerahkwa the natural way, and Tawiskaron ("Flinty Rock"), who decided he would be born from under his mother's arm. His birth mortally wound her and she died soon after the birth of her sons.[37]

The first son mourned his mother, expressing his deep sadness to his grandmother Sky Woman. Eventually, Skyholder decided to bury her and visited his mother's grave every day. Within a short while, he noticed buds springing from the ground where his mother was buried. Where her feet lay, the potato plant grew; from her fingers came beans; squash sprang from her abdomen; the tobacco plant grew near her forehead; and finally, from her breasts sprang corn. Thankful that her grandson had tended his mother so lovingly, thereby nourishing new life, Sky Woman declared: "By these things we shall hereafter live, and they shall be cooked in pots with fire, and the corn shall be your milk and sustain you. You shall make the corn grow in hills like breasts, for from the corn shall flow our living."[38]

The Wabanaki story of Corn Mother as related by Lisa Brooks is in general similar to that of the Haudenosaunee, although the details of her death are different. In this story, the husband of First Mother noticed she was becoming increasingly discontented—their children were hungry and asking for food. She promised her children they would have enough to eat and asked her husband to kill her with a stone tool and to tend to and bury her body in a particular way. Her husband reluctantly consented and followed her instructions. Within a short time after her burial, enough corn to feed her children grew from her flesh, as well as tobacco to "give strength to their thoughts" that came forth from her bones. Her husband declared to the people: "As we are all brothers, divide among you the flesh and bone of the first mother, and let all shares be alike, then the love of your first mother will have been fully carried out." As Lisa Brooks explains, both the Haudenosaunee and Wabanaki stories designate the "transformation of Native space through the body of a woman . . . the common pot that births and feeds us all."[39]

Among the Haudenosaunee, it was a woman who held the title of Djikonsä'së (Jigonsase in English), meaning Mother of All Nations or Ye-go-wa-neh (Great Woman). She had been the first to understand and implement the messages of the Wendat prophet Peacemaker and his Haudenosaunee neophyte Hiawatha urging the cessation of hostilities.[40] Because of her role in keeping peace, she became the head clan mother of the Haudenosaunee. She was a direct descendant of the Lynx and Sky Woman, and embodied the Lynx from the time when brother fought against brother, threatening to destroy the entire nation.[41] The first Jigonsase is said to have been of the Attiwandaronk or Neutral nation, which was closely allied to the Wendat. The Attiwandaronk were Iroquoian, and their original homelands placed them in what is now central-southwest Ontario, Canada, before they were dispersed and absorbed by the Haudenosaunee in the mid-seventeenth century. Their territory may also have extended as far west as Lake Erie, which would have placed them in the region of Detroit.[42]

Jigonsase came to be known variously as "the Peace Queen," "the Fire Woman," and "the Maize Maiden." She cultivated both corn and peace and her duties included feeding war parties and all visitors to Iroquoia, no matter what their nation of origin. During this process, she was also responsible for discovering the business of these visitors. Her longhouse was a place of sanctuary, and she was charged with keeping the peace through mediation and negotiation at every level: individual, clan, and nation. If war could not be avoided, she had the right to assemble and command armies. Because of her, only women could declare war since they held the peace in their hands. As the head clan mother, she convened all meetings of the clan mothers and sent their decisions on issues forward to the men's Grand Council, who could not act on these matters without the prior consensus of the Mothers. Together with the Peacemaker and Hiawatha, she was cofounder of the Great Law of the Confederacy.[43]

A seventeenth-century Jigonsase emerged as a savior of her people in 1687 when French Governor General Denonville was ordered by King Louis XIV to invade Seneca territory and quash Haudenosaunee resistance to the French. Denonville put a plan into action, inviting the Haudenosaunee men's Grand Council and some of the clan mothers to attend a peace meeting. Once they were gathered, Denonville seized them and sent them to France to serve as slaves. By so doing, Denonville believed he had effectively leveled the Haudenosaunee government. Denonville was unaware, however, that he had not captured Jigonsase because it was customary for her to send representatives to official meetings while she remained in her home territory. Jigonsase immediately assembled a war party that consisted of several women and appointed war chiefs, leading this army herself in a decisive battle at Ganondagan (known as La Chine in French). Jigonsase drove Denonville out of Seneca territory and back to Montreal. The next year, Denonville was forced by Jigonsase to abandon the French fort at Niagara. She also demanded the return of the members of the Haudenosaunee government who had been sent to France. She was only successful in reacquiring thirteen of this group because the rest had died as slaves in the French navy.[44] As historian Brett Rushforth points out, Denonville's behavior was viewed by the Haudenosaunee as an "egregious violation of North American laws of war" because he had invited them to meet under the "pretext of friendship" and peace.[45]

The importance of corn and its gendered connection can be found in the origin stories of other Indigenous groups. The Myaamia, traditionally patrilineal, were successful producers of maize and known in particular for a distinctive type of sweet white milky corn that was grown exclusively by them. Although the Myaamia story of corn's origin is strikingly similar in many details to that of the Lynx and Nigawes, their rendition of how corn entered their world as a powerful source of sustenance features a man, rather than a woman. Myaamia Chief Clarence Godfroy related the story set in a time before the arrival of Europeans.

At that time, food and game were scarce and the Myaamia were greatly troubled because their people were on the point of starvation. A large council consisting of chiefs and prophets convened to consider a solution. Several talented prophets were sent into the forest to seek answers. The prophets remained in the woods for many days and nights and eventually, they returned one by one without any food. There remained one prophet who had not returned, however, and the other prophets set out to look for him. A few days later, they encountered him on his way back to the camp. When asked if he had found food, he answered yes, and proceeded to tell them the story. This last prophet had met a handsome man in the woods who asked him why he was alone in the forest. The prophet answered that he had come to seek guidance because there was famine in his country. On hearing this, the handsome man declared that the prophet was required to fight a duel with him, and then kill and bury him on the spot on which they were standing. The prophet was hesitant—he told the man that he had no quarrel with him and therefore no reason to kill him. The handsome man replied that if the prophet expected to save his people from starvation, he was required to do as he had been instructed. The prophet reluctantly complied and a strenuous battle ensued.

The prophet killed the handsome man and buried him at the designated location on a little knoll. The next morning, the prophet returned to the place of the burial and saw a large stalk (*miincipaahkwi*) growing on the grave.[46] Upon closer examination, the prophet saw that there was food on the plant, which he took with him on his trip back to his people. The prophet had declared that if the stalk was planted, the people would never starve again. The Myaamia complied and sowed their first crop, and from that time forward, the people never went hungry again. The food was called *miincipi,* which later became known as Indian corn.[47] Tending crops was usually the work of women among Algonquian and Iroquoian groups, but interestingly, the agricultural activity in which Myaamia men would participate was the planting and hoeing of corn.[48]

The milk of the corn grew from the mounds of earth and the handsome man's body, just as it emanated from the breasts of Sky Woman's daughter "the Lynx," representing the quintessential maternal gift of sustenance. In Iroquoian societies, the maize mother Jigonsase worked to maintain peace over those who favored war. In the Myaamia corn origin story, maize is the only crop that springs from the body of the slain handsome man, and is the only crop men will grow. It rises from the ground as a stalk bearing the "milky" seeds that will allow it to continue to sustain the people, acting as the quintessential phallic/paternal gift of sustenance. In all of these stories, violence must take place before corn can be grown. But at the same time, in order to grow, it requires a space free from the threat of war. In essence, it signifies the subtle balance between war and peace that must be maintained if a society hopes to prosper.

For Europeans establishing posts in the upper country, corn was an essential crop that they adopted from local Indigenous groups, and Cadillac frequently mentioned it as an indicator of Detroit's viability as a place of settlement. It represents the adaptation by Europeans of Indigenous concepts of settlement and sustenance because without corn, Europeans could not build their empires in the upper country. At Detroit, multiple nations interpreted corn and the ground from which it grew according to gendered distinctions. Corn became a symbol of the generative principle of male and female combined, an attenuated creative force that made it the most important crop for all Indigenous nations and eventually, for Europeans as well.

Both Europeans and the multitude of Indigenous nations at Detroit had to learn to navigate and negotiate within a world crossed with these subtle gendered distinctions. When Cadillac and other contemporaries spoke in council with Indigenous groups, they often assumed the role of both father and mother at the same time in a hybridized version of the penultimate parent. Indeed, the role of Onontio very closely resembled that of Jigonsase. Onontio was required to be a generous mediator and arbiter of peace who could propose but not demand that a course of action be followed. It was only when the rituals of peace were no longer effective that Onontio was expected to call for war. Indeed, in many Indigenous nations, uncles—brothers of a man's mother—wielded the most powerful influence, not the fathers, who were more often seen as mediators.[49]

Onontio also adopted the metaphor of breastfeeding from Indigenous peoples to communicate a willingness to provide resources and acknowledge the political importance of clans. For the Anishinaabe, as Heidi Bohaker points out, one's *nindoodem* or clan/kinship network was named for an other-than-human progenitor being (beaver, bear, wolf, otter, crane). All those of the same *nindoodem* considered themselves related to one another and as having kinship obligations to each other, locally and across distances.[50] One's *nindoodem* or clan was inherited from one's father, and according to Brenda Child "was quite literally the breast from which milk and sustenance derived and . . . the center of one's spiritual identity."[51]

Historian Gilles Havard has recovered multiple instances in the French imperial record where the metaphor of the breast or of breastfeeding was utilized by Onontio and Indigenous representatives in their official speeches. Using the ritualized language of diplomacy, Indigenous men abandoned the ways of war to drink at the breast of Onontio, a father-nurturer. In 1690, the French invited the Haudenosaunee "to come and see their old father [Frontenac] who came to give them succor." The calumet, a symbol of peace, often constituted a substitution for the breast. La Potherie reported that during a visit to the Mascouten, Nicolas Perrot "had them smoke his calumet, telling them that this was his breast that he had always presented for them to suckle." The metaphor of the breast also explained the protective function of Onontio. His children were "held to his breast," explained Charlevoix, and would therefore benefit from French military protection. This type of "feeding" augmented the social relation between the metaphoric father and his children.[52]

Cadillac evoked this idea in a speech delivered to an assembled group of Odawa leaders at Detroit. Hoping to reassure them of their importance to the French, he proclaimed, "I hold you all pressed to my breasts; I take you into my breast to die with you."[53] Cadillac's words likely communicated two things: he would continue to supply the Odawa with resources in return for their economic and military support, and he would respect and maintain clan coherency at Detroit. Three years later, in 1706, the Odawa were frustrated by the fickle nature of French backing, a situation that had contributed to the division of Odawa *nindoodemag* between Michilimackinac and Detroit. Skirmishes had broken out between the Odawa and the Myaamia and Wendat at Detroit—the latter of the two nations rumored to be in league with the Haudenosaunee—resulting in the deaths of several Myaamia and two Frenchmen.

An Odawa contingent traveled to Montreal to meet with Governor General Vaudreuil to address French demands for the surrender of Le Pesant, the Odawa leader blamed for the incident. Using the metaphor of familial relationship to express their concerns, the Odawa representatives reminded the French of the prominence of the diplomatic relationship originally forged by the two nations: "We remember perfectly that our father told us that we are in his breast, and the Iroquois also our brothers, with this difference though that these last are in the right breast, and we at the left, we are together well lodged in his heart."[54] The Odawa speech clearly delineated the degrees of intimacy between the French father-nurturer and the Odawa and Haudenosaunee. The following year, the relationship between the French and Odawa remained significantly damaged. The Odawa felt that the French had not only failed to protect them during the altercation with the Myaamia and Wendat, but had also aligned themselves with these two aggressive nations. Outoutagan, one of the principal chiefs of the Odawa Sable *nindoodem* who was known to the French as Jean Le Blanc declared to Vaudreuil that Cadillac had relinquished his role of father-nurturer and had left his children in a vulnerable position:

> My father my father, Monsieur de La Mothe [Cadillac] has done as the porcupine who doesn't suckle its young, it's he who called us the four Ottawa nations to Detroit, but after having made an opening in the tree as the porcupine does to give suckle to its young, he left us.[55]

Outoutagan references Cadillac as an inept parent who eschews or misunderstands his hybridized role as both mother and father. Creating the opening in the tree opens a space within which the porcupine mother faces her children and offers the soft breast that nourishes, rather than the painful prick of the quill that wounds and potentially kills. In calling the Odawa to Detroit, Cadillac purported to offer a safe place for them to live and trade, but he ultimately turned his back, refusing to support and protect them. Outoutagan's concern that his nation had lost their original position at the left breast of the French father-nurturer had been realized. At a meeting held two months after his speech to Vaudreuil, Cadillac told the Odawa that while they were at Detroit, they had been elder sons, but once they left for Michilimackinac, they had become younger sons, and the Wendat had taken their place.[56]

As was discussed in the previous chapter, Cadillac had made a general appeal for wampum with which he could enter into diplomatic talks with local nations and address any grievances. Vaudreuil had begrudgingly assented to this request, thereby empowering Cadillac to act on his behalf, but not as Onontio. Nevertheless, Cadillac had assumed the role of the father-nurturer despite Vaudreuil's protestations. La Blanche, who like her kinsman was a leader among the Odawa, accused Cadillac of offering wampum to Odawa women to compel them to remain at Detroit during the first year of French settlement.[57] Cadillac had later used wampum to address the situation between the Odawa, Myaamia, and Wendat in a manner he felt local circumstances required. But Le Blanc/Outoutagan's fears of abandonment by Cadillac had materialized, and Cadillac's perceived mishandling of the situation would sink him further in the eyes of imperial authorities. This was a crucial moment in the local enactment of the metaphorical nurturer/father-child relationship between the French and Indigenous communities.

The milk from the breasts of the father-nurturer could symbolize the gifts that attended the enactment of friendship between the French and Indigenous nations. It could also represent alcohol. Pierre Potier, a Jesuit in residence at Detroit, made note of a Wendat expression that made this connection: "We hope that our father will have breasts full of milk and will give us good brandy."[58] Historian Bruce White noted that rum, brandy, and other forms of alcohol "crystallized the idiom of kinship more than any of the other gifts." Rum became the symbol of a mother's milk, and in diplomatic negotiations, the exchange or gifting of rum indicated the seriousness of these talks to the Anishinaabe and other Indigenous nations. White points out that among the Ojibwe, only when a mother was nursing her son could she exhibit an authority over him that was equal to that of his father. He also postulates that drinking alcohol could induce childlike behavior in the person imbibing, thereby strengthening the metaphorical parent-child relationship.[59]

For the elite of New France, becoming intoxicated symbolized their desire for freedom from the constraints of morality.[60] Religious authorities viewed drunkenness and luxury—the pursuit of pleasure as an end in and of itself—as interconnected, and they therefore denounced the abuse of alcohol.[61] Members of the religious orders who worked among Indigenous groups feared that the consumption of alcohol would disrupt the fabric of their society and encourage sexual liaisons between French men and Indigenous women. It may also have been perceived as a dangerous "leveler" of gender barriers, since women were encouraged to abstain from drinking alcoholic beverages, the belief being that these drinks would warm their blood.[62] Throughout the eighteenth century, the correspondence and reports of Euro-Americans were littered with references to how Indigenous women were equally or often more unruly than their men when they became intoxicated.

In order to promote settlement at Detroit, Cadillac needed to maintain a flow of goods and alcohol that would grease the wheels of his ongoing negotiations with local Indigenous nations. He needed to nurture as a woman and protect (with its promise of military intervention) as a man. Cadillac had experience while in command at Michilimackinac with the Wendat and Odawa, and was mindful of the agency of Iroquoian clan mothers who straddled the line between war and peace. He attempted to model both feminine and masculine traits in a manner that would help him to maintain a viable diplomatic position and allow him to tread delicately, particularly in his interactions with the Haudenosaunee, who were perceived as being a constant threat to peace and settlement at Detroit, even after the Great Peace of 1701. A threat equal to that of Haudenosaunee aggression was Haudenosaunee and English access to the Algonquian nations of the *pays d'en haut*. Detroit both provided a barrier to Haudenosaunee/English penetration into the upper country and made contact between the Haudenosaunee and Algonquian nations easier.

At a metaphoric level, Cadillac and his contemporaries assumed the transgendered role of father-nurturer because it was demanded by their Indigenous allies. It was a persona that was not always successfully enacted, but the performance would be repeated through to the end of the French regime. It is highly likely that two things resulted from this set of circumstances: European men, like Cadillac, recognized the integral roles played by Iroquoian clan mothers and Algonquian women leaders, and adopted or modeled characteristics of these women in their negotiations and interactions. Cadillac may have displayed womanly traits because he was aware that Iroquoian and Algonquian women determined whether a space would be used for peace or for war, and that in Iroquoian and Algonquian nations, the land on which crops were grown and settlements erected was gendered female. Cadillac modeled both feminine and masculine characteristics in his efforts to keep his Indigenous allies ready for war while also recognizing the necessity of creating a settlement at Detroit that allowed for peaceful cohabitation so that trade could be conducted.

French women would utilize the transecting gender norms available at Detroit in their own ways that would allow them to defy the state, even as their presence concomitantly represented European ideals of women as a generative force. The French state also attempted to control them and their families by designating women markers of men's rootedness to an agricultural lifestyle. They would defy this stricture, however, by modeling Haudenosaunee and Algonquian women, who held systemic political power, operated at the highest diplomatic channels, and moved freely through the extensive territory of their nations. Also, like their counterparts at court in Versailles, elite French women operated as mediators and close advisors to their husbands and other male members of their families. They actively worked to build and maintain political ties and commercial enterprises and to challenge and even destroy competing interests.[63]

Marie-Anne Picoté de Belestre (Madame Tonty), who we met at the beginning of this chapter as she and Madame Cadillac arrived to the caresses and celebratory musket fire of local Indigenous nations, would be accused of setting the fire that destroyed most of the fort in 1703.[64] After her death, Alphonse Tonty would marry Marie-Anne de La Marque, who before this marriage had run afoul of French authorities when she was accused of working together with a French trader and a Haudenosaunee man to illegally traffic in English stroud.[65] La Marque appears on at least three occasions to have occupied her husband's position of commandant at Detroit during his tenure from 1717 to 1727. Church records refer to her on three occasions in 1722 as "commandant of said place."[66]

La Marque would also act as her husband's *procuratrice,* a power of attorney under the French legal system Coutume de Paris that allowed her to operate on her husband's behalf as his equal.[67] La Marque acquired the goods he needed to operate in Montreal and at Detroit, petitioning imperial authorities for compensation for her own expenses and to maintain Indigenous alliances and the commandant's residence. Tonty, his first wife Picoté de Belestre, and second wife La Marque would all stand accused of illegal activities in the first three decades of the eighteenth century.[68] Like Cadillac, Tonty would be called to Quebec to answer for his actions, and in his absence, his second wife would act on his behalf as Detroit's commandant. By enacting French and Indigenous gendered models, the women were able to optimize their potential for commercial success, and at times to avoid the dangers or penalties associated with transgressing the boundaries of European notions of proper womanly behavior. Just over a decade later, Marie-Anne Picoté de Belestre's sister-in-law, Marie Catherine Trottier DesRuisseaux, would continue the women's work of this extended family, acting as a *procuratrice* for her husband François Marie Picoté de Bellestre at Detroit.[69] Their son, also named François, would be Detroit's last French commandant.

Fathers who suckled their young, corn mothers, and women commandants combined attributes from across European and Indigenous nations that would undergird Detroit's development as a spiritual, economic, and political midpoint in imperial agendas. In all of these cases, power was available when women and men called upon a variety of gendered practices, and recognized the importance of these behaviors for moving across and utilizing the land and its resources. Even before Cadillac and the French had arrived, Detroit was already a contested space, an arena for political diplomacy, and a site of economic development. Imperial officials such as Cadillac stumbled through complex negotiations, calling upon a mix of gendered symbols and practices. They were obligated to act on behalf of the king and the interests of the state. But when they exploited this obligation and embodied the king to benefit themselves politically and economically, they risked imperial censure and removal. In either situation, they were precluded from operating outside official channels and the metaphoric ties of parent-child kinship that came with representing Onontio.

Detroit's terrain would present another set of possible intersections between Indigenous and European worlds. Located within the liminal space designated as a hunting territory by Iroquoian and Algonquian groups, Detroit would continue to be defined by overlapping and sometimes competing Indigenous and European hegemonic claims through the eighteenth century. Patricia Albers and Jeanne Kay point out that the key to jointly utilizing lands in a peaceful fashion was the establishment of "extensive kinship ties connecting the involved groups."[70] More enduring models of family would take root at Detroit and fill the vacuum left by the state's often ineffectual and more contrived performances of relatedness. These alternative ties of kinship would operate outside the ritualized world of diplomacy and become part of day-to-day activities in which the French-Indigenous family networks engaged. Members of the networks could call on the tools of ritualized kinship when they represented or responded to the state. They could also cast aside these tools when they chose to adopt other models that benefited them and their families, or when they were threatened by imperial censure. As well, they would also stretch this range of kinship ties across vast distances, utilizing Detroit's status as a transitional location and center point of overlapping concepts of settlement as a pivot point for their activities.

Imperial alarm was often based on the fear that persons skilled at navigating French and Indigenous worlds controlled the entire economic and political apparatus in the upper country, forcing the state to meld its strictures and operations in response. Their activities were often deemed illegal by the state because they defied rules and regulations that attempted to control access to Indigenous communities and to the complex and highly lucrative trade based on furs. Indeed, sometimes the state would play "catch-up" to make activities of the family networks fit within a legal context, so that trade and amicable relations with Indigenous nations could continue. But families on the ground led much more complex lives. Indigenous and French men and women came together, creating family networks that operated sometimes within and sometimes in spite of imperial edicts. Like the state, these networks attempted to control the flow of goods and persons in order to maximize economic and political clout as a hedge against imperial intrusions. Members also used their resources to build their own corporate identity through the elaboration of and performance of a distinct culture. Their loyalties were to their family first, even when this obligation ran counter to the state.

The next chapter will provide an examination of how the French-Indigenous family networks would gain complete ascendancy in Detroit and the upper country by the mid-eighteenth century. These families were built on connections that predated French imperial establishment at Detroit. Trade at the fort in its first crucial decade depended on the cooperation of these networks. Those commandants who managed to maintain this goodwill, such as Cadillac, met with some success in trade. Those who did not found themselves on the wrong side of relations with both local French and Indigenous communities. Cadillac struggled to maintain control as the agent of the state/Onontio/father-nurturer, but the activities of the family networks would ensure Detroit's economic ascendancy. Sometimes, alternative concepts of territorial occupancy and kinship exhibited by the networks would clash with imperial expectations and erupt into warfare. This would be the case in 1712 as the activities of French, Myaamia, and Meskwaki (Fox) families clashed with the state's determination to make war. At the center of this dispute, as it first broke out at Detroit, would be a woman connected to the French-Myaamia family of Pierre Roy.

CHAPTER 3

War, Slavery, and Baptism

The Formation of the French-Indigenous Networks at Detroit

Un sauvage chassant dans ces bois,
Ayant faim de manger du pain,
Dessur un Français il s'est en allé
Tout épouvanté, disant:—Sauve-toé.
Il lui a dans ces bois beaucoup d'Iroquois
Qui vont mettre à yâ-yor les Français.

Bourdignon qui est un homme sans façon
Il dit:—Camarades allons!
Tout en continuant sur le commandant
Il s'est en allé, disant:—Monsieur Roy
Faites rassembler tous vos garnadiers,
Un homme pour interpreter.

Aussitôt qu'le commandement fut donné,
Tout à chacun fut rassemblé.
Et les sauvages contents avec leur butin,
Ils s'en allaient tous, ils criaient:—Ya oin!

Oh les Mascoutens patagos malins,
Tous chargés de ce bon butin.[1]

A man named Monsieur Roy appears in "Les Mascoutens," a French song collected
and recorded by folklorist and musician Marcel Bénéteau in River Canard,
an area that is part of the original community of le Détroit. Most of the other
compositions gathered by Bénéteau feature melodies or lyrics that appear
whole-cloth or as portions of other songs imported from France or French North
America. "Les Mascoutens," however, is unique to le Détroit and references specific
historic events that took place there. Bénéteau speculates that this is probably
because the Mascouten, an Algonquian Great Lakes nation for whom the song
was named, figured especially prominently at one particular juncture in Detroit's
history.[2]

The lyrics tell the story of an Indigenous man hunting in the woods who is
very hungry. He encounters a Frenchman who he warns of an impending Iroquois
attack. The alarm is sounded, and members of the community flee in fear. Once
everyone has gone, the Mascouten arrive, steal the goods left behind, congratulate
themselves on their success, and set off on their way. The song ends with the French
surprised and angry at the deceit that has been perpetrated upon them. The song
contains colloquial expressions—buoys marking the cultural landscape of early
eighteenth-century Detroit and the upper country. One of these expressions, *yâ-
yor*, plays an important role, indicating what the Iroquois hiding in the woods are
prepared to do to the French. The second expression, *Ya oin*, acts as an exclamation
of victory by the Mascouten who have managed to steal merchandise from under
the noses of the French at Detroit. The third word, *patagos*, functions as a quality
used to describe the victorious Mascouten. According to Bénéteau, the three words
may be vocables or vestiges of Indigenous languages that have been altered over
time through oral transmission by French speakers, making it difficult to discern
their original meaning.[3]

Although the meaning of *ya oin* remains elusive, it is possible that *yâ-yor* is
a local variation of the French "dehors," meaning "outdoors" or "outside." In this
context, the sentence would literally translate as "who [referring to the Iroquois]
are going to kick the French outdoors," or remove the French from the area. It is
a compelling interpretation, especially because the Haudenosaunee considered
Detroit to be part of their hunting grounds, and the song begins with an Indigenous
man hunting at Detroit. According to Bénéteau, it is easier to be more precise about

the third word, *patagos,* which is Algonquian-based.[4] In the last verse, when it has been discovered that the Mascouten have made off with considerable plunder, the song's narrator exclaims: "Oh les Mascoutens patagos malins." Bénéteau identifies "patagos" as possessing the prefix "pata," which in some Algonquian languages implies "evil, sin, or damage." The line, roughly translated as "oh the cunning and evil Mascoutens," leads us to believe that the threat of an Iroquois attack was part of the ruse, and that the reputed legions of Iroquois warriors hiding in the woods may never have existed. The Indigenous messenger involved in the plot could therefore have been a Mascouten man with multiple loyalties, and a person trusted by the French at Detroit.

Throughout the song "Les Mascoutens," panicked movement expressed through repetition of the phrase "il s'est en allé" (he went on his way) or "ils s'en allaient tous" (they all went on their way) propels the actors forward. In a cycle that repeats itself each time the song is sung, the threat of attack becomes the means by which the day-to-day affairs of Detroit are disrupted and assets redistributed. This circular movement also makes it difficult to discern alliances and to determine who, if anyone, has emerged as victor in this staged attack. The song hints at the complex layers of relationship between the French, Mascouten, Haudenosaunee, and possibly—as allies of, in French eyes, and motivators behind Iroquois aggression—the English. It is a song in which Indigenous participants, directing the complexities of local politics and utilizing the power of French fear of the Iroquois and the English, control the outcome of events. Ultimately, the French are defeated by this fear generated not at Detroit, but in Quebec by an ineffectual and embattled Onontio/king/state whose resources are ultimately stolen and absorbed into the local economy.

"Les Mascoutens" tells us that the threat of an Iroquois attack continued to resonate in French and Indigenous communities. Eleven years after the Peace of Montreal of 1701, at which the Haudenosaunee had promised to cease their raids against Algonquian nations in the upper country, the possibility of their continued aggression still struck fear. The song also likely relates a fragment of the story of the Meskwaki (Fox) and Mascouten attack of the French fort at Detroit in 1712. The Meskwaki, purported to be in conversation and perhaps alliance with the English and Haudenosaunee, nearly succeeded in destroying the French settlement. But fear of the Haudenosaunee and the reality of the peaceful presence of both the Haudenosaunee and mixed French/Algonquian/Wendat/Haudenosaunee families stand in sharp contrast, and hint at Detroit's unique status. Was this a war between nations, or a dispute between particular members of the same settlement? Could it be that this place of plural and intersecting networks, a center of mobility by virtue of its long-standing status as a space for hunting and war, resisted imperial efforts to settle and claim it according to European conceptions? To consider these questions, it is necessary to more closely examine the people and events that led to this outbreak of violence at Detroit. This conflagration would launch a decades-long French genocidal campaign against the Meskawaki referred to by historians as the Fox Wars.

There are two renditions of these events, one generated by the state and another that is locally based. At the juncture of these two stories is the Monsieur Roy referenced in the song "Les Mascoutens." He and his Myaamia-French family were pivotal members of French-Indigenous kinship networks who were already utilizing Detroit's central location in the upper country. The family members diverted resources, including slaves, to bolster an alternative configuration of power relations that crossed European and Indigenous nations. During the same year that members of the networks would introduce slaves into Detroit hailing from locations further west, a wave of Meskwaki families arrived to join the Detroit community. Two years later, fueled by the availability of war captives from the failed Meskwaki attack on Detroit, trade in enslaved persons would explode. If we make assumptions about Detroit's political, economic, and cultural viability based solely on the exhortations expressed in imperial correspondence, it would seem that the locality was constantly threatened by war and abandonment by its inhabitants, whether Indigenous or French. Imperial representatives repeatedly attempted to get to the bottom of what seemed to be fundamental problems in Detroit's infrastructure, and condemned Detroit as a moldering site of illegal and dangerous activities. What looked in the eyes of a succession of governors general to be the inability of Detroit's citizens and its commandant to curb incessant violence and questionable business practices, however, was actually the parsing-out of power relations within French-Indigenous family networks. The strength of the networks would be enhanced as members diverted resources to bolster an alternative configuration of power relations that crossed Euro-American and Indigenous worlds. Imperial correspondence hints at the existence of conflicting versions of events at Detroit around the outbreak of the Fox Wars, which reflected these alternative viewpoints.

The Background: Fear, Violence, Alliance, and Peace

Historians have postulated that there was more to the attack and the motivations behind it than may have seemed readily apparent. Algonquian communities of the upper country were already united in their intense dislike of the Meskwaki, and seeing an opportunity to eliminate them, provoked them into battle at Detroit, while also preventing the French from intervening. The Meskwaki-allied Mascouten had headed to Detroit to escape repeated attacks by Anishinaabe (who had had a contentious relationship with the Mascouten for over a hundred years) and sought refuge at the French fort. The resident Meskwaki grew progressively angrier when they heard of the ill-treatment the Mascouten had suffered at the hands of the Odawa and Potawatomi. Jacques-Charles Renaud Dubuisson became convinced that the Meskwaki meant to launch an attack on the French and responded militarily, igniting the conflict. The wars that resulted were due to French arrogance expressed through excessive force by which they sought to control rather than mediate in the world of Indigenous politics.[5]

The Fox Wars could have erupted due to the efforts of French-allied Indigenous nations of the upper country to limit growing French influence by turning against the Meskwaki. By attacking the Meskwaki, who the French were trying to bring into an alliance, the French-allied nations attempted to dictate the development of Indigenous-French relations.[6] It could also be that amidst the escalating internal wrangling that characterized French imperial policy, the destabilizing and radical machinations of one man in particular, Cadillac, touched off a level of excessive violence.[7] Cadillac's efforts to embody Onontio locally created an imperial crisis, coming to a head during an uneasy period when two commandants resided at Detroit. Both men would vie to control the messages of diplomacy with Indigenous nations.

The Fox siege marked a decisive moment in Detroit's evolution as a flashpoint in the increasingly complex world of Indigenous-European relations in the upper country. The previous conflict between the Odawa, Myaamia, and Wendat that had played itself out during Detroit's first decade as a French settlement had been a highly localized battle of wills, both European and Indigenous. It had largely been a contest between Cadillac and his Odawa partners on one side, who wished to bring all of that nation, including the Sable, Kiskakon, and Sinago *nindoodemag* to Detroit, and on the other side, the Jesuits and their Odawa allies who wished to remain at Michilimackinac. This battle of wills, riding the coattails of perennial and persistent rumors of Haudenosaunee and English involvement, had grown to include other resident groups. It pitted the Myaamia and Wendat, purported to be in league with the Haudenosaunee, against the Odawa. The French had held the Odawa *ogimaag* Le Pesant responsible for having ordered an ambush of several Myaamia leaders on their way to visit the Wendat fort at Detroit. For their part, the Odawa had acted on information that a combined Myaamia/Wendat force intended to attack their fort and seize their women and children while they were away on a raid of the Dakota. When the resident Recollet priest Father Constantin Delhalle and a French soldier were killed during the battle that ensued, French imperial agents demanded that reparations be made by the Odawa.[8]

Governor General Vaudreuil called for the surrender of Le Pesant, who hailed from the Sable, and Cadillac prevailed upon members of Le Pesant's community to hand him over to be executed; these included Outoutagan (known also as Jean Le Blanc, the Odawa leader who had signed the treaty forged at the Great Peace of Montreal in 1701); his brother Miscouaky; Kinongé (known to the French as Le Brochet, another leader of the Sable); and Onaské (a member of the Kiskakon, who were particularly attached to their residence at Michilimackinac). It was the first true test of Cadillac's change in status within the imperial power structure working on behalf of the king and governor general after the Compagnie de la Colonie had discontinued its funding of the fledgling settlement at Detroit. Almost immediately after this change in status, Cadillac had been called to Quebec to answer for irregularities and illegalities in his operation of the fort and was briefly incarcerated as a result. He was in the process of exonerating himself in 1706 when the Le Pesant affair broke out at Detroit. Cadillac seemed to stumble along in his response on multiple fronts. He disputed warnings of the Jesuits at Michilimackinac that the war made Detroit too dangerous for Indigenous and French habitation. He appeased both Vaudreuil and the Odawa by capturing Le Pesant and then somehow allowing him to escape before he could be executed. He staged a poorly planned and ineffective attack on the Myaamia fort at Detroit meant to satisfy the Odawa while also inflicting minimal damage on the Myaamia.[9]

In his 1708 report on the state of the forts in the upper country, imperial agent François Clairambault d'Aigremont related Cadillac's misdirected military efforts and a myriad of other complaints about him. Aigremont was convinced that Detroit was not only of little use to the French in the upper country, it was detrimental. Aigremont reported that there were only sixty-three inhabitants at Detroit, and of that number, only twenty-nine were practicing agriculture. Cadillac was a despot, exacting exorbitant taxes from inhabitants, Indians, soldiers, blacksmiths, traders, and gunsmiths. He was also charging artificially high rates for wheat and peas. The populace was miserable and the soil and peltries were of bad quality.

Aigremont pointed out that the post was a threat to the colony because it brought French-allied nations such as the Wendat and Myaamia into close contact with the Haudenosaunee and the English, sending all commerce to New York. The gathering of so many different Indigenous communities in one place had caused quarrels to develop among them. According to Aigremont, Cadillac's continued efforts to have the Odawa of Michilimackinac relocate to Detroit would cause the majority of the beaver of Canada to pass into English hands by means of the Haudenosaunee. If this happened, the colony would lose the entire northern trade at Lake Superior, which was the source of the highest quality fur in New France. Indeed, according to Aigremont, from the time that the fort at Michilimackinac had been closed, most of the northern peltry was already making its way to the English at Hudson Bay.[10]

The "Iroquois menace" surfaced in Aigremont's report, just as it had run as an unsettling undercurrent in the Le Pesant conflict two years earlier. Vaudreuil wrote his superiors in Versailles that the Haudenosaunee were "more to be feared than the whole of New England."[11] The alliance between the Myaamia and Wendat against the Odawa was of great concern to the French because of the influence of the Haudenosaunee among the Wendat. The French were also well aware that the Myaamia were already making their way to Albany to talk trade with the English. A few years later, the Meskwaki attack would similarly cause French imperial agents to fear that the Haudenosaunee and English were at work among the Indigenous nations of the upper country. Vaudreuil would report that the Meskwaki had moved to Detroit—which they claimed as part of their homelands—in order to be closer to the English.[12] Dubuisson would emphasize the external threat represented by the Haudenosaunee, telling imperial authorities that the Meskwaki and Mascouten had been encouraged by the Haudenosaunee and English to attack Detroit and kill all of the French there.

There are inconsistencies and contradictions that complicate imperial versions of events leading up to the hostilities in 1712. This includes the fact that local French and Indigenous communities did not consider all Meskwaki to be enemies, nor did they consistently or uniformly perceive the Haudenosaunee as a threat, two dispositions that ran counter to official French imperial policy. There was a myriad of relations among the French, Wendat, Algonquian, Meskwaki, and

Haudenosaunee nations that complicated official French policy. French imperial agents may have used fear of the Haudenosaunee to galvanize and organize its colonists, but at Detroit, there were many resident Haudenosaunee well integrated into the community. In 1704, Cadillac reported that there were thirty Haudenosaunee families settled there.[13] Church records of several baptisms attest to the presence of these families in the first few decades of the eighteenth century. They hailed from various communities and locations, including Mohawk from Sault St. Louis and Sault au Recollet (French-allied settlements near the Lachine Rapids and Montreal, respectively); Oiongouinis (Cayuga); and Lonontouans (Onondaga). Some Detroit-based Haudenosaunee women were married to Wendat men, meaning their children would have been raised as part of their mother's Haudenosaunee clan.[14] Twenty-five Haudenosaunee warriors would join with the Wendat to defend the settlement against the Meskwaki in 1712.[15]

The Meskwaki had also been encouraged to settle at Detroit by Cadillac, before his removal from Detroit and subsequent appointment as governor of Louisiana and they began to arrive in 1710. Their movement en masse two years before the 1712 outbreak of violence would be the last such large-scale migration initiated as part of Cadillac's original plan to gather large numbers of Indigenous nations at Detroit. Although the Meskwaki had been increasingly marginalized by many Algonquian nations in the upper country as the eighteenth century proceeded, some of these nations, including the Atchatchakangouen Myaamia, Ouiatenon (Wea), and Piankashaw, had a history of peaceful relations with the Meskwaki and had lived among them and fought alongside them against the Dakota. Communities of Odawa had also resided with the Meskwaki at Chequamegon Bay at the southwest corner of Lake Superior in the mid-seventeenth century. Indeed, Governor General Vaudreuil had equivocated in seeking the Meskwaki as friends or considering them enemies.

In 1710, only one year before he warned the Meskwaki at Detroit that they should curb their bad behavior or risk bringing all the other nations against them, Vaudreuil described them as allied to all of the tribes of the Great Lakes, with the exception of the Salteaux (Ojibwe), who were attempting to get the Nipissings, an Algonquian nation closely associated with the Ojibwe, to make war on the Meskwaki and their allies the Sauk. Vaudreuil considered this a matter of great importance, declaring that the French should do everything they could to stop these nations making war on each other "so as to have it in our power to make use of them in case of need, should the Iroquois happen to declare against us." Vaudreuil hastily dispatched a representative to convince the Ojibwe to suspend their hatchet.[16]

When two Odawa leaders spoke with Vaudreuil in July 1712 after the Fox attack, one of them, Koutaouiliboé, was anxious to wreak vengeance and sought French approval to descend on the Meskwaki at their old dwelling place at Baie des Puants (Green Bay), where they had retreated after the Detroit debacle. The other leader, Ouilamek, urged caution, telling Vaudreuil that matters were not as simple as Koutaouiliboé described. According to Ouilamek, not all the Meskwaki were culpable. Those that lived at the farthest side of Green Bay had not been involved in the events at Detroit and should not be attacked. He added that the Meskwaki had many alliances among the nations that had fought them at Detroit, who might be regretting their actions against the Meskwaki.[17]

The transition by imperial French agents from viewing the Meskwaki as allies before 1712 to enemies afterwards occurred while one former commandant (Cadillac) and another newly appointed commandant (Dubuisson) were briefly but simultaneously at Detroit in a state of uneasy cohabitation. Cadillac had been dismissed from his position and waited to depart for Louisiana. Dubuisson was thrust into temporary command when Cadillac's designated replacement, François Dauphin de La Forest, was too ill to travel to Detroit.[18] Dubuisson's reports on the outbreak of hostilities with the Meskwaki in 1712 belie his relative lack of knowledge of local politics, but these same reports offer us a window through which to contextualize the involvement of French-Indigenous family networks and their role in the events leading up to and after the hostilities with the Meskwaki.

Inconsistencies and Intricacies: Stories of the Fox Wars

The family networks combined French, Odawa, Myaamia, Wendat, and Haudenosaunee members at Detroit, where, as Andrew Sturtevant has pointed out, an Odawa north-south power axis centered at Michilimackinac intersected with a Wendat/Myaamia/Haudenosaunee east-west power axis that stretched to the English at Albany.[19] Members of the networks included the Odawa woman leader La Blanche operating at Michilimackinac; her kinsman Outoutagan/Jean Le Blanc; Outoutagan's wife Isabelle Couc (later called Madame Montour by the English); Waapankihkwa, referred to by the French as Marguerite Ouabankikoué and member of the powerful Myaamia Atchatchakangouen/Crane band known in French as Grue; and her husband Pierre Roy, a French voyageur who would figure in military and diplomatic events in early Detroit and the upper country.[20]

Dubuisson related nothing of the ties of family between these kinship networks and the Meskwaki. His rendition instead emphasized how in the face of overwhelming odds, he turned certain French defeat into decisive French victory. He described how despite initial aggression by the Meskwaki that would have led to the complete annihilation of the fort's residents, the tables had been turned against them by French-allied Indigenous nations hailing from near (Anishinaabe [Ojibwe, Odawa, Potawatomi], Myaamia), and far (Illinois, Missouri, and Osage). Responding to Dubuisson's messages for help, these groups had made haste for Detroit and forced the Meskwaki and Mascouten to withdraw into their fort. This siege continued until the Meskwaki and Mascouten were on the point of starvation. Trying unsuccessfully to negotiate a surrender, they fled under cover of darkness, only to be pursued by the French-allied groups, who killed over a thousand people and enslaved many of them, predominantly women and children.

The song "Les Mascoutens" offers several clues that help in recontextualizing Dubuisson's official version of the events of 1712. This version has the French fleeing rather than staying to fight the Haudenosaunee/Iroquois, ostensibly because there were not a sufficient number of bodies to defend the fort. During the attack, the fort was almost completely defenseless because Indigenous men of the settlement were away hunting. There had also been a loss of ten French soldiers two years earlier in 1710, when Vaudreuil had decided to withdraw the garrison to decrease expenses.[21] Anticipating at that time that further cuts in expenditures would deprive the settlement of the resident priest, Cadillac and forty-six inhabitants of Detroit had agreed to contribute funds and to provide support for a cleric Cadillac would request from the bishop of Quebec.[22] Ultimately, the church and the homes of several families were left outside the protective walls of the palisade when the size of the fort was decreased by Dubuisson as part of Vaudreuil's plan.

In addition to Madame Cadillac and her children (Cadillac had not been present), Pierre Roy and others, including the Parent and Campeau families, had been left outside the walls in 1710.[23] Just as the Mascouten man in the song seems cognizant of these facts, so too, it would seem, did the Mascouten and Meskwaki who attacked in 1712. This knowledge would have circulated because these nations had been in regular contact with French-allied Indigenous communities resident at Detroit, including the Ouiatenon, a nation closely allied to the Atchatchakangouen Myaamia.[24] Also, in the case of the Meskawki, large numbers of their citizens were already living at Detroit and had been absorbed into the community by local members of the French-Indigenous networks.

By focusing ever closer on the topography of Detroit's Euro-Indigenous relations, it is possible to discern how this gateway had been constructed through constantly shifting allegiances that were more tightly drawn than imperial records might have us believe. If we examine kinship relations and connections, it appears that at least some of the members of the French-Indigenous families had a distinct and more favorable relationship to the Meskwaki and Mascouten that were resident at Detroit, a position at odds with that of Detroit's commandant Dubuisson. There were several Meskwaki families at Detroit the year before the Meskwaki-Mascouten attack who had baptized their children there between 1710 and 1712 and had members of Detroit's French and Indigenous communities as godparents; this included Pierre Roy and his Myaamia wife Marguerite Ouabankikoué.

If we listen closely to Dubuisson's report of the outbreak of hostilities, he tells us that the entire conflagration began with Meskwaki coming into the French fort to stab an inhabitant named La Jeunesse and a girl belonging to a man named Roy, perhaps the Monsieur Roy referred to in the song "Les Mascoutens."[25] La Jeunesse was a soldier at the fort. The Roy referenced was almost certainly Pierre Roy, who as Dubuisson would later report, was holding gun flints, powder, lead, and shot necessary to defend the fort. These supplies had been mysteriously lost during the Meskwaki attack when they were needed the most, and reappeared, still in Roy's possession, a month later. Cadillac had entrusted Pierre Roy with these materials and all of the departing commandant's extensive goods before Cadillac departed for France and Louisiana. Roy's possession of these items drew him into an acrimonious dispute between Cadillac, La Forest (Cadillac's designated replacement), and Dubuisson.[26] Pierre Roy was also the same man whose family, together with those of other leading French-Indigenous families and Cadillac's wife and children, had been turned out of the protective walls of the fort by Dubuisson himself the year before.[27] Were efforts by the Meskwaki—at least as Dubuisson reported after the fact—to assault the girl belonging to Roy the opening salvo of the battle at Detroit? And what is the significance of the highly localized events for the twenty years of war waged against the Meskwaki that would follow?

Members of the Meskwaki contingent charging into the French fort were specific in their reference to a grown daughter or girl belonging to Roy. Pierre Roy and Marguerite Ouabankikoué had baptized three daughters and one son at Detroit between 1704 and 1710. The eldest daughter, aged eight in 1712, would not have been considered grown and is unlikely to have been the focus of the Meskwaki's wrath. French baptismal records routinely used the term "belonging to" (*appartenant*) to refer to the relationship between a slave and his or her owner. As well, although it represented an older definition of the word, *appartenant* could also refer to the relationship linking someone who had been adopted by another.[28] In April 1709, Intendant Raudot had issued an ordinance "formalizing the legal status of slaves in New France and guaranteeing that they would be protected as property."[29] Within a year, slaves began appearing in Detroit's church records, including a seven-year-old boy listed as belonging to Pierre Roy. The girl targeted by the Meskwaki could have been a slave belonging to Roy who hadn't been baptized and therefore doesn't appear in church records. She could also have been a girl adopted by Pierre Roy's Myaamia wife Marguerite Ouabankikoué.

Marguerite Ouabankikoué had stood as godmother to three Meskwaki children in 1710, when the large contingent of Meskwaki families had arrived to settle at Detroit. She performed her designated role as "spiritual mother" and witness at these three baptisms all in one day, September 22, 1710. Two of the baptized were brother and sister: "Jean," who was named, in all likelihood, for the soldier Jean Contant (who, like Marguerite, godparented for both siblings), and "Marie," a common baptismal name for both French and Indigenous girls. The names of the children's Meskwaki mother and father, Mounamahan and Michapiahan, were duly noted, as were those of their godparents (Contant and Ouabankikoué), a customary format for every baptism entered into the church record, whether French or Indigenous (unless the identity of one or both of the parents was unknown).[30]

For two years, between August 18, 1710, and April 16, 1712, thirty-two Meskwaki individuals were baptized at Detroit and the names of their parents and godparents recorded.[31] More baptisms of Meskwaki occurred during this period than of any other Indigenous nation, including Detroit's largest resident populations of Wendat and Odawa, and far outstripped baptisms of French infants.[32] All together during this two-year span, twenty-five Wendat individuals, thirteen Odawa, four Sauk, one Illinois, eleven French, and one child of mixed Indigenous-French parentage were baptized. This variety of Indigenous nations and the small number of French in relation testifies to Detroit's status as a center of mobility, where the constant comings and goings of Indigenous peoples occupied the majority of inhabitants' time and were the driving force in maintaining a sense of community.

When the Meskwaki arrived, baptism opened a transitional space in which the process of integration could be ritualized and carefully enacted. Community members worked to incorporate the new arrivals, at times baptizing several individuals in a one- or two-day period. At the same time, through this medium the

Meskwaki sought to establish symbolic ties of kinship to members of the resident family networks.[33] Indeed, the very first Meskwaki individual on record in 1710, a son of Akouemesouissgri and Attarissikoupe, received the baptismal name Louis. This was not the name of his godfather, but it was in all likelihood bestowed in homage to the king of France, Louis XIV, as had transpired three years previously when the Wendat Bear clan leader, called Quarante Sols by the French (also known as Michipichy or Cheanonvouzon), was baptized as Louis Antoine, the second name acknowledging Quarante Sol's godfather Antoine Cadillac. Receiving the baptismal name of the king of France and being the first baptism performed by the resident priest may indicate that this Meskwaki individual had one or both parents who were prominent in their nation.

Beginning fewer than two months later, on June 6, 1712, however, the baptisms of Meskwaki began to take on a different form and meaning. The same act, with its symbolic words and gestures that had formerly operated as the gateway to community integration, now became the means of depersonalizing Meskwaki and rendering them outsiders. Hostilities with the Meskwaki had just ended, and members of that nation had been brutally subdued and relegated by the French and allied Indigenous nations of the upper country to the category of enemy. The eleven baptisms of Meskwaki that followed between June 1712 and November 1713 were of individuals who had become slaves and been forced to shed their former identities.[34] The manner in which these baptisms are recorded testifies to this transition—there are no names of parents listed. Each Meskwaki is listed as a slave "belonging to" one French man, the latter of whom in almost all cases was a member of the French-Indigenous family networks involved in the fur trade, with either an Indigenous wife and/or complex ties to one or more Indigenous nations.

The enslaved continued to have godparents, who were, in many cases, the same individuals who had acted in this role for the Meskwaki welcomed as family before the 1712 battle. These godparents, however, were now either the owners of their "spiritual charges," or the family and business colleagues of these owners. It was mandated in New France that slaves be baptized and raised as Catholics.[35] Although this requirement was difficult to enforce, the church would practice greater vigilance in ensuring this act was carried out as the eighteenth century unfolded. The register of Ste. Anne at Detroit contains numerous records of the baptisms of slaves with strict instructions as to how their owners should see to their spiritual needs. These "contracts" between the priest and the slave owner obligated the priest to perform the baptism, as long as the slave owner promised that in the event the slave was sold, he/she could only be purchased by a Catholic.

Baptism in fur-trade communities had always been, according to historian Susan Sleeper-Smith, "more about trade than the nature of religious faith."[36] God-parents were the means of integrating the families of the Meskwaki baptized in 1710 into the greater community at Detroit. For the enslaved Meskwaki, godparenting satisfied a legal requirement while also cementing trade alliances. For Marguerite Ouabankikoué, the stint as godmother for the three Meskwaki individuals on September 22, 1710, was the first time she had stood as godmother at Detroit. But in June 1714, she would act again in this capacity, this time for a three-year-old Mascouten boy slave belonging to the voyageur and trader Louis Gastineau, who had stood as godfather for some of Marguerite and Pierre Roy's children. Baptism and the roles of spiritual mother and father completed the circle and created a bond among network family members.[37]

We may never know the circumstances of the Meskwaki demand for and threat against the Roy girl, but Dubuisson portrays it as the event that drove him to take up arms. In his report, it is described as a separate incident occurring just before the arrival of the Mascouten who were fleeing the Odawa and Potawatomi. We cannot entirely trust the accuracy of Dubuisson's report. His short tenure at Detroit meant he would have had at best a cursory knowledge of the complex nature of political and military affairs. Also, his hatred of and frustration with Cadillac and Cadillac's confederates likely colored how he reported on their activities. Dubuisson may have had limited understanding of the nature of the situation between the Meskwaki and Roy, causing him to misconstrue Meskwaki intentions and react with force. We may even question whether the Meskwaki intended violence against the girl belonging to Roy. Perhaps the Meskwaki, seeking instead to undo the ties of spiritual kinship that had been created at a very different moment two years previously, were asking for the return of the Meskwaki girl baptized as Marie, for whom Roy's wife Marguerite Ouabankikoué had stood as spiritual mother. It is possible that the incident did not occur at all, although reference to specific individuals involved suggests at least a degree of verity. For all that Dubuisson did not comprehend about Detroit, he was aware of the influence of members of the French-Indigenous family networks such as Roy. He was also aware of the kinship ties between them, as he illustrated when he linked Roy with the young woman who belonged to him.

Dubuisson's description of the detailed method of proposed violence and the intended victim suggests there was unfinished business between the Roy family and the Meskwaki in question that had gone suddenly awry, spilling over the bounds of, and ultimately threatening, the French imperial presence at Detroit. As they would continue to solidify their control of trade in the eighteenth century, members of family networks would be highly motivated, as historian Brett Rushforth points out in his study of slave-holding French merchants, "to support warfare in the West, because they could profit both from the captives generated by the conflict and from the provisions they offered for its resolution, charged to the king at a profit." By the mid-eighteenth century, French imperial authorities were frustrated with and unable to curb the activities of these individuals, who they accused of making "a great commotion" and starting "wars in connection with private incidents of trade of but little interest to the nation."[38] The reported animosity involving Roy and the Meskwaki likely marked such a moment much earlier in the eighteenth century, when a denouement in trade relations accelerated into an imperial crisis at a crucial location in the string of French-Indigenous installations in the continental interior.

There is little doubt Roy possessed considerable power in the period leading up to the outbreak of war with the Meskwaki in 1712. This clout had no doubt been built upon his earlier marriage to Marguerite Ouabankikoué, who belonged to the influential Myaamia Crane band. In Cadillac's absence, Roy controlled access to a vast array of private goods possessed by Cadillac the trader, and imperial goods owned by the king and claimed by Cadillac the commandant. Suddenly designated "Sieur" in church records, Pierre stood as godfather at the baptism of the son of Wendat-Petun, Deer clan leader and French ally Sasteresti in 1711, acting in much the same way as Cadillac had done in 1707 when he had godparented for Wendat Bear clan leader Michipichy. Pierre Roy would operate as Cadillac's designate and from a powerful position in a network that included Odawa, Myaamia, and Haudenosaunee members, blurring the lines between private and imperial interests. But something happened, causing relations to sour with Meskwaki. Additionally, the singling out of a woman at a moment when peace was threatened and war was imminent would be a persistent theme when interests of the family networks collided with matters of the state. Because women of the French-Indigenous families were often the primary agents of trade, their presence at these critical junctures demonstrates the tight and intricate link between economic and political affairs.

As commandant, Cadillac had begun 1710 with an invitation for the Meskwaki to join the Detroit community, confident of the fiscal backing of the state. By the time they arrived, however, Cadillac had been ordered to Louisiana, and for all intents and purposes, stripped of any imperial authority or financial backing that would have allowed him to continue to put his plans into action. The governor general withdrew military and spiritual protection and rebuilt the fort, leaving Cadillac, his allies, and the church outside the walls and outside the pale of imperial support and protection. But they would band together to oppose Vaudreuil's efforts. They went so far as to make plans to hire and maintain their own cleric in an agreement dated two months before the arrival of the Meskwaki, who were baptized en masse, first as an effort toward community integration, and two years later, as part of a transition into legalized slavery. The fact that the resident Recollet priest never left Detroit during this time, however, suggests Cadillac and his allies had successively challenged Vaudreuil's plans and signals Cadillac's efforts to control spiritual matters at the local level as he prepared to absorb the Meskwaki into the Detroit community. The outbreak of the Fox Wars forced the imperial government to reinvest in Detroit and rescued the French installation from almost certain dissolution.

Almost twenty years later, in 1730, the story of how another group of French officers, soldiers, and Indigenous warriors defeated a Meskwaki contingent would be related in exactly the same way and with the same result. Commandant of Fort St. Joseph Nicolas-Antoine Coulon de Villiers, described the Meskwaki as on the point of starvation in their fort and surrounded by French and Indigenous armies when they attempted to flee during a violent storm at night, only to be discovered and subdued. One nineteenth-century historian would remark that the Meskwaki seemed to miraculously rise over and over again from near total obliteration at the hands of the French and repopulate themselves. Like the Iroquois menace, the fear of a ruthless, arrogant, and willful Meskwaki nation would prove a useful mechanism for maintaining the alliance between the French and other Indigenous nations of the upper country, and is considered by historians to have contributed to finally ending the long-standing animosity between the Myaamia and the Illinois.[39]

In addition to Monsieur Roy, another man is mentioned by name in the song "Les Mascoutens" of whose identity we can only conjecture: Bourdignon. There was a soldier at Detroit in 1710 named Didier Bourgoin dit St. Paul who stood as godfather three times that year—twice to Wendat-Petun and once to an Odawa. A soldier is a good fit for the individual in the song who brings the warning of an impending Iroquois attack to the attention of the commandant.[40] A stronger case can be made for Étienne de Véniard de Bourgmond/Bourgmont, who had connections to the family networks and whose activities at Detroit link the hostilities of the Le Pesant affair and the Fox Wars. He figures prominently in the late seventeenth- and early eighteenth-century history of Detroit, the Illinois Country, Louisiana, and the Southwest. He acted in Cadillac's place as commandant while the latter was in Quebec in 1706, during which time hostilities between the Odawa, Myaamia, and Wendat broke out, culminating in Le Pesant's capture. That same year Bourgmont left the fort (perhaps in response to the official censure of his actions during the altercation) but stayed in the vicinity of Detroit, taking up residence with the French-Algonquin Isabelle Couc, who would later become known as Madame Montour. He lived eighteen months among the Mascouten until 1712, during which year he would have been present for the attack of the Meskwaki and Mascouten on the French fort at Detroit. After 1712, he went south to live among the Missouri. He was considered by French imperial authorities (both secular and religious) to be a dangerous agent who encouraged English trade in the upper country and had a negative effect on the Illinois tribes.[41]

Ultimately, the Fox Wars had provided the opportunity for French-Indigenous family networks to engage in trade in Indigenous slaves. The 1709 French mandate regularizing slavery gave these transactions by family members the veneer of legality, which meant they could be carried out on behalf of the state and Onontio. For the Mascouten in Marcel Bénéteau's song, furs would be the ultimate wartime booty. For the family networks, however, slaves would become an early means to greater wealth, first through their labor, and later as a status symbol that would mark family members' burgeoning wealth at Detroit.[42] The mass baptism of Meskawki slaves would further ensure Detroit's status as a location where merchandise and people were revalued as they transitioned between French and Indigenous worlds. The unique significance of Detroit as a center at which multiple nations converged allowed for the burgeoning power of French-Indigenous family networks whose members navigated the political and economic contingencies brought about by this plethora of Indigenous voices.

Who, then, was the Monsieur Roy in the song "Les Mascoutens?" The lyrics tell us he is a person of influence to whom the community at Detroit turns to organize its exodus because he understands the devastating implications of an Iroquois attack. He is an interpreter on a number of levels: uniquely qualified to determine the gravity of the situation, and possessing facility and competency in Algonquian (Mascouten) and Iroquoian languages and customs. Pierre Roy almost certainly knew Iroquois languages because he had been born and raised near Montreal in close proximity to the Mohawk community at Sault au Recollet, and because he had been traveling in the *pays d'en haut* for several decades. He was a man who hovered on the periphery of imperial reports in veiled references made to his role in the skirmish with the Fox and in Cadillac's bitter disputes with French officials. He is the key to understanding how nation-based wars that ran roughshod over entire communities in the upper country were based in highly localized squabbles that bubbled to the surface at Detroit.

Pierre Roy, the man who could very well have been the "Monsieur Roy" called upon in the song "Les Mascoutens" to take action against the proposed Iroquois threat, traveled a path that brought him into constant contact with the Cuillerier, Fafard, Couc, Ménard, Rivard, Turpin, and Bizaillon families who would become prominent as part of the kinship networks. Through his marriage to Marguerite Ouabankikoué and into the family of a pivotal French-alliance leader of the Myaamia nation, Pierre carved a unique niche for himself at the center of imperial politics. By the middle of the eighteenth century, Pierre Roy's children and grandchildren and his extended family would control the means by which trade was conducted at Detroit and radiated westward. Thirty years after the events described in the song "Les Mascoutens," the Mascouten would be fully integrated into Roy's family, producing Mascouten-Myaamia-Ouiatenon leaders who would figure prominently in the complex world of intertribal and French, British, Spanish, and American relations until the end of the century. The crucial element that distinguished Roy from other hired men on the many voyages from the St. Lawrence valley to the upper country was his marriage to Marguerite. When he became kin to one of the most powerful Indigenous nations in the Great Lakes and Ohio Valley, unlimited avenues for commerce opened to him. Marguerite was the agent of transformation and the means by which the Roy family would form a network that stretched from Detroit to the Illinois Country and Louisiana.

With the Fox Wars, fear of the Haudenosaunee influence among the Wendat, Myaamia, and Meskwaki would become absorbed into a war that had much larger geopolitical points of demarcation. It was the threat of, or potential for, war as much as war itself that elicited fear and disrupted the lives of people at Detroit and in the upper country. Words warning of war, negotiating for war's postponement, or reconfirming and repairing diplomatic relations after war constituted the bulk of imperial conversation. Just as war required an outlay of resources, so too were there costs associated with the language of diplomacy and the keeping of peace. Members of the family networks, as the designated speakers and interpreters, stood to gain the most from these conversations.

Detroit's second decade would launch its status as a center point at which the vicissitudes of the politics of the upper country would be amplified. Detroit would become the place where European and Indigenous policymakers threw their voices into the highly complex world of political negotiation regulated according to a multitude of diverging Indigenous agendas. The French-Indigenous family networks were the vein that carried those voices from east to west in an ever-widening arc that would transform Detroit into its own center of diplomacy and commerce. Earlier members of the networks had carved inroads in the seventeenth century, as they traveled full-circle from the St. Lawrence valley to the upper country and back again, altering, with each journey, the configuration of Euro-Indigenous relations. The next chapter will examine the intricacies of the multiple points of kinship within the networks, situating members in time and space as pivotal conduits that altered imperial politics, sometimes for the good of the state, but always to maintain the resilience of the networks and their advantage in trade.

CHAPTER 4

Ils s'en allaient tous

Roots and Routes of the French-Indigenous Family Networks

A t Detroit, conflict seemed to be pervasive as wars were waged and peace disrupted by individuals seeking to shore up authority and maintain order. Imperial agents were not always the ones who stood to benefit under these circumstances, nor was the traditional imperial impetus to concentrate power in one place the best method to benefit politically or economically. Indeed, the French-Indigenous families did not focus all of their efforts at Detroit. They looked to alternative centers of trade located in the villages of their Indigenous members, with networks crossing vast spaces and nations, including Anishinaabe, Myaamia, Wendat, and Haudenosaunee, as well as French and English domains. The first generations of the families were widely traveled over a geography that stretched from the Atlantic coast to Albany and Hudson Bay and to the border between French Louisiana and northern New Spain.

Members of the kinship networks lived in the interstices between French, English, and Indigenous worlds. Imperial correspondence and reports are replete with warnings about individuals of the networks who traversed borders between these worlds, spaces which remained frustratingly undefined in the vast expanse of the interior of the continent. The English described the border dwellers as too French and potential turncoats who were not to be trusted. They were "alien," "spies," and "very dangerous persons" who "kept private correspondence with the Canada Indians and the French, entertained strange Indians in remote and obscure places and muttered suspicious words." Anglo-American imperial authorities were vigilant in their distrust of the French traders, and had them followed, interrogated, fined, and sometimes jailed.[1] French authorities could be equally unforgiving, but the greater issue was making clear the chain of command and the position these individuals held within the French imperial system. In order to do so, French imperial authorities had to either compel them to operate within the colony's legal parameters, or alter those boundaries to include them. In their letters and speeches with representatives from Indigenous communities about the traders, imperial officials were as much concerned with maintaining their authority and power as they were with the threat that rogue traders were in league with the English.

Operating in the constantly changing world of Euro-Indigenous trade and policy could therefore mean that the same activities and relationships sanctioned at one time by governments were rendered illegal or even treasonous at others. An inordinate number of persons associated with the family networks at one time or another ran afoul of the French government, which suspected them of trading illegally with the English. Some of the persons so accused were subsequently jailed for their activities, while others were fined and warned to cease their practices. These accusations began in the first decades of the eighteenth century, as the French-Indigenous family networks were becoming established, and tested the nature and strength of their ties to the state. Members of the family networks became adept at navigating these shifting perceptions in order to buttress their importance to imperial agendas. Once they used these skills to become indispensable agents of economic expansion and political negotiation, governments were often forced to redefine categorizations of legality to operate in tandem with their activities.

At Detroit, members of the families slipped in and out of the role of imperial representative, either as multilingual interpreters and communicators of Onontio's message, or as imperially sanctioned traders working on the king's behalf. One of these families, the Cuillerier dit Beaubiens, would eventually establish a pivotal presence at Detroit and become increasingly powerful while members of the Bizaillon family would represent a more fleeting presence. Both networks utilized the region's status as a center of mobility and imperial way station to legitimize their economic and political claims. Individuals prominent in one family were also often part of another through kinship ties. In order to understand how these layers of influence and authority functioned to allow the families to dominate, this chapter parses out the sinews of relation in the Bizaillon and Cuillerier families and follows the numerous linkages that created and would continue to strengthen the families throughout the eighteenth century. We will also see how these families converged at Detroit, where the value and meaning of their pursuits were transformed in the eyes of imperial authorities.

The Bizaillon-Fafard Network

In 1714, French imperial officials took legal action against Michel Bizaillon, training their attention on the nature of his activities across a territory that stretched from the southern reaches of the Illinois Country to Detroit and Michilimackinac. Bizaillon was accused of lèse-majesté, violation of the king's person, a charge that reflected the governor general's frustration over the state's inability to recover an individual perceived as being not only beyond French jurisdiction but also outside French cultural norms.[2] Branding Bizaillon a criminal who had lived a profligate life and had endeavored to unite the Illinois nations with the English at Carolina, the governor general would appeal to his superiors in France, asking that the king "lay hands" on Bizaillon by bringing charges of treason. Such a profound violation in the eyes of the state suggested a willful disengagement from the king and a repudiation of imperial service in a region where Indigenous sovereignties could make alternative and competing claims.[3] A few years later, however, the governor general would reverse his position and claim that Bizaillon's temperament had been favorably transformed. He would be depicted as having unflaggingly and single-handedly protected French interests. In the end, Bizaillon had not altered his behavior, but his usefulness for imperial ambitions dictated whether this behavior was exemplary or dangerous.

The road to state censure and dueling interpretations of Bizaillon began in 1710 in Detroit with his marriage to Marguerite Fafard, who was part of a family with extensive ties to Indigenous communities. Michel was thirty-five years of age and Marguerite one month short of her fifteenth birthday.[4] In the first census taken at Detroit that same year, neither Marguerite nor any other women were enumerated by name, although Bizaillon was listed as a Canadian with a wife at Detroit.[5] Michel did not opt to take up land to farm, purchasing instead a site on St. Anne Street inside the fort, an option common among men who plied the fur trade and were highly mobile.[6]

Marguerite was the daughter of François Fafard, who had arrived with his cousin Louis Fafard dit le Longval as part of the fifty-two-man contingent sent to establish the French fort at Detroit in 1701.[7] François, his brothers Jean and Pierre, and their cousin Louis were multilingual interpreters and voyageurs, and two were or had been married to Indigenous women. François was the official interpreter at Detroit for the Wendat and Odawa. His brother Jean Fafard dit Makours was married to the half-French/half-Algonquin Marguerite Couc, which made Jean a brother-in-law to her sister, the interpreter and trader Isabelle Couc, known as Madame Montour to the English.

Jean Fafard dit Makours (also spelled Macouce or Maconce) had been a soldier from Fort Frontenac when he was hired by René-Robert, Cavalier de La Salle for a trip to the upper country. La Salle's contingent encountered Daniel Greysolon Du Luth at Lake Superior in 1679, who had been attempting to settle a treaty with the Dakota to commence trade. La Salle reported that as Du Luth had no interpreter, he enticed Jean Fafard away from La Salle's expedition and then sent Fafard with a contingent of Dakota and Ojibwe to the western end of Lake Superior to explore the area. Fafard, who La Salle described as a young man (he would have been twenty-two years old at the time) had performed his duties as interpreter well, reporting back to Du Luth that there was an abundance of beaver furs. Fafard had also been one of the voyageurs traveling with the Jesuit and Odawa interpreter Jean Enjalran in 1684 near Michilimackinac as part of an unsuccessful campaign waged by Governor General La Barre against the Haudenosaunee. Fafard delivered Enjalran's letters to Governor General La Barre.[8]

Louis and another Fafard cousin named Joseph had been hired in 1690 by an agent of François Dauphin de La Forest (future commandant of Detroit) to travel from Montreal to Saint-Louis-des-Illinois to obtain beaver and other peltry to sell in Montreal; La Forest and Henri Tonty held the trading concession at the St. Louis fort. The terms of their contract did not allow the Fafards to tap into La Forest and Tonty's business by trading at the fort or in the Illinois Country, but they were allowed to carry merchandise to conduct trade of their own anywhere they wanted outside these designated areas. They were given a canoe and provisions for the journey, as well as a gun, lead, and powder in order to hunt for themselves if their voyage extended longer than anticipated and their original provisions were exhausted.[9]

Like his brother Jean, the third brother, Pierre Fafard dit Boisjoly, was traveling in Anishinaabewaki and trading with Odawa near Michilimackinac at the end of the seventeenth century. Pierre's eventual marriage to an Indigenous woman made him typical of the men who were part of the French-Indigenous family networks. What was unusual about Pierre's marriage to Marguerite Anskekae at Kaskaskia would be the intrusion of the state in defining the union's legitimacy.[10] In 1723, Pierre sought legal action against his wife on charges she had committed adultery. Three witnesses provided testimony in the case, and judgment was made in Pierre's favor. He was given permission to have Marguerite taken into custody, if he was able to catch her, and to have her "shut away wherever the said Sieur shall find appropriate, and to remain there for the period of two years, during which time the said Sieur Faffart may take her back if he pleases."[11] As will be discussed in the next two chapters of this book, interference by the state in marriages of the French-Indigenous networks illustrates efforts—sometimes violent—by men in the families and/or those in positions of imperial power to control women's movement and restrict their participation in trade.

Marguerite Fafard and Michel Bizaillon would leave the Detroit community after their marriage in 1710. One of the last functions Marguerite performed there that year was to act as godmother for a seven-year-old *panis* slave belonging to Pierre Roy. The term *panis,* originally a reference to enslaved peoples of the Skiri Pawnee, South Band Pawnee, Arikara and Wichita, and other Great Plains and Southwest nations, would become a generic designation used by the French for all slaves.[12] In a speech to Vaudreuil two years later, the Peoria-Illinois leader Chachagouesse discussed Michel Bizaillon, the complexities of French command in the upper country, and the alternative models of Onontio that existed within Indigenous communities. Chachagouesse's words reveal a multitude of imperial power arrangements operating simultaneously. According to Chachagouesse, Michel Bizaillon had told the Illinois he was speaking on their behalf, and that he had taken their concerns to Cadillac. In 1712, the year in which Chachagouesse made his speech, Cadillac's position within the imperial framework was in a state of transition. He was no longer commandant at Detroit, but he hadn't yet been ensconced as governor of Louisiana. The Illinois were in a similar position of liminality, existing on the geographic edge of two provinces of the French North American empire, Canada and Louisiana, and two channels through which French imperial authority flowed.[13]

Through Michel Bizaillon, the Illinois had asked Cadillac why they had been abandoned, to which Cadillac had answered that he was no longer in charge and advised them that they should write to "Monsieur Le Gouverneur" about their concerns.[14] Chachagouesse was attempting to ascertain who was the preeminent

French authority, and to hold that individual accountable for the fragile state of the diplomatic relationship between the Illinois and the French. In his speech, Chachagouesse referred to both Cadillac and Vaudreuil as "father," revealing that Cadillac had been operating as a localized version of Onontio at Detroit, and that Detroit functioned as a localized version of Quebec in its status as a center of negotiation in the upper country.

After the Meskwaki attack had taken place at Detroit and the French had fully invested in war against them, Detroit's geographic importance had been reinforced and enhanced. It became the point from which French imperial resources were launched westward, and the stream of captives and slaves resulting from the war flowed eastward for the next two decades. Michel Bizaillon had been an agent linking Chachagouesse and the Illinois to Cadillac and Detroit. In the speech Vaudreuil delivered in response to Chachagouesse, he attempted to sever this tie to Bizaillon and regain his own authority as Onontio. He told Chachagouesse that the Illinois should not listen to Michel Bizaillon, who was a bad spirit among them. The Illinois were counseled to listen only to the person who brought Vaudreuil's orders and acted as the king's representative—Pierre-Charles de Liette.[15]

It seems that Vaudreuil's attempts to reestablish his authority by excluding Bizaillon and inducing the Illinois to work with de Liette were not entirely successful. Bizaillon remained a threat and two years later, Governor of Montreal Claude Ramezay would make the charge of lèse-majesté against him. He accused Bizaillon and two accomplices of fomenting a division between the Illinois and the Myaamia, two nations that de Liette (for the Illinois) and Jean-Baptiste Bissot de Vincennes (for the Myaamia) had been working to reconcile in order to unite them against the Meskwaki.[16] Ramezay also warned that it was impossible to prevent Bizaillon and his partners Bourdon and Bourgmont from bringing the Illinois together with the English of Carolina. In response to Ramezay's letter, French imperial authorities in France ordered the arrest of the three coureurs de bois.[17]

Michel Bizaillon's business partners were a man named Bourdon and Étienne de Véniard de Bourgmont. As discussed in the previous chapter, Étienne de Véniard de Bourgmont had been in command temporarily at Detroit in 1706 when a battle broke out between the Odawa, Myaamia and Wendat. Bourgmont later partnered with Isabelle Couc, ran afoul of French imperial authorities, and spent most of the rest of his life in the Illinois Country and Louisiana. There were two Bourdon brothers active at Kaskaskia, Jacques and Pierre. Jacques godfathered several times at Kaskaskia for children of French fathers and Indigenous mothers between 1704 and 1717. The brothers were sons of Marie Ménard, a sister to the Michilimackinac indigenous language interpreter Maurice Ménard. As nephews to Maurice and his wife Madeleine Couc, the Bourdons were linked to Madeleine's sister Isabelle Couc (Madame Montour), the French/English trader and interpreter.

Michel Bizaillon responded to the charges leveled against him by painstakingly reciting all that he had done for the king over the past seventeen years. In a detailed report written in 1716, Bizaillon appeared to have single-handedly directed and defended the course of French influence among the Illinois and Myaamia. Bizaillon is consistently described as having acted on behalf of the king rather than furthering his private interests, which he attempted to prove by enumerating the many services he had rendered to his government. He had ferried the priests of the Seminary of Quebec to their mission among the Quapaw without conducting any trade of his own, and he had traveled with the permission of imperial authorities to the Illinois Country with the Jesuits Gravier and Charest. He had attempted to protect Gravier and all the other French who were with him from the Illinois who wanted to kill them. When, despite his best efforts, Gravier had been wounded, Bizaillon had taken him to the cabin of someone known to Bizaillon, where Gravier was protected by fifty men until he was able to depart.[18] After the incident with Gravier, Bizaillon had brought one hundred cabins of Illinois to the mission of Jean Bergier at Cahokia, with which Bergier had been greatly pleased, and had stayed for two years, attending to the needs of the spiritual community. Upon Bergier's death, Bizaillon had gathered the priest's belongings and entrusted them to the Jesuits.[19]

After leaving the Illinois Country, Bizaillon made his way to the Ouabache (Wabash River) where the Ouiatenon lived, a nation Bizaillon described as having behaved badly toward the French. He was intent on continuing to Detroit, but the low level of the rivers prevented him from departing, and he accepted the offer of the Ouiatenon to stay with them until the winter. According to Bizaillon, while he was at the Ouabache, an Indigenous man had arrived with five collars of wampum sent by the English to induce the Myaamia to join them in attacking Detroit. Bizaillon and three colleagues promptly departed for Detroit to alert the inhabitants there of the impending attack, and to assist in defending the fort. The contingent was forced to travel by land due to the low water levels and Bizaillon guided the party along the route.[20]

Before leaving the Ouiatenon, Bizaillon had warned them not to join with the English or they would be destroyed. He also placed all neighboring Indigenous nations on alert and asked them to come together in eight days to defend Detroit.

The nations paid heed to his message and promptly left their winter hunting grounds to meet him at Detroit. Cadillac had been surprised at Bizaillon's quick success in gathering so many Indigenous warriors. He sent Bizaillon to the Myaamia to speak on behalf of the governor general, which Bizaillon had done "without any private interest." Bizaillon explained that he had been happy to act as ambassador, and brought fifty Myaamiaki to Detroit to meet with Cadillac. After this service, Bizaillon returned to the Illinois, acting on Cadillac's behalf to put the Illinois under the authority of the king. When the Illinois asked him who he considered to be his master, Bizaillon pledged himself to the governor of Canada. Bizaillon then asked the Illinois who they held to—the governor of Canada or the governor of Mobile. The Illinois responded that they would remain faithful to the governor of Canada and proved their loyalty by giving Bizaillon three slaves, one each for the governor general, the intendant, and the governor of Montreal.[21] A year later, Bizaillon transported the slaves to Michilimackinac at his own expense.

Bizaillon indicated that the intendant, for whom one of the three slaves was designated, had died in the course of the time Bizaillon was holding the slaves at Michilimackinac. Bizaillon reported having arranged with the resident Jesuit Marest to have two of the slaves forwarded to Montreal. What, then, happened to the third slave? It is impossible to know for certain, but the church records at Detroit provide a potential clue. On March 10, 1710, the first baptism of a slave at Detroit took place—an eighteen-year-old young man belonging to Michel Bizaillon. The slave was referred to as Joseph Mikitchia and he was listed as the son of Kik8neuta and of a mother whose name he was unable to remember.[22] He was designated as having been Tête-Plate (Flathead), a term the French used in reference to either the Choctaw or Catawba.

The Choctaw, who lived in the mid to lower Mississippi area, were allies of the French, but a considerable number of them had been enslaved by the English. If Bizaillon and the Illinois had been engaging in trade with the English (as feared in Montreal), a Choctaw slave could have been transferred from the English to the Illinois. The Catawba, on the other hand, who lived on the border of what are today the states of North and South Carolina, were allied with the English. A Catawba individual could therefore have been captured by the French or Illinois. The most compelling evidence for this slave having been one of the three given to Bizaillon by the Illinois is the slave's name. "Mikitchia" means "bald eagle" in the Miami-Illinois language.[23] The godfather at Joseph Mikitchia's baptism was none other than Bizaillon's business partner Pierre Bourdon, who had been accused with Bizaillon and Bourdignon of working to keep the Myaamia and Illinois from making peace and of attempting to unite the Illinois and English of Carolina.

After recounting his service to the king, Bizaillon's letter finished with damning words against de Liette, Vaudreuil's chosen ambassador to the Illinois. According to Bizaillon, when de Liette had arrived in the Illinois Country, he had delayed in delivering the presents he brought from Vaudreuil. He refused to speak with principal leaders and criticized Bizaillon to the Illinois. Believing de Liette to be jealous of the affection the Illinois had for him, Bizaillon had responded to his poor behavior by remaining quiet. Bizaillon claimed that de Liette was responsible for creating a division among the Illinois that had led to their growing discontentment with the French. A year after de Liette had arrived, the English sent presents to the Illinois, who had accepted the gifts. When the principal Illinois leaders held a meeting on the matter and subsequently asked Bizaillon how they should proceed, Bizaillon had responded that the Illinois could not accept diplomatic gifts from two opposed kings. Bizaillon counseled the Illinois that they should stand behind their first obligation to the French because the English only wanted to destroy them. In response, the Illinois leaders reassured Bizaillon that they planned to remain loyal to the French.

With this letter, Bizaillon not only denied involvement in bringing the English and Illinois together, he pinned the blame on de Liette. By that time, however, Governor of Montreal Ramezay seemed to have changed his mind about Bizaillon. Ramezay's son Louis, Sieur de Monnoir had participated in a disastrous and poorly planned summer campaign against the Meskwaki, during which Bizaillon had proven himself by assembling two hundred Illinois to join the French. Bizaillon had also acted as interpreter between Ramezay's son and the Illinois.[24] Ramezay Sr. now presented Bizaillon as a suitable representative to send to the upper country because he was considered to be a son by the Illinois, Myaamia, and Ouiatenon. Even Vaudreuil was forced to acknowledge Bizaillon's contributions, reporting to France that Bizaillon and Le Sieur Pachot, a cadet in the troops and interpreter of Wendat at Detroit, had been well prepared for the strike against the Meskwaki, and had been the only two Frenchmen who had participated.[25]

Despite serious reservations as to Bizaillon's loyalty, imperial officials had no choice but to reintegrate him into the French colonial fold by covering his activities with the French flag and allowing him to speak for the king. In his letter attesting to Bizaillon's exemplary service during the skirmish with the Meskwaki, Ramezay also claimed that Bizaillon's character had changed. Bizaillon had apologized to the Jesuit Vaillant and to Sieur de Liette for having shown them disrespect. After listing those illegal activities in which Bizaillon was suspected of having engaged, including joining his brother with the English at Carolina and transporting a large amount of money (1,000 écus) consigned to him by a merchant at Montreal named Desauniers, Ramezay concluded that Bizaillon couldn't be held accountable. As for the currency that had made its way to the Illinois Country, Ramezay concluded that if the transaction had been effected to profit the king, it was not illegal, and Bizaillon, therefore, had conducted himself properly.[26]

Michel Bizaillon had been in the employ of the Pennsylvania government and merchants during the same period he chronicles having worked to keep the Myaamia and Illinois in alliance with the French. He acted as a guide for a party headed by Pennsylvania governor John Evans and three prominent Pennsylvania businessmen who were venturing to the Susquehanna River to meet with Seneca, Shawnee, and Nanticoke delegations at the Shawnee village of Pequehan.[27] As historian James Merrell describes, in the course of the expedition, Michel suddenly disappears from Evans's account of the trip.[28] It is possible that at this juncture, Bizaillon left his employment with the Pennsylvania government to take on a role as ambassador between the French governor general and the Illinois. Although we cannot rely entirely on the accuracy of the timeline in Bizaillon's letter to French authorities, it seems likely that Bizaillon's tenure working for the French, the English, and the Illinois overlapped.

Neither the French nor the English entirely trusted Bizaillon, but they did make use of his familiarity with the upper country. In the correspondence generated by both these governments, reference is made to his ability to navigate the region's topography. He leads the Pennsylvania governor through the complex and multinational Indigenous world of the Susquehanna River region. Working for the French king during the same period, he guides the French men in his party on a complicated overland route to Detroit that he has likely previously traversed before, but with which they, traveling normally by the system of rivers, are unfamiliar. For Bizaillon and other members of the French-Indigenous family networks, the upper country was not a dichotomized region hanging in the balance between French and English kings. They also understood that there were many Indigenous nations acting in their own diplomatic and military interests that sometimes aligned with or clashed with those of Europeans.

The governor general of New France was as concerned with ensuring the Illinois maintained ties to Canada, rather than Louisiana, as he was with preventing English influence among the Illinois. In the Anglo-American world, New York merchants complained as loudly over the activities of their Pennsylvania counterparts in the west as they did about any ill effects of illegal trade with the French. Members of the family networks understood that many different levels of political identity operated in tandem in the upper country. The ease with which they moved between these states made them both ideal vehicles for the propagation of imperial presence, and conversely and ironically, a persistent threat to its continued existence. As the eighteenth century unfolded, agents of Indigenous and Euro-American nations of the upper country would single out members of these networks as the reason for the various ills that plagued their increasingly complex diplomatic relations.

Historic records allow us to speculate about and sometimes substantiate the existence of children of traders such as Michel and his brother Pierre Bizaillon who were born of their relations with Indigenous women. We can postulate about the significance of these relationships and the children they produced to the larger metaphoric family Euro-Americans and Indigenous peoples were attempting to establish and maintain. In his 1712 speech in which he had discussed Michel Bizaillon's status among the Illinois, Chachagouesse noted that Bizaillon had offered to carry a message to Vaudreuil that the Illinois wanted to make an alliance with the French by marrying all of their daughters to worthy French men.

As historian Sophie White points out, Illinois women were "crucial intermediaries" in "fur trade exchanges and the broader alliances that facilitated them."[29] In Algonquian kinship systems, daughters and sisters created lateral alliances through marriage that crossed geographical distances, a fact of which the French had always been well aware.[30] Relations between the French and the Peoria were tenuous, and the Peoria desire to arrange these marriages reflected their willingness to smooth these differences and promote trade and military cooperation.[31] Chachagouesse also implied that Bizaillon was a central agent in these relations, noting that he was well liked by the Illinois, and the only regret they had about him was that he was already married, otherwise each of the Illinois men would have offered Bizaillon his daughter.[32]

It would be Bizaillon's past relationships with Illinois women that determined whether or not the state viewed his behavior as immoral and illegal. Bizaillon claimed to have been married according to Catholic rites to two Illinois women (one likely Kaskaskia and the other Metchigamia) who had passed away before his marriage in 1710 to Marguerite Fafard.[33] It was this situation that likely frustrated French imperial officials who, understanding the symbolic importance of marriage between French men and Illinois women, were loath to recognize the power Bizaillon held because of these previous marriages. Claude Ramezay's recitation of Bizaillon's past bad behavior had included the charge that he had been with a number of Indigenous women, suggesting these were not Catholic marriages. This had brought him to the attention of the Jesuits in the Illinois Country. In his attempt to convince his superiors that Bizaillon could be trusted, Ramezay had included the testimonial of the Jesuit Vaillant who insisted that since his Catholic marriage to Fafard, Bizaillon had changed, and a gentleness had returned to his demeanor.

Chachagouesse's statement about Bizaillon's status in relation to his French wife and the Illinois women is meaningful in a number of ways. Bizaillon was part of the network of influential French-Indigenous families at Detroit that operated in close association with Cadillac. The issue of marriage between French men and Indigenous women had pitted Cadillac and Vaudreuil against one another, with Cadillac pushing these associations and Vaudreuil refusing to allow them. Michel Bizaillon's offer to Chachagouesse to take a message to Vaudreuil advocating marriage between Illinois women and French men was made after Bizaillon told the Illinois that Cadillac was no longer in a position of authority, and that they had to appeal directly to Vaudreuil with their concerns. Knowing this, it is possible that Bizaillon and perhaps Cadillac himself were looking to put pressure on Vaudreuil by forcing him to tell France's Indigenous allies that he did not want to make political alliances with them through the marriages of French sons and Illinois daughters.

When Vaudreuil made his response to Chachagouesse, he denounced Bizaillon as a bad influence, but did not directly address the issue of Illinois women marrying French men or Bizaillon's past marriages to Kaskaskia and Metchigamia women. Vaudreuil ended his speech to Chachagouesse by giving gifts to him and his daughter as a mark of the governor general's gratitude for the journey they had made to Quebec to meet with him.[34] Vaudrueuil's actions suggest he was savvy enough to acknowledge the political importance of the Peoria women to the French-Illinois alliance, while sidestepping the larger issue of French-Indigenous marriage that he had officially prohibited at Detroit. If he had allowed Cadillac to sanction marriages of Indigenous women to French men, he would have empowered Cadillac in his efforts to channel the power of Onontio. As a likely confederate of Cadillac, Bizaillon was an unsuitable and perhaps dangerous agent whose dubious relations threatened to divert power from the governor general.

Imperial records carefully couched Bizaillon's behavior, suggesting he had engaged in illicit sexual relationships with Illinois women but had supposedly abandoned this behavior after his Catholic marriage of 1710.[35] If true, in the eyes of the Peoria, this too may have constituted a potential threat to the alliance with the French. Because Bizaillon was already respected by the Illinois and considered a son, based no doubt on his past relationships with Illinois women, the issue of whether there had been a change in his temperament and behavior would have resonated differently in the eyes of the Peoria than it would have for French imperial officials. The activities that had previously endeared him to the Illinois had threatened his status among the French as an emissary for the king. Whether he had changed and could be trusted to speak for the king among the Illinois hinged on how his marriage to Marguerite Fafard was interpreted. Bizaillon seemed to have been aware of this fact.

Sometime between late 1713 and early 1714, Bizaillon was at Michilimackinac at the same time as French officer Claude-Charles Dutisné. Dutisné was preparing to lead a group to the Ouabache to construct a fort to prevent contact of the Myaamia and Natchez with the English, and to explore an area of mines around Kaskaskia. Dutisné asked Bizaillon to accompany him because he had been told that Bizaillon would be a crucial addition to the expedition. Bizaillon responded that because he wished to see his wife he could not accompany Dutisné, but countered that if the governor general wished it, he would go in service to the king.[36] Bizaillon may have had many reasons, besides wishing to return to his wife, for refusing Dutisné's invitation. He may have wanted to avoid taking part in an operation meant to counter English influence. In the end, Bizaillon forced the choice of his involvement in the expedition on Vaudreuil, one of the imperial officials who had been so critical of Bizaillon's behavior. The question of whether Bizaillon should return to Montreal and honor his Catholic marriage to a French woman, or if he should work on the king's behalf among the Illinois rested with the governor general. Because of his kinship links through past relationships to Illinois women, Bizaillon was a powerful political emissary whose allegiance to the French empire could never be fully ascertained.

How genuine and in whose eyes was Bizaillon's "conversion" from rakish philanderer and wily traitor to monogamous and gentle husband and obedient servant to the French king, and had it been realized through the medium of his Detroit marriage to Marguerite Fafard? Vaudreuil and other agents of government, including religious officials and Indigenous leaders such as Chachagouesse, couched

Bizaillon's character and behavior in these dichotomous terms, but on the ground in the upper country, there were many other choices as to how one could operate. After all, Marguerite Fafard hailed from a family skilled at navigating French, English, and Indigenous worlds, and combining matters of business with matters of marriage and family. When Michel left Michilimackinac with the remaining slave given to him by Chachagouesse, he kept with him a gift meant to symbolize Illinois loyalty to the king. We have no way of knowing if the slave ever reached the new intendant or whether Bizaillon retained ownership. In continuing to possess the slave, Bizaillon would have been acting on the basis of his private interests and no longer as an agent of the king. This action could have disrupted or threatened Illinois-French diplomatic relations.

We do know that Bizaillon stopped at Detroit, had his slave baptized, and married Marguerite Fafard, all within three months. Bizaillon's prior relationships to Illinois women held significance for French imperial officials only as part of the narrative arc tracing the transformation of Bizaillon's character. This purported change in Bizaillon would not have held similar significance for the Illinois who considered him a son. His marriage became a pivotal marker in time between these two disparate states of being. Performed at an imperially sanctioned location, the marriage functioned as a version of the "certificats de bonne moeurs" French officials had considered demanding of individuals who traveled to the upper country. Detroit operated as a center of political and economic importance by virtue of its status as an Indigenous point of origin, threatening the authority of Quebec officials. The Bizaillon marriage held a unique and powerful meaning in both worlds.

Michel's brother Pierre Bizaillon seems to have taken a somewhat different route than his brother in his interactions with the Illinois and other Indigenous nations. Pierre Bizaillon had begun his North American life as a voyageur. In 1686, he traveled with René Cuillerier (who we will meet later in this chapter) as part of Henri Tonty's contingent sent down the Mississippi to find the missing René-Robert Cavelier de La Salle. Two years later, Pierre made himself available to the English and, like his brother, was working with business contacts in Pennsylvania to further trade in the upper country. He became part of a short-lived agency called the New Mediterranean Sea Company launched by Pennsylvania doctor Daniel Coxe, who was looking to establish a trading center on the south shore of Lake Erie.[37] Although this venture was never successful, Pierre maintained his contacts in Pennsylvania. The group's activities would challenge the trading networks of New York and also bring Bizaillon to the attention of eastern-based Philadelphia merchants who were concerned for their own profits.[38]

The parish register for Notre Dame de la Conception at Kaskaskia lists the baptisms of several children with the last name Bizaillon in the final decade of the seventeenth and first decade of the eighteenth centuries. In 1703, Pierre and an Indigenous woman named Marie Thérèse baptized a son named Pierre, and in 1712, another son (named Michel) of Pierre and of a woman named Apeusamacoué was baptized. The birth of a girl named Marie Bisaillon in 1699 is attributed to a man named Bisaillon and an Indigenous woman named Marie. It is impossible to know the first name of the father, and to determine, therefore, if the infant had been fathered by Michel or Pierre.[39]

We do know, however, that Pierre fathered a daughter sometime between 1685 and 1689 with a woman named Jeanne or Johanna Sioute, who may have been Dakota. A poignant letter written from New York in 1701 by the girl—named for her mother—to her father tells us that by the age of twelve, she had lived all or most of her life apart from both of her parents:

> Beloved Father—My only Desier is that my dier father would be pleast to Remamber me, for I understand that you are my only father, my mother Jahanna Sioute She take noe care of me for Shee gave me away hwen I was a Little Child to Anna Couvenowen whare I have bin these 12 yeare and a halfe and have bin well brought up. . . . Now my only Desier is that my beloved father would be pleas to Remamber his Diere Child; and Sned me few word back again that Should mak me glad and Satisfigd in my mine that I hav a father in life; My hombey Respect to my Diere father for ever Petter Belelion. Jahanna Beselion[40]

At twelve years of age, Johanna had seemingly never met her father, but her letter communicates a strong sense of connection. This might only have been possible if someone, perhaps Johanna's Dakota mother or her Euro-American adopted mother, had spoken of Pierre/Peter. The stories of Pierre allowed Johanna to cultivate an imagined relationship to a distant father that prevailed for over a decade, despite the multiple dislocations associated with life in the upper country. It remained to be seen whether the king of France would maintain his metaphoric fatherhood with Indigenous nations of the upper country and whether members of the family networks would continue to operate as emissaries and embodied representations of the father-king.

Pierre Bizaillon had chosen one of many possible paths in the upper country. He eventually removed himself completely from any role in the French imperial system and became part of Pennsylvania's colony. Perhaps he made his way to New York for a reunion with a daughter he likely had never known. All of these children became markers of the disparate worlds traversed a hundred times in the course of a lifetime in the upper country. The Bizaillon brothers linked the governments of Canada, Louisiana, Pennsylvania, Carolina, and through their familial contacts, New York. One brother allowed his marriage in the Catholic Church to function as a symbol of his willingness to operate within the French imperial system when it served his purposes. The other brother, however, seems to have abandoned this path, and to have chosen instead to pursue relations only with Indigenous women. This behavior effectively separated Pierre Bizaillon from the French king.

There were other choices to be made in crafting both a relationship to the father-king and a position within the imperial system. Children of men such as Michel and Pierre Bizaillon would become the new power brokers in the upper country as the eighteenth century unfolded. The circumstances of their births and early lives would influence the nature of their role in imperial politics. Members of the extended Cuillerier dit Beaubien family would follow paths that sometimes diverged and at other times converged with the Bizaillons in their efforts to negotiate multiple Indigenous and Euro-American worlds. Indeed, the worlds of these two families would overlap and come together at Detroit.

The Cuillerier dit Beaubien Network

René Cuillerier had migrated from France to New France only two years before he was taken captive by the Oneida in 1661, as he and other workers quarried stone outside Montreal for the building of the city's first seminary. Once back in Oneida territory, he was adopted by an Oneida woman to replace her brother who had died in battle. Cuillerier spent nineteen months among the Oneida engaged in various occupations, including accompanying a pregnant woman of his adoptive family on a trip to bring supplies to her husband at the family's winter hunting grounds.[41] In 1663, while hunting with French men and Oneida in Mohawk territory, Cuillerier left or escaped, heading to Fort Orange in New Netherland. From there, he made his way to Boston and then journeyed back to Montreal.[42] He proved himself a keen observer of his adoptive community, and was able to provide detailed descriptions of the Oneida-Haudenosaunee political system, gender roles, and religious customs for the Sulpician priests for whom he had been working when he was taken captive. The report of his captivity experience was incorporated into the *Jesuit Relations* for the years 1664–1665.[43]

René eventually settled at La Chine, and between 1673 and 1713, he and his family converted what had been Samuel Champlain's fur-trade operation established sixty years earlier, first into a wooden fort, and later a stone trading post that became known after 1676 as Fort Cuillerier.[44] René's experience among the Haudenosaunee launched him into the world of European-Indigenous trade and diplomacy, and his La Chine residence provided a base from which he acted on behalf of the state, allowing him to steadily gain economic and political clout. Acting as official interpreter at one critical juncture, he met with the Onondaga leader Teganissorens (known also by the hereditary title Niregouentaron) at Fort Cuillerier and reported back to Governor General Frontenac on the fragile state of Haudenosaunee-Illinois relations.[45]

Cuillerier extended his operation steadily west and south. In 1681, he was granted a license by Robert Cavelier de La Salle to send two or three men to the country of the Kiikaapoi and Meskwaki, located in an area that ranged from what is today northern Wisconsin (predominantly Meskwaki territory) to central Illinois (predominantly Kiikaapoi territory). To the permit was added a proviso that the men not engage in trade with the Odawa, a stipulation that likely protected preexisting trading networks.[46] This meant that, although the contingent would have traveled via the waterway system from Montreal through the straits of Mackinac in Anishinaabewaki, the men would not have been allowed to trade there. In 1686, Cuillerier accompanied Pierre Bizaillon and Henri Tonty on a trip down the Mississippi River to look for the missing La Salle, during which time the men established a trading post at the Quapaw village of Osotouy on the lower Mississippi.

Just before a 1689 Haudenosaunee attack on La Chine, René—now listed as a merchant—and his associates, including his son René Hillaire and son-in-law Michel Descaris, were in Montreal settling accounts for a previous trip to the Illinois Country.[47] Cuillerier could have avoided the Haudenosaunee attack by luck alone, seeing as his business in Montreal may have detained him there. It is also possible that because Cuillerier had kinship connections among the Oneida, had acted as a Haudenosaunee-French interpreter, and engaged in trade with the Haudenosaunee of Kahnawake, he may have had advance warning. He was not only able to avoid injury to his person and property, he also profited from the hostilities. He was paid by the French government for ferrying ammunition from Montreal to La Chine and for storing it at Fort Cuillerier. In addition, acting Governor of Montreal Vaudreuil and his troops rested at Cuillerier's home after the disastrous (for the French) battle.[48] This battle was part of the same war initiated by Jigonsase, the head clan mother of the Haudenosaunee, in reprisal for Governor General Denonville's seizure and enslavement of members of the Haudenosaunee government.

By 1698, René had relocated to Montreal and while still operating as a merchant, held the title of chief surveyor of the Island of Montreal. René's sons followed their father into the family business and his daughters married men who were similarly inclined. One daughter and one son married siblings from the Trottier dit DesRuisseaux family, which would also figure prominently in Detroit's French-Indigenous family networks. His son Lambert, eighteen years of age at the time, and son-in-law Joseph Trottier dit DeRuisseaux were first accused in 1700 of having conducted illegal trade at Fort Frontenac for which they had employed Haudenosaunee of Kahnawake (called Sault St. Louis by the French). Further charges of participation in illegal trade at Fort Albany followed, for which the men were eventually jailed.[49] Lambert and his brother-in-law had not only followed their father/father-in-law into trade with Indigenous nations, they also followed the routes he had taken through Haudenosaunee territory and to the doorstep of the English colonies, making them potential threats to French imperial aims. These early interactions across multiple European and Indigenous nations would form the basis for the economic and political power of the burgeoning French-Indigenous family networks.

Despite his implication in the affair of 1700, Lambert was part of the expedition that set out from Montreal with Cadillac to establish the French fort at Detroit in July 1701, and two years later, he would be given permission to travel with a contingent to the Illinois Country.[50] Lambert operated in accordance with imperial policies for trade at Detroit, but his brother-in-law Joseph Trottier dit DesRuisseaux ran afoul of these same regulations. During the winter of 1701, Joseph was accused of engaging in trade with Indigenous nations of Lakes Erie and Ontario in defiance of the edicts of the king and the Conseil Supérieur, for which he was jailed. The thirty-four-year-old Joseph, described as living with his father-in-law Cuillerier, was interrogated in the matter, as was an Indigenous man named Gaientarongouen Sanontanan, requiring the use of two translators.[51]

In the twenty-five years following the 1681 proviso that had prevented René from trading with the Odawa, the Cuillerier family had not only managed to defy this stipulation, they were also acting as imperial representatives in Anishinaabewaki.

In 1706, a member of the family, possibly Lambert, together with Maurice Ménard, the interpreter of Indigenous languages at Michilimackinac, provided gifts from their private stores for the Odawa at a perilous moment in French-Odawa relations. Marest, the resident Jesuit, urged Governor General Vaudreuil to compensate the men for these expenses incurred on the king's behalf, since the king's boat had not contained sufficient goods for settling troublesome matters.[52] In this way, Cuillerier and Ménard's trade goods were transformed into tools of diplomacy used to bring peace on behalf of an impoverished king who lacked the resources to prevent war. Correspondingly, family networks gained economically as the value of their goods was enhanced at conveniently auspicious junctures in French-Indigenous relations.

The incident that had allowed Cuillerier and Ménard to gain their advantage in trade with the Odawa was associated with the Le Pesant affair that had broken out at Detroit and pitted the Myaamia and Wendat against the Odawa. The goods contributed by the two men had gone to two influential Odawa women who were seeking to avenge the French killing of their brother by calling Odawa warriors to attack the French at Michilimackinac. To maintain peace, the women demanded gifts and the privilege of purchasing trade goods at a price they would determine. The women relented only when their demands were met and they had learned that the French had not taken part in a second attack on the Odawa at Detroit.[53]

The intercession of Cuillerier, Ménard, and the Odawa women may have been both a fait accompli and an opportunity they created to enhance their economic and political power at Detroit and Michilimackinac. The extended Cuillerier network included the powerful Odawa leader Outanagan—at the center of negotiations over the Le Pesant affair—and his wife Isabelle Couc (Madame Montour). As well, one of the Odawa women demanding gifts and control of trade was likely La Blanche, kinswoman to Jean Le Blanc (Outoutagan). In charging the king for diplomatic gifts they provided and demanding the right to adjust the price of trade goods, all to resolve a crisis they likely had a hand in creating, Cuillerier, Ménard, and La Blanche had fixed the system to their benefit. The basis for their power lay in their extended kinship network with its multiple connections across French and Indigenous nations. Members were essential to imperial projects not only because they were able to harness resources across these nations, but also because their connections made them consummate diplomats and interpreters who could counsel either war or peace.

The Cuillerier dit Beaubien Network: Ménard, Couc, and Montour

The same year Lambert and Maurice Ménard worked together to appease the Odawa women at Michilimackinac, Lambert stood as godfather for a child of Maurice's brother-in-law Jean Baptiste Couc and Couc's wife, an Abenaki woman named Anne. The following year, in 1707, Lambert Cuillerier would marry Maurice Ménard's niece, Marguerite Ménard.[54] Lambert Cuillerier's business partner and now uncle by marriage, Maurice Ménard was a well-traveled interpreter. Over the course of several decades, he was frequently utilized by imperial officials as a liaison between the French and a multitude of Indigenous nations, including the Abenaki (the nation into which he had married), the Odawa at Michilimackinac, and the Meskwaki during the Fox Wars.

Maurice was married to Madeleine Couc, sister to Isabelle Couc (Madame Montour) and daughter of Pierre Couc and the Algonquin Marie Miteouamigoukoue. The Couc family was one of Detroit's earliest and most powerful of the burgeoning French-Indigenous families. As we learned earlier in this chapter in the discussion of the Bizaillon family, Madeleine and Isabelle Couc's sister Marguerite was married to Jean Fafard, member of a family of interpreters of Wendat and Odawa languages at Detroit. A brother, Louis Couc dit Montour, would be murdered in 1709 by Louis-Thomas Chabert de Joncaire, a prominent and influential leader among the Seneca who worked at maintaining good relations between the Seneca and the French.[55]

Governor General Vaudreuil had ordered Chabert de Joncaire to kill Louis Couc dit Montour on charges he was a traitor who was allied to the English. Vaudreuil cited the bad character of the half-French/half-Indigenous Louis as the reason for Vaudreuil's denial of Cadillac's request to allow marriages between French men and Indigenous women at Detroit.[56] Chabert de Joncaire was Vaudreuil's designated agent for speaking and acting on behalf of the king with the Haudenosaunee while Louis Couc dit Montour performed this role for Cadillac. With relations strained between Vaudreuil and Cadillac as both men sought to embody Onontio, it was not surprising that their interpreters were also at odds and that the messages they relayed and carried diverged dramatically. Cadillac regarded Chabert de Joncaire with as much suspicion as Vaudreuil had expressed of Louis Couc dit Montour, with Cadillac accusing Chabert de Joncaire of undermining his influence by turning the Seneca against him. In response, Vaudreuil claimed that Joncaire had single-handedly diverted a war by the Seneca against the French set in motion by comments Cadillac had made when passing through Seneca country.[57]

Not all members of the Couc dit Montour family formed alliances with Cadillac. Isabelle Couc, an interpreter herself, became the object of Cadillac's derision when he claimed she had joined the growing group of individuals working to ruin him. Early in the eighteenth century, Isabelle split her loyalties between the French and English, and formed several partnerships with prominent French and Indigenous men, including the Odawa leader Outoutagan. By the mid-eighteenth century, she would be firmly entrenched in the interests of the English, becoming known as Madame Montour. She and her son Andrew functioned as interpreters whose information and advice were pivotal to English success in negotiations and alliances with Indigenous nations.[58]

After Lambert Cuillerier died in 1709, his widow, Marguerite Ménard, married another trader with French and Indigenous ties who had been a business associate of her first husband. François Lamoureux dit St. Germain had been charged, along with Lambert, of engaging in illegal trade. St. Germain's maternal grandfather had been an Algonquin medicine man named Pigarouich or Pigarouisnunepiresi and his maternal grandmother an Ojibwe woman named Marguerite Pataouabanoukone or Oupitaouabamoukou.[59] The same year that St. Germain married Lambert's widow, he was again engaged in illegal commerce, for which he, his partners Pierre and Nicolas Sarrazin (the latter of whom traded at Baie des Puants/Green Bay), and their *panis* slave Joseph were accused and prosecuted.[60] St. Germain and Sarrazin were mentioned in the 1708 report condemning Detroit by imperial representative Aigremont as having witnessed the diverting of furs by French-allied Indigenous groups to the Haudenosaunee and English. Aigremont complained that this practice was so widespread, it drastically reduced the number of skins Cadillac sent to the king.[61] Almost twenty years later, in 1726, St. Germain and wife Marguerite Ménard would be accused of trading brandy for furs with two Indigenous men, an incident the court was not willing to ignore because the couple had been engaging in this practice for a long time.[62]

The Cuillerier dit Beaubien Network: Expansion and Slavery

There was a clear disparity between commercial success and political affluence on the one hand and periodic bouts of imprisonment or punishment for illegal activities on the other that marked the early days of the Cuillerier family network. Indeed, as the family prospered economically, their members would continue to walk the thin and constantly shifting line that separated imperial persecution from imperial sanction, which at times had them operating as political appointees. A member of the Cuillerier family, likely René Cuillerier's son René Hillaire, resided for six years at Fort Bourbon on Hudson Bay and was entrusted by French imperial authorities to assist with the transition from French to English control following the Treaty of Utrecht in 1714, a job that required Cuillerier to travel to England.[63] On the return trip aboard a British navy ship, he accompanied the English commandant designated to assume control at Hudson Bay. He was also ordered to be present during an account by Fort Bourbon's outgoing French commandant of the fort's personnel and property, to sign this inventory on behalf of the French government, make his own report, and arrange passage of French goods, officers, and hired men (*engagés*) out of Fort Bourbon.

The second decade of the eighteenth century also marked a pivotal shift in trade practices for the Cuillerier family. Roughly five years after his service to the king at Hudson Bay, René Hillaire had sexual relations with Elisabeth, a Patoca (Padouca/Plains Apache) woman, resulting in the birth of a daughter.[64] We cannot be entirely certain that Elisabeth was or had been a slave, although this is likely. At the end of the seventeenth century and the beginning of the eighteenth, Great Plains nations joined with French slave raiders to attack the Plains Apache who were allies of the Spanish. The targets of their raids were Apache women and children, who were sold to the French for guns and other items.[65] The Cuillerier family and members of their network were likely already involved in an informal trade in slaves as members moved about the continental interior between Louisiana, the Illinois Country, and Hudson Bay, but the legalizing of the trade by the French government in 1709 and the outbreak of the Fox Wars at Detroit in June 1712 had brought slaves into imperial and church records.

The Cuillerier family name first appears in the church register of Ste. Anne's at Detroit in April of 1713, when René Hillaire baptized a Meskwaki slave Jean Baptiste, named for his godfather Jean Baptiste Quenet.[66] A year previous to this baptism, Jean Baptiste Quenet had stood as godfather in Detroit for another Meskawki on June 24, 1712—the first day of mass enslavement and baptism of Meskwaki captives immediately following Meskwaki defeat at Detroit. The Quenet and Cuillerier families would have been well known to each other because both families were based in La Chine, and their patriarchs (René Cuillerier Sr. and Jean Quenet Sr.) had for a long time been engaged in trade with Indigenous nations and had built wealth and prestige as royally sanctioned merchants and holders of royal titles. For the Quenet family, the acquiring of captives was already a family business. Jean Quenet Sr. had purchased a New England captive from Haudenosaunee at Montreal. This young girl, named Sarah Allen, had been taken during the French-Indigenous raid on Deerfield, Massachusetts, in 1704. She had been baptized, given a French name, and joined the Quenet household as a domestic.[67] Ultimately, the Quenet and Cuillerier families would strengthen their trade alliances by means of a family union that crossed generations when Jean Quenet Sr. married René Hillaire's sister Françoise Cuillerier in 1718. At the time of the marriage, the bride was thirty-three and the groom seventy years old; both had been widowed.

The Cuillerier dit Beaubien Network: Trottier dit DesRuisseaux

Before her second marriage to the elder Quenet, Françoise Cuillerier had been married to Joseph Trottier dit DesRuisseaux, and her brother Jean had married Joseph's sister Marie Catherine Trottier dit DesRuisseaux. It was this latter marriage that would produce subsequent generations of power brokers in Detroit and at the Ouabache/Wabash/ Myaamionki in the mid to late eighteenth century. Alexis, another of the Trottier dit DesRuisseaux siblings, would marry Marie Louise Roy, a daughter of Pierre Roy and the Myaamia Waapankihkwa/Marguerite Ouabankikoué. Another brother, Julien, purchased land at Detroit in 1707 within the fort's walls, providing an anchor for the family's business operations that pivoted east and west for decades.[68] By 1722, Joseph, Alexis, and Julien had a well-established business partnership that was augmented by the involvement of women of their family. Their sister Marie Catherine was a *procuratrice* who acquired thousands of livres of merchandise from her brother Julien to establish her family's trade at Detroit.[69]

Other members of the family, both men and women, maintained integral trade relations with Haudenosaunee communities in the St. Lawrence valley. One of the oldest of the Trottier siblings, Pierre Trottier dit Desauniers, was a merchant who had operated with Michel Bizaillon in the Illinois Country. Pierre's daughters Marguerite, Marie-Anne, and Marie-Madeleine were fluent speakers of Iroquoian languages who would eventually launch their own trading enterprise at Kahnawake in 1727, building on their family's decades-long connections in that community to advance English goods to the upper country. Historian Jan Noel describes the sisters as *filles majeures/non mariées* (having attained the age of majority and unmarried) and moving easily between French and Indigenous worlds. Their position of power was undoubtedly influenced by norms set by Haudenosaunee women who dominated the trade between Montreal and Albany.[70] Twenty-seven years after their Uncle Joseph Trottier dit DesRuisseaux had been accused of engaging in illegal trade with Haudenosaunee of Kahnawake, the sisters would face similar scrutiny as their business flourished and they were perceived as a threat by French officials.

Targeted by imperial authorities, including the king of France, who sought for years to put a stop to the sisters' activities, in 1750 the governor general finally took measures to destroy their trade. In his exhortations against the sisters, he referenced two levels of influence—one economic and the other political—that made them and other members of the French-Indigenous family networks powerful and potentially dangerous. He first charged them with conducting contraband trade with the English at Orange/Albany and Chouaguen (the French name for the British Fort Oswego) in New York. His second charge was more serious in its implications. He accused the sisters of launching an "Empire" and fomenting a spirit of independence and rebellion among the Haudenosaunee, and ordered that they be removed from Sault St. Louis/Kahnawake.[71]

The governor general's command was carried out by Daniel-Marie Chabert de Joncaire, who would have had a number of reasons for relishing the opportunity to expel the sisters. He had recently constructed a fort, over Haudenosaunee objections, at a location where he could intercept furs before they were taken to Chouaguen/Oswego. The ubiquitous Empire of the Desauniers sisters threatened his efforts. Once the sisters were gone, he was given a monopoly on trade and promoted to lieutenant.[72] Additionally, his family had a decades-long rivalry with members of the Cuillerier family network. As we learned earlier, Daniel-Marie's father Louis-Thomas Chabert de Joncaire, Governor General Vaudreuil's interpreter with the Haudenosaunee, had murdered rival interpreter and Cadillac intermediary Louis Couc dit Montour in 1709. Over forty years later, the two families were functioning in similar roles—the Joncaires acting on behalf of the French governor general and the extended Cuillerier network occupying a more uncertain position of periodic defiance and independence that threatened French imperial aims.

While the Desauniers sisters composed numerous letters to the government and to the trading corporation Compagnie des Indes requesting permission to return to Kahnawake to recoup their goods and salvage their reputations, their cousin Julien Trottier dit DesRuisseaux dit Desrivières would capitalize on his family's extensive network. By 1755, he had become a *négociant* (wholesaler) at the

Vincennes post located on the lower Ouabache among the Piankashaw, a member community of the Myaamia nation. There is little doubt his Desauniers cousins and their Haudenosaunee partners had provided the goods for Julien's business. Haudenosaunee war leader Teganagouassen reported to French authorities that the sisters and their associates exchanged beaver furs for English goods obtained from Albany that were subsequently sent to the posts in the upper country.[73] The trading network through which those goods flowed also circled back to other members of the Cuillerier family network. The sisters' business had been bolstered early on by 800 pounds of beaver provided by the Quenet family of La Chine.[74]

Hailing from French, Haudenosaunee, Anishinaabe, and Myaamia communities and whose induction had been achieved either through capture and adoption or by virtue of marriage or geographical proximity, early members of the extended Cuillerier family network became ideal agents in Euro-Indigenous economic and political relations. Their sons, daughters, and grandchildren who helped forge the multicultural community at Detroit did not arrive, therefore, without the requisite skills, experience, and connections to realize commercial success. Because of them, Detroit became a prominent location in a network stretching across the continent. Both the Bizaillon and Cuillerier family networks utilized Detroit's status as a transitional location and center of mobility to conduct trade and expand power and influence in both French and Indigenous worlds.

Both families anchored themselves at Detroit with landholdings while also extending their economic reach in every direction. The Bizaillons' tenure at and through Detroit would reach its peak during the early Fox Wars and the pivotal second decade of Detroit's establishment as a French-provisioned fort. The Cuillerier dit Beaubien family would operate in the vicinity of Detroit first during the second decade of the eighteenth century and strengthen their economic base in the years leading up to the Seven Years' War. Both families maintained power by linking their activities at Detroit to Myaamionki and the Illinois Country. The path between these locations would grow in importance just as the families who expertly traversed it strengthened their economic and political presence.

Members of the networks understood the dichotomized existence that came with working for the king or Onontio while attempting to bolster their private interests. They knew that when they represented the king in interactions with Indigenous nations, their commercial activities were imperially sanctioned because this trade was acknowledged as part of the necessary mechanism for establishing and maintaining diplomatic relations. When they were perceived to have stepped out of the role of representative of the king, however, they were harassed, reprimanded, and even jailed for illegal activities that threatened the imperial presence.

Members of the networks lived in and were an integral part of the day-to-day life of multinational communities like Detroit that were dependent on good relations with resident Indigenous nations. The embodied selves of network members engaged in a thousand daily activities devoid of any overarching symbolic meaning. This ran counter to, and perhaps at times weakened the impact of, the amplified and metonymic persona of the king they were supposed to represent when it was demanded of them. Individuals at the top of the colonial hierarchy, such as Governor General Vaudreuil, were the most threatened by the ease with which members of the family networks moved into and out of the role of king's representative. Vaudreuil's insecurity originated in the slippery quality of this ontological duality, which historian Nancy Shoemaker has described as the difficulty of "how to locate political authority when any person, not only European monarchs, might have 'two bodies': the 'Body natural' and the 'Body politic.'"[75] The line between public and private was continually being crossed and renegotiated, creating a constantly shifting distinction that imperial officials found difficult to interpret and police.

CHAPTER 5

On Such Does the Fate of Empires Depend

Women of the French-Indigenous Family Networks

We briefly glimpsed in the previous chapter how the Desauniers sisters, operating out of Kahnawake, established a powerful economic empire that cut across Indigenous and European nations and threatened the French state in the years leading up to the Seven Years' War. At times their commercial activities allowed them to be integrated into the imperial system, while at other times, that same system sought to control and even expel them. The French state had always attempted to control women's bodies, including through practices used to recruit French women to the colony and by seeking to limit their movement outside the colonial capital at Quebec. It also attempted to convert Indigenous women to French standards of behavior and to police their manner of reproduction. These efforts clashed with the agency exhibited in many Indigenous nations, including the Haudenosaunee, where women held systemic political power and female leaders operated at the highest diplomatic channels, moving about within the extensive territory of their nation. Indigenous women's power surprised and frustrated imperial authorities.

The ultimate indication of the failure of imperial authorities to regulate the fur trade was the burgeoning agency of the French and Indigenous women who participated in this commerce. They ventured far outside the sphere of state control and drew their power from a multitude of norms for gendered behavior. These women succeeded in thwarting Euro-American attempts at control by navigating the multicultural world of the trade and crafting a hybrid gendered identity. This chapter considers some of the ways in which women of the French-Indigenous networks expressed their authority in the multicultural world shaped by the fur trade. In every instance, women smoothed the road for economic exchange through marriage, acted on behalf of or sometimes in spite of their husbands in their handling of family businesses, conducted trade on their own that frequently escaped the notice and censure of imperial authorities, and initiated trade between nations at the request and with the approval of these same authorities. They also engaged in illegal trade, participated in wars, took multiple husbands, and fled abuse at the hands of some of these men. Their trails through imperial correspondence crossing vast distances is evidence that they used their mobility to escape situations limiting their autonomy, or in some cases, threatening their lives, to seek greater opportunity elsewhere. This ability to disappear into alternative gendered worlds, however, could be used against them by French imperial agents and their own kinsmen.

Controlling Bodies: Women and Empire in New France

In the first decades of French presence in the St. Lawrence valley, French men vastly outnumbered French women. For every woman between the ages of sixteen and thirty in the colony, there were twelve unmarried men of the same age range.[1] In order to address this discrepancy and increase the population of the colony, Intendant Jean Talon had conceived of the idea of the *filles du roy* or daughters of the king. These were young women hailing largely from orphanages in France whose passage to Canada was paid and a royal dowry of fifty livres attached in exchange for their immediate marriage in New France. Between 1663 and 1673, just under one thousand such women had made this trip and 80 percent of them married within six months of their arrival in North America.[2] Jean Talon's project had been successful—the presence of the *filles du roy* made possible a significant demographic increase.[3]

Catherine Ducharme was one such *fille du roy* hailing from Paris. Within a year of her arrival in New France in 1672, she married Pierre Roy, who had been hired as an *engagé* in the French port city of La Rochelle. After their marriage at Notre Dame

Cathedral in Montreal, the couple established themselves in LaPrairie, a location immediately southwest of Montreal known as Kentake to the Haudenosaunee. It was settled initially by Oneida, and there had been a large influx of Mohawk families at roughly the same time the Roy family arrived.[4] Catherine performed her reproductive duties well, bearing nineteen children, the third of whom, also named Pierre, would eventually marry the Myaamia woman Waapankihkwa/Marguerite Ouabankikoué at Detroit.[5] By 1666, Pierre Sr. was working as an *engagé* for one of Montreal's most influential merchants, Jacques Le Ber, whose extensive trading interests stretched between Montreal, Albany, and France.[6] Pierre and Catherine were able to assemble a respectable dowry to place their eldest daughter Marguerite at the age of fifteen in the sororal religious community Congrégation de Notre-Dame in Montreal, the same age at which her younger brother Pierre Jr. was engaged for the first time to travel west to Anishinaabewaki in the upper country.

When Marguerite Roy took her vows in July 1698, the forty-year-old order had been reinvigorated only a few weeks before by the consecration of a new chapel, built through the generous donations of Jeanne Le Ber and her father Jacques, the same man who had employed Pierre Roy Sr. thirty years previously. Indeed, the women who would staff the Congregation hailed predominantly from families with extensive ties to the fur trade with Indigenous nations. René Cuillerier placed his daughter Marie-Anne-Véronique in the Congregation at the same time Pierre Roy Sr. placed his daughter Marguerite. Marie-Anne-Véronique Cuillerier would become the official secretary and annalist of her order from 1725 to 1747; her accounts of contemporary events are still used today by historians.[7]

Marguerite Trottier, who also hailed from another prominent French-Indigenous family, was in the order during the same period as the sisters Cuillerier and Roy (Trottier witnessed the 1698 ceremony in which Marguerite Roy made her profession), becoming superior general in 1722. The religious bond between sisters Cuillerier and Trottier further entrenched the connection between the two families we read about in chapter 4, made through marriages of two Cuillerier siblings to two Trottier siblings. It would have been a mark of status to have a daughter in the Congregation or the Ursulines. Pierre Roy Sr. might have benefited as much from his daughter's standing as his own when in 1705, he was entrusted with the care of the ornaments and furnishings of his local church while it was being torn down and rebuilt.[8] Many of the upwardly mobile merchants of the St. Lawrence valley would be similarly honored with this position of "marguiller" (churchwarden), as would members of the French-Indigenous family networks at Detroit.

The Congrégation de Notre-Dame was one of very few holy orders in New France for women, and was unique among these groups because it allowed its members to remain uncloistered. This freedom was an unintentional result of a few accidental occurrences and contingencies.[9] The Congregation's founder Marguerite Bourgeoys had left her order in France to found its offshoot in New France before she took her final orders and became cloistered. This set the tone for the Congregation in Montreal, which did not require the seclusion of its members and was regarded as a "secular" order. Cloistering was a way of curtailing the free movement of women, which was seen as especially important for protecting the chastity of single women living without the protection of fathers.[10] Marguerite Bourgeoys further eschewed this confinement by offering the Virgin Mary as the standard by which Bourgeoys wished to live. Christ's mother, after all, had not been cloistered and had traveled wherever she was needed, and like La Vierge, Bourgeoys was committed to working among the people who could benefit from her ministrations.[11]

Despite Bourgeoys's efforts, cloistering of the nuns of the Congregation remained a contentious issue. The superior general of the order took her case against the practice all the way to the king and was successful in gaining his support against it. From a practical standpoint, it seems that the religious women were more useful to the imperial project working in the community than if they remained within the walls of their convent.[12] But the formal taking of vows and cloistering were synonymous in all women's religious orders of the time. The superior general found herself in an ironic situation—to have complete freedom of movement, the nuns could not take formal vows (only cloistered nuns could take vows). By not taking vows, however, the order could not exist in an official capacity equal to other communities of religious women, with all of the attendant privileges.[13] The superior general opted to protect the freedom of her members while having novices take their vows in secret. It was a solution uniquely suited to the demands of the society of New France and is entirely emblematic of the ways in which women skirted strictures that restricted their liberty while creating new models of community. When Governor General Beauharnois commented that "Canadians had little taste for cloistering," and a "love of liberty," his comments could be viewed as equally applicable to the women of the Congregation as to members of the French-Indigenous networks he and his predecessors tried in vain to control.[14]

Working together with the Sulpicians among Montreal's diverse French and Indigenous populations, the women of the Congregation had considerable influence and authority. Within this order, Marguerite Roy stood out as exhibiting unlimited amounts of ambition and zeal, and possessing a strong vision that led her to skirt the normal hierarchical channels of her order. She had enough of a belief in the importance of her plans to bypass the priest/confessor of her community and communicate directly with the bishop of Québec Jean-Baptiste de la Croix de Chevrières de Saint-Vallier. The bishop was intent on realizing a long-held aim to establish teaching missions in Acadia and Louisbourg. Marguerite offered to travel to Louisbourg to bring about his dream, despite the fact that neither her order nor the French crown possessed sufficient funds to establish her there." Her efforts in opening a school in Louisbourg and admitting pupils were at first successful, but her lavish spending led her into trouble. Because of her strained relations with people within her own order, she was denied the assistance to continue, and in 1733 she was recalled to Montreal. Saint-Vallier's successor, Bishop of Quebec Pierre-Herman Dosquet reported that no priest wanted Marguerite in his parish. He accused Marguerite of having caused trouble everywhere she lived and described her as "the most deceitful, the most scheming nun, and the one most filled with illusions that I know."[15]

For the most part, young women like Marguerite Roy who entered religious orders hailed from families of means, and many were the daughters of merchants. Placing their daughters in a convent required a dowry for novitiates, which was often equal to a share of their parents' inheritance, a sum that many families of more modest income would not have been able to afford.[16] Unlike the English colonies, which observed the legal principles of primogeniture (the estates of parents were inherited by the eldest son) and coverture (the wife and all of her goods became the property of her husband upon marriage), New France adhered to the Coutume de Paris. This legal tradition declared that all children were entitled to an equal share of their parents' estate. Upon marriage, women maintained ownership and control of whatever goods or wealth they brought into their marriages. With their husbands, they formed a *communauté de biens* (marital community) that was made official by a contract drawn up at the time of the marriage.[17] At the death of one of the marital partners, the surviving spouse took half of the estate and divided the other half among the couple's children. If there were no children, the surviving spouse had the use of the entire estate for life. The wife also had access to a "douaire" (dowry), which was guaranteed to her if her husband died.[18]

Control of financial assets did not mean that French women had a greater voice in family matters than English women. French husbands still had the final word in all fiscal matters and were considered the heads of the household.[19] The

Coutume de Paris subjected a wife and children to the *puissance paternelle* or fatherly authority of the adult male. He was considered the overlord or "seigneur" of the couple's joint property, and his consent was required for all legal acts and property transactions engaged in by his dependents.[20] Still, the status of French women was commented on by outsiders as extraordinary. Writing as late as 1812 after a visit to Louisiana, Amos Stoddard found that French women had "more influence over their husbands than is common in most other countries" and that "they not unfrequently assume the management of property."[21] Some women were able to use these levels of agency inherent in French legal customs to realize exceptional economic and political clout.

A French woman known by her married name as Isacheran Pachot to English officials at New York held extensive commercial interests and operated between Albany, Montreal, and Haudenosaunee territories. She would play a key role in the resumption of trade after the War of the Grand Alliance between Britain and France ended in 1697. Colonel David Schuyler and the Reverend Godfrey Dellius, both influential negotiators for the English government, traveled to Montreal after peace had been restored to meet with French officials. Governor of Montreal Louis-Hector de Callière (who in a matter of months would become governor general) was anxious to talk business with the Englishmen, and asked Madame Pachot to delay a planned trip to join in the discussions.[22] Pachot did postpone her journey and attended all of the meetings, despite the fact that she was in her last month of pregnancy at the time (a situation, in any case, that would not have prevented her from undertaking her original travel plans).

She met Dellius and Schuyler at Montreal, where she resided, and they and their party departed in four canoes for the six-day journey to Quebec to meet with Callière. The two men from New York stayed ten days, during which they were entertained by Madame Pachot and others. Dellius and Schuyler brought lemons, oranges, and coconuts imported from Barbados and Curaçao, as well as oysters that were available in New York but not easily obtained in Quebec. Among other delicacies offered by Madame Pachot, Dellius and Schuyler sampled fresh salmon, a rare commodity in New York. Upon discovering that they had enjoyed the fish, Pachot promised to send them a pickled variety once they had returned to New York.[23] While at Montreal, Dellius and Schuyler met with another rich and influential woman, Jeanne Le Ber, who as previously mentioned was the daughter of Jacques Le Ber, one of Montreal's most prominent merchants. The Englishmen visited Jeanne at her lodgings in the Congrégation de Notre-Dame, accompanied by Bishop of Quebec Jean-Baptiste de la Croix de Chevrières Saint-Vallier, the same cleric with whom the nun Marguerite Roy would develop a close alliance.

Isacheran Pachot was the highly influential and savvy Charlotte-Françoise Juchereau, whose commercial successes would allow her to attain the title of countess. Charlotte-Françoise was sister to Louis Antoine Juchereau de Saint-Denys, who would extend French trade in the south in the second decade of the eighteenth century from New Orleans to Natchitoches and to the Spanish at Rio Grande. Like his sister, Louis Antoine became accustomed to moving between Euro-American and Indigenous worlds. He married Manuela Sánchez Navarro, the granddaughter of the Spanish commandant at San Juan Bautista presidio, and would be accused by the French of illegal trade with the Spanish and of spying for the French by Spanish authorities. Charlotte-Françoise was married to François Viennay-Pachot, a leading merchant and director of the Compagnie du Nord, until Pachot's death in 1698.[24] François was part of the crew that traveled with Cadillac in the summer of 1701 to formally establish Fort Pontchartrain at Detroit.

Through her marriages and business practices, Charlotte-Françoise amassed a considerable fortune, bought the Île d'Orléans after her first husband's death, and with it the title of Comtesse de St-Laurent and became more openly defiant of imperial authority. In 1706, she was given power of attorney by Antoine Cadillac just before her trip to France to manage his affairs there. She subsequently married Captain François Dauphin de La Forest, who would be designated commandant of Detroit in 1712. Charlotte-Françoise, her brother Charles, and La Forest funded numerous trade expeditions to the Mississippi and other western locations, many of which were illegal because they had been conducted without imperial approval, bringing the trio to the attention of colonial authorities. Minister of the Marine Jérôme Phélypeaux, comte de Pontchartrain called her a "dangerous woman," and intendant of New France Antoine-Denis Raudot, who was involved in protracted legal proceedings with Charlotte-Françoise, referred to her as "haughty and capricious."

Charlotte-Françoise became a very prominent businesswoman who regularly advanced large sums of capital to a number of individuals involved in the trade with Indigenous nations, paving the way for her children to succeed in trace and diplomacy. It is certainly a mark of Charlotte-Françoise's considerable wealth that she and her second husband, La Forest, did not draw up the usual marriage contract establishing a "communauté de biens" or community of goods that protected the survivor when one of the marital partners died. This was an unusual arrangement that was acknowledged in legal records. The language of many of the contracts of Charlotte-Françoise's business dealings describe her as the wife of La Forest who has not entered into a marriage agreement.[25] This addition to the language of the contract was almost certainly inserted to alert business partners that she was not responsible for her husband's debts, and as importantly, he was not responsible for any of her business losses. Charlotte-Françoise's son Jean Daniel Marie Viennay Pachot served as a paid interpreter for the Wendat at Detroit during and after his stepfather's command, distinguishing himself for keeping the Detroit nations, including the Myaamia, out of the English orbit, and for his heroics in military expeditions during the Fox Wars against the Meskwaki, Mascouten, and Kiikaapoi.[26]

Women such as Charlotte-Françoise lobbied on behalf of their sons for commissions and titles and expanded their families' economic prospects, often to the great chagrin of business rivals and imperial agents attempting to maintain control at forts in the upper country. At Detroit, Alphonse Tonty experienced this challenge to his position as commandant and to his commercial activities at the hands of a woman who controlled the sale of brandy. A centralized system for dispersing the substance to Indigenous nations throughout New France had been established in the hope that these communities would buy from the French, rather than the English. Marie Magdelene Thunes dit Dufresne became the designated agent for sale and control of brandy at Detroit, to the frustration of Tonty. He accused Dufresne of having committed fraud on several occasions and claimed that she had been ineffective in preventing local Indigenous peoples from trading with the English for alcohol. Tonty appealed to Governor General Vaudreuil, suggesting the state-sanctioned system be discontinued. Vaudreuil concurred, allowing the brandy on hand to be sold before its sale was discontinued. Magdelene Dufresne was permitted to leave her supply with her son to sell on her behalf while she was in Montreal. When it was revealed that brandy continued to be traded at Detroit despite the prohibition, Tonty used the example of Magdelene to warn of the escalation of private trade outside of his control that took place at Detroit.[27]

Tonty's efforts were directed at women of fur trade families who threatened his interests but as we have seen, both of Tonty's wives hailed from similar backgrounds and participated in activities deemed illegal by imperial authorities. Before her marriage to Tonty and move to Detroit, second wife Marie-Anne de La Marque had been the widow of Jean-Baptiste Nolan, a very successful merchant at Montreal. Their son Charles Nolan LaMarque built his own career in the fur trade on the clout established by both parents, demonstrated through his use of both their last names.[28] La Marque had been engaged in trade of an item that served a similar purpose as brandy in the state's efforts to maintain alliances with Indigenous nations. As previously discussed, she, Jean Quenet, and a Haudenosaunee man named Thomas Leguerrier (Thomas "the warrior") were accused of illegally trafficking in English stroud. Two pieces of the cloth were found in a room La Marque was renting to Quenet and were said to be designated to pass via Leguerrier to Kahnawake, where residents routinely traded at both Albany and Montreal.[29]

The English-made material was much in demand in Indigenous communities, and the French were attempting to control importation of British goods. The same year in which Marie-Anne de La Marque was accused of the illegal commerce, the French exported samples of the material to France and an imitation was manufactured in Languedoc. When the French-made material, called "écarlatine," was introduced in Canada the following year, however, the imitation was detected straight off and rejected.[30] Ultimately, it was the price of the materials that became the largest point of contention. French imperial officials felt that they could prevent Indigenous buyers from trading with the English if they could offer the cloth at the same price as the English. In the end, the French colonial government felt it had no other choice than to allow Montreal merchants and wholesalers to acquire the cloth from Albany to sell to Indigenous customers. They concluded that if too much pressure was put on the merchants to discontinue commerce in an item demanded by buyers, this would disrupt the trade networks and allow the English to gain a foothold in the upper country.[31] The irony may have been lost on French officials who felt it was necessary to acquire English goods in order to hedge against English encroachment.

Women who managed the bulk of the trade, including Charlotte-Françoise Juchereau, Marie-Anne de La Marque, and the Desauniers sisters determined the state's acquiescence in this way through their practice of engaging in multinational trade. Because the French and English states were frequently at war in Europe and in their colonial domains in North America, trade between them was strictly regulated and often prohibited. Despite this interdiction, as we have already seen, individuals and their families involved in French-Indigenous commerce continued their activities, to the chagrin of imperial officials who were powerless to stop them.

In cases involving women of the French-Indigenous family networks who freely crossed English, French, and Indigenous national boundaries, their freedom of movement could be used against them. One such example was the court case mounted in New Orleans in 1739 by Louis Turpin, brother of the deceased Jean Baptiste Turpin, who was attempting to extinguish any claim that Jean Baptiste's widow had to the couple's shared goods. The couple had been married at Detroit, and their activities while residing there became the crux upon which the widow's family challenged Louis's efforts to exclude his sister-in-law in the division of the deceased's estate.

Jean Baptiste Turpin had married Marguerite Fafard in 1710, within a month of the wedding of Marguerite Fafard's cousin (also named Marguerite Fafard) to Michel Bizaillon. Turpin's wife Marguerite Fafard had a father who was a voyageur and interpreter of several Indigenous languages, and her mother was Marguerite Couc, the half-French/half-Algonquin sister to Madame Montour. At the time of Jean-Baptiste Turpin's death in 1737 in New Orleans, he and his wife had been living separately for many years. Jean-Baptiste's brother Louis arranged to have his deceased sibling's goods inventoried in May 1739, and an equitable division of the estate instituted, as was duly noted in New Orleans's notarial records. It appears, however, that the surviving spouse, Marguerite Fafard, was not included as a recipient of the proceeds of her husband's inheritance.

Marguerite's brother-in-law Louis Metivier, who with Marguerite's sister Marie resided at Fort Chartres in the Illinois Country, challenged Louis Turpin, filing a petition in October 1740 to have the case heard before the Superior Council of New Orleans. Metivier claimed that, because Louis Turpin had "obtained false judgement in his sister's absence," he had "been obliged to appeal and prays to be allowed to produce evidence of Marguerite Fafart's good conduct and to prove that the separation with her husband was due only to his ill treatment and in order to preserve her life and that of her son." Metivier's request for a hearing was accepted. He was able to produce several witnesses who had lived at Detroit with Jean Baptiste Turpin and Marguerite Fafard who attested to Turpin's violent behavior toward his wife.

In February 1741, Metivier produced his first witness—Michel Vien, who was still living at Detroit. Vien reported that on two occasions Turpin had attacked Marguerite, once with an axe and once with a gun with "intent to kill." Two months later, additional witnesses, all now living at Kaskaskia, gave testimony on Marguerite's behalf. One of the men stated that "if Turpin's wife left him it was owing to ill treatment and to save her life." A third man claimed that Marguerite Fafart was "a good and honest woman who was compelled to leave her husband by ill treatment," and a fourth witness called her "brave and honest." Finally, Jean Paré, who like the others (except for Vien) was now living in the Illinois Country, testified that when he was at Detroit, "he heard the inhabitants speak of Jean Baptiste Turpin as ill treating and beating his wife."[32]

It appears that Marguerite Fafard had indeed fled her abusive marriage with Turpin. A 1717 imperial report relates the critical moment at which Marguerite may have left Detroit. Detroit's commandant Jacques Charles Sabrevois wrote with alarm to Governor General Vaudreuil about the arrival of an Indigenous man named Ouytaouikigik who was attempting to convince the Detroit tribes to trade with the English. According to Sabrevois, Ouytaouikigik brought rum and wampum as enticements and took La Turpin to the English.[33] Sabrevois's description leaves open the possibility that La Turpin, who was most assuredly Marguerite Fafard referred to by her married name, may not have left Detroit willingly.

We cannot be entirely certain under what circumstances Marguerite departed her husband and Detroit, but we do know that she found her way to the English colonies. She became known by the name "French Margaret" and was referred to by Moravian missionaries in Pennsylvania as "sister's daughter"—a designation that highlighted the importance of her relationship as niece to Madame Montour. She married the Kahnawake Mohawk man Katarioniecha, also known as Peter Quebec, and had four children with him. In 1733, the two were living at Shamokin, but by 1745, they had moved to the Alleghany River, where a missionary encountered Marguerite/Margaret at her cousin Andrew Montour's home. In 1744, French Margaret was present with her aunt at the proceedings of the Lancaster Treaty. By 1753, she had assumed a position of authority and leadership at a settlement close to Madame Montour that became known as French Margaret's Town, where she prohibited liquor.[34]

French Margaret may not have been in need of the proceeds from her French husband's estate. Perhaps she was unaware of the death of a man she had long since ceased caring for, and at whose hand she had suffered physical abuse. In separating herself physically from Turpin and moving out of the home they had shared at Detroit, she had, for all intents and purposes, divorced him. She had also taken another husband, was raising their children, and had become a person of influence and authority in her Mohawk-English community. Indeed, she was operating in another corner of the vast territory covered by the extensive family networks. From what we know, she was not directly involved in the legal proceedings of Turpin's inheritance at New Orleans and we only hear about her travails and her person through the words of others.

Her sister and brother-in-law may have pressed her case in order to obtain some or all of her portion of what would have been a sizable estate, since the Turpin family members were wealthy residents of Kaskaskia.[35] For his part, in settling his brother's affairs, it is possible Louis Turpin also believed that his brother and Marguerite were divorced according to local customs. He may have assumed she would not learn of Jean Baptiste's death and press her case since she lived at such a great distance. Married to Dorothée Mechiper8eta, a wealthy woman of the Kaskaskia nation who was well-connected in the Illinois Country, Louis was intimately acquainted with the enhanced power of Indigenous women and would have understood what he needed to do to navigate any potential claims of Marguerite Fafard.[36]

The testimonies on Marguerite's behalf were meant to counter potential challenges to her right to the community of goods she had shared with Jean Baptiste Turpin. The witnesses rebuffed any effort Louis Turpin might have made to disparage Marguerite's character—by claiming she had made light of her marriage to Jean Baptiste and had casually wandered away from him, or that her move to the English colonies meant she was not to be trusted. This latter point is suggested by the fact that Marguerite's sister (Metivier's wife) had submitted an affidavit signed by the superior of Foreign Missions stating that "little Turpin" killed by the Chickasaw appeared not to have changed his religion. This was a reference to Marguerite's deceased son by Jean Baptiste and speaks to the pivotal issue of whether or not this son had been converted to or practiced a Protestant religion while residing with his mother in Pennsylvania.[37]

The freedom of movement of women of the French-Indigenous family networks could be read in a variety of ways and constituted a potential threat, depending on the context in which the women were operating and the vested interests of the men with whom they interacted. Marguerite's sister and brother-in-law went to great lengths to counter any suggestion that Marguerite Fafard was a dishonorable and treacherous woman by presenting evidence that she had left Detroit to save her life and the life of her child. Detroit commandant Sabrevois connected her departure to affairs of state in reporting she had been taken by an English-allied Indigenous man. Indeed, knowing as we do that Marguerite was niece to Madame Montour and a member of a powerful extended French-Indigenous family network alerts us to the significance of Sabrevois's solitary reference to Marguerite in his report. It may also tell us something about Sabrevois.

He either had little or no understanding of the extent of the political clout of local French and Indigenous families, or he knowingly misrepresented the agency of these families. He may have felt powerless to curb their activities and check their movement across French, English, Haudenosaunee, and Algonquian nations. By couching their activities in the language of imperial politics, he avoided calling attention to his inability to command at Detroit. Sabrevois blamed French authorities for Marguerite Fafard's removal, claiming that, because the governor general had removed Sabrevois's interpreter, the commandant was unable to confront the Indigenous emissary allied to the English and prevent him from communicating with local nations and taking away Marguerite. Sabrevois invoked fear of English influence to divert attention from his ineffective efforts at economic and political control. Other French and Indigenous women like Marguerite would operate across nations, and their activities would intersect with and directly affect political and economic policies and practices.

Warriors and Diplomats: Indigenous Women

Despite the fact that imperial correspondence infrequently mentioned Indigenous women either in the St. Lawrence valley or at Detroit, there are clues as early as the seventeenth century that tell us these women actively participated at every level as members and representatives of their nations. In the course of a meeting held in 1682 between Governor General Louis de Buade de Frontenac and the Onondaga leader Tegannissoren, Frontenac expressed his pleasure that Teganissorens had taken/resuscitated his grandfather's name of Niregouentaron. As Onontio, Frontenac considered the elder/deceased Niregouentaron, Niregouentaron's wife and his niece to be friends, and had adopted this niece as his daughter.[38] Frontenac's offering of diplomatic gifts not only to Niregouentaron but also to pivotal women of the family was appropriate and essential, given the power of women among the matrilineal and matrilocal Onondaga, a member nation of the Haudenosaunee. For his part, Tegannissoren/Niregouentaron needed to maintain the connection to his mother's clan in order to maintain his prominent political position with the French.

Niregouentaron's claim to his grandfather's name and position required the approval of clan matrons, and Frontenac sought to maintain strong diplomatic ties to Niregouentaron's female kin. Their presence buttressed the legitimacy of the younger/resuscitated Niregouentaron's authority in the eyes of the French. Frontenac clearly referenced this sororal power in discussions with Niregouentaron and focused on maintaining pivotal metaphoric kinship ties in his role as Onontio:

Here are some beads, which Onontio gives you for the wife of the deceased prince, and for your sister who is at the fort, and whom, you know, Onontio adopted as his daughter, in order that they may remember him until he shall see the former at the meeting next spring at the fort, whither he invites her, when he will have it in his power to give her greater evidence of his friendship, and also bewail there the death and cover the grave of Oniacony, the father of the latter.

Frontenac gave scarlet cloth trimmed with gold and a dress to Niregouentaron for Onontio/(Frontenac's) "daughter," for whom, Frontenac claimed, "he evinces great love."[39] It is difficult to know whether this father-daughter relationship between Frontenac and the niece of the elder Onondaga chief had an overarching ritualized status, akin to that exhibited by the male members of various Indigenous nations as sons to their father Onontio, but it is strongly suggested in this passage. The woman in question was described as having been adopted by Onontio, the metaphoric father, and Frontenac also participated in the symbolic gestures of diplomacy with this daughter (providing gifts and covering the grave of her father).[40]

There were other occasions at which the French engaged in diplomatic talks with Indigenous women who were pivotal in maintaining good relations. As was discussed in chapter 4, at a meeting in Quebec held to discuss strained relations between their two nations, Governor General Vaudreuil met with and gave ceremonial gifts to Peoria leader Chachagouesse and his daughter. Chachagouesse pledged to Vaudreuil that his daughter would carry Vaudreuil's "letters and your word," but warned that under the prevailing fragile state of affairs "my daughter and I may both die in doing so."[41] Chachagouesse's statement suggests that because both he and his daughter acted as emissaries, they carried different messages intended for different audiences, likely men and women. Chachagouesse's daughter not only traveled to Quebec as a diplomatic representative of her nation, but in carrying and delivering Onontio's message, risked her life acting as his representative among her people. There would be other points at which Indigenous women communicated dispatches meant solely for women and exhibited similar authority at moments of political crisis.

Anishinaabe women had the power to decide whether their nation went to war. As we saw in chapter 4, two Odawa women, one of whom was likely La Blanche, kinswoman to the Odawa leader Outoutagan, determined whether their nation would go into battle. This could have ignited a conflagration that would have spread beyond Detroit and Michilimackinac in 1706.[42] La Blanche's importance as a political ally would be explicitly acknowledged later, at a critical moment in the weeks following the outbreak of the Fox Wars in 1712. Governor General Vaudreuil sent gifts to Michilimackinac that were designated for La Blanche, described by the local Jesuit Marest as the daughter of a chief and a close friend of the French who was a wise and capable woman of her nation.[43] Maintaining her favor was therefore of utmost importance to the governor general as the French plunged headlong into war with the Meskwaki and sought the support of their Indigenous allies.

Odawa women may have held the peace in their hands and decided whether their men would go to war, but they could also participate in battle. During the 1706 skirmishes that pitted the French, Myaamia, and Wendat against the Odawa, a contingent of Odawa sought to negotiate an end to the fighting. The Myaamia and Wendat were immediately suspicious of the good intentions of the party. They commented that the party was too sizable to be a peace contingent, its members were outfitted for war, and they recognized two Odawa men and one Odawa woman who had fought against them.[44] Other women of Great Lakes Indigenous nations were documented as having participated in hostilities. In 1716, as the Fox Wars raged across the upper country, Vaudreuil made an official report of a battle in which the Meskwaki had been engaged by the French and their Indigenous allies. The Meskwaki were defeated, despite the fact that they possessed a larger fighting force, including, according to Vaudreuil, five hundred Meskwaki warriors and three thousand Meskwaki women. Vaudreuil described the women as "fighting desperately on these occasions."[45] By setting them apart from men as waging war with an exceptional degree of intensity, he demonstrated his shock at the prospect of women engaged in battle. The victory of the French and their allies over the Meskwaki is depicted as remarkable not only because they were outnumbered, but also because they faced an exceptionally violent and large contingent of Meskwaki women.

Other Indigenous women of Great Lakes nations were similarly empowered by specific responsibilities or activities in which they took part. We have already seen how French women of Pierre Roy's family flouted traditional gender roles because of unique opportunities brought about by the contingencies of their family participation in trade with Indigenous peoples. Pierre's Myaamia wife Waapankihkwa/ Marguerite Ouabankikoué, hailed from the Atchatchakangouen band and was likely a member of the family of, and possibly a sister to, the band's *akima* (leader) Wisekaukautshe, who by the mid-eighteenth century would become known to the French as Pied Froid (Cold Foot).[46] In the early eighteenth century, the French chose to recognize the Crane band as the most powerful of the Myaamia confederacy (which also included the Ouiatenon and Piankashaw), and Waapankihkwa's band or clan identity would have been of central importance, despite her marriage to a Frenchman. Waapankihkwa had married Pierre Roy in 1703 and their children had been baptized at Detroit. The children's godparents were other members of the French-Indigenous family networks, including Isabelle Couc (Madame Montour), daughter of a French voyageur and Algonquin mother who was an influential interpreter at Detroit and Michilimackinac.

Pierre's relationship with Waapankihkwa allowed him to be integrated into the Myaamia community. The term *nilenkwalehsa*, meaning "my cross-nephew" could have been applied to Pierre by his wife's uncle, making Pierre honorary kin and therefore a member of the powerful Crane band.[47] Pierre might also have been called *kiilimonan* or brother-in-law by his Myaamia family because of his marriage to a Myaamia woman. As a *kiilimonan* he would have called his wife's sisters, aunts, or nieces *niilimwa* or "my cross-sex sibling-in-law," a relationship that would have allowed him to take these women as wives, as long as he was able to provide for them.[48] It is entirely possible that the baby girl he fathered in 1717 who was baptized at Detroit and listed as an *enfant natural* (illegitimate child), and did not have his wife Waapankihkwa as mother, could have been her niece, grandniece, or cousin.[49]

Imperial correspondence tells us just how important Waapankihkwa and her family were to imperial politics beginning in the second decade of the eighteenth century. For the first decade and a half, a community of Myaamia had lived at St. Joseph, from where they had traveled the relatively short distance to conduct trade at Detroit. After the Meskwaki attack at Detroit in 1712, the Myaamia and the Ouiatenon had moved back to the Ouabache (Wabash), one of their original sites of habitation in the seventeenth century. Vaudreuil feared that the Myaamia were at greater risk of being influenced by the English the further they were from Detroit and in 1719, he pressured them to move back to St. Joseph, claiming they had promised to return. The Myaamia refused to relocate.[50]

A year later, Vaudreuil had become increasingly impatient with Myaamia unwillingness to remove to St. Joseph. He ordered all trading permits and merchandise that had come down from Montreal for the Myaamia be held at Detroit until he was certain the nation intended to move back to St. Joseph. He also asked that an order be sent without delay to Pierre Roy, instructing him to gather his wife and his children and all of their goods over the course of the winter and leave the Wabash settlement for Detroit. The urgent tone of Vaudreuil's letter and the instructions that singled out Roy and his wife and children tell us that Vaudreuil was aware of Waapankihkwa's status among the Myaamia. If this pivotal woman and her family relocated to the Detroit region, the entire Myaamia contingent forming Pied Froid's band would hopefully follow.[51] Like Cadillac, who had heralded Haudenosaunee clan mothers' sanctioning of the Detroit settlement in 1701 and attempted to compel Odawa women to remain at Detroit to ensure the settlement there would flourish, Vaudreuil was well aware of the importance of women's presence to the maintenance of an economically viable and peaceful space.

Vaudreuil would also have likely been aware that beginning in 1718, Pierre Roy and his brother François had established a trading enterprise among the Myaamia on the upper Wabash.[52] The two brothers were not about to disrupt a commerce that would have been sanctioned by their kinsman Pied Froid and the Crane band.[53] Indeed, the Myaamia, Ouiatenon, and Piankashaw were in an enviable position as French and British polities vied for their allegiance and business. In 1717, the Illinois Country had been formally annexed to Louisiana and was no longer administered by Quebec. In 1721, it was formally designated as a district within Louisiana's system of governance.[54] The French at Kaskaskia were encouraging the Piankashaw, Ouiatenon, and Myaamia to stay at the Wabash, rather than follow Vaudreuil's orders to move to St. Joseph and Detroit. These Kaskaskia residents promised the Piankashaw that they would be provided with merchandise, and attempted to convince them that they now came under the charge of the French at Illinois. At the same time, the British were acknowledging the importance of the Myaamia in their plans to wrest control of the interior of the continent from the French.

The extended Roy family maintained a position that placed their interests between the imperial powers that vied for their loyalty. They did not move to St. Joseph, but after the Meskwaki attack of 1712, some had stayed at Detroit, a crucial point on the water route between Montreal and the Myaamia villages. As members of the Roy family continued to reside at and move through Detroit, the network of families that formed part of this conglomerate grew in tandem. A number of brothers of Pierre Roy remained at or moved through Detroit. Etienne Roy was described as living at Detroit when he acted as godfather in 1712 and again in 1715. François Roy was present for his nephew François's baptism (son of Pierre Roy and Marguerite Ouabankikoué) in 1713. Between 1720 and 1726, Louis Roy and his wife Marguerite Dumais baptized three children at Detroit, while Dumais acted as godmother to a slave belonging to her brother-in-law François Roy.[55] Within a few years, Louis and Marguerite had relocated to New Orleans.

Pierre remained among the Myaamia while François spent a large portion of his time hiring voyageurs and outfitting teams to take merchandise to his brother at the Myaamia post. François was given numerous *congés* (permits) over the years for these journeys. Etienne Roy acted for a time as a third partner at New Orleans in the trade with his brothers. Named for Etienne Bizaillon, his godfather and the brother of Michel and Pierre Bizaillon (whose activities were detailed in chapter 4), Etienne Roy married Marguerite Catherine Neveu. Marguerite Catherine was the daughter of Jacques Neveu, a merchant and trader with Indigenous nations, and Michelle Chauvin, sister to the wealthy and powerful Chauvin dit Lafresniere brothers who were among the richest merchants and landowners at New Orleans.[56] Jacques Neveu, his wife Michelle Chauvin, and three of their young daughters godparented exclusively for Indigenous children at Detroit between 1716 and 1720 before making their way to the post in Myaamionki.

Etienne Roy's marriage into such a prominent New Orleans family undoubtedly gave him a crucial leg up in trade. In a 1722 census of Natchitoches, he was listed as a discharged soldier who had become a farmer and had only his wife living with him. Just two years later, in a 1724 census taken of people living at New Orleans along the eastern shore of the Mississippi, Etienne was one of a small number of residents referred to as "Sieur," a title denoting a position of privilege. He was described as a nephew of Monsieur Chauvin, a designation that communicated prominent social standing, and as living on Bienville's land. In addition to his wife, he had an Indigenous woman slave and one cow as part of his household, and the census noted that he was served by his slave and with the help of fourteen black day workers who removed stumps from the land on which he grew sugar cane. His commitment to this crop determined his growing dependence on slave labor, which was borne out two years later. Etienne, now a resident of "Petit Dezeri" (Little Wilderness), a New Orleans settlement, was part of a group of wealthy residents who were requesting black slaves.[57]

In May 1728, Marie Magdelene Roy, daughter of Pierre Roy and Waapankihkwa, married Pierre Chesne dit LaButte at Kiihkayonki (Fort Miami). The commandant of the French post in Myaamionki, Nicolas-Joseph Noyelles de Fleurimont, signed the marriage register one day after he had signed a contract establishing a partnership with Pierre and François Roy to control trade at that location.[58] Following in such quick succession, the timing of the two events illustrates the integral relationship between matters of commerce and family in French-Indigenous kinship networks. It is easy to imagine that wedding festivities held the day after business was conducted provided a foundation of good feelings and intentions for both partnerships. Indeed, just four months later, François and Pierre Roy sent Pierre's new son-in-law 1,000 livres worth of trade goods.[59]

In October of 1732, Waapankihkwa would die of smallpox. One month later, her daughter Marie Magdelene, wife of Pierre Chesne dit LaButte, would follow, along with a thirteen-year-old Patoca (Plains Apache) slave named Antoine who belonged to LaButte. Marie-Anne-Véronique Cuillerier, sister and annalist of the Congrégation de Notre-Dame who served in the order with Marguerite Roy (Waapankihkwa's sister-in-law), would document this smallpox outbreak that raged at Montreal, Detroit, and Kiihkayonki. The disease had erupted in several New England towns, including Boston, and spread to Philadelphia, Albany, and Montreal. In Kiihkayonki, it killed many of the Myaamia community's leaders, and then spread to the Illinois Country and north to Lake Superior and Hudson Bay.

The trail of devastation of smallpox followed the pathways of French-Indigenous families along the system of rivers that stretched across Indigenous, French, and British nations. Women of the families who moved across these regions likely and unwittingly facilitated the spread of disease. They also documented its destruction and perished because of it, as had been the case with Waapankihkwa. Without the pivotal connection provided by Waapankihkwa and the powerful Myaamia Crane band, the Roy brothers would not have been able to establish their extensive trade network. In the early eighteenth century, women who were part of the French-Indigenous kinship networks became adept at navigating the shifting demands of trade and linking the needs of their home communities to those of the French imperial state. For decades, these women directed trading activities at several locations in the North American continental interior, ranging from the St. Lawrence valley to the Illinois Country. Their ability to procure the items that constituted the trade, and their control of the networks by which goods circulated made them invaluable to their families and communities and to Euro-American and Indigenous imperial agents. By the mid-eighteenth century, as British, French, and Indigenous nations vied for political, military, and economic control, the women's essential role in trade made them targets of distrust and censure from imperial authorities. As the British attempted to regularize the trade with Indigenous peoples, they sought to limit the participation by French-Indigenous families while also controlling and ultimately limiting women's roles in this trade.

By the time the British arrived at Detroit in 1760, women of the family networks had so skillfully fused the multiple strands of gendered behavior of European and Indigenous worlds, they became sought-after marriage partners to English merchants. Once their expertise had been incorporated in this manner, however, these same men regarded the "Indian-like" behavior of these women as base and unbefitting the wives of affluent businessmen. Indeed, it was the mobility of the women of the networks that the British would condemn. The events of Pontiac's War in 1763 would demonstrate the threat these women were perceived to have made to the imperial project.

CHAPTER 6

Unveiling the Conspiracy

Women at the Heart of Pontiac's War

I n March 1761, only a few months into British occupation of the formerly
French-held fort at Detroit, newly installed commandant Donald Campbell
penned a letter to his superiors. The missive was written in English and French
and was devoted in equal parts to the logistics of establishing British military
protocols and musings on peoples and events. According to Campbell, local women
"surpassed" his expectations, although he considered the men "very indifferent."
An occurrence he had never before witnessed drew particular notice, which he
described in French: "Il ya Assemblée toutes les dimanches au Soir, chez Monsr
le Commandant au y se trouvent une Vightaine des Personnes des deux Sexes."
("There is a gathering every Sunday night in the home of the commander, where
there are to be found about twenty people of both sexes.") He proclaimed of the
event: "You have no such doings at Fort Pitt."[1] Switching from English to French
in his letter to the Swiss-born Colonel Henry Bouquet, Campbell transitioned
from the public voice of martial observation to the coded whisper of more private
reflection.

This pattern of intermittent personal disclosure in British imperial correspondence in the period immediately following the Seven Years' War suggests general
uncertainty and guarded vulnerability. Fort Pitt had been a British installation

Plan of Detroit with its environs, 1764

from its establishment in 1758 and social conventions there had followed British norms. But at Detroit, the weekly cultural event Campbell described had a different precedent, and its participants would not be deterred by a change in leadership or empire. Nowhere could this insistence on tradition be more compellingly enacted than in Campbell's home, a space that for all intents and purposes remained under French control. The new British commandant was renting his quarters from the former French commandant, François Marie Picote de Belestre, who was a member of the French-Indigenous family networks and son of *procuratrice* Marie-Catherine Trottier DesRuisseaux by her second husband.

In describing the "exceptional attributes" of local women in his letter, Campbell might have been referencing the essential role in trade played by women such as Marie-Catherine. He may also have been describing their physical appearance and commenting on their sexual natures. In either case, the women of Detroit, more powerful than their male kinsmen in the eyes of the British, freely entered the quarters of the new commandant—a space they would continue to control. Campbell's comments also tell us that British expectations of proper gendered behavior differed from those of local peoples at Detroit. The mixing of men and women was a potential threat to the new imperial order, as had been the mixing of French and Indigenous blood that had threatened the French imperial state several decades earlier. Campbell seemed unaware of, or unconcerned with, potential ramifications of these cultural differences. Within a year, however, he appeared to be regretting his openness with the local populace. "It requires judgement and temper to command at one of these posts," he noted in 1762. "The French inhabitants and Indians are soe much connected that if you disoblige one of them, the other takes part ."[2] "I begin to know the people too well," he commented darkly. "I do not think they improve on a long acquaintance."[3]

It was not the first nor would it be the last time British elites spoke disparagingly of French and Indigenous peoples. Historians have traced these early ruminations through May of 1763, when the Odawa leader Pontiac and warriors of Great Lakes nations brought down all British-occupied installments in the upper country, except Forts Detroit, Pitt, and Niagara.[4] Pontiac's War generated reams of correspondence, much of it produced by British military agents frustrated by the lack of information emanating from Detroit—a location at the apex of the disturbance—as it lay under siege. As British men faltered in their efforts to understand and control political, military, and economic affairs at Detroit, they expressed their frustrations and fears in negative references to local Indigenous and

French women. A plethora of men, from contemporary British imperial agents to antiquarians writing histories a century later, would ascribe the uncertain course of the war to a woman.

The reality of Indigenous and French women's activities at Detroit was much more complex than these histories would have us believe. Not only were these women often operating as diplomatic representatives and political operatives, they also managed the trade on which Indigenous/Euro-American relations depended. Because they often controlled both of these essential components, they just as often became the targets of censure and accusation. As historian Kyle Mays has pointed out, elite white men have told stories of Pontiac and his war to solidify their precarious socioeconomic and political positions.[5] This chapter will examine accounts of the women purported to have been at the center of Pontiac's War, situating these narratives within the context of their authorship by British imperial agents who perceived themselves to be in physical and emotional distress. Only then is it possible to expose the manner in which women continue to be excluded from this history and to recover the complex economic and political roles they played at Detroit. Historians of Pontiac's War have repeatedly recounted gruesome atrocities visited upon the British by Indigenous combatants, including the death of Donald Campbell, but none of these histories have addressed the violence reserved for the Indigenous woman at the heart of multiple versions of this story.[6]

Carry'd on by Their Women: Gendered Peril and Prospect

British imperial agents who arrived at Detroit and in the upper country after the Seven Years' War made frequent anxious exclamations that the region to which they had been dispatched was a "wilderness detached from the world" that would cause profound change by making "great alterations in peoples tempers."[7] British officers considered themselves banished from the "civilized world" and living in exile, and the farther west they traveled, the greater the perception that they had been relegated to a harsh fate. Captain Lewis Ourry, in command at Fort Bedford in Pennsylvania, decried his isolation but thought it less offensive than that of men of his battalion who continued their trek westward: "I cannot Complain of my Fate, when I reflect on . . . that of the poor Lads that have past Detroit, in their Way to their respective Banishments, but I cannot help deploring the cruel Destiny, of (what I must Still call), *our* unlucky, dispersed Battalion."[8]

The apprehension of the men was at times coupled with frustration at the unhindered agency of women. Kathleen Wilson has described this dis-ease as "intense male anxiety" exhibited in response to "intrusions of the feminine into the political sphere at times of national emergencies."[9] At some points, the anxiety was temporarily resolved through statements attesting to the sexual prowess and power of British elites over local women. These men, as Kathleen Brown has described, used metaphors of military conquest and aggression to counter fears of female domination.[10] French and Indigenous women would prove threatening because they prevailed in their control of trade and in their freedom of movement, challenging British perceptions of gender roles. As crucial economic agents, but in light of the general distrust of interracial intimacy that pervaded British imperial views, Indigenous women in particular occupied a paradoxical position in the British imaginary. Superintendent of Northern Indian Affairs Sir William Johnson exhibited the complex nature of this position. Johnson was married to a white woman while also maintaining a home with Mohawk matron Molly Brant, who was instrumental in his rise through the ranks, his integration into Haudenosaunee circles, and his economic success. It was Johnson who encouraged Indian agent George Croghan to publicly shame political and commercial competitors by accusing them of engaging in sexual relations with Indigenous women.[11]

In early 1763, the intense anxiety over the unrestricted agency of a woman would spill over at Detroit as British imperial agents continued their struggle to control trade and strengthen political authority. Captain Donald Campbell, no longer commandant but still in residence, suspended a short recitation on the fort's garrison, devoting the bulk of his letter to Bouquet in addressing an urgent situation pertaining to an officer. "Poor Lieut MacDonald has been troubled with a Melancholy disorder for sometime past. It proceeded from a Love affair with one of our Young Ladys. The Doctor thinks he would get the better of it, if he leaves this Plase, and if he continued here it would Still be the worse with him. Major Gladwin has consented to give him leave to goe to Fort Pitt, but desires you will Send an Officer to Releive him." Campbell's attention to MacDonald's fragile psyche suggests his belief that lovesickness was compromising the officer's physical well-being, and that removal from Detroit and from the woman who was the source of his anguish was the only remedy.

Whether he was more worried that an enfeebled MacDonald might threaten British military strength, or that news of his condition would demoralize others or damage Lieutenant MacDonald's reputation, Campbell asked Bouquet not to make public MacDonald's situation. He thought it best to hide the reason behind MacDonald's removal, suggesting that "we put on the footing of his goeing to settle his Accompts with the Pay master."[12] MacDonald's lovesick descent into melancholy hovered as an ominous subtext alongside Campbell's comments on the fragile state of relations between the British and Indigenous nations.

All of Donald Campbell's efforts to preserve James MacDonald's life and well-being would ultimately come to nothing. By the time Henry Bouquet received Campbell's letter on May 19, the fort at Detroit was under siege, and almost all other British installations in the upper country had fallen to a combined force of Indigenous warriors led at Detroit by the Odawa leader Pontiac. There would be no more time for discussion of James MacDonald's compromised state. MacDonald would remain at Detroit, thrust into a central role as part of a small British military contingent that struggled to maintain the fort.

In a July letter to Bouquet written at the height of the six-month siege, Mac-Donald proudly touted his "full account of all that transpired in this district," which featured "every material circumstance that has happened." He finished with a French declaration on the subject of his former melancholy. "Mon Cher Ami Monsieur Campbell, me montroit une Lettre qu'il vous avoit ecrit daté dans l'Avril dernier dans laquelle il vous informoit que j'etoit maladif, et par cette raison que Je doit Aller a Fort Pitt, mais maintenant Dieu (Dieu merci) mes yeux sont Ouvert, et Je vois que les plue courtes folies sont les meilleures." ("My Dear Friend Mr. Campbell showed me a letter that he had written you dated during last April, in which he informed you that I was ailing, and for this reason that I should go to Fort Pitt; but now God (thank God) has opened my eyes, and I see that the shortest episodes of madness are the best.")[13] MacDonald's French disclosure betrayed a vulnerability perhaps rising from a perception of shared physical and psychological ordeal and, for MacDonald, the loss of Donald Campbell three weeks earlier.

James MacDonald had previously spent time at Detroit during the Seven Years' War as a captive, where he was held for several months by the Wendat after he had been taken at Fort Duquesne in 1758.[14] Returning to Detroit a few years later, now as part of the incoming British imperial presence, the people and surroundings would have likely seemed familiar. It is possible that MacDonald sought reintegration through relationship with a French or Indigenous woman he may have already known. We do not know, nor is it ultimately pertinent, whether this woman returned his affections or rebuffed him, or if she was aware of his obsession. But we do know based on reports of his superiors that he lacked the strength to fight a melancholy that threatened his physical and mental well-being. With "eyes opened" (had he fallen out of love or begun to perceive local peoples as a threat, or both?), he would ultimately break from this affection, the intimacy of local ties, and his own lovesickness and recommit himself to the British imperial cause.

MacDonald's account found its way to men at the highest levels of the British military and Indian Department, including commander in chief of British forces Jeffery Amherst, military governor of Montreal Thomas Gage, superintendent of Northern Indian Affairs William Johnson, and deputy Indian agent George Croghan. This same narrative was used as evidence in court proceedings held by Detroit's commandant Henry Gladwin in August 1763 to ascertain the level of participation of local French in the July 4 death of Donald Campbell at the hands of an Ojibwe *ogimaa*.[15] The story would also form the basis for a published account and play written by British officer and ranger Robert Rogers, who had resided at Detroit. Like Antoine de la Mothe Cadillac before him, Rogers had an elevated sense of his own importance; a belief that his empire did not appreciate him or appropriately reward his efforts; and a flair for drama. His sensationalized rendition of events at Detroit in 1763 would set the tone for histories of Pontiac's War for centuries to come.[16]

Narrating Pontiac's War

James MacDonald had begun his account of events at Detroit with references to a confidential exchange and an unidentified informant: "On Friday the 6th of May we were privately informed of a conspiracy being formed against us by the Indians, particularly the Ottawa nation." The information gleaned allowed the British to prepare for the proposed attack. When the Odawa came into the fort to visit merchants the next day, they had been surprised to find the shops closed and to see armed soldiers and officers stationed throughout. In council with Henry Gladwin and Donald Campbell, Detroit's first and second in command, the Odawa had demanded to know the reason for the presence of the armed men, to which Gladwin had replied "that he had certain intelligence that some Indians were projecting mischief and on that account he was determined to have the troops always under arms upon each occasion." Gladwin fell back on protocol, explaining that "they being the oldest nation and the first that had come to council that spring needed not be astonished at that precaution as he was resolved to do the same to all nations." The disconcerted Odawa departed, crossing the (Detroit) River to their settlement.

Several hours later (MacDonald is precise with his times—Odawa departing council at 2 p.m. and returning at 6 p.m.), six young Odawa warriors returned "and brought an old Indian woman prisoner with them who they aledged had accused them falsely." Gladwin replied that the prisoner "had never given us any kind of information. They then insisted upon naming the author of what he had heard with regard to the Indians, which he declined to tell them, but acquainted them that he was advised by one of themselves, whose name he promised never to reveal." After eating two loaves of bread, the warriors "went off," carrying the woman prisoner with them. Here MacDonald takes his first opportunity to mock Pontiac's authority as an Odawa *ogimaa* before describing the fate of the woman prisoner: "When they arrived at their camp Pontiac their greatest Chief (or King as they are pleased to call him) seized on the prisoner and gave her three strokes on the head with a stick which laid her flat on the ground, and the whole Nation assembled round her, and called repeated times, kill her, kill her."[17] MacDonald's rendition of the events of May 6 ends abruptly with this anecdote and does not resume until the 8th of May.

This account, which would find its way to Sir Jeffrey Amherst, is virtually identical to versions written for Colonel Henry Bouquet and deputy Indian agent George Croghan. One of the few points of difference is MacDonald's description of the proposed informant. She is "an old Indian woman prisoner" in the reports to Bouquet and Amherst, but to Croghan, she becomes "an old Squaw prisoner."[18] MacDonald and Croghan knew each other well. Use of the word "squaw" is a marker of that familiarity and their shared experience living and working among Indigenous peoples at Detroit and in the upper country. Originating in an Algonquian term, Indigenous nations used variations of the word to refer to a woman. In some cases "squaw" signified a young woman and in others a woman leader. In adopting the term, eighteenth-century Europeans collapsed cultural and tribal distinctions, using the word to lump all Indigenous women, regardless of their roles, duties or personalities into one category.[19] This stereotyping also came to include negative allusions to the dangerous and potentially destructive sexual nature of these women who were perceived to do what white men wanted "for money or lust."[20] MacDonald's use of "squaw" with Croghan likely invoked this generically racialized and sexualized woman. Although we can't be certain of MacDonald's proclivities, Croghan was involved in his own intimate relationship with a Mohawk woman named Catherine, a fact he never disclosed in official correspondence.[21]

In describing the woman's treatment at the hands of Pontiac, MacDonald departs from his eyewitness account. If he had not been present himself, we may wonder, how could he have known what happened to the woman at the Odawa settlement? Who, if anyone, had told him, and if they had, why didn't he divulge his source for this information? Without this information, the trials endured by the woman are disturbing hearsay, with MacDonald using the violence perpetrated against her to temporarily resolve mounting hostility and to end the confidential exchange with which he began his story. We do not learn if the woman was killed and we never hear of her again. She becomes a flattened specter and plot device used to portray Pontiac as ruthless and bloodthirsty. If MacDonald had suspected his readers had been interested in knowing the circumstances of her life, he would have included testimony as to her fate. Instead, his larger aim is to atone for any potential breach of protocol caused by his lovesickness, and for any damage his lapse in judgment may have caused in bringing on a war that came within a hair's breadth of destroying British imperial presence in the upper country. In declaring himself cured and painstakingly compiling his account, he is eager to convince Bouquet that there are no more intimacies or secrets shared with the local Indigenous and French populace.

We may wonder if there had been violence perpetrated against this particular Indigenous woman. We do know that a short time before the outbreak of war, Gladwin had executed a *panis* enslaved woman who with a *panis* man had killed the British trader who owned them while all were en route to Detroit. The man had managed to escape to the Illinois Country, but the public execution of the woman was meant to serve as a "terror to others from being guilty of such crimes for the future."[22] We do not know if Pontiac hit the woman in question, but Pontiac as character in MacDonald's chronicle does perform this role. MacDonald channels his own rage, shame, and fear through Pontiac, to whom MacDonald assigns the task of brutally punishing the woman. This allows MacDonald to maintain a bureaucratic demeanor and emotional distance while simultaneously ascribing excessive violence to the enemy.

As he continues his account, MacDonald broadens his scope at several points, further positioning himself as an authoritative source. This bird's-eye view also allows him to describe in detail how each of the occupied forts in the upper country fell to Indigenous forces, although he must again rely on the testimony of others to describe the magnitude of British loss. It is in this context that he forefronts an Indigenous woman for a second time in order to communicate the dangers of sexual encounter. As had been the case with his discussion of the proposed woman informant at Detroit, MacDonald's accounts of this second woman differ. To Croghan he writes: "On Sunday the 5th of June we were informed" ["we were acquainted" in the report to Bouquet] "that Fort Miamis was taken—that Ensign Holmes who commanded there, had been informed by two Frenchmen ... of Detroit being attacked by the Indians, which he would hardly believe, and threatened to imprison the French for that report—that an Indian woman had betrayed him [Ensign Holmes] out of the fort, by pretending another woman was very sick, and begged him to come to her cabin, and bleed her, and that when he had gone a little distance from the fort, was fired upon and killed."[23]

In the account received by Amherst, MacDonald credits a Canadian with the information regarding the fate of Ensign Robert Holmes at Fort Miami, and describes that post as dependent on Detroit's garrison, which helps to explain Holmes's shock and disbelief on hearing the news of the attack on Detroit. MacDonald provides a more detailed description in this report of Holmes's demise at the hands of a number of Indians in ambuscade "who fired on him and killed him." The most explicit information MacDonald added to this account pertained to the Indigenous woman who had lured Holmes to his death. She was an Indian woman *with whom he* [Holmes] *had been intimate.*[24] Why had MacDonald held back this particular detail description in his report to Croghan? Perhaps MacDonald suspected the story was apocryphal and hesitated to share it with Croghan, who may have also doubted the story's veracity. It is possible that Croghan may already have been aware of the relationship between Holmes and the woman in question, and restating this fact would have been unnecessary. It is most likely that the practice of engaging in or forcing intimacies with Indigenous women was so widespread in the upper country, it was not worth noting to Croghan. In any case, this component of the story would not have elicited in Croghan the particular reaction MacDonald desired.

In adding this detail on sexual relations between Holmes and the Indigenous woman, MacDonald likely meant to alarm Amherst and British imperial decision makers of the magnitude of Indigenous involvement, which now extended far beyond Pontiac and his warriors and made every Indigenous person a potential threat to British lives. As commander in chief of British forces, Amherst was in the best position to bring men and resources to bear in seeking large-scale "retribution" against this threat. The story of Robert Holmes presented British manhood at its most fragile and vulnerable—a dangerous position induced by passion for a woman. That she was also Indigenous further deepened a rage already in play against

Pontiac and his confederates. It is possible that MacDonald saw himself in the story of Holmes and relished his own deliverance from a lovesickness that would ultimately kill Holmes. The women of MacDonald's account become emblems of the fraught and muddied relationship the British held with French and Indigenous communities and of the struggle of each British man against the excesses of his own passions.

The Forgotten Story of Pontiac's War: Catherine

The identity of the person who informed Henry Gladwin of Pontiac's plan remained a matter of conjecture in the years and centuries following the incident. Historians in the nineteenth and early twentieth centuries felt it necessary to discover who had acted as informant, and devoted a considerable amount of space in their books and papers to the subject.[25] Although there were a few individuals put forward as having acted in this capacity, later accounts and histories eventually settled on two "suspects"—Catherine, an Ojibwe-Catholic or Potawatomi-Catholic woman who may have been an *ogimawkwe,* and Angelique Cuillerier dit Beaubien, member of one of Detroit's powerful and well-established French-Indigenous family networks.[26]

Historian Helen Humphrey noted that all of the reports by Euro-Americans present at the time of the siege, whether French or English, inferred that allies of Pontiac accused an Indigenous woman of divulging the information to the British, even though no one could prove she was the perpetrator. None of the testimony, therefore, was provided by people who had spoken to the woman or by anyone to whom this woman had entrusted the story. As we have already seen, reports circulated by British officers present during some portion of the six-month period of Pontiac's siege, beginning with and based on James MacDonald's account, are similar in identifying an Indigenous woman and describing her punishment. One anonymous French source, however, differed in its description of the woman and her fate.

The sinews of French support for Pontiac or the British were highly complex and difficult to discern for British imperial agents commanding at Detroit. Indeed, viewed through the lens of these agents on whose records historians have long relied, it is as problematic for twenty-first-century readers to discern French motives and loyalties. Even within the ranks of the family networks, some members worked, at least ostensibly, to support the British, while others actively worked against them and in support of the Indigenous cause. Pierre Chesne dit LaButte, for example, is frequently mentioned in British correspondence in his capacity as interpreter between Gladwin and Pontiac. Pierre's nephew, the Indigenous-language interpreter Isadore Chesne was similarly helpful to the British while Isadore's brother Eléopolle (known as Mini) and their Uncle Jacques Godefroy (brother-in-law to Pierre Chesne dit LaButte), both also Indigenous-language interpreters, appear in imperial correspondence as allied to the Indigenous cause. Mini and Godefroy, acting on Pontiac's orders, traveled to the Illinois Country to solicit military support from Indigenous nations residing there. They also took part in the successful Indigenous attack on two British forts located in Myaamionki, including Fort Miami.[27] It may therefore not be surprising that the French account of the events of 1763 offers an alternative version of how the British came to learn of Pontiac's plans to take the fort and the role played by the suspected woman informant.

In this version, it was an Odawa man named Mahigama who related Pontiac's plan to the British commandant. He is described as having only "feeble" support for Pontiac's cause and to have come to the gates of the fort at night to request a meeting. When Donald Campbell offered to send for interpreter Pierre LaButte, Mahigama had refused, insisting he spoke sufficient French to make himself understood to Campbell. Mahigama may have wished to deliver his information quickly and did not want to wait for LaButte's arrival. It is also possible, however, that Mahigama refused LaButte's assistance because he feared the interpreter would share the sensitive information with Pontiac or others of the Odawa nation. Mahigama described Pontiac's plans in detail, begging the commandant to keep his identity secret because he feared for his life, which Campbell and Gladwin promised to do.[28]

Having perceived his plans to have been discovered, Pontiac is described as "struggling with different emotions—anger, fury, and rage." He ordered the "traitor of his nation" found, proclaiming that the individual "must be killed." At about 4 o'clock in the afternoon (another effort to make precise note of time) "a *false* rumor came to the Odawa leader that a Sauteaux [Ojibwe] woman had given them away, and that she was present in the village of the Foxes." Pontiac ordered four men to bring the woman to him. Crossing the river to the Fox settlement located southwest of the fort, they surprised the woman, who had no knowledge of their intent. They did not take her directly to Pontiac as ordered by him, transporting her by force instead to the home of the commandant, where they demanded to know if she had been the source of the information. The commandant did not answer and they left "not better satisfied than if they had kept quiet," after the commandant had given them and the woman bread and beer. The Odawa men then "took her to their chiefs in the village."[29] The French report provides no further information on the fate of the woman, but the anonymous author's suggestion of the woman's innocence leaves open the possibility that she may have been spared. The author provides further details about the activities that took place in French and Indigenous communities during the siege, which we do not see in MacDonald's report. This French account is the source from which we might expect to have heard firsthand about the violence perpetrated by Pontiac on the woman informant. But on this the account is silent, upholding the woman's innocence and eschewing the violence against her.

After the resolution of Pontiac's War, Detroit merchant John Porteus was the first to refer to the woman informant as Catherine, who he described as "an old Popish [Catholic] Squaw of the Poutewatomy Nation."[30] Five reports dictated to antiquarian Charles Trowbridge in 1824—sixty years after the events of 1763—provided by French men and women who were either present at the time or had testimony from family members who had been present, differ in their identification of the informant, with some naming Catherine.[31] The story featuring Catherine was widely circulated in the published works of Jonathan Carver, who heard it at Detroit during his North American travels in 1766.

With Carver's narrative, a substantial amount of contextual information is added to the prevailing accounts. Carver described Catherine as "an Indian woman who had been employed by Major Gladwyn to make a pair of Indian shoes out of curious elk-skin" for his friend. When she came to visit him to give him the shoes, he was so pleased that he asked her to take skins to fashion a pair for Gladwin. He paid the woman and "dismissed her." But the woman did not leave immediately, even though the gates of the fort were about to be closed for the evening. She lingered in the street, eventually coming to the attention of Gladwin. He beckoned her to return and asked what was troubling her. She told him that she could not take the skins because she would never be able to return the finished product. She then related what Pontiac had planned for the following day—the calling of a meeting inside the fort with the purported purpose to talk friendship with the British and the presentation by Pontiac of a wampum belt communicating peace. Pontiac's associates would have sawed-off guns under their blankets that they would brandish as soon as Pontiac gave them the signal—the presentation of the belt in a reversed position. The woman asked that Gladwin not divulge that she had warned him, and he promised to keep her confidence.

Gladwin prepared for the next day's conference, stationing extra soldiers inside and outside the fort and advising them to be prepared to draw arms when Pontiac presented the belt. Surprised by this unexpected behavior by the British, Pontiac and his followers were forced to conclude the conference as it had been originally pretended—a meeting advocating peace. Carver comments that Pontiac had been prevented from carrying out his planned attack by "an apparently trivial and unforeseen circumstance," commenting wryly, "on such does the fate of empires frequently depend." Carver has Gladwin call into question the woman's information when he consults with second-in-command Donald Campbell as to its veracity. Although Campbell casts doubt on the woman's reliability, "considering the information as a story invented for some artful purposes" and advising Gladwin "to pay no attention to it," Gladwin "thought it prudent to conclude it to be true, until he was convinced that it was not so."[32] Thomas McKenney and Lewis Cass, authors of many articles and books on Indigenous culture and history in the early nineteenth century, adopted this story virtually whole-cloth from Carver and included it in their publications. Like Carver, Cass derided the woman and her information, declaring that it was "fortunate that her warning was well received."[33]

The story changed shape in 1851 with the publication of Frances Parkman's *The Conspiracy of Pontiac and the Indian War after the Conquest of Canada*. Parkman had visited Detroit to research his book in 1845, which included interviewing local peoples about the events of 1763. The mayor of Detroit, who was descended from some of the area's eighteenth-century French peoples, told Parkman that he thought "Pontiac or his Indians was overheard speaking of the plot by one of the French who understood French-Indian, and that by means of a French woman it was conveyed to the fort. The woman made it known to the interpreters, who told the officers . . . the woman's name was Labutte, daughter to the interpreter of that name."[34] The mayor's account highlights an Indigenous-French patois used by both local French and Indigenous peoples, while also acknowledging a woman to have been the source of the information. The interpreter of Odawa Pierre LaButte, however, did not have a daughter, which may mean that the mayor had conflated different accounts of the historic episode.

Although Parkman would also rely on the oral testimony of local French previously recorded by Trowbridge, Parkman chose not to use the mayor's version of the story (which the mayor admitted he had heard from someone else). Instead, Parkman romanticized the Carver account by re-creating the character of Catherine as a beautiful young Ojibwe maiden living in the Potawatomi village who "could boast a larger share of beauty than is common in the wigwam." In addition to maligning the physical appearance of all Indigenous women in comparison, Parkman hinted that Catherine had carried on a sexual relationship with Gladwin. In Parkman's account, as in those of Carver, McKenney, and Cass, Catherine visited Gladwin for the purpose of giving him elkskin moccasins ornamented with porcupine work that he had requested her to make. Parkman ascribes an emotional vulnerability and deference to Gladwin's authority to Catherine when he relates that instead of leaving immediately, she lingered, her face "sad and downcast."[35] When questioned by Gladwin, she eventually divulged the information on Pontiac's impending attack. Parkman cited Henry Rowe Schoolcraft as the source of this information.[36]

Schoolcraft, another well-published writer of the Indigenous experience, married to the Irish-Ojibwe Jane Johnston of Michigan, claimed to have heard the story from Detroit Indian agent Henry Connor, who told Schoolcraft he had met the Ojibwe woman informant in her older age. Schoolcraft noted that "the affair had other motives than [Jonathan] Carver imagines" and provided a description of her as "a very handsome person in her youth, being nearly white, though of Indian blood," who had "thought more of saving the life of Major Gladwyn than of saving the whole Anglo-Saxon race."[37] In his description of Catherine, Schoolcraft used the concept of race-based blood quantum to separate Euro-American from Indigenous states of being. He explains that despite the illusion of whiteness offered by Catherine's physical appearance, her true identity is Indigenous. This is a matter that has considerable bearing on her suspected role in Pontiac's conspiracy. His dichotomous description leaves out mixed-blood identity entirely and the implications this might have had on Catherine's loyalties.

Schoolcraft further disparages her historical influence by depicting her as a betrayer of two men from two cultures, one of whom punished her for her actions. Her Indigenous husband had "bit off her nose" "owing to her gallantries" with Gladwin. She meets an ignoble and painful end that is ascribed to her perfidy. As an old woman she had become "intemperate" and "in such a state had fallen backward into a kettle of sap" at a sugar camp on the Clinton River. Schoolcraft concludes his description with a moral denouncement that is meant to justify the horrifying nature of her death: "truly the way of the transgressor is hard."[38] Schoolcraft's narrative and Parkman's subsequent reinterpretation do place an Indigenous or mixed-blood woman at the center of one of the most pivotal moments in Detroit history . But they curtail her agency by suggesting that she was led more by emotion in her love for an elite white man than by any political or economic motive that would have bearing for her community. Indeed, Schoolcraft depicts her as immoral, sexually dissolute, and alcoholic, reflecting contemporary views of his time of Indigenous women.[39]

Catherine's appearance within the fort and at the commandant's residence to deliver the moccasins is trivialized in nineteenth-century histories as taking place outside the world of commerce because the transaction is perceived to have unfolded in a private sphere of romance and sexual intimacy. But however minimized, the moccasins provide a clue as to the role played by Indigenous women in trade at eighteenth-century Detroit. Indigenous-made elkskin moccasins were highly prized as footwear by both Indigenous peoples and Europeans at Detroit because their manufacture made them more soft and supple than European varieties of shoes. It was Indigenous women who traditionally oversaw the entire process of their construction at Detroit and other centers of trade in the Great Lakes.[40] In addition to making the moccasins, Indigenous women would have been the agents designated to trade them and other goods.

An eighteenth-century letter written by Detroit's commandant in the period immediately following Pontiac's siege speaks directly to Indigenous women's commerce. The British remained suspicious that Indigenous nations at Detroit would unite to launch another attack on the fort. To counter this possibility, a law was passed limiting the number of Indigenous men who could be within the walls of the fort at any one time to between thirty and forty. The British commandant felt that this regulation of the men would not provoke or anger them because they would realize it stemmed from their actions during Pontiac's War. He also expected that the men would not complain of the law adversely affecting commerce, since as he pointed out, their trade was "carry'd on by their women."[41] The law reflected British efforts to achieve military dominance by controlling Indigenous men while at the same time safeguarding the lucrative trade on which the British depended. This arrangement continued to allow for the free movement of Indigenous women and the recognition and legitimization of their role as vital contributors to economic well-being in the greater effort to secure British power.

Catherine's appearance at the British commandant's quarters to relay information would also have been in keeping with the pivotal role that Anishinaabe women played in communicating issues of importance to the community.[42] As previously discussed, eighteenth-century Anishinaabe women had traditionally held leadership roles, with the power to call men to war and to take part in diplomacy and political negotiation while also controlling commerce and the value of trade goods. If Catherine had been at the British commandant's quarters, she most likely was acting for economic or political reasons, and her presence there would not have been viewed as extraordinary.

Perhaps the most provocative rendition of the story of the woman informant was offered by Mary Catherine Crowley, whose 1902 book of historical fiction on the life of a French girl named Angelique brings together the two women suspected of having divulged Pontiac's plot. In *A Heroine of the Strait: A Romance of Detroit in the Time of Pontiac,* Crowley presents Catherine, a Catholicized Ojibwe woman and daughter of a chief whose love for the British commandant Gladwin is rejected because she is Indigenous. Catherine learns that the commandant is in love with Angelique and she determines to somehow punish her. Catherine discovers Pontiac's plan to attack the fort and divulges just enough information to Angelique to raise her concern, but not enough to allow her to do anything to prevent the attack, knowing, as Catherine tells the Jesuit priest, "being a French girl, she could do nothing, since if she tried to warn him by word or signal, the anger of Pontiac would fall upon her."[43] Angelique declares that she does not love Gladwin and pleads with Catherine to tell him of the plot. Catherine initially balks, but eventually, after praying to the Virgin Mary, she relents and tells Gladwin of Pontiac's plot. When the Odawa ask Gladwin if Catherine is the informant, he denies her participation, but she is still taken to Pontiac, who beats her. In her book, Crowley refers to Catherine as Nedawniss, daughter of Makatépelicité.[44]

According to historian Richard Middleton, Mackatépelecité was an Odawa chief second only to Pontiac in influence in that nation.[45] Nedawniss is an Algonquin word for daughter, which would further underscore the importance of Catherine's relationship to a powerful father and her own likely position as a leader.[46] Perhaps Catherine was involved in or overheard plans for the attack on the fort from her father and Pontiac. Historians and antiquarians suspected Angelique had gained the information at her home in conversations between Pontiac and her father, Antoine Cuillerier. Crowley's story knits together the French and Indigenous threads of the most prominent versions of the story of the woman informant.

The Forgotten Story of Pontiac's War: Angelique

The other candidate for the role of informant was Angelique Cuillerier dit Beaubien. When she was born at Detroit in 1735, her family had been engaged in trade with Indigenous nations for seventy-five years. As we learned in chapter 4, her great-grandfather René Cuillerier had provided the means by which the family entered this lucrative commerce. After his experience as a captive and adoptee among the Haudenosaunee in the mid-seventeenth century, he had launched a lifelong career in trade and diplomacy that had taken him from Montreal, Boston, and Albany to the Illinois Country, Michilimackinac, and Detroit. His great-granddaughter Angelique would become an influential and well-connected businesswoman who put her family's connections and experience to good use in the upper country. Angelique was also the daughter of Antoine Cuillerier dit Beaubien, a pivotal power broker of the French-Indigenous family networks and leading merchant. His wife/Angelique's mother Angelique Girard was her husband's *procuratrice* and managed the family's extensive trading business.[47]

Antoine had a close relationship with Pontiac and ties to the Odawa, as well as other local Indigenous communities, which led the British to suspect him of having participated in the siege. Angelique was purported to have divulged Pontiac's plan when it was revealed to her father at his home because she wished to save the life of her British husband. This alternative narrative of the divulging of Pontiac's surreptitious plans was circulated by historians Clarence Burton and George Catlin in the late nineteenth and early twentieth centuries. In these versions, yet another woman is driven to participate in the political world controlled by men for entirely nonpolitical reasons.[48]

In the course of the Indigenous siege, Antoine Cuillerier had donned a hat and lace clothing—items likely gifted to Pontiac by the British in 1761—and sat in a designated chair in the middle of the largest room in his house. Pontiac named him commandant of the French fort and addressed him as "his father come to life."[49] An observer professed to have never seen Cuillerier in the clothes or posture, underlining the highly ritualistic nature of this event. We can view the Pontiac/Cuillerier performance as mimicking the ceremonies attending diplomatic meetings between Onontio (normally channeled through the French governor general) and Indigenous leaders. In wearing the ceremonial garb, Cuillerier transformed himself into Onontio and British gifts into a symbol of French-Odawa alliance.[50]

The family networks had for decades enacted a local "creole nationalism" that had buttressed and threatened in turn the French king's power and remained in force at mid-century. The performance by Pontiac and Cuillerier maintained the power of the networks by keeping a version of Onontio at Detroit. In fact, with the French imperial state and its king gone from the upper country in the wake of

French defeat in the Seven Years' War, the families could operate openly as the only embodiments of Onontio left standing between Quebec and the Mississippi River. Because Detroit functioned as a hub for Indigenous nations and now for the British in the upper country, the Pontiac/Cuillerier diplomatic ritual reinscribed Detroit's central status as a multinational political center. Knowing that French-Indigenous family members had enacted Onontio locally since the turn of the century, we can shed new light on what Angelique may have heard and on the role played by the Cuillerier family during a period at mid-century when Detroit's economic growth and population increased dramatically.

Angelique had made her first appearance in British records in the journal of Northern Superintendent of Indian Affairs William Johnson during his first official visit to Detroit in September 1761. During the first half of the century as a French colonial outpost, Detroit's population had almost doubled, growing slowly at first from 270 French men and women in 1707, to 483 in 1750. In the next fifteen years, the number would double again to over 900 in the transition from French to British imperial presence. French colonial officials had abandoned efforts to dismantle the settlement, committing instead to enlarging and strengthening the fort. Growth outside of the walls had also greatly increased, due to the brisk deeding of land in the 1730s called for by Governor General Beauharnois in order to make Detroit self-sufficient in supplying its own grain. In relatively short order, Detroit possessed a sufficient number of people from various socioeconomic ranks to support good trade in diverse consumer goods.[51]

The trade with Indigenous nations was generating record profits for merchants and their families at Detroit. Two main entrepôts, Detroit and Michilimackinac, served as interior headquarters and transshipment points for forts further west. These and other factors provided ideal circumstances for the French-Indigenous family networks to consolidate their status as the richest inhabitants in Detroit. Between 1749 and 1750, a large wave of immigrants from the St. Lawrence valley arrived at Detroit, settling across the river from the fort and next to the Wendat community. These immigrants were mostly farmers, and they created a new French suburb with its own Jesuit-led church. Their arrival provided a more substantial sedentary class of people who added a "thick" layer of agriculturalists to the class system that was solidifying at Detroit.

With more farmers in the area, Detroit became a major supplier of agricultural produce for the western posts. It also maintained its position as a central location in the operation of the fur trade. In 1754, a record number of canoes came from

Montreal, carrying merchandise to Detroit and returning to Montreal with furs from the interior. The largest concentration of Indigenous peoples in the Great Lakes basin could be found at Detroit, increasing from 2,160 in 1731 to 3,120 in 1763, and far outnumbering the French population.[52] The French-Indigenous family networks profited by supplying the new arrivals with the necessities to establish themselves, and by absorbing them and their resources into existing kinship conglomerates.[53]

With unprecedented wealth came cultural florescence. In 1754, Simple Bocquet, Detroit's resident cleric, had begun using the words "bourgeois" and "négociant" in church records to refer to Pierre Chesne dit LaButte, Antoine Cuillerier, and other members of the family networks. The eighteenth-century *négociant* was a wholesaler who was wealthier than a merchant and many nobles in the colony. *Négociants* modeled themselves as closely as possible after nobility, obtaining commissions as officers in the militia and evincing a "mode parisienne" to mimic the manners of France's high society.[54] Members of the family networks used their wealth to buy various cultural markers that displayed their prominence, including slaves. Pierre Chesne dit LaButte made many contributions to the church at Detroit, at one time giving 1,000 French livres in goods. This sum was roughly equal to six years' salary for a member of the laboring class, and one year's salary for military captains in the upper country.[55]

By the mid-eighteenth century, two generations of the networks containing the richest individuals were operating simultaneously at Detroit. Pierre LaButte, son to Pierre Chesne dit LaButte and son-in-law to Antoine Cuillerier (LaButte Jr. had married Marie Anne, another of Antoine's daughters), was also listed as a *négociant* and *bourgeois* of the city ("bourgeois de cette ville") in church records, and like his father, he engaged in extensive commercial transactions.[56] These included receipt of 2,000 livres from the Odawa/French trader and interpreter Charles de Langlade in 1758 and a promise to Langlade to deliver a twelve- to fifteen-year-old female *panis* slave. By 1760, Pierre Jr. had formed a company with his cousin Paul Trottier dit DesRuisseaux, receiving in one transaction 7,000 livres from a soldier who had mortgaged all of his real and personal property to purchase several barrels of brandy to trade.[57] By the time the British had arrived, the family networks had fully entrenched themselves as Detroit's most powerful residents. Their role as power brokers in diplomatic and economic relations with Indigenous nations gave them influence and wealth that outstripped that of British officers.

When he arrived at Detroit in 1761, William Johnson would enlist LaButte and other pivotal members of the networks to assist him in investigating rumors of an impending uprising of Indigenous peoples against the British and to dispel Indigenous concerns about the new British imperial presence. In advance of his visit, Johnson had sent wampum belts to Detroit that he expected would circulate further west to call Indigenous nations to a grand council at the fort. During his stay at Detroit, troops and provisions were organized and sent west from Detroit to the posts at Michilimackinac, Kiihkayonki (Fort Miami), and Ouiatenon, while Indigenous representatives came to Detroit in such large numbers that Johnson was forced to hold the official council outside. Johnson reassured the Odawa and Wendat, the two largest resident communities at Detroit, of British friendship and confronted the Seneca messengers who had brought wampum belts to Detroit advocating war.

As the official interpreter for the Odawa, LaButte, known also by his Wendat name of Onditsouoa, was called on frequently by Johnson.[58] Attesting also to his elite status as a leading merchant, LaButte was invited on several occasions to dine with Johnson, commandant Donald Campbell, and British officers. Johnson also spent time in the company of women of the French-Indigenous networks. One morning he reported that "four of the principal ladies of the town" came to visit him and he served them "rusk [a crisp bread] and cordial." Another morning, Campbell escorted some of the "town ladies" to Johnson's quarters, and he served them "cakes, wine, and cordial." Johnson also hosted several balls for the city's well-heeled residents that lasted through the night, and in at least one case, until seven the next morning. At one such occasion, he led Angelique Cuillerier in the first dance of the evening, noting in his diary: "I opened the ball with Mademoiselle Curie—a fine girl." Johnson promised her he would write after he had returned to his home in the Mohawk Valley.[59] Johnson's interactions with women are couched solely as social events in his journal, belying the importance of these women to Johnson's efforts to solidify British imperial aims. Indeed, that these women were deemed "principal" by Johnson and were introduced to him by Campbell suggests that these meetings involved discussions of trade. It is likely that Johnson met not only with Angelique Cuillerier, who was niece to Detroit's last French commandant, but also with her mother and Cuillerier family *procuratrice* Angelique Girard.

Detroit's pivotal location would prove as advantageous for the British as it had been for the French. Detroit became the headquarters for all the British army garrisons in the upper country, and traders from Pennsylvania and New York now had an opportunity to compete with French and Indigenous merchants in Detroit. But while many British traders waited for their Indigenous customers to return from their winter hunting grounds in early spring to conduct business, members of the French-Indigenous family networks traveled to or with Indigenous communities to their hunting grounds and traded on the spot. As a result, the families consistently outproduced their British counterparts.

Early efforts by British imperial agents to control commerce by controlling the movement of the French-Indigenous family traders would prove unsuccessful, but James Sterling, an Irishman who had served with the British army in the Seven Years' War, would prove an exception to this general state of affairs. Sterling's accounts and letters provide a window into British efforts to assert economic prominence at their newly won forts, while also highlighting the essential role local family networks continued to play in these efforts. Sterling came to Detroit in 1761 from a successful business at Niagara, bringing the financial backing of his business contacts in Oswego, Schenectady, and Niagara with him. Although he had his own trade network in place that had allowed him to thrive in the east, he spent his first few years at Detroit attempting to gauge the tastes of his French and Indigenous clientele. Sterling seemed well aware that his stiffest competition was with members of the French-Indigenous family networks.

Sterling had to pay dearly for the basics that the family networks already possessed, a fact that may account for the consistent tone of contempt he used in references to the French. He fumed as he waited on the arrival of clerks from Oswego he planned to send to Kiihkayonki to fetch goods, a situation he insisted could not be avoided because it was "rare to get a Frenchman here that can be depended on or entrusted with goods."[60] Although he could speak and write French, Sterling was forced to budget for an Indigenous language interpreter, paying thirty pounds a year to a Mohawk man who was proficient in English, French, and other Indigenous languages.[61] Sterling demanded an additional allowance per day for "living in exile." This cant, as has been previously discussed, that was used by newly arrived British officers and traders to express their frustration with perceived differences between them and the Indigenous and French communities in which they were settling. Sterling's dress and demeanor marked him as an outsider and prevented him from establishing a thriving commerce. Judging by the acerbic tone of his request for funds to purchase clothing, he was keenly aware of this lack of status. He resented that he was "obliged to support in appearance the empty name of what the French call 'un gros marchand' [a successful merchant] which has very much effect with the sort of cattle I have to deal with."[62]

Keeping up appearances became even more costly when Sterling asked his partners back east for funds to buy a furnished house inside the fort that was located on a desirable street for trade. Here too, Sterling's frustrations communicate a larger dilemma faced by the British. The newcomers—military and civilians alike—were forced to rent properties from the French, who owned the majority of the structures within the walls of the fort.[63] Sterling rented the same house that had been previously occupied by Indian agent George Croghan. Although both men believed the rate was exorbitant, they had no other choice than to pay what was demanded by their landlady, Marie Catherine Godefroy, referred to by Sterling as Madame DesRuisseaux, her married name. It would have been risky for Sterling to challenge her over rent. Marie Catherine's uncle was Pierre LaButte and her brother Jacques Godefroy was in interpreter and trader among the Illinois who was a close associate of Pontiac. She was also the second wife of Alexis DesRuisseaux, who hailed from the influential Trottier/Cuillerier dit Beaubien family. Alexis had first been married to one of the daughters of Pierre Roy (Pierre LaButte's former father-in-law) and Roy's Myaamia wife Waapankihkwa (Marguerite Ouabankikoué).

Although Sterling may have begun to dress the part of the successful merchant, his particular aesthetic proclivities continued to differ from those of local French. Marie Catherine Godefroy/Madame DesRuisseaux was surprised and angered when she discovered that Sterling had converted a bedroom into a storeroom in the house he was renting, and had mounted shelves on a wall, driving nails through an expensive tapestry.[64] DesRuisseaux reported the damage to the owner, who sent word from Montreal that he intended to come back to Detroit to occupy the house, and that Sterling should cease making any further damages. Women would control every aspect of Sterling's efforts to establish himself and succeed commercially at Detroit. Like George Croghan and other British traders and government agents, Sterling engaged in sexual relations with Indigenous women, to whom he obliquely referred in rare instances. In 1762, at the same time he was complaining of his inability to tap into Detroit's market and expressed his disdain for local residents, he told a British officer that business had left him little time to meet women and he had been "obliged" to seek the company of "that of a copper hue."[65]

In 1765, Sterling's fortunes and the anti-French tone of his letters shifted dramatically when he met and eventually married Angelique Cuillerier. In a letter to one of his eastern partners, Sterling gushed over his new wife and the material advantages she and her family would provide:

She is a very prudent woman and a fine scholar; she has been raised to trade from her infancy and is generally allowed to be the best interpreter of the different Indian languages at this place. Her family is in great esteem amongst the Indians, so much that her father was suspected to have been chosen by the Indians to command here in case they had succeeded, which only arose from his being more in favor with them than the rest of the inhabitants. He has offered me to go with goods to some of the posts in case I should have more than I can dispose of here. He is pretty rich; he has given me with his daughter to the value of near a thousand pounds in houses, money, and peltry. He has already given me possession of the houses in the fort, has paid part of the money and peltry and is to pay the remainder in one or two years, as I may think proper to demand it. The Indians flock here daily since our marriage and lament our not having Indian goods, as they would trade nowhere else but here, if we could supply them. We shall carry on trade much better and with a great deal less expense than formerly, my wife serving as interpreter and she and I myself as clerks which I would much rather do than pay dear and be under obligations besides.[66]

Sterling had already attained a measure of acceptance in the French community during Pontiac's War when he had become engaged to Angelique. His marriage completed his transformation to insider, allowing him to eliminate the costs of an interpreter, the rent on his house in the fort, the need to hire agents from the east to transport his goods west to the Myaamia, and the expense incurred in maintaining patronage networks. He had also gained a trade partner who was well acquainted with the local economy. Most importantly, the marriage acted as an immediate signal of Sterling's credibility to Indigenous nations, who promised him exclusive trading privileges. Sterling wasted no time writing a letter to Sir William Johnson, aware that his betrothal to Angelique would raise his position in the eyes of the superintendent of Indian Affairs. He relayed the news of his marriage and Angelique's compliments to Johnson, and followed with a request that he be employed in the Indian service.[67] As interpreter and fellow merchant and with a connection to British power brokers, Angelique changed her husband's business prospects and allowed him to compete with French traders in the Great Lakes.

For her part, Angelique continued to conduct business in her own right. After her marriage, she sold a house she owned at the fort. She bought items such as silver and gold—popular trade goods among Great Lakes Indigenous nations—through her husband's eastern business partners for sale at Detroit and other locations in the upper country, while selling pelts and rare and unusual items of fur clothing in eastern markets.[68] In one of his letters to his trading partner John Duncan, Sterling conveyed a message and gift on Angelique's behalf to Duncan's wife. Angelique asked that her compliments be given to Mrs. Duncan, as well as a northern fox-fur muff that Angelique had acquired from a local French man who, in turn, had procured it from an Indigenous man at the far end of Lake Superior. Sterling stressed the singular and valuable nature of the muff, commenting that "it is look'd upon as curious here."[69]

Angelique helped Sterling bring Indigenous goods into the British North American marketplace, where they became highly valued. Sterling reserved such special items as gifts to curry favor with influential individuals in British North America. When a commanding officer at Niagara thanked Sterling for a beaver blanket, Sterling affected an attitude of humility in reply, while also showcasing his connection to Indigenous communities and setting himself apart from other merchants as a purveyor of unique articles. He responded that he had given "but a few Indian baubles" for the blanket, "which were so very trifling that it was not worth while making any charge of them. I beg you will do me the honor to accept it and shall be glad of an opportunity of procuring any Indian trinkets that are curious and may be agreeable to you."[70] Sterling's comment reflects his efforts to devalue some Indigenous commodities while inscribing others as Euro-American luxury goods within the British colonial marketplace.

Sterling asked John Duncan to sell four packs of fur belonging to Angelique to cover the cost of an enslaved black woman Angelique had previously purchased from Duncan and intended to keep "for her own use." Black slaves had been relatively rare during the French period, and as a result, were worth twice as much as their Indigenous counterparts. Most of those in the upper country during that time came through the English colonies and New York. But even after the British conquest, their number remained low in relation to that of Indigenous slaves, which explains why possession of black slaves acted as a mark of social status for those able to afford them.[71] As historian Tiya Miles has discovered, Sterling regularly traded in black slaves over the course of several years, and also utilized their multilingual abilities in French, English, and Indigenous languages.[72]

Angelique's father Antoine Cuillerier held two slaves, with the majority of Detroit residents holding at least one.[73] Because of their kinship connections and participation in trade with Indigenous nations, other members of the family networks continued to acquire slaves. The 1762 census of Detroit listed Pierre Chesne dit LaButte as in possession of one slave while his son Pierre LaButte held three, one of whom was black.[74] Indeed, one of the oral accounts of Pontiac's War collected in 1824 and the contemporary 1763 French version of those events may confirm the existence of a slave community, or shared sense of community, at Detroit. In his early nineteenth-century testimony, Jacques Parent claimed to have been told by Pontiac that an "old squaw" had communicated Pontiac's plans for the attack on the fort to "Pawnee wenches" who shared this information with the British.[75] Pawnee (a version of the French *panis*) was a generic term for enslaved peoples and its use here describes a group of enslaved women. The 1763 French version referenced a village of the Fox—a nation that been enslaved in large numbers by the French after 1712—as the location from which the woman informant had been taken by force by the Odawa on Pontiac's orders.

Angelique Cuillerier dit Beaubien's trading activities appear within the framework of her husband James Sterling's letters to his trading partners, just as the particular commerce in which she engaged transpired alongside Sterling's business dealings with the British government. Angelique dealt in goods and on terms different from those of her husband. She relied on well-established kinship networks that linked to Indigenous communities throughout the Great Lakes to buy and sell specialized luxury items, including "Indian curiosities," and the black slave she obtained from Duncan. Sterling maintained a brisk trade predominantly in foodstuffs and other necessities needed by the British garrison, including alcohol, pork, firearms, and ammunition.[76]

At the same time Sterling was attempting to control the value of the "Indian curiosities" his wife traded, he was also marginalizing that portion of his wife's activities that marked her behavior as connected to Indigenous peoples. Writing to his partner John Porteus on the subject of an interpreter he promised to send, Sterling assured him that he could spare the man in question as "Mrs. Sterling will answer the end of an interpreter, tho' not to ride after the Indians which is now the mode here."[77] Sterling's statement reflects his view that it was unacceptable for his wife to travel to Indigenous communities to conduct trade and he intended to limit her mobility by ensuring she remained at home, as prescribed by British gender norms. Indeed, he had demonstrated the same determination to restrict the movements of others he owned or who worked for him, including an escaped black slave Sterling had diligently pursued and vowed to confine upon his recapture.[78]

James Sterling continued to benefit from Angelique's family connections and business acumen. In 1763, Angelique may have shared crucial information with

Sterling that she had heard regarding Pontiac's planned attack and the involvement of members of French communities at Detroit and in the upper country to contribute resources to the Indigenous campaign. Sterling may then have disclosed this intelligence to British command.[79] He eventually learned to speak the Wendat language, an ability perhaps gained through instruction by his wife or immersion in the trade to which his marriage had given him full entrée.

In 1773, Detroit commandant Major Henry Bassett described conditions identical to those that had been faced by Henry Gladwin, Donald Campbell, and James MacDonald ten years previously. Indigenous peoples "seemed restless" and "were not much to be trusted." Bassett believed that "some French traders amongst them helped to stir them up." Unlike previous commandants, Bassett was unable to speak French, a serious disadvantage in a settlement with 1,300 French-speaking residents and a community of Wendat, who often used the French language in council. Bassett communicated his need for a French interpreter, requesting that Sterling, the "first merchant at this place and a gentleman of good character," be given the position. For all intents and purposes, Sterling had already been acting as Bassett's proxy. He had been translating into English from French all proceedings from Wendat councils and the legal disputes between inhabitants, as well as writing Bassett's French letters, which Sterling had performed "without any gratuity," according to Bassett. Pressing his case further, Bassett extolled Sterling's abilities and a rather unique family history based in the events of Pontiac's War calculated to placed Sterling beyond reproach:

> During the late war through a lady that he then courted from whom he had the best information, [he] was in part a means to save this garrison, this gentleman is now married to that lady and is connected with the best part of this settlement [and] has more to say with them than anyone here; the Indians can't well begin without his having information of their designs.

Bassett offered an additional impetus for the hire, explaining that Sterling could act as both French and Wendat interpreter, thereby cutting costs for the government.[80]

Bassett's glowing description of Sterling bore a striking resemblance to the enthused account Sterling had offered of Angelique following their marriage. The crucial means of entrance for Sterling into the world of the family networks had been through this marriage, just as it had been for Pierre Roy through marriage to Waapankihkwa (Marguerite Ouabankikoué). Sterling's eventual success as a merchant, facility in at least one Indigenous language, and familiarity with local Indigenous communities continued to be gained through Angelique. The story of Angelique's role in saving the British imperial state from destruction at the hands of Pontiac resonated ten years later and acted as evidence of her husband's trustworthy nature.

Eighteenth- and nineteenth-century narratives of Pontiac's War managed to foreground a woman as a proactive agent, but these same accounts featuring Catherine and Angelique curtailed the woman's agency by suggesting that she acted out of love rather than for the political or economic good of Indigenous or French communities. We cannot be entirely certain of Catherine's status or even her tribal identity, although in most cases she is identified as Anishinaabe. She may have been a leader among her people, and like the Odawa La Blanche fifty years before, her power would have resided in her regulation of trade, war, and peace. In this role, her visit to the home of British commandant Gladwin takes on added dimensions. Aware of Pontiac's plans, she may have attempted to bargain for peace by threatening to call Odawa men to war and demanding a beneficial trade arrangement. Angelique's agency also resided in her participation in trade. As a member of the family networks who easily crossed fluid boundaries between French and Indigenous worlds, she too controlled the manner in which commerce and diplomacy intersected.

Recent scholarship on Pontiac's War does not address in any depth the issue of the person responsible for warning the British of Pontiac's plans. In these histories, the point is moot and contributes little to an understanding of the highly complex relations between Indigenous and European nations. At mid-century, members of Detroit's French-Indigenous networks had transformed resources of the upper country into luxury items by manipulating the means by which these resources were valued. British belief that they could control this system of exchange was at first illusory. They underestimated the complexity of the family networks and members' adherence to a distinct lifestyle that had flourished for over fifty years. In the course of the six-month siege waged by Pontiac, they were ultimately unable to determine or direct the loyalty of the networks. As the first decade of British rule at Detroit came to an end, they would soon discover that the biggest challenge to British hegemony came from a particular enclave within the ranks of the family networks—Indigenous communities on the western edges of Detroit's trade network. The next chapter will examine the continued proliferation of French-Indigenous kinship ties in the period after Pontiac's efforts to reassert

Indigenous sovereignty in 1763. Key members of the networks had worked and sided with Pontiac. This cooperative effort had cemented familial ties and brought British suspicions and retribution to bear on family members. In the years following, however, some would choose to align themselves with British imperial interests, while others maintained a reliance on and loyalty to a French-Indigenous collective identity, including the Myaamia-French children and grandchildren of Pierre Roy and Marguerite Ouabankikoué.

CHAPTER 7

Bastards and Bastions

Domestic Disorder and the Changing Status
of the French-Indigenous Family Networks

n late August of 1764, Captain Thomas Morris left Detroit with official orders from General John Bradstreet to "take possession of the Illinois Country in his Britannic Majesty's name" and counter any lingering influence of Pontiac. Morris spent time in Odawa and Myaamia communities on the Maumee River and met Pontiac and other Odawa leaders, but he never made it past the Myaamia villages. Odawa, Wendat, Shawnee, Kiikaapoi, Ouiatenon, and Lenni-Lenape, as well as Pontiac himself, still considered the British enemies and were suspicious of Morris's motives. His narrative of his trip is filled with details of constant councils and the arrival and departure of Indigenous diplomatic emissaries, some of whom rebuked and threatened him.

At one point, an Odawa leader more sympathetic to Morris emerged dressed in "a laced scarlet coat and a laced hat," gifts that had been bestowed upon the man when he had conducted William Johnson to Detroit in 1761. The clothing is remarkably similar in its description to the "laced hat and coat" that had been worn by Antoine Cuillerier as he and Pontiac enacted French-Odawa diplomatic alliance at Detroit in 1763. It is not at all unlikely that such highly significant gifts conferred to solidify newly established British-Odawa relations by Johnson, the superintendent of Indian Affairs had in turn been given by Pontiac to Cuillerier for purposes of replacing British imperial agency with that of the French. After Pontiac's War, the clothing would have been transported from Detroit and its meaning transformed as Pontiac and the Odawa moved west to the Maumee. In 1764, the Odawa leader wearing the clothes effected friendship to Morris and resituated the clothing within the symbolic context they had been originally bestowed by the British on the Odawa.[1]

Also present in Morris's narrative were French men who had been sympathetic to Pontiac's cause in 1763, including Morris's guide Jacques Godefroy. The Godefroy family had been active among the Illinois and Myaamia for more than fifty years, and Jacques, as we learned in chapter 6, was brother-in-law to Odawa interpreter Pierre Chesne dit LaButte and had been closely allied with Pontiac during the events of 1763. Godefroy had not gone willingly on the trip with Morris. The British had imprisoned him at Detroit and planned to hang him for treason for his role in Pontiac's War. Describing him as speaking "all of the Indian languages," Bradstreet offered that if Morris thought Godefroy could be of use on his trip, Bradstreet would pardon the Frenchman. Godefroy would prove essential, translating multiple Indigenous languages into French for the bilingual (English-French) Morris.

However, while Godefroy remained relatively safe from harm and served as interpreter throughout, Morris barely escaped with his life from angry Odawa warriors who chased him into a cornfield. When he made his way to the Myaamia villages, he perceived himself to be in equally dangerous circumstances. Myaamia warriors captured and restrained Morris, leading him to expect that his torture and death were imminent. At the moment when Morris feared he was being led to this fate, Pakaana, described by Morris as "the king of the Miamis nation and just out of his minority," arrived and loosed his bonds, demanding that Morris be released. The warriors complied and Morris expressed his gratitude to Pakaana. Morris was sent to one of the Myaamia dwellings, where he was visited by Pakaana's sisters, described by Morris as "handsome." One of these young women was almost certainly Tahkamwa.

The event may have been staged by Pakaana's family to demonstrate his fitness for leadership. It was certainly dramatized by Morris, whose romanticized portrayal of Tahkamwa and others he encountered was undoubtedly influenced by literature he was reading in the course of his trip. Tahkamwa was designated a "princess" to his "happy Don Quixote," and it is easy to see Quixote's faithful companion Sancho Panza in the depiction of Jacques Godefroy, described by Morris as of a "low station" and "indebted" to him "for his liberty, if not his life." Morris also carried a volume of

Shakespeare's plays gifted to him by an Odawa man, to which Morris made frequent reference as he read the "tragedy of Antony and Cleopatra."[2]

Like the Roman Antony, who hailing from the military ranks of a colonizing empire is finally conquered himself, Morris the British officer sees his own imperial status subverted. Morris's liberty and masculine privilege are ultimately controlled by Pakaana and Tahkamwa while he is a prisoner among the Myaamia. He becomes a political pawn used to validate Pakaana's masculine virtue as leader.[3] Cast as the Egyptian Cleopatra to Morris's Antony, Tahkamwa exercises a gendered political authority residing outside the Roman/British empire. Just as "Rome shapes its Egyptian imperial struggle around the contours of Cleopatra's sexualized and racialized black body," Morris casts Tahkamwa as the Indigenous princess whose danger to the empire lies in her desirability. As had been the case in the multiple accounts of the women at the heart of Pontiac's War, Morris's chronicle of the power and sexual agency of Tahkamwa communicated a larger threat to the British in the upper country.[4]

Illustrations of this gendered peril are revealed in Morris's journal and his encounter with a fellow captive Englishman that tie all of these women together. The only survivor of the Indigenous raid on Fort Miami a year earlier during Pontiac's War, the man related the story of the fort's doomed commandant Ensign Holmes, who had been "enticed" out of the fort to his death by the "young squaw whom he kept." Morris's fellow captive had escaped certain death through the intercession of an "old squaw" who agreed to adopt him. Not only is this the same vignette of the killing of Holmes that James MacDonald had included in his account in 1763, it also brings together the figures of the old and young squaw who would feature in the many stories of Pontiac's War. Both of these women, as well as Tahkamwa, exercised power accorded them in their respective nations, even if its expression was misconstrued and misrepresented by British men threatened by them and by Indigenous agency in general.

In seeking to subdue the influence of one Indigenous leader—Pontiac—Morris had unwittingly allowed himself to become the instrument for the growing influence of another. Whether or not Pakaana's demonstration of his leadership abilities in the sparing of Morris's life had been prearranged, Pakaana had won his authority at a crucial point in British/Myaamia relations, and Myaamia women had in all likelihood been involved in its enactment.[5] Years later, Tahkamwa would devise the rescue of an American captive by her son Jean Baptiste Richardville, thus ensuring his succession to the leadership position of his uncle Pakaana.[6] With her participation in Morris's liberation from captivity and the arrangement of her son's performance to solidify his authority among the Myaamia, Tahkamwa's power would be at the center of imperial crisis across decades.

Tahkamwa and the Myaamia-French Family Network

On September 18, 1774, Captain Richard Berringer Lernoult of the King's Eighth Regiment and commander of the Detroit post and its dependencies arbitrated a case that had the potential to upset a tenuous alliance between the British and Indigenous nations in the upper country. Possessing military authority at a fort that continued to serve as an economic and political center for the British, Lernoult acted as a representative of the king of England and as metaphoric father in talks with Indigenous diplomatic representatives at Detroit. The entire mattered rested on the troubled marriage of Tahkamwa and her French husband Richardville (also known as Richerville). Her brother Pakaana and other family members had come to Detroit to argue her case and that of Charles Beaubien—the man with whom she had taken up residence—against her husband.[7]

Richardville had broken ranks with his Myaamia in-laws and together with a business partner Alexis Maisonville, sought to oust the Myaamia from their position of economic control. The larger effort on the part of the Myaamia family was to maintain control of capital in the form of slaves, cattle, corn, and wampum, and of a pivotal portage that Tahkamwa held by virtue of her influential lineage. For the Myaamia, ancestral rights, commercial success, and political authority into the future were at stake. For the British, an alliance with the Myaamia made more likely the maintenance of an imperial presence in an area increasingly contested by English settlers and Indigenous nations. While Captain Lernoult heard the details of the case and considered whether he should decide in favor of either the wife and her family or her husband and his associates, it became clear that decisions and judgments rendered in the case of this woman's marriage would determine the shape of already tenuous British and Myaamia relations.

Just as it had been for other women of the French-Indigenous family networks, Tahkamwa's status and activities, expectations of her behavior, and treatment by men became the basis for a complex trope around which her family and European agents structured their arguments. Dueling narrations by British, French, and Indigenous men placed Tahkamwa at the center of a political and economic groundswell that threatened the foundations of European-Indigenous relations. British imperial efforts at controlling this influence were contingent on navigating the complex networks of kin, as well as recognizing and responding to cues for proper gendered behavior in the ritualized world of political negotiation.

Metaphors of kinship and gender were indistinguishable in the rhetoric of formal speeches made between Indigenous nations and between these nations and the British. The father/child metaphor was a frequently used form of address and hierarchical constructions of relatedness and authority were often expressed when individuals referred to one another as male relatives, such as uncle and nephew, or elder or younger brother. These gradations of power were also invoked more globally, when nations were referred to as women, demonstrating that these gendered exchanges stressing dominance and submission were increasingly expressed through references to sexuality.[8]

The highly ritualized and metaphoric language of the council house, where Europeans spoke with Indigenous administrators or where these administrators spoke to each other, was in general remarkably uniform across time and space in the eighteenth century. But in the years leading up to revolt by colonists against the British empire and to increased warfare between Indigenous nations and colonists in the contentious area of the upper country, this language and its gendered imagery reflected specific experiences of individuals and collectives. In this world, the Wendat, a matrilineal group that traced *otara* (clan descent) through its women and placed great importance on the role of clan mothers, continued to use the term "father" when addressing the French and British.[9] In this world, *akimaa* (male leaders) of the Myaamia referred to themselves as children of the *akimaahkwia* (queen) of their village. In this world, women of the French-Indigenous family networks engaged in behavior often viewed by British imperial agents as unbefitting their gender. In this world, a localized French language patois continued to be used in council meetings, even when the British were present and presiding. In this world, members of the French-Indigenous family networks remained a dominant presence, presenting unique challenges for the British.

The parties involved in the set of circumstances involving Tahkamwa used familiar tropes in new ways to address local concerns, with each discussion referencing a distinct history. Indigenous, French, and British speakers brought this history into negotiations to help set precedent or remind other parties of promises or responsibilities. Using gendered terminology to express their wishes and concerns was the most expedient way to communicate because widely utilized gendered kinship metaphors had been intertwined with the notion of British patriarchal authority under siege beginning in those first tentative years after the Seven Years' War.

In 1774, when Tahkamwa sought her release from Catholic marriage to Richardville, the men of her family would assert alternative models of masculinity and force the British Onontio to adopt a transgendered version of the proper parent, just as they had done with Cadillac over seventy years before. For her part, Tahkamwa moved between Myaamia and French worlds, avoiding the dangers and penalties associated with transgressing British gender norms. Three generations of women in her kinship network had been central to European imperial visions of profitable settlement. It was Tahkamwa's indigenous identity and economic and political clout among the Myaamia that would force these officials to recognize and support her efforts to maintain her family's trade empire.

Tahkamwa's French-Indigenous network had linked Myaamia, Mascouten, and other Indigenous communities to Detroit for almost seventy-five years. She was known as the wife of Richardville to British officials, and according to French church records we can infer her last name before marriage to have been Pacanne dit Roy.[10] She had been born in the course of the 1740s and was the daughter of an unknown mother who may have been Mahican, and of a father hailing from the Roy family, likely André Roy, who was half-French and half-Myaamia.[11] Indeed, this parentage would have made Tahkamwa granddaughter of Pierre Roy and Waapankihkwa (Marguerite Ouabankikoué). At the time of the conference held between Lernoult, her brother Pakaana and other relatives, Tahkamwa had already left the home she shared with her husband Antoine Joseph Drouet de Richerville, a trader among the Myaamia and a former French nobleman. Richerville had been engaged in commerce with the Myaamia since 1750 and had fathered two sons and two daughters with Tahkamwa. He had also produced children with other women, but these progeny were not in dispute in the discussions of 1774. Indeed, the four children of Richerville and Tahkamwa and the question of which parent could claim them was one of the points of contention between the two.

The Myaamia considered Tahkamwa and Richerville to have once been married and they were referred to as such several times in the course of the proceedings at Detroit. The fact that Richerville denied being married to Tahkamwa, when asked by Lernoult, testifies to his acknowledgment that according to Myaamia custom, the marriage was considered to have ended once he and Tahkamwa took up separate residences. By leaving her husband, Tahkamwa had divorced him. She subsequently moved into the home of Charles Beaubien, another Frenchman, and a highly influential merchant also operating among the Myaamia.

Shortly after her change in residence, she had asked Beaubien to retrieve her belongings from her former home. According to the parameters of the Coutume de Paris's *communauté de biens* (marital community property) that had been in force when she married Richerville, she was entitled to these possessions. She was also a Myaamia *akimaahkwia* (female civil chief) likely part of the powerful Atchatchakangouen (Crane) band and member of her nation's traditional medicine society whose family played a prominent role in Euro-Indigenous diplomacy. Finally, as the probable daughter of a Mahican woman hailing from a matrilineal culture, Tahkamwa's rights were multi-layered and spiritually, politically, and economically anchored. This was the crux of the entire case, namely, that her marriage was read in a variety of ways by the participants involved.

Richerville/Richardville invoked Myaamia norms to divest himself of Tah-kamwa, answering "no" when asked if he and Tahkamwa were married. He also endeavored to convince Lernoult that she had not brought property into their union, stating: "When I first took in the squah, she had less value than half a broach and I can prove it." Following French legal norms, this meant that there was nothing pre-existing the marriage to which she could lay sole claim after the union's dissolution, even though everything acquired afterwards (their *communauté de biens*) should have technically been split in half. Finally, Richardville may have followed Lernoult's lead in his use of the British legal concept of coverture. Lernoult began their discussion with reference to Richardville's ownership of Tahkamwa, asking him: "What things did Mr. Beaubien take from you, besides your wife?." In addition to equating her value to an object (broach), Richardville responded by adding Tahkamwa to the list of possessions to which he would be entitled under British Common Law, "Mr. Beaubien has taken away my slaves, cattle, Indian corn, wampum, silver works and my children.." If Richardville "owned" Tahkamwa, he also owned everything she claimed to possess, entitling him to every piece of property under discussion, including their children, and undermining the Coutume de Paris and Myaamia norms.

Gendered Threats: The Many Channels of Tahkamwa's Authority

Tahkamwa shared a mother with a brother named Mihšihkinaahkwa (Little Turtle) who would eventually become a war chief among the Myaamia at the end of the eighteenth century. From the eastern seaboard, Mahican contingents had begun moving west in the latter half of the seventeenth century and by 1680, two communities had been established among the Myaamia. Mahican women played pivotal roles in political decision-making, dictating the timing of wars and the taking of captives, and maintaining control of their family's property.[12] Tahkamwa shared a different lineage with her brother Pakaana. As previously noted, their father was likely the half-Myaamia/half-French André Roy, known also as Pakaana. The younger Pakaana would eventually become civil chief of the Myaamia.[13]

In the early eighteenth century, the French had recognized the Myaamia Atchatchakangouen or Crane band as the most powerful. As probable members of this band, Tahkamwa and Pakaana would have possessed an elite pedigree as the great-niece and great-nephew of the *akimaa* Wisekaukautshe, known to the French as (Pied Froid). It is likely that Wisekaukautshe's family gained power and prominence in the vacuum left when several Myaamia leaders were killed at Detroit in 1706 by the Odawa. Eight Myaamia had been on their way to attend a feast at the Wendat fort when they were fired upon by an Odawa contingent that included Le Pesant and Miscouaky, igniting the local war that would come to be known as the Le Pesant affair.

In his report to Governor General Vaudreuil about the incident, Miscouaky had described himself as a friend to Pacamakona, who was among the leaders in the Myaamia party. Miscouaky had given a signal to Pacamakona moments before the Odawa launched their attack, providing him an opportunity to make his escape. As a result of Miscouaky's actions, Pacamakona, who may have been related to Wisekaukautshe, was the only Myaamia leader who survived the killing of his nation's leaders.[14] In fact, it was almost certainly a kinship connection that had saved Pacamakona's life. Miscouaky was brother to Outoutagan (Jean Le Blanc), who was a brother-in-law and later husband to Madame Montour. She had godparented for a child of Pierre Roy and Waapankihkwa. As the probable sister to Wisekaukautshe, Waapankihkwa, in turn, would have also been related to Pacamakona. This series of familial links overrode the larger skirmish between the Odawa and the Myaamia.

Pied Froid had been a pivotal French alliance chief up until his death in 1752 of smallpox. Fifty years later, at the end of the eighteenth century, the location of his village was still designated by his name on maps.[15] Charles Trowbridge collected information from Myaamia in the 1820s (including the leaders Le Gros and Pinšiwa [Jean Baptiste Richardville], son to Tahkamwa and nephew to Pakaana) who spoke of Pied Froid as having been "one of the most distinguished and powerful members" of the Medicine Society. They described his abilities as a shape-shifter who was able to produce "different changes . . . by dint of his professional power." He was reported at times to have "passed the village in the form of a bear, a buffalo, or a buck, and when the young hunters had chased him a mile or two, they would find him in his natural shape."[16]

The elder Pakaana, father of Tahkamwa and likely Pakaana Jr., had worked in much the same manner as his uncle Wisekaukautshe. In the period leading up to the Seven Years' War, when the Myaamia were split between pro-French and pro-British factions, he allied with French imperial agents against British encroachments. After the French gave ground to the British in the upper country, Pakaana remained a pivotal leader in Euro-Indigenous politics, and sought to strengthen his nation's position further by maintaining an alliance with the Spanish. At a 1765 meeting of the Ouabache/Wabash tribes with the Spanish at the post among the Quapaw (Arkansas), both Pakaana and his brother Menoquet were in attendance, where Pakaana was also acknowledged as representing the Kiikaapoi of the lower Wabash.[17]

Tahkamwa and her brothers had come into the world during a time of political volubility for French, British, and Indigenous nations in the Ohio Valley. In 1747, the year Pakaana Jr. and Little Turtle had been born, a Piankashaw warrior known by the French as La Demoiselle, and by the British as Old Briton, broke away from the pro-French Myaamia and established his own village in Pennsylvania.[18] It was also at this time that the family networks linking French and Indigenous peoples between Detroit and the Ouabache/Wabash became most entrenched. Key persons, including Claude Gouin—who was married to Marie-Josèphe Cuillerier, another of Antoine's daughters—and other members of the Cuillerier family, acted as agents for the commandants of several posts. A Sieur Cuillerier (almost certainly Antoine) who operated from a base at Detroit was listed as the agent for trader Charly St. Ange, who was active among the Myaamia. Cuillerier underwrote the costs associated with the trip of a group of Myaamia representatives to Detroit who were accompanying the French commandant of the Myaamia post. Among these expenses, Cuillerier listed a salary for the interpreter Pakaana and presents for the son of Pied Froid, as well as gifts for the nephew of the war leader Le Signe.[19]

Indeed, at mid-century, one extended family conveyed Myaamia diplomatic contingents to and from Detroit, bore the costs of maintaining and transporting them and providing gifts, and acted as interpreters between the Myaamia and the French. In addition to Cuillerier and Gouin (whose son would eventually marry a Myaamia woman), the French relied on Pied Froid; Pakaana/André Roy; Pakaana's brother François Roy; Kaweahatta (Le Porc-Epic/The Porcupine), who was chief of the Myaamia's Kilatika division and father-in-law to Pakaana; Menoquet (Le Temps Clair/Fair Weather), Mascouten leader and brother to Pakaana; and Le Garloup, brother-in-law to François Roy, to counter the effects of other Myaamia leaders, such as Demoiselle, who were more sympathetic to British interests.[20]

From the period just before the Seven Years' War, tensions between the British, French, and Indigenous nations of the upper country increased and would continue to mount in the years leading up to the American Revolution. Simultaneously with this uptick in political unrest, the British had bolstered their colonial authority in accordance with a particular "system of household governance," within which gender roles were unequally structured. The British had applied this system much more stringently than their French predecessors to order their relations with Indigenous nations.[21] In the latter part of the eighteenth century, this more hierarchical ordering of gendered interaction was increasingly utilized as an ideological ballast against perceived threats to British hegemony.[22] The siege mentality that had taken root at the end of the Seven Years' War and with Pontiac's War placed increased importance on the maintenance of the domestic sphere and its powerful patriarch. At the same time, economic growth brought material comforts into this domestic sphere, further bolstering the symbolic importance of the patriarch father and elevating the significance of the home as a material reflection of his authority. Throughout the British empire, a stable and well-appointed home reflected clearly differentiated gender relations between fathers, mothers, and children, with the father-patriarch dominant.

In colonial outposts such as North America, and particularly in the upper country where British order was threatened from multiple directions, manliness became "bound up with defending the domestic," and debates "resounded with talk about the duties of men to families."[23] The threat of violence existed in potential conflict between the authority of the parent and the "liberty of the child-subject."[24] Colonized peoples were seen either as needing protection or as requiring reprimanding in the eyes of their metaphorical British father. Conflict along these "gender frontiers," where Europeans and Indigenous peoples interacted, was directed at "resistance, accommodation or adaptation" to British efforts at keeping their metaphorical house in order.[25]

Tahkamwa's case and relations with the Myaamia in general took a particular shape at this moment of gendered conflict. The larger issue in the proceedings before Lernoult at Detroit became bound up with British efforts to control the Myaamia and determine their right to a pivotal portage. In the years leading up to the trial in 1774 that pitted Tahkamwa and her brother Pakaana against Tahkamwa's husband Richardville and Richardville's business partner Alexis Maisonville, contentious relations with the Myaamia had made British imperial agents wary. Multiple factors, including illegal occupation of Myaamia land by Euro-American settlers, escalated tensions, destabilizing British control. The crucial water route through Myaamionki was increasing in importance for the British which required that they develop a stronger alliance with the Myaamia.

The portage between the Maumee and Ouabache/Wabash Rivers at Kiihkayonki in the Myaamia homeland offered a shortcut to western territories.[26] One of the privileges of membership in the powerful Crane band was control of this portage and a number of others. In 1774, when Pakaana took his sister's case to Lernoult, the Myaamia reminded the British of the portage's rightful ownership and the importance of good relations between the two nations. At this time and in this place, the British were more reliant on the favor of their Indigenous allies than they were loyal to Frenchmen such as Richardville and Maisonville whose own dedication to the British was difficult to gauge. Tahkamwa's competing familial and marital ties reflected and symbolized this larger issue of imperial control.

The Myaamia had abandoned many of their portages in the seventeenth century during Haudenosaunee raids. Upon their return at the turn of the eighteenth century to the forks of the Ouabache/Wabash River, however, members of the Crane band fell back on tradition and claimed the right to live near and control access to the Maumee-Wabash portage. Ignoring this ancient ownership, General Thomas Gage, commander in chief of British forces in North America, had given control of the portage to Alexis Maisonville in 1764 at the urging of Superintendent of Northern Indian Affairs Sir William Johnson. Maisonville had proven himself loyal to the British cause by saving the lives of British officers during Pontiac's War, for which he had been rewarded with control of the portage. Johnson had also seen this as an opportunity to keep a close eye on the activities of the Myaamia. He instructed

Maisonville to "constantly, or by every opportunity make me acquainted with what passes amongst the Nations in that quarter, and let me know their numbers, connections, and politics."[27]

Traffic across the land bridge continued to increase through the eighteenth century, and those who transported materials for others could make a handsome profit. Pakaana and Tahkamwa had each carried goods and charged tolls, reaping the material benefits of their thruway. Maisonville's activities deprived them of this livelihood. Pakaana complained in the petition to Lernoult: "I have been at the farther end of the carrying place with horses expecting to get a load back but was obliged to return without any as the French traders who were there told me the carrying place belonged to Maisonville and that I must not carry."[28] Tahkamwa's husband Richardville had broken with his wife's family and joined Maisonville in his enterprises at the portage. In his discussions with Lernoult, Pakaana challenged this alliance of the two Frenchmen by discrediting Richardville as a husband which provided the means for a larger effort to oust Maisonville and regain a traditional source of Myaamia economic viability.

What it meant to be a good husband in Richardville's case was difficult to assess for Lernoult and the British, something Pakaana perhaps counted on. Because Richardville was a Frenchman but also part of the Myaamia community through marriage, there were multiple standards for manliness in play. Holding him within British gendered parameters, Pakaana described Richardville as "lazy." Tahkamwa's erstwhile husband, complained Pakaana, did "nothing but sit and smoke his pipe." This was acceptable behavior for Myaamia men, but it was imperative that Pakaana refrain from depicting Richardville according to Myaamia measures of manhood. Accordingly, he appealed to British sensibilities by painting Richardville as dissolute and an inadequate husband and father who did not provide for his family and whose household was therefore in a state of disorder.

Where Richardville had failed through neglect and inaction, however, Tahkamwa's natal family had actively sought to ensure her well-being and that of her children. As he discredited Richardville in one breath, Pakaana inserted Tahkamwa's Myaamia family into the role of provider in another, stating that Richardville's failure as a husband had "obliged my sister's relations to contribute toward her and her sons' subsistence." By giving Tahkamwa skins from their hunts, she was able to establish a trading business, and to assure a stable standard of living for her family. Tahkamwa's involvement in trade was traditional among Myaamia women and had not, therefore, been necessitated by Richardville's neglect; but once again, Pakaana posited her behavior in a manner that would play to British concepts of gender roles, which saw women as economically dependent on their husbands. As Richardville had taken no part in his wife's and her family's livelihood, he should therefore not be entitled to any property that came to Tahkamwa as a result. Pakaana drew the circle tightly around his sister's Myaamia family, excluding Richardville on the basis of his inadequacies as a husband and merchant concerned only with his own profits. The only role left for Richardville to play in the eyes of British imperial agents was the rogue Frenchman working against the British and their efforts at alliance with the Myaamia and other Indigenous nations.

In this arena of continued political turmoil, Indigenous women appeared more frequently in European imperial records. Historian Richard White has noted that in the first half of the eighteenth century, agents of diplomacy in imperial records had been mostly limited to Indigenous men and French and British officials. In the second half of the century, however, Indigenous women, as well as traders, missionaries, and settlers, became more visible as political intermediaries.[29] There are many possible reasons for this growing agency of women. Like those of other upper country Indigenous nations, Myaamia women held authority through their control of the extended domestic sphere, including the planting and harvesting of crops, the butchering and preparation of meat, and the making of clothes.[30]

The constant warfare that came with political instability placed greater importance on women's work in cultivating the necessary surplus foodstuffs to feed war parties, traders and other transient populations.[31] Escalating warfare also skewed gender ratios.[32] The rising prominence of Myaamia women in European records occurred at the same time leading Myaamia men faced immense challenges. Pied Froid's ability to shape-shift into various animal forms eventually led to his death at the hands of fellow Medicine Society members jealous of his power, according to testimony recorded by Trowbridge over fifty years later. Pied Froid's son enacted revenge by destroying all those who had killed his father, resulting in the deaths of many Myaamia power brokers.[33] Richard White postulates that this series of events roughly parallels the deaths that resulted from the power struggle between Demoiselle and Pied Froid in the late 1740s and early 1750s and the demise of both Pied Froid and his son from smallpox in 1752.[34] Myaamia women, who filled the power vacuum left by the loss of these many men, found themselves in possession of greater authority. The increasing frequency of their appearance in the letters, journals, and testimonials of their kinsmen and British imperial agents is evidence of their growing agency and of

British apprehension of their power which exceeded the boundaries of propriety expected of British women.

This level of frustration is certainly evident in the journal of British lieutenant governor Henry Hamilton, who in 1778 was making a fateful journey to Myaamia territory to wrest back control of Fort Vincennes from rebellious local French traders. Hamilton depicted Myaamia women as willful and acting independently of Myaamia men. In describing the range of insults that could be expressed among the Myaamia, he ascribed greater fervor to women, due to two behaviors deemed inappropriate: drunkenness and physical violence; "to spit in a man's face is the penultimate indignity, to bite off his nose the ultimatum, but this usually is done when liquor has possession of them and happens more commonly among the soft sex than among the men."[35] Pakaana made reference to such conduct when he admitted to Lernoult that a cow belonging to Maisonville had been killed by the Myaamia. Pakaana claimed no responsibility, explaining "it was our squahs who did it." Maisonville had retaliated by stripping "himself naked to fight with them."[36]

By ascribing willfulness and violence to the women, Pakaana and Hamilton expressed the volatile and unpredictable nature of Myaamia-British relations. At times, Myaamia women seemed to threaten the normal course of diplomacy. Henry Hamilton expressed his frustration with a woman who refused to exchange a French for a British peace medal he offered. Noting that her husband, a Myaamia leader, had already chosen to wear a British medal, Hamilton deemed it appropriate that the wife would do the same. Unlike her husband, however, the woman chose instead to wear both medals and to keep the jewelry Hamilton had presented as an impetus to make her change her mind.[37] Other examples of acts of women's defiance also appear in Pakaana's 1774 petition to Lernoult. When asked to explain his appearance at the Myaamia portage during the night, Alexis Maisonville's brother François offered an excuse that if not true, was certainly one he felt would be acceptable, namely, that "a squah that his brother had formerly kept and lately turned away intended seizing his packs at the carrying place."[38] François explained an Indigenous woman's actions as stemming from her desire for revenge against a Euro-American man who has rejected her, rather than the commercial activities in which she took part.

Between the lines of male-authored accounts, such as the legal case at Detroit and Henry Hamilton's journal of his time among the Myaamia, we can glimpse these women-centered narratives. Myaamia and other Indigenous women also created lines of communication that connected them. Hamilton alluded to such an avenue when he noted the arrival of a wampum belt sent by Great Lakes women and addressed to the women of the rivers, including the Myaamia. The belt, which urged them to "work hard with their hoes, to raise corn for the warriors who should take up the axe for their father the King of England," was doubly gendered.[39] It was women who routinely constructed the wampum belts containing messages that connected the farthest eastern regions to the upper country and beyond. In this specific instance, women had not only fashioned the belt, they had composed a message meant only for other women.

At the time of Tahkamwa's birth, at least two women leaders were in positions of political control, including the mother of the *akimaa* Le Gris, who ran his chiefly affairs until he reached his age of majority. Years later, Tahkamwa would herself act in a similar capacity as regent to her son Pinšiwa (Jean Baptiste Richardville) until he was old enough to become an *akimaa*. An elite woman's authority could be augmented in the increasingly contentious political climate of the eighteenth-century upper country by additional factors, including personality and unique circumstances within her family. In Tahkamwa's case, if she had in fact had a Mahican mother, she would have been raised in a matrilineal tradition, which would have influenced Tahkamwa's expectations about control of her home and surrounding territory. At his meeting with Lernoult, Pakaana may have made reference to this when he described Tahkamwa's possessions as belonging to her and not her husband because they had been inherited from her mother. Pakaana's statement suggests that Tahkamwa's mother, having amassed valuables in her own right, had the right to pass these to her daughter, and that Tahkamwa had come into her marriage to Richardville with her own belongings. This ran counter to Richardville's claim that she had entered their marriage having no worth.

As a Myaamia *akimaahkwia* or woman civil chief, Tahkamwa would have been raised to be a role model, to exhibit initiative and leadership qualities, and to act as an effective political and cultural broker.[40] Her position would have been inherited through her father Pakaana, who was an *akimaa*.[41] These women exercised an enhanced gendered authority in their supervision of women's work. They oversaw the preparation of feasts, and collected the skins, moccasins, sinews, and other materials made by other women, presenting them to departing war parties. They could prevent warriors from engaging in hostilities by appealing as mothers and relatives to the war chief on behalf of the warriors.[42] They also watched over the affairs of their village, and relayed this information to male leaders. As active participants in the Medicine Society, Myaamia women leaders were able to undertake human-animal transformation and took part in the induction of new members.[43]

There are numerous references in the eighteenth century to this type of woman's leadership. At a meeting held a year before the Detroit conference with Lernoult, Pakaana and the *akimaa* Le Gris operated from a position of peaceful, albeit guarded expectations with the British, partly under the authority of a woman they described as the "Queen of the Village," who they said had "given us some branches of wampum, thanking us that we have taken pity on the women and children."[44] This is a reference to the woman village or civil chief who was responsible for protecting the interests of women and children. It is also likely that the "Queen" to whom they referred was Tahkamwa. This position brought with it an authority above reproach and question, but it was in turn enhanced by the personality of the woman who held it. One Myaamia informant reported of women chiefs that "no attempt was made to prevent the execution of their designs" and they exercised their authority through "powers of persuasion."[45]

The source of the enhanced authority and prestige exhibited by Myaamia women leaders in the latter half of the eighteenth century thus came about through an intersection of traditional avenues of authority for women, and the unique demands of the highly unstable political and economic world of the upper country. Born into this set of circumstances, Tahkamwa modeled the behavior of other Myaamia women leaders, while taking advantage of especially favorable individual and family circumstances. Although the Myaamia were patrilineal, in that individuals traced their lineage through their father's line, the position of *akimaa* or leader was passed through the *akimaa*'s sister. Thus, when the *akimaa* either died or deemed it appropriate to allow a successor to his position, his nephew, the son of his sister, could expect to inherit the office. When there were more than one of these nephews, it became incumbent upon the sister of the *akimaa* holding office to choose among her sons. When she had made this choice, she arranged for a public display of this son's prowess and a demonstration of his fitness for the position.[46] Suitability for this role thus rested on the ability of a sister to state the case of her son. Tahkamwa witnessed and perhaps played some part in this ritual when her brother Pakaana became *akimaa* under dramatic circumstances connected to the visit of Thomas Morris. She would play a direct role in her own son's elevation to *akimaa* years later.

As Myaamia leaders, Pakaana and his family were central to an Anglo presence in the upper country. To the British, however, Tahkamwa's influence had grown to dangerous proportions because she held authority through her kinship ties to men viewed by the British as power brokers among the Myaamia, and to Frenchmen, such as Beaubien, viewed as threats to British hegemony. Writing at the time of the Detroit conference with Lernoult, Lieutenant Jehu Hay, British Indian agent at Detroit, described the pivotal role played by Tahkamwa in the precarious political situation in the west:

> While I was at the River Miami, I learned that the messages sent by Sir William last year which were taken by the Huron to the Miami, have been lying there ever since, and are now in the possession of one Beaubien, the Indians I suppose have given them to him to keep for them, or perhaps worse. He is a man whom the rest of the French Traders say is dangerous there. He has taken the Wife of one Richarville from him, and Richarville complained against him at Detroit. . . . As the Woman is of the Pacanne Family of that Nation, she is capable of doing a good deal of mischief, and the rest of the French Traders are under some apprehension she will, through the instigation of this Beaubien.[47]

This image of a willful and powerful Tahkamwa capable of crippling or destroying the entire British imperial project operated concurrently with the image of Tahkamwa as helpless victim of violence, evoked by her brother Pakaana and second husband Beaubien, and as valueless possession, put forward by Richardville. In the case before Lernoult, Beaubien accused Richardville of having "abused the squah so much . . . she could no longer live with him and she left him for that reason." Richardville "had threatened to kill her so often," Pakaana "had told him to do so." Richardville's domestic abuse was ascribed to his jealousy of Beaubien and Tahkamwa's relationship, compelling Beaubien to feel himself "under an obligation to provide for her" and take her in "with the consent of her brother Pacanne and their family." The varying levels of agency and violence inherent in these depictions of Tahkamwa had direct bearing on how larger issues of imperial control were presented and interpreted.

The trope of victim was also utilized by Pakaana and members of his contingent during the meeting with Lernoult to describe their perceived status as disinherited within the political and economic family headed by their British father. Pakaana reproved his British father—as he did Richardville for his treatment of Tahkamwa—for shirking his parental responsibilities and leaving his children destitute. At a meeting between the Myaamia and the Wendat, at which the Wendat acted as ambassadors for the British, the Myaamia expressed their anger over the lack of British support. They addressed the Wendat as elder brethren—an acknowledgment of that nation's longer relationship with the British—while at the same time pointing out their own unenviable position within the same political family network. "Now you are come to tell us that we are all as one people, wherefore we receive Governor Johnson's belt, with both our hands, notwithstanding that we are worthy of compassion, having ever since the English are in possession of the country, been looked upon as Bastards."[48]

A year later, at a meeting between the Myaamia and the Wendat, Pakaana and fellow ambassadors abandoned the position of victim, adopting a more threatening posture. Wendat leader Sasteresti and his entourage traveled from Detroit to visit Mascouten, Kiikaapoi, Ouiatenon, and Myaamia communities at two locations on the Maumee and Ouabache/Wabash Rivers to smooth relations with the British. A small group of Wendat addressed representatives of these nations as brothers, as they had done on previous occasions. They first presented wampum belts from William Johnson, metaphoric father to the Haudenosaunee, Wendat, and Lenni Lenape, that encouraged the Wabash nations to maintain peace. At their next stop, the Wendat delegation was kept waiting three days by the Myaamia who refused to address Johnson's request. When the entourage continued on to the Ouiatenon, Kiikaapoi, and Mascouten villages, members were made to wait fifteen days without getting an answer.

When the Wendat spoke to their Ouiatenon hosts about the bad treatment, they were told that the Meskwaki and Iowa had advised the Ouiatenon not to listen to their British father or to the Wendat. Although the contingents met in council, lighting and smoking the calumet, one Wabash nation leader and four warriors spat out the smoke. The Wendat reproached them for their disrespectful behavior, for listening to bad counsel, and for ignoring the Wendat who had come "with good messages to them from our Father." In response, one of the elder leaders, likely Myaamia *akimaa* Pakaana, and several young warriors threw off their breech cloths and, as the Wendat later explained to Lernoult, "exposing their privy parts desired us to look and see if they were men." The Myaamia then seized the British flags carried by the Wendat and throwing them in a heap, threatened to burn them, demanding to know why the Wendat had chosen to display them rather than white flags.[49] Confused and alarmed, the Wendat interpreted this behavior as directed not at them, but at William Johnson, the Haudenosaunee, and the Lenni Lenape.

On September 11, 1774, Sastaresti and twenty-six Wendat leaders held a council in Detroit with Captain Lernoult to report on these meetings with the Myaamia. They explained that because they felt the injury more acutely when it was directed at

Johnson and the other allied nations, they answered Pakaana's physical affront with a verbal threat: "Being much nettled at their behaviour we reproached them, saying, you shew your bravour as we are but three, but notwithstanding your number, we dare also shew our nakedness as well as you and convince you that we are men too." In this contest of masculinity, the Myaamia had sought a position of dominance as well as to relegate the Wendat, who operated from within an Anglo-Indigenous metaphorical family, to a submissive role.

The Wendat had visited the Myaamia and Ouiatenon expecting to have their more foundational position of authority in the British Covenant Chain acknowledged. By exposing themselves, the Wabash groups reminded the Wendat, British, and Haudenosaunee that their power and authority as men trumped a womanly submission demanded of them as younger brothers. The response of the Wendat exposed their fear of their emasculation and loss of authority in the hierarchical relationship that linked them to the Haudenosaunee and the British. The masculine prerogative of the Wabash nations was a serious threat that could disrupt this metaphorical family, and with it, British-Indigenous relations in the Ohio Valley.

Sastaresti reported that the Wabash nations were holding back twenty-four belts recommending peace, some of which had been delivered a full year prior to the latest tense conference. In 1774, the series of belts had neither been answered nor circulated further, which made the way too dangerous for Seneca representatives and British officials from Detroit to travel to the Illinois Country in an effort to contain the increasingly vicious skirmishes between the Shawnee and Virginia settlers. The Wabash nations were sitting on messages that had the potential to assist or undermine British efforts at keeping large-scale war from breaking out in the upper country. Added to the threat posed by colonists who were meeting in Philadelphia in an official body as the Continental Congress at the same time, British imperial agents became increasingly alarmed. The stalled belts and their messages remained at the Wabash, controlled by Tahkamwa—sister to Pakaana who had openly scorned the Wendat—and Tahkamwa's second husband, the Frenchman Beaubien.

It was one week after the Wendat conference with Lernoult over their bad treatment at the hands of the Myaamia that Pakaana, his sister's first and second husbands, and other principal men of the Myaamia had the meeting with Lernoult at Detroit over control of the Myaamia portage and Tahkamwa's marital status. They did not mention the recent "contest of masculinity" in which they had engaged with the Wendat, nor did they admit that they were holding wampum belts. Instead, perhaps knowing they were a threat to their British father's authority and operating from a dominant position attained at the expense of the Wendat, they argued over control of the pivotal and lucrative portage in Myaamia territory. Like Jehu Hay, who had used Tahkamwa and her kinship status to communicate the dangers to British hegemony in the upper country, Pakaana presented his sister's marital state as a point of contention upon which British-Myaamia diplomatic relations uneasily rested. Pakaana argued for his sister's right to her extensive goods and property, despite her first husband's efforts to deny her. Arguments and threats exchanged by the first and second husbands over this situation threatened the peace of the entire Myaamia village. Pakaana backed Beaubien's authority by acknowledging his relationship with Tahkamwa. Coming on the heels of Jehu Hay's news of the languishing wampum messages controlled by Tahkamwa and Beaubien, the Myaamia contingent was in a powerful position.

Rather than taking an openly threatening posture, as they had done by exposing themselves to the Wendat the year before, they adopted another tactic, meant to challenge their British father's metaphorical transgendered authority. The Myaamia accused the British of failing to act as father-provider, just as they had accused Richardville of having shirked his duties as husband and father. Pakaana reproved Lernoult: "It is very true our women and children are naked and it's you that make them so; they formerly gained wherewith to cover themselves by carrying goods at the carrying place. Have charity, have consideration for your children; it is now ten years the Frenchman holds the carrying place, it is enough. I demand he shall pay an annual rent for the time he has had the carrying place; I speak not for myself, it is for the benefit of the women and children in general."[50] Using women and children to represent economic need was a common trope in speeches between Indigenous nations and the British. Pakaana made use of this metaphor to shame the British father into performing his duties, a position of dominance he was able to attain because Tahkamwa held the belts that would otherwise be urging peace among the nations of the upper country. Pakaana's speech was full of metaphorical references to his childlike submission to the British father. But this language was a thin veneer over a more threatening posture adopted by this powerful Myaamia leader, who was revered and referred to as grandfather by other Myaamia allied nations.[51]

Pakaana's kinsman Hibou (Owl) echoed Pakaana's insistence that the British honor their responsibilities as father-provider and evoked an overarching order of paternal authority: "You are our father but he that is above is your father; he is ours also and wills that we should be all equal and that we should subsist on the land he gave us. God made all and is master of all and you are master of us and have it in your power to clothe us." The Myaamia had assumed the role of fatherless/ bastard victim at some points, while at others denouncing it as an emasculated state they would not tolerate. Owl combined these disparate positions in one principal motif as the ideal by which the British should operate in their relations with the Myaamia: "Those of your children you now see here are poor and naked; we hope your breasts are not gone dry and that you will give us a little of your milk."[52] The Myaamia were instructing Lernoult to act as both mother and father by exhibiting nurturing qualities while at the same time using a masculinized political, legal, and if necessary, military authority to protect Myaamia interests. This was yet another example of how multiple expectations of gendered behavior operated simultaneously.

Owl repeated the message that had been delivered to the Wendat a year before when the first series of wampum belts had been offered to the Myaamia: "All of us who are now here present said when we lost our French father—ah! It is hard, we are now bastards and we have looked upon ourselves as such even till now." This was the second time in a year the Myaamia had referred to themselves as parentless in relation to the British. In restating it, the Owl repudiated the system of submission and dominance inherent in the kin-based language of elder and younger brothers and harkened back to another more favorable Euro-imperial model. The request by Owl to "give us a little milk" communicated a desire to restore metaphoric kinship relations, as well as a request for economic assistance. Owl extended this metaphor further, however, by questioning the ability of the British to provide resources. By mentioning breasts explicitly, rather than only referring to milk, the Myaamia could also have been expressing their perception of the political and military submissiveness of the British by calling them women. This message, coming on the heels of dramatic displays by Myaamia and Mascouten leaders of their manliness, communicated the doubts of upper country nations that the British could maintain their imperial hegemony and provide for the needs of Indigenous allies.

In late eighteenth-century Britain and in the British colonies, breasts were "going public" as more elite women were breastfeeding their own babies instead of employing wet nurses. As historian Kathleen Wilson explains, images of breasts abounded in popular publications, and a particular ideal shape and size of breasts became synonymous with the respectability of certain classes of women and their ability to give good milk.[53] The Reference to the British father's dry breasts by Owl may have held a similar meaning for Lernoult, emphasizing the inadequacies and ultimate failure of the British as father-provider. The Onontio constructed early in the eighteenth century by Great Lakes Indigenous diplomats had combined multiple gendered attributes in a manner that emphasized strength and nurturance. The Father called out by the Myaamia several decades later, however, with his breasts flat and dry, represented the disintegration of this gendered hybridity and the impending failure of British-Myaamia relations.

The British could neither act as mother nor father. In attempting to quell open warfare, British officials sought to contain Indigenous nations by urging them to be quiet, or to not be men. Hunting and making war, activities of men of the nations of the upper country, were threats to British control in 1774. The British struggled to keep these men from making war with Virginian colonists hungry for Indigenous land, and areas coveted by the Virginians were most often the hunting territories of particular Indigenous nations. Correspondence of British imperial agents at this time is rife with anxious allusions to the risk posed by these manly pursuits. But not all forms of masculinity constituted threats. Wendat ambassadors and negotiators displayed their manliness in the dominant role of elder brother to the Wabash nations' younger brother within the framework of the British-Indigenous Covenant Chain.

Lernoult responded to both the complexities of Tahkamwa's status and behavior and that of the Myaamia by awarding her and her family most of what they demanded. He accepted Pakaana's rendition of his sister's affairs and activities over that of her first husband, and ruled that the property in question belonged to Tahkamwa. He further decreed that the property in question did not belong to Beaubien either, since Tahkamwa had only asked Beaubien to retrieve them from Richardville on her behalf. Lernoult's decision reflects larger critical issues he was facing in the upper country. He was attempting to prevent Indigenous nations at Detroit from allying with the Shawnee in their war against the Virginians and to stop French traders (including Detroit-based Pierre Drouillard, who we will meet in the afterword) from providing arms to the Shawnee and inciting other nations against white settlers squatting on Indigenous land.[54]

With his decision on Tahkamwa's case, Lernoult ensured the continuing legitimacy and authority of the Myaamia Crane band by preventing the source of their revenue from falling into the hands of Frenchmen (Richardville and Beaubien) who presented unknown threats to British hegemony in the upper country. Finally, Lernoult reinscribed the traditional Myaamia privilege of Pakaana and Tahkamwa to carry at the portage and charge tolls. He did not dispense entirely, however, with maintaining some measure of British control at the pivotal location. He decreed that Alexis Maisonville—who had saved British lives during Pontiac's War and provided William Johnson with information on Myaamia activities—would still be allowed to maintain the lands around the portage by keeping roads clear and open. Four years later, Pakaana would declare that the "carrying place of the Miamis was in good order." At that point, he, François Maisonville, and Myaamia leaders Hibou/Owl and Le Gros Loup would be working together when they met with Detroit commandant Henry Hamilton, who was on his way to Vincennes to regain control of the fort taken by anti-British colonists.[55]

Pakaana had put forward a multilayered description of his sister's activities and set of expectations for her behavior. Tahkamwa was represented as the victim of abuse and property of one man who drove her to seek protection from another. But she also carried goods across a Myaamia portage, collected tolls, conducted a lucrative business in skins and rum, and held considerable property in her own right. Myaamia women such as Tahkamwa dictated protocol and procedure in the negotiations of head chiefs, communicated with other Indigenous women across vast distances, and stole and destroyed property and livestock. Myaamia custom for women allowed for many of these activities, but it was Tahkamwa's status as an *akimaahkwia* and member of the powerful Crane band whose cooperation was essential to the British that placed an exceptional level of importance on her position. It is unlikely that her case would have been heard by Lernoult had she not constituted a threat to British or Myaamia political and economic control. Otherwise, her concerns would have been addressed locally and within her "blood" family, rather than through the larger metaphorical family represented by Lernoult.

It was, in fact, the enhanced agency of Tahkamwa and other Myaamia women at this pivotal moment that had contributed to the men's perception that their masculinity was under threat. When Alexis Maisonville, who was competing with Tahkamwa for control of one of the most lucrative portages in the upper country, stripped himself naked to fight Myaamia women, he enacted his rage on them. Like Pakaana, he exposed himself in order to reestablish an economic privilege he felt he was owed. The stories of other Indigenous women, such as François Maisonville's companion who attempted to flee with her possessions, appear only in passing in the transcript of the proceedings of Tahkamwa's case, and are not presented as reminders to the British of their larger political and economic parental responsibilities. Tahkamwa would continue to exert considerable influence almost twenty years after her case was heard at Detroit.

By the 1780s, the Myaamia portage controlled by Tahkamwa and Pakaana became "the most important confluence . . . in the Old Northwest."[56] In 1780, Augustin
de La Balme, a French officer working on behalf of the American government
who was attempting to gain Myaamia support for an attack on Detroit, seized a
large warehouse of trade goods held by Tahkamwa's brother Mihšihkinaahkwa
(Little Turtle) and her second husband, Charles Beaubien, at the portage. His
victory was short-lived, however, when Pakaana, Mihšihkinaahkwa, and Myaamia
warriors killed La Balme and defeated his forces, further enhancing the power of
Tahkamwa's family.[57] Unlike Angelique Cuillerier, whose husband James Sterling
had sought in 1765 to limit her mobility by preventing her from "running after the
Indians," Tahkamwa would be described in 1790 as "gone into the Indian Country
(*dans les Terres* as the French term it)" to her trading place, which was roughly
eighty-five miles from Kiihkayonki.[58] Her former husband, Antoine Joseph Drouet
de Richardville, had moved to Trois Rivières near Montreal. She resided with her
son Pinšiwa (Jean Baptiste Richardville) when she was not at her camp, and spoke
on his behalf in council while he presided at Kiihkayonki in the absence of his uncle
Pakaana, who was away in the Illinois Country.[59] In the end, Antoine Richardville
had not managed to control three "items" he purported to own: his son, Tahkamwa,
and the Myaamia portage.

The remarkable quality of Tahkamwa's situation lay in her personal qualities of
confidence and business acumen, opportunities afforded by access to the prestige,
authority, and wealth of her family, and to contingencies of constantly shifting
relations between the British and the Myaamia. Tahkamwa the *akimaahkwia*
was both exceptional and typical, as the details of her life demonstrate. If her
voice cannot be directly heard through historic records, her treatment by men
and their depictions of her activities bring us closer to a more nuanced portrait.
Euro-American and Indigenous men used multiple interpretations of Tahkamwa to
press claims and determine policy. Tahkamwa's Myaamia family had asked Captain
Lernoult to determine the rights of a sister. They also used her case to seek British
approbation of their tenuous position of dominance. As historian Toby Ditz points
out, "women come between men" and access to them "creates solidarities and
hierarchies among men."[60] Indigenous nations were cognizant of British notions
of the inferior status of women in relation to men, and at times used this image of
weakness and denigration to facilitate communication with British power brokers.
The feminine was represented in a multitude of ways, and its figurative use by these
groups reflected different motivations and concerns around the maintenance of

peace, order, and good relations. In such cases, the approval of the British would act as a hedge against the encroachments of "illegitimate" claims, both within and outside the family.

The plight of Tahkamwa as the victim of abuse at the hands of her husband was used by the Myaamia to represent the larger state of their own poor treatment by the British. It was no more respectful for Richardville to mistreat and threaten his wife than it was for the British to exploit the Myaamia in a similarly disrespectful manner. Pakaana demanded that he and his kinsmen be treated as men, even when that treatment combined attributes of a metaphoric quality of diplomatic dependence ascribed by both the Myaamia and the British to women and children. He also demanded recognition of the Myaamia in making politically- and economically-motivated decisions that were of equal importance to those of the British in the maintenance of peace and order in the upper country.

The agency and mobility of the French-Indigenous family networks, including the French-Myaamia family of Pakaana and Tahkamwa, had persistently led British imperial agents to perceive them as a threat. In 1767, George Trumbull, the commander of Detroit, had written his superiors about the practice of French families selling their houses inside the fort to British newcomers. He reasoned that containing the French within the walls of the fort would prove beneficial in two ways: keeping them close would provide the British with a good source of intelligence about Indigenous peoples , and if fire broke out in the fort, it was preferable to lose French rather than British lives.[61] In 1770, Detroit commandant James Stevenson shared his concerns with William Johnson about local French families who he described as having "slip'd away to the Miamis under a pretence to trade," but who were "prevailing on the Indians to grant them lands [since] they propose to make a settlement there." Stevenson ordered them to quit their movements west because of his fear that "our back settlements will feel the effects of it whenever we have a war with France."[62] In 1778, Henry DuVernet, an officer accompanying Henry Hamilton on his trip from Detroit to Vincennes, commented on the French living among the Myaamia, describing them as "a worthless set, deserters from Canada or Detroit" whose settlement consisted "of a few dirty huts."[63] At this moment of mounting tension between colonists and Indigenous nations in the upper country, Stevenson viewed the traditional movement of the families to and from Myaamionki as a threat, rather than a boon to British interests.

By 1774, continued overlapping conversations had been taking place between officials representing the British and Indigenous nations. Such conversations had been a regular and long-standing occurrence between these groups. But heightened states of anxiety, fear, anger, and sometimes resignation formed an undercurrent to the 1774 discussions, and hinted at the potential breakdown of a tenuously held status quo. Toward the end of the eighteenth century, both the British and Indigenous agents shared a notion of gender and kinship as inseparable and hierarchical constructs. Used in discussions and negotiations, these two concepts continued to function in the representation of shifting power relations in the period before open revolt by American colonists, when the British imperial household became completely disordered.

In 1774, Indigenous and British administrators anxiously sought to control each other through words and actions that combined explicit and implicit references to sexuality and gender. Indigenous nations seized this critical moment to renegotiate their relationships to each other and to the British using metaphors that gained new meanings in this constantly evolving context. These constructs or tropes had their own history and been used before in discussions and negotiations between Indigenous, French, and British agents. But as easily as they could function more generally, they could also be tailored to fit particular situations and act as rhetorical shortcuts promoting mutual intelligibility and cutting across gendered binaries for the parties in discussion. Looking at use of these metaphors offers us a chance to see how critical junctures in British and Indigenous relations are tied to specific notions of intimate relations between individuals or communities. Old roles and attitudes were becoming increasingly inadequate and even dangerous in addressing new challenges presented. In this rapidly changing political milieu, French-Indigenous families would continue to act to assure their survival in a region stretching west from Detroit to the Mississippi, an arena that would continue to be hotly disputed well into the nineteenth century.

Afterword

I n 1793, several Quakers traveling west from Pennsylvania stopped in Detroit. Their intended destination was Sandusky, where the group was to participate in a grand council with Great Lakes and Ohio Valley Indigenous nations and United States commissioners. A Christian sect that abjured violence, one of their purposes was to redirect rising tribal resentment over illegal occupation of Indigenous lands into a resignation to the inevitability of settler presence. But Detroit offered its own diversions, and the men were sufficiently intrigued to devote several pages in their journals to its description.

The Quakers noted the "different tribes of various appearances and languages" gathering at and moving through Detroit, a "thoroughfare of all northern Indians."[1] Hundreds of Indigenous diplomats arrived from as far north as Michilimackinac on their way to the general council, and messages came from as far south as the Cherokee homelands. Also assembling at Detroit were British and American imperial agents who were busily planning meetings with tribal representatives and vying with each other for Indigenous support. Although pro-British sentiments were stronger, the Quakers were tolerated based on their professed commitment to remain outside Euro-American politics. Ultimately, the British-Indigenous council

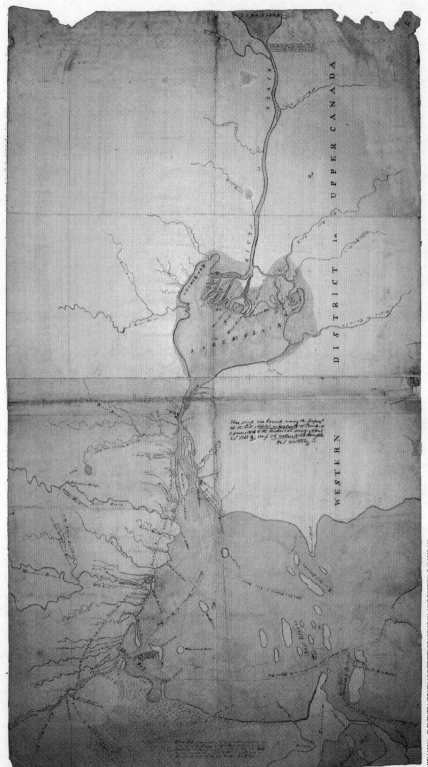

would meet at the forks of the Maumee River, but the American-planned council did not take place as planned and the Quakers would never arrive at Sandusky.[2]

While they were at Detroit, however, the Christian visitors kept themselves busy. Tribal leaders expressed outrage over the broken promises of governmental officials who had promised the Ohio River as a permanent border between settler and Indigenous territories. The Quakers worked hard to quell this anger by preaching the benefits of acquiescence as a divinely inspired commitment to peace. They wrote with thinly veiled condescension about the manners and customs of local residents, reserving critical scrutiny for the interpreters of Indigenous languages upon whom the Quakers were dependent. The burial of one man in particular, Isadore Chesne, was sufficiently noteworthy to have been recorded in more than one Quaker journal.

Chesne was described as "an old Indian interpreter, supposed to have shortened his days by the immoderate use of strong drink."[3] They commented with disapproval on the "religious parade" of his funeral, led by bare-headed ecclesiastics "growling a sentence or two of Latin over and over" and followed by a mass at the "Roman chapel" where there was "a good deal of form and ceremony, in their way." Distinguishing the Roman Catholic "Gentile superstition" of Chesne's funeral from their own "Christian simplicity," the Quakers were frustrated at the cultural impasse presented by these differences.[4] They noted that they "sometimes find great difficulty in conversing with the Indians, in such manner as we wish, on account of our interpreter's sentiments and prospects differing in some respects so widely from ours."[5]

Known also as Shetoon-Hayanemadae, Isadore was French, Wendat, and an adopted Ojibwe. He had married three times, to a Pekowi-Shawnee woman, a Kishpoko-Shawnee woman, and an Odawa-French mixed-blood woman, by whom he had several children. He had taken part in major military conflicts in the Ohio Valley, fighting in the Seven Years' War, and with Shawnee leaders Blue Jacket and Cornstalk in 1774 as they defended Shawnee lands against encroaching white settlers.[6] He had also participated in an attack on Boonesborough in 1778, with, among others, Tahkamwa's second husband, Charles Beaubien—a campaign that had led to the capture of settler Daniel Boone. He had served as interpreter between the British and Indigenous nations during Pontiac's War, and in the decades following, he had spoken on behalf of Odawa, Ojibwe, Wendat, Mascouten, and

OPPOSITE: Map of the western end of Lake Erie, Lake St. Clair, and the St. Clair River, 1813

Lenni Lenape at treaty negotiations. In 1780, the British had labeled him a dangerous man, demonstrating that like many other members of the French-Indigenous networks, the nature of his allegiance was often in question.[7] Indeed, only one year after his death, as British and American imperial agents grappled to control the peoples and resources of the upper country, members of the networks made clear their independence from Euro-American political structures. They declared that although the British claimed them and their land, they had "nothing to do with the English" and considered themselves a separate people."[8]

A hundred and fifty years after the Quakers' visit to Detroit, historian Milo Quaife would also address the multinational status of the region's French-Indigenous family networks. In April 1945, he penned a peremptory letter to the superintendent of the Oregon Historical Society addressing an article that had appeared in the *Oregon Historical Quarterly*. The piece in question, a reconstruction of the roster of the Lewis and Clark expedition, seemed innocuous enough. Among the forty-seven persons listed, however, Quaife quibbled with the description of one in particular—George Drouillard. The article's author had devoted more space to Drouillard than he had to expedition co-leader Meriwether Lewis:

> the interpreter and hunter. Half Indian, (mother a Shawnee) and half French. Son of Pierre Drouillard of Kentucky who was a friend of George Rogers Clark whom he served as interpreter. George was tall, straight, black hair, brown eyes, reserved, stoic. Could write and was adept at Indian sign language. An excellent runner and extremely valuable man to the expedition. Was killed in 1810 by the Blackfeet while a member of Manuel Lisa's party. He was exempted from guard duty while with Lewis and Clark.[9]

Secretary-editor of the Burton Historical Collection at the Detroit Public Library, Quaife had published extensively on the history of the fur trade and had also produced his own edited collection of journals from the expedition. He contested the article's depiction of George's father, Pierre Drouillard, as hailing from Kentucky and having a friendship with George Rogers Clark (brother to William Clark of the Lewis and Clark expedition). Quaife doubted the friendship and refuted the notion of a Kentucky home, describing Pierre as "very much a Detroiter" and a subordinate official of the British-Indian administration who was still being damned in the mid-twentieth century by "Kentucky orators and patriots."[10] Quaife allowed for hackneyed stereotypes attributing reserve and stoicism to George Drouillard to go unchallenged, but he would not allow the British sympathies of George's father and connection to Detroit to go unrecognized.

The crafting of George Drouillard's persona and concurrent reinvention of his French and Shawnee cultures had begun in the course of the two-year Lewis and Clark expedition. Before their return to St. Louis in September 1806, Meriwether Lewis and William Clark carefully crafted a letter dramatizing their success in making a transcontinental crossing. First published in Kentucky newspapers and then across the United States, the letter elevated members of the expedition to mythic status by stressing their admirable moral characteristics and exceptional physical skills in facing extraordinary challenges.[11] A year after the return of the expedition, in a letter to the secretary of war, Meriwether Lewis described Drouillard as "a man of merit" who had been particularly useful for his knowledge of Indian sign language and his "uncommon skill" as a hunter and woodsman. Drouillard had conducted himself with "ardor, good faith, and honor."[12] Historian Reuben Thwaites included Lewis's letter in the first edited collection of journals and correspondence relating to the expedition, timed to coincide with its centenary in 1904.

Depicting Drouillard as hero, Lewis set him apart as exceptional in comparison to other French-Indigenous members of the expedition and to Shoshone guide and interpreter Sacagawea, while Reuben Thwaites cast the Lewis and Clark expedition as American national legend.[13] But neither Lewis nor Thwaites elaborated on Drouillard's French-Shawnee lineage. When M. O. Skarsten published his biography of Drouillard in 1964, he similarly made no mention of Drouillard's Frenchness and addressed his Shawnee heritage only to offer it as the reason for Drouillard's natural abilities in the woods. To Skarsten, George Drouillard the hunter-guide was incongruent with the George Drouillard who in 1809 had penned a tender letter to his half-sister in Detroit. In order to marry the two personas, Skarsten concluding that Drouillard had had the benefit of schooling, and even if he had dictated and not actually written the letter in question, "the solicitude revealed by the letter suggests that its author was, if not a man of refinement, then at least one blessed with some knowledge of the social amenities."[14] What made the story poignant for Skarsten was that Drouillard had promised his half-sister he would visit her in Detroit after his return from a three-year expedition to the Upper Missouri. He never made the trip because he was killed in the course of that expedition. Like Meriwether Lewis, Reuben Thwaites, and Milo Quaife, Skarsten portrayed Drouillard as exceptional in his time and place and straddling social classes, rather than French-Shawnee worlds or British-American national identities.

Scholars have recently begun to offer more nuanced discussions of George Drouillard's multi-layered world. Robert Englebert proposes that French-Shawnee kin groups very likely worked to establish their own distinct position within Shawnee society in Upper Louisiana, where George Drouillard lived before and after his stint with Lewis and Clark.[15] Further clues to George Drouillard's multifaceted cultural identity lie in the address to which the letter to his sister had been sent: Sandwich Detroit. This geographical designation puts Drouillard's sister in both British Canada and the United States during the first decade of the nineteenth century, demonstrating the fluidity of national boundaries. The Drouillard family lived on either side of the Detroit River and of a vaguely defined international border between the Territory of Michigan and Upper Canada. Upper Louisiana (encompassing today's cities of St. Louis and Cape Girardeau, Missouri) had similarly diverse borders shaped by British, Spanish, and Indigenous polities that included Chickasaw, Choctaw, Cherokee, Osage, Lenni Lenape, Quapaw, Shawnee, Myaamia, Wabanaki, Peoria, and Kaskaskia. Here, Drouillard would have likely encountered the Myaamia *akiima* Pakaana in the last decade of the eighteenth century. A regular visitor to the region, Pakaana had relinquished his British medal to the Spanish in 1790, only to travel four years later to Detroit, where he met with British lieutenant governor of Upper Canada John Graves Simcoe in the wake of the murder of Pakaana's father-in-law by Virginians.[16] Both Pakaana and Drouillard had well-established familial ties to Detroit.

The men and women of these extended families owed their enhanced status to the unique intersection of individual opportunity with competing imperial agendas. In the first half of the eighteenth century, they acted as ambassadors for a French empire that desired political and economic control of the continental interior but was unwilling or unable to provide the considerable resources needed for such an ambitious plan. The first generation of French members of the family networks came from the region around Montreal, the economic center of the fur trade where French and Indigenous individuals had mingled from the early seventeenth century. Long before the establishment of a French fort in Detroit in 1701, they had been accustomed to living and conducting business both at Montreal and in the upper country with Iroquoian and Algonquian nations.

Indigenous members of the family networks, many of them women, hailed from the ranks of leaders and speakers of their nations—those who interfaced most regularly with European representatives. The women acted as pivotal marriage and commercial partners for French men and as cultural emissaries to French imperial agents, providing the foundation for the first multinational families. The Meskwaki siege of 1712 at Detroit, which launched the Fox Wars in the upper country, provided the fuel for the growth of these first families of the networks. Many Meskwaki were taken as slaves after the unsuccessful siege. As a result, slavery developed into a commercial enterprise, with members of the kinship networks gaining wealth and prestige from their participation. The highly mobile French-Indigenous family networks transformed Detroit into a clearinghouse where they could control the value of slaves and imperial resources that flowed through the region.

By the 1740s, key families had increasing power over policy in Detroit. At the same time, Great Lakes and Ohio Valley Indigenous nations began to splinter in their support of either French or British policy. Family network members became cultural brokers and interpreters for the French government in its attempts to maintain good relations with Indigenous nations in the face of increasing influence by the British. At this time of competing solidarities, a third generation of French-Indigenous family members was born that would further entrench its indigeneity by marrying into other Iroquoian and Algonquian nations. The merchants and traders of the family networks strengthened their economic position and established themselves as Detroit's elite and burgeoning bourgeoisie at mid-century. They became commercially powerful by providing materials to new immigrants who were part of a large government-sponsored influx of settlers from the St. Lawrence Valley in 1749 and 1750. By the outbreak of the Seven Years' War, the networks had increased in size and density. French-Indigenous families possessed unlimited possibilities for increasing trade at Detroit and in the upper country because of their multiple connections across Indigenous communities. Marriage and godparenting patterns that connect these families demonstrate that the networks grew in power and members maintained their authority.

With their victory in the Seven Years' War, Britain gained control of France's posts in the upper country. British officials traveled to Detroit and engaged with French-Indigenous family members in an effort to determine the sentiments of Indigenous nations toward the British newcomers, and gain economic support of the networks. Family members acted as interpreters and intermediaries for the British and as agents working against British hegemony at key moments, including in 1763 when the Odawa leader Pontiac led a movement to reassert Indigenous sovereignty. Irish and Scottish traders would marry into the family networks in order to ensure their survival in the increasingly competitive trade at Detroit, gaining a foothold through wives raised in the culture of indigeneity of the upper country. These women pursued a lifestyle of mobility, like the men of their families, and worked together with their husbands, fathers, and brothers to build familial commercial empires. Mobility was imperative to the conduct of good trade, and the French, who had developed shared kin networks with Indigenous communities, continued to use these connections to ensure safe passage to and from Detroit.

In the decades following British imperial control at Detroit, family ties within the networks proliferated. The key members of the networks who had worked with Pontiac in his failed attempt cemented familial ties and brought British suspicions and retribution down on members. With the installation of American imperial polities at the end of the eighteenth century, these French-Indigenous family traders and interpreters had become ever more proficient in negotiating and communicating the language and cultural proclivities of Great Lakes Indigenous nations. They had also become equally essential to British and American state agents in interpreting the local patois utilized by French and Indigenous peoples and the distinct culture upon which it was based.

Some members chose to align themselves with British imperial interests, while others maintained a reliance on, and loyalty to, a French-Indigenous hybrid identity. Some of these factions would eventually evolve into pro-American and pro-British camps during the American Revolution. By looking closely at the case of Tahkamwa, a Myaamia *akimaahkwia* who was both sister to an *akimaa* and wife of a French husband from whom she was seeking to wrest back her property and income, we can see how individuals and families that constituted the French-Indigenous family networks dealt with the increasingly complex world of Euro-Indigenous relations, with its multiple and conflicting loyalties. The family networks would fight in support of both American and British causes in the War of 1812, maintaining a devotion to members of their extended kin networks and a French-Indigenous hybrid identity over loyalty to a particular Euro-American nation. Their allegiance to family and community overrode Euro-American concepts of nation and citizenship.

Detroit's urbanity—the shaping of a unique local culture with complex economic, political, spiritual, and gendered dimensions—had been initiated by multiple Indigenous nations before the eighteenth century and the arrival of Europeans. The growth and diversification of the citizenry of Detroit, explosion of agricultural activity, continued settlement outside the walls of the French and English forts, and constant threat of war that made peaceful relations with and between Indigenous nations ever more essential, all combined to make the French-Indigenous family network members wealthy and influential. They used this wealth to bring consumer goods and luxury items into Detroit, as well as property in the form of slaves.

The common thread throughout this period were the opportunities presented by Detroit's geography. Detroit was defined by the ease by which one could travel through the region and the opportunities presented for economic development. It was a political hot point in imperial agendas because of the nations that utilized and at times threatened it. Because it was the only post in the upper country that consistently had a full-time priest in residence, it was a spiritual way station for the French and their slaves. Acting as both center and hinterland in European and Indigenous perceptions of space and place, and with Albany and Montreal as satellites, Detroit's name emphasized its status as a center of mobility.

There were different sets of gendered configurations of settlement and family for Indigenous and European communities resident at Detroit in the eighteenth century. In the first decades of French presence, there were also shifting perceptions and support by imperial authorities of marriage between French men and Indigenous women. Because of the real and symbolic importance of these unions to political and economic relations between Indigenous and French nations, their women persistently functioned as key agents in the maintenance of trade and peace. The presence of these women in contemporary narratives of the Fox Wars and Pontiac's War and romanticized portrayal in subsequent accounts of these events, demonstrates this crucial role, even as their complex lives were essentialized and obscured by historians over time. The basis of their multifaceted participation in diplomacy and commerce was a diverse series of gendered parameters in their nations. French and Indigenous men and women had access to this expanded pool of behavioral norms and used this to further trade and communicate expectations for imperial leaders operating as metaphoric fathers. These representatives of state used the parent-child metaphor predominantly in their negotiations with Indigenous communities, but within these communities, other symbols of kinship were equally powerful. The French-Indigenous family networks had access to a much larger variety of metaphoric kinship relationships to develop and solidify their connections to each other and to tie imperial European representatives to an expanding series of obligations.

At Detroit, a location of strategic economic and political importance and gateway to the upper country, members of the French-Indigenous kinship networks became invaluable. Empowered in this climate, they extended their influence and diversified within their own ranks, producing individuals with varying levels of allegiance to community and nation. Although Anglo-American power ebbed and flowed, the influence of Indigenous-French intermediaries persisted and families remained intact. Historian Lucy Murphy has illustrated how French-Indigenous fur-trade families in Midwestern states such as Illinois, Wisconsin, and Michigan navigated American political and economic systems meant to exclude or marginalize them.[17] Well into the nineteenth century, these families would maintain a cultural identity independent of any particular nation. How the French-Indigenous families of Detroit examined in this book prevailed and adapted into the nineteenth century, as American and Canadian governments increasingly enacted race-based policies, is a story for another day and another book.

Creating Community at Detroit

Witnessing the Marriage of Michel Bizaillon and Marguerite Fafard

The marriage contract of Michel Bizaillon and Marguerite Fafard was mandated by law under the Coutume de Paris and was signed on June 27, 1710, three days before the church wedding. The template was standard for documents defining the legal dimensions of this type of partnership. It declared that the two parties were entering into matrimony of their own free will and with the approval of their parents and friends. In this capacity, Pierre Roy (husband of the Myaamia Waapankihkwa/Marguerite Ouabankikoué) witnessed on behalf of Michel Bizaillon, and Antoine de la Mothe Cadillac, his wife, and daughter witnessed for Marguerite Fafard. The marriage partners agreed to own everything in common once the church wedding had taken place, with neither one to be held responsible for the debts of the other that were incurred before the wedding. A dowry of 1,000 livres was provided for the couple—an amount that once paid was required to be set aside in the future for the surviving spouse. The survivor would own all goods, real estate, and personal property acquired by both parties during the marriage. The marital *communauté de biens* created by the union would be considered dissolved on the death of one of the partners. In the event of the husband's death, the wife was entitled to everything she had brought to the partnership, including her dowry, real estate, clothes, linen, jewelry, bed, and bedding. The legal document was signed by Cadillac, his wife, daughter, and son; the mother and sister of the bride; the husband of the wife's cousin; the fort's surgeon (who was also a voyageur); and two other voyageurs: Jacques Cardinal and Nicolas Rivard. Three people were unable to affix their signatures because they could not write: Pierre Roy, the bride, and the groom.[1] Among the witnesses to the church marriage three days later were leading members of the French-Indigenous family network: Pierre Roy, Joseph Parent, Jean Baptiste Turpin, and the brothers Nicolas and Joseph Rivard.

Joseph Parent and Family

Joseph Parent was a beer maker (*brasseur*), master toolmaker (*maître taillandier*), and blacksmith (*forgeron*) at Detroit. As a toolmaker and blacksmith, Parent was able to produce and repair guns, which were essential as a means of procuring food and providing protection. A blacksmith could perform minor adjustments and repairs to firearms, but master toolmakers and gunsmiths (*armuriers*) were trained craftsmen who possessed a thorough knowledge of firearms. Indigenous communities often requested the services of a man who could repair guns, and from the seventeenth century up to the end of the Seven Years' War, the French routinely provided a blacksmith or gunsmith to Indigenous allies at no charge.[2] In its first two decades, Detroit had two master toolmakers/blacksmiths (Joseph Parent and Louis Normand dit la Brière), three gunsmiths (Guillaume Bonnet Deliard, Yves Pinet, and Laurent Trutaud), and five men designated solely as blacksmiths (Jacques Langlois, Joseph Senecal, the brothers Estienne and Jacques Campeau, and Jean Baptist Trutaud).[3]

Because they were pivotal to the colony's safety, metalworkers, more than any other tradesmen, stood to capitalize on their talents and correspondingly rose quickly through the socioeconomic ranks, occupying a position of importance in both French and Indigenous communities. The Detroit blacksmith Jacques Langlois, for example, had Cadillac as godparent for one of Langlois's sons in 1709, who was named Antoine after his godfather. The only other time Cadillac godparented during his tenure as commandant was for the Wendat leader Michipichy (Quarante Sols), who was baptized a few days before his death. In turn, Cadillac and his wife acknowledged Langlois's social standing by asking Langlois's wife Anne Toupin dit Dussault to stand as godmother to a child of Cadillac's in 1707. This was an equally rare event because the Cadillac children born at Detroit routinely had either their older siblings or highly ranked and titled officers as godparents.[4]

As a testimony to the close relations with Indigenous communities that their trade provided, Langlois and other metalworkers and their kin godparented as frequently as did voyageurs and their families at the baptisms of Indigenous individuals. Langlois's wife, for example, was godmother to a daughter of Pierre Roy and Waapankihkwa in 1708. They also tended to marry into other blacksmithing families and those with Indigenous members. Joseph Parent's son Gilbert would marry Susanne Richard, daughter of the blacksmith Jean Baptiste Richard and Marie Anne You de Ladécouverte, a half-Myaamia and half-French woman. Richard would move from Detroit to Myaamionki, eventually managing to successfully ply his trade at the Ouiatenon post on the Ouabache (Wabash) River.[5]

Joseph Parent's daughter Marie-Magdeleine married the blacksmith Jean Baptiste Truteau, who had multiple connections to the Myaamia and to Pierre Roy and his family. Pierre had been hired by Jean Baptiste's father in 1692 to make a trip to Odawa country.[6] Ten years later, Pierre and Jean Baptiste were working together and hired men to make a voyage to Detroit in 1713.[7] Jean Baptiste stood as godfather for a Mascouten slave belonging to Pierre in 1714, and again in 1717, at the baptism of Pierre's illegitimate daughter ("enfant naturel"). In 1712, Jean-Baptiste Truteau's brother Laurent, a gunsmith, godparented with Pierre Roy's wife Waapankihkwa for a slave belonging to the blacksmith Senecal. Jean Baptiste, Laurent, and their brother Jacques godparented exclusively for Indigenous individuals and Indigenous slaves at Detroit between 1710 and 1717. A fourth brother, Pierre Truteau, was married to Marie-Charlotte Ménard, niece to Maurice Ménard, the influential interpreter at Michilimackinac. A fifth brother, Joseph Truteau, was at one point a carpenter at Detroit, and together with Pierre Roy carried messages from the Illinois Country to Montreal during the early years of the Fox Wars.[8] A sixth brother, François Truteau, established himself as a master carpenter in Louisiana, acquiring land and slaves and ranging as far afield in his profession as Pensacola where he worked for the Spanish.[9]

Jean Baptiste Turpin and Family

Another of the witnesses at the wedding of Michel Bizaillon and Marguerite Fafard was Jean Baptiste Turpin, who had married Marguerite's cousin the previous month. His wife, also named Marguerite Fafard, was the daughter of Jean Fafard dit Maconce and Marguerite Couc, and niece of Marguerite Couc's sister Isabelle Couc (Madame Montour). Jean Baptiste Turpin had been in La Rochelle, France, when he engaged himself to accompany Pierre Le Moyne d'Iberville in 1699 on a voyage to Biloxi, during which time Iberville built a second fort on the Mississippi and entered into negotiations with resident Indigenous nations to hold back the English of Carolina.[10] That same year, Jean Baptiste Turpin's father, a Montreal merchant named Alexandre, was also in Europe. He traveled to England and Holland to establish business contacts with manufacturers who might be interested in buying beaver pelts to make hats.[11]

Like many other individuals associated with the family networks, Alexandre had been briefly incarcerated for suspected involvement in illegal trade in the west.[12] He had begun his career in the fur trade as a "cabaretier," an individual who provided a venue for the consumption of alcoholic beverages. In 1685, he and several other *cabaretiers* had petitioned the governor general to prohibit Quebec City *cabaretiers* from coming to Montreal in the summer and early autumn.[13] Such a move would undoubtedly have been made to protect the lucrative business of selling alcohol to Indigenous traders when they came to Montreal in the summers for the annual trade fair. In addition to Jean Baptiste, Alexandre had two other sons who were voyageurs and traders. Jacques Turpin operated at Kaskaskia, as did his brother Louis, the latter of whom married Dorothée Mechipoueoua, a woman of the Illinois-Kaskaskia nation.

Nicolas and Louis Joseph Rivard dit Loranger and Family

Nicolas and Joseph Rivard dit Loranger, the other witnesses to the Bizaillon-Fafard wedding, had both been godfathers at several baptisms of Odawa and Wendat individuals at Detroit in 1710. Their family had a well-established and extensive involvement in trade with Indigenous nations. Their father, Robert, had been one of the men sent in July 1684 with instructions from Governor General La Barre to Michilimackinac's commandant Olivier Morel de la Durantaye, ordering him to gather French and Indigenous men for an attack on the Haudenosaunee.[14] In 1690, Robert Rivard and his business partner Michel Roy dit Châtellerault entered into an agreement with the Compagnie du Nord (a precursor to the Compagnie de la Colonie, which funded the establishment of Detroit) for trade at Lakes Abitibi and

Témiscamingue, which lay at a crucial juncture between the St. Lawrence valley and Hudson Bay.[15] Two of Robert's other sons, Mathurin and Claude, had been part of the first contingent of French men who came to Detroit in 1701. Claude was also an interpreter at Detroit and was married to the daughter of Châtellerault, his father's business partner.

In a lengthy report in which he had answered to numerous charges laid against him by the Compagnie de la Colonie, Cadillac accused Claude Rivard dit Loranger and Claude's father-in-law Michel Roy dit Châtellereau of having conspired against and stolen from him. Cadillac labeled Claude a perjurer and insisted that he was incapable of understanding the Odawa language, despite his official position as Odawa interpreter. Michel Roy dit Châtellereau, a clerk for the Compagnie at Detroit, was alleged by Cadillac to have left for Montreal with two other clerks in a canoe loaded with goods without informing Cadillac. They were discovered as they were about to leave and imprisoned on Cadillac's orders.[16] Almost every individual mentioned by Cadillac in his report was characterized as having conspired against him, reflecting the threat they likely posed to his efforts to establish commercial and political supremacy.

In Batiscan, a town in the St. Lawrence valley from which Claude Rivard dit Loranger and his family hailed, each of four Rivard siblings stood as godparent in 1715 and 1716 for four Meskwaki slaves who had almost certainly been transported through Detroit in the aftermath of the failed Meskwaki attack of 1712. Three Rivard sisters (Marie Charlotte, Marie Catherine, and Marie Françoise) stood as godmother in 1715 and 1716 for three Meskwaki slaves, and their brother René-Alexis stood as godparent for a Fox slave in 1715, with his sister-in-law Marie-Anne Lafond dit Mongrain. René-Alexis's brother-in-law Jean Mongrain godparented on two occasions with René-Alexis Rivard's sisters Marie Charlotte and Marie-Catherine. Of sixteen slaves listed by historian Marcel Trudel as having been held in Batiscan between 1710 and 1762, almost half (seven) had some connection with the extended Rivard family, being either owned by the Rivards or having them and their relatives as godparents.[17]

The influence of the Rivard family in the political and commercial affairs of the colony was evident in marriage partners and extended family. A brother-in-law of the Rivards, François Dumontier, had held a position as secretary to Governor General Vaudreuil. Their cousin Paul Guillet maintained the king's storehouse at Detroit, eventually following in his uncle Robert Rivard's footsteps and becoming the leading trader at Fort Témiscamingue. Paul Guillet would stand as godparent at

Detroit in 1710, together with the blacksmith's daughter Marie Magdeleine Parent, at the baptism of Marie Magdeleine Roy, daughter of Pierre Roy and Marguerite Ouabankikoué. A year later, Guillet and Parent would godparent for a young Meskwaki girl named Magdeleine, likely named for her godmother. The baptism took place before the 1712 Meskwaki attack transformed the status of baptized Meskwaki from spiritual kin to war captives and slaves.

The Rivards and Guillets were interrelated via multiple blood and marriage connections and like other French families that could number up to nineteen children, intermarriage across generations was common. Nicolas and Joseph Rivard's grandmother Jeanne St. Pré and her sister/their great-aunt Catherine St. Pré had married Guillet brothers. An uncle of Nicolas and Joseph Rivard was also their great-uncle—Nicolas Rivard dit Lavigne, older brother to their father Robert, was also second husband to their great-aunt Catherine St. Pré. This continuing series of kinship events helped to maintain links between the Guillet, Rivard, and St. Pré families over time.[18]

Antoine Rivard, cousin to Nicolas and Joseph, married at Mobile in 1704, becoming a leading planter and merchant. His wife Marie Briard was one of the young women sent by the king of France in 1704 to help populate Louisiana.[19] The Rivard brothers' nephew Alexis Maisonville would become a prominent merchant and British ally during Pontiac's War and would challenge the Myaamia grandchildren of Pierre Roy and Waapankihkwa to ownership of a pivotal portage in Myaamionki in 1774. The families of the French-Indigenous networks had been linked through their involvement in the fur trade since the seventeenth century, and would remain bound to each other throughout the eighteenth century.

Notes

INTRODUCTION

1. Hazel Mary Lauzon Delorme, *Family Tree of Labute, LaBute, Labutte* (Windsor, ON, 1977).
2. For the concept of hiding in plain view beneath the cover of whiteness as it refers to mixed-blood women in the late nineteenth century in the Great Lakes, see Susan Sleeper-Smith, *Indian Women and French Men: Rethinking Cultural Encounter in the Western Great Lakes* (Amherst: University of Massachusetts Press, 2001), 139. Sleeper-Smith adopts this terminology to refer to strategies these women used in the face of American opinions of Indigenous racial inferiority.
3. For the idea that family histories exist outside the realm of traditional histories of the nation, see Anne McClintock, *Imperial Leather: Race, Gender and Sexuality in the Colonial Conquest* (New York: Routledge, 1995), 39. McClintock traces this primacy of patrilineal genealogies to the Victorian era and western industrialists seeking to shore up their social, cultural, and political influence.
4. These marriages were instead often performed "à la façon du pays" or according to the rites of the country or nation from which an Indigenous woman hailed. There has been extensive scholarship on these marriages, beginning most notably with Sylvia van Kirk's *Many Tender Ties: Women in Fur Trade Society in Western Canada, 1670–1870* (Winnipeg: Watson & Dwyer, 1980).

5. Peter Burke, "History as Social Memory," in *Memory, History, Culture and the Mind,* ed. Thomas Butler (Oxford: Blackwell, 1989), 108.

6. Michel-Rolph Trouillot, *Silencing the Past: Power and the Production of History* (Boston: Beacon Press, 1995), 27.

7. Frederick Cooper, *Colonialism in Question: Theory, Knowledge, History* (Berkeley: University of California Press, 2005), 139.

8. Nicholas J. Entrikin, *The Betweenness of Place: Towards a Geography of Modernity* (Baltimore: Johns Hopkins Press, 1991), 5.

9. Ann Stoler, "Tense and Tender Ties: The Politics of Comparison in North American History and (Post) Colonial Studies," *Journal of American History* 88, no. 3 (December 2001): 864.

10. Ann McGrath, *Illicit Love: Interracial Sex and Marriage in the United States and Australia* (Lincoln: University of Nebraska Press, 2015), xv.

11. Heather Devine, *The People Who Own Themselves: Aboriginal Ethnogenesis in a Canadian Family, 1660–1900* (Calgary: University of Calgary Press, 2004), 13, 16.

12. Carolyn Podruchny, "Werewolves and Windigos: Narratives of Cannibal Monsters in French-Canadian Voyageur Oral Tradition," *Ethnohistory* 51, no. 4 (2004): 279.

13. Daniel Laxer, "A Reservoir of Voices: Franco-Ontarien Folk Songs," *Ontario History* 1, no. 1 (Spring 2009): 46.

14. Karen Marrero, "'Fait Chorus': Telling New Histories of Detroit's French Community." *Michigan's Habitant Heritage,* 39, no. 4 (2018): 167.

15. Julie Cruikshank, "Oral History, Narrative Strategies, and Native American Historiography: Perspectives from the Yukon Territory, Canada," in *Clearing a Path: Theorizing the Past in Native American Studies,* ed. Nancy Shoemaker (New York: Routledge, 2002), 5.

16. James C. Scott, *Seeing Like a State: How Certain Schemes to Improve the Human Condition Have Failed* (New Haven, CT: Yale University Press, 1998), 313.

17. Marcel Bénéteau, "'Les Mascoutens': Chanson de composition locale," from À la table de mes amis: Vieilles chansons du Détroit, vol. 3 (Disques Petite Côte Records, 2001), compact disc.

18. Sheldon Pollock, "Cosmopolitan and Vernacular in History," *Public Culture* 12, no. 3 (2000): 596.

19. See Victor Lytwyn and Dean Jacobs, "'For Good Will and Affection': The Detroit Indian Deeds and British Land Policy, 1760–1827," *Ontario History* 92, no. 2 (Spring 2000): 24; Marcel Bénéteau and Peter Halford, *Mots choisis: Trois cents ans de francophonie au Détroit du Lac Érié* (Ottawa: Presses de l'Université d'Ottawa, 2008), 136, 203–204; and Timothy D. Willig, *Restoring the Chain of Friendship: British Policy and the Indians of*

the Great Lakes, 1783–1815 (Lincoln: University of Nebraska Press, 2008), 63–64. The Anishinaabe are the original people of the three fires: Odawa, Ojibwe, and Potawatomi (Bodéwadmi).

20. Peter W. Halford, *Le français des Canadiens à la veille de la Conquête: Témoignage du père Pierre Philippe Potier, S.J.* (Ottawa: Les Presses de l'Université d'Ottawa, 1994), 65, 83, 247; and Bénéteau and Halford, *Mots choisis,* 136.

21. David T. McNab, *Circles of Time: Aboriginal Land Rights and Resistance in Ontario* (Waterloo, ON: Wilfrid Laurier University Press, 1999), 154–155.

22. Victor Lytwyn, "Waterworld: The Aquatic Territory of the Great Lakes First Nations," in *Gin Das Winan: Documenting Aboriginal History in Ontario,* ed. Dale Standen and David McNab, no. 2, Occasional Papers of the Champlain Society (Toronto: Champlain Society, 1996), 15.

23. Dean Jacobs, "Indian Land Surrenders," in *The Western District,* ed. K. G. Pryke and L. L. Kulisek (Windsor, ON: Essex County Historical Society, 1983), 65, 67. The Chenail and other waterways have also been pivotal because they act as borders between the United States and Canada.

24. Lisa Philips and Allan K. McDougall, "Shifting Boundaries and the Baldoon Mysteries," in *Lines Drawn upon the Water: First Nations and the Great Lakes Borders and Borderlands,* ed. Karl S. Hele (Waterloo, ON: Wilfrid Laurier University Press, 2008), 133.

25. McNab, *Circles of Time,* 147. Walpole Island is called "Bkejwanong" by its Anishinaabe residents, meaning "the place where the waters divide." Dean Jacobs explains that the English name comes from "warpoles," wooden staves in the ground carved with Indigenous emblems that were seen by early visitors to the area. The "island" is composed of 6,900 hectares of diverse wetlands and 58,000 acres of land that stretch across six islands, with Walpole as the largest (Dean M. Jacobs, "'We have but our hearts and the traditions of our old men': Understanding the Traditions and History of Bkejwanong," in Standen and McNab, *Gin Das Winan: Documenting Aboriginal History in Ontario,* 1).

26. Yvan Lamonde, *Trajectoires de l'histoire du Quebec* (Ottawa: Musée de la civilization, 2001), 11.

27. Gilles Havard, *Empire et métissages: Indiens et Français dans le Pays d'en Haut, 1660–1715* (Sillery, QC: Les Éditions du Septentrion, 2003), 55; Robert Englebert and Guillaume Teasdale, "Introduction," in *French and Indians in the Heart of North America, 1630–1815,* ed. Englebert and Teasdale (East Lansing: Michigan State University Press, 2013), xiii.

28. Christophe Horguelin, "Le XVIIIe siècle des Canadiens: Discours public et identité," in *Mémoires de la Nouvelle France: De France en Nouvelle France,* ed. Philippe Joutard and Thomas Wien (Rennes, France: Presses universitaires de Rennes, 2005), 218–219.

29. Jay Gitlin, *The Bourgeois Frontier: French Towns, French Traders, and American Expansion* (New Haven, CT: Yale University Press, 2009), 27; and Robert Englebert, "Merchant Representatives and the French River World, 1763–1803," *Michigan Historical Review* 34, no. 1 (Spring 2008): 66.

30. John Francis McDermott, *Glossary of Mississippi Valley French, 1673–1850* (St. Louis: Washington State University, 1941), 50.

31. The word "dit" meaning "also called" was frequently used among the early French. The latter name was often a sobriquet that in many cases later became a family name.

32. Jodi Byrd, *The Transit of Empire: Indigenous Critiques of Colonialism* (Minneapolis: University of Minnesota Press, 2011), xxx.

CHAPTER 1. CREATING THE PLACE BETWEEN: BUILDING INDIGENOUS AND FRENCH COMMUNITIES IN EARLY DETROIT

1. Infant mortality in England and France compared to that of their colonies in North America was virtually the same, with the only difference occurring in particular regions of the colonies. Southern English areas such as Virginia and Maryland saw a higher level, based on the climate and its attendant diseases, compared to the Massachusetts colony. Urban areas, like Philadelphia, also had higher rates—due, it is supposed, to the greater population density and the ease of spread of disease. In Quebec, infant mortality rates increased steadily between 1659 and 1728, with spikes in rates corresponding to four major epidemics in that period (George Alter, "Infant and Child Mortality in the United States and Canada," in *Infant and Child Mortality in the Past,* ed. Alain Bideau, Bertrand Desjardins, and Héctor Pérex Brignoli [Oxford: Oxford University Press, 1997], 94–95).

2. There is no record of the birth, baptism, death, or burial of the infant because a fire at Detroit in 1703 destroyed Ste. Anne's church and all its records for the period 1701–1703. The church's register begins in April 1704 and continues to the present day.

3. The entire French passage (original spelling retained) reads: "il n'est pas possible que nos familles peussent demeurer dans un lieu qui ne seroit habité que par des sauvages; leur misere seroit extreme; puis quelles seroient sans aucun secours, comme il en arrive au Madame Tonty qui a veu mourir son enfant pour avoir manqué de lait, a quoi elle ne s'attendoit pas. Je crains que la même chose n'arrive a ma femme qui êtoit sur le point d'accoucher quand je suis parti, celle n'en pas extraordinaire, suivre que ces dames seroient nourrir leurs enfans, ainsi il n'ya suis a balancer de les faire decendre des l'année prochaine, si on ne permet pas a quelques familles d'aller s'y êtablir, affin quelles se puissent soulager dans ces facheuses conjonctures." Original French passage from

"Mémoire de Lamothe Cadillac au Ministre donnant la description du Détroit," Québec, 25 septembre 1702, Série C11E, Correspondance générale, vol. 14, Folio 120, Bibliothèque et Archives Canada (hereafter shortened as BAC). Translation used here appears in M. La Mothe Cadillac, "Description of Detroit," *Michigan Pioneer and Historical Society Collections,* vol. 33 (Lansing, MI: Robert Smith Printing Co., 1904), 139.

4. "Mémoire de Lamothe Cadillac au Ministre donnant la description du Détroit," Folio 126.

5. Suzanne Sommerville, "Who Was the Anonymous 1702 Wet Nurse for One of Lamothe Cadillac's Children? Additional Documentation for the Birth of a Cadillac Child at Fort Pontchartrain in 1702," *Michigan's Habitant Heritage* 26, no. 1 (2005): 21–27.

6. Catherine Rollet, "The Fight against Infant Mortality in the Past: An International Comparison," in *Infant and Child Mortality in the Past,* ed. Alain Bideau, Bertrand Desjardins, and Héctor Pérez Brignoli (Oxford: Oxford University Press, 1997), 53.

7. Dorothy McLaren, "Fertility, Infant Mortality, and Breast Feeding in the Seventeenth Century," *Medical History* 22, no. 4 (October 1978): 378.

8. Allan Greer, *The People of New France* (Toronto: University of Toronto Press, 1997), 66; and Denise Lemieux, *Les petits innocents: L'enfance en Nouvelle-France* (Quebec: Institut québécois de recherche sur la culture, 1985), 116.

9. Lemieux states (*Les petits innocents,* 177) that elite women of Quebec sent their newborns to wet nurses in the suburb of Charlesbourg.

10. Guillaume Aubert, "The Blood of France: Race and Purity of Blood in the French Atlantic World," *William and Mary Quarterly* 61, no. 3 (July 2004): 442.

11. Hierosme Lalemant, "Relation de ce qui s'est passé en la Nouvelle France, és années mil six cent cinquante neuf et mils six cent soixante," in *The Jesuit Relations and Allied Documents,* vol. 46, ed. Reuben Gold Thwaites (Cleveland: Imperial Press, 1899), 90.

12. Richard Steele, 1711, in Ruth Perry, "Colonizing the Breast: Sexuality and Maternity in Eighteenth-Century England," in *Forbidden History: The State, Society, and the Regulation of Sexuality in Modern Europe,* ed. John C. Fout (Chicago: University of Chicago Press, 1990), 124–125; Lemieux, *Les petits innocents,* 116.

13. Bob Antone, "Reconstructing Indigenous Masculine Thought," in Warren Cariou, Daniel Heath Justice, and Gregory Scofield, *Indigenous Men and Masculinities: Legacies, Identities, Regeneration* (Winnipeg: University of Manitoba Press, 2015), 26.

14. Michael McKeon, *The Secret History of Domesticity: Public, Private, and the Division of Knowledge* (Baltimore: Johns Hopkins University Press, 2005), 193.

15. "Le ministre à M. de la Mothe Cadillac," Versailles, 6 mai 1702, Série B, Lettres envoyées, vol. 23, Folio 94v, BAC. Cadillac wrote to Versailles three times in October of 1705 alone, once again prompting the displeasure of Phélypeaux, who told him that he should reread

his letters to eliminate useless and boring repetitions that wasted a lot of the reader's time ("Le ministre à M. de La Mothe Cadillac," Versailles, 9 juin 1706, Série B, vol. 27, Folio 275, BAC). As Sara Chapman points out, Cadillac eventually paid heed to these warnings, writing in more spare prose in future reports, and his 1702 grand narrative of Detroit's beginnings was subsequently published in a literary journal in France (Chapman, "Détroit to France and Back: Political and Cultural Networks and Colonial Exchanges during Louis XIV's Reign," paper delivered at the 64th Annual Meeting of the Society for French Historical Studies, Pittsburgh, March 8–10, 2018 [my thanks to Sara for sharing this conference paper]).

16. Richard Weyhing, "'Gascon Exaggerations': The Rise of Antoine Laumet dit de Lamothe, Sieur de Cadillac, the Foundation of Colonial Detroit, and the Origins of the Fox Wars," in *French and Indians in the Heart of North America, 1630–1815,* ed. Robert Englebert and Guillaume Teasdale (East Lansing: Michigan State University Press, 2013), 98.

17. Sara E. Chapman, "Reluctant Expansionists: Louis XIV, the Ministers of Colonies and the Founding of Détroit," in *The Third Reign of Louis XIV c. 1682–1715,* ed. Julia Prest and Guy Rowlands (London: Routledge, 2016), 93; and Chapman, "Détroit to France and Back."

18. Jean Blain, "Picoté de Belestre, Pierre," in *Dictionary of Canadian Biography,* vol. 1 (Toronto: University of Toronto/Université Laval, 2003–), http://www.biographi.ca/en/bio/picote_de_belestre_pierre_1E.html.

19. C. J. Russ, "Tonty, Alphonse, Baron de Paludy," in *Dictionary of Canadian Biography,* vol. 2 (Toronto: University of Toronto/Université Laval, 2003–), http://www.biographi.ca/en/bio/tonty_alphonse_2E.html.

20. E. B. Osler, "Tonty, Henri," in *Dictionary of Canadian Biography,* vol. 2 (Toronto: University of Toronto/Université Laval, 2003–), http://www.biographi.ca/en/bio/tonty_henri_2E.html.

21. For Champigny's letter, see "Lettre de Champigny au ministre," Québec, 24 octobre 1694, Série C11A, Correspondance générale, vol. 13, Folios 93v–94, BAC. For biography of Champigny, see W. J. Eccles, "Bochart de Champigny, Jean, Sieur de Noroy et de Verneuil," in *Dictionary of Canadian Biography,* vol. 2 (Toronto: University of Toronto/Université Laval, 2003–), http://www.biographi.ca/en/bio/bochart_de_champigny_jean_2E.html.

22. Robert Michael Morrissey, *Empire by Collaboration: Indians, Colonists, and Governments in Colonial Illinois Country* (Philadelphia: University of Pennsylvania Press, 2015), 47, 59–60.

23. W. J. Eccles, "Brisay de Denonville, Jacques-René de, Marquis de Denonville," in *Dictionary of Canadian Biography,* vol. 2 (Toronto: University of Toronto/Université Laval, 2003–), http://www.biographi.ca/en/bio/brisay_de_denonville_jacques_rene_de_2E.html.

24. Michael Witgen, *An Infinity of Nations: How the Native New World Shaped Early North America* (Philadelphia: University of Pennsylvania Press, 2012), 18.

25. Michael A. McDonnell, *Masters of Empire: Great Lakes Indians and the Making of America* (New York: Hill and Wang, 2015), 23.

26. "Mémoire de Lamothe Cadillac au Ministre donnant la description du Détroit," Folio 118.

27. "Mémoire de Lamothe Cadillac au Ministre donnant la description du Détroit," Folio 120v.

28. "Lettre de Martin Lino au ministre," Québec, 15 novembre 1703, Série C11A, vol. 21, Folios 208–208v, BAC.

29. It is possible that the Abenaki group, referred to as the Oppenago by Cadillac, came to Detroit at his invitation because he had encountered them when he lived at Acadia in the 1680s. In 1692, he had also conducted reconnaissance of the New England coast with them, the Caniba (also known as Kennebec—members of an Abenaki confederated tribe), and the royal cartographer Jean-Baptiste-Louis Franquelin.

30. "Mémoire de Lamothe Cadillac au Ministre donnant la description du Détroit," Folio 120v.

31. "Lettre de Lamothe Cadillac au Ministre à propos de l'établissement du Détroit," Détroit, 31 août 1703, Série C11E, vol. 14, Folio 156, BAC. Cadillac made reference in particular to a "Frenchified" Odawa chief who was eager to offer the king his services.

32. Joyce E. Chaplin, *Subject Matter: Technology, the Body, and Science on the Anglo-American Frontier, 1500–1676* (Cambridge, MA: Harvard University Press, 2001), 314.

33. "Lettre de Champigny au ministre [Phélypeaux]."

34. Mark Rifkin, *Manifesting America: The Imperial Construction of U.S. National Space* (New York: Oxford University Press, 2009), 140.

35. Gilles Havard, *Histoire des coureurs de bois Amérique du Nord, 1600–1840* (Paris: Les Indes Savantes, 2016), 184–185.

36. For contemporary meaning of "moeurs" see *Dictionnaire de l'Académie Française*, 1st ed. (1694), *Dictionnaires d'autrefois* at ARTFL Project, Department of Romance Languages and Literatures, University of Chicago, https://artfl-project.uchicago.edu/content/dictionnaires-dautrefois.

37. "Mémoire de Denonville à Seignelay," janvier [1690], Série C11A, vol. 11, Folios 187v–188, BAC.

38. Rony Blum, *Ghost Brothers: Adoption of a French Tribe by Bereaved Native America* (Montreal & Kingston: McGill-Queen's University Press, 2005), 121.

39. Julia Adams, "The Rule of the Father: Patriarchy and Patrimonialism in Early Modern Europe," in *Max Weber's 'Economy and Society': A Critical Companion,* ed. Charles Camic,

Philip S. Gorski, and David M. Trubek (Stanford, CA: Stanford University Press, 2005), 240.

40. Sylvia Van Kirk, "From 'Marrying-in' to 'Marrying-out': Changing Patterns of Aboriginal/Non-Aboriginal Marriage in Colonial Canada," *Frontiers: A Journal of Women Studies* 23, no. 3 (2002): 1. Van Kirk distinguishes "marrying-in" that occurred during the early years of Indigenous-European interaction from "marrying-out" in the later nineteenth and twentieth centuries, which saw Indigenous women who married white men losing their status as members of their tribes and nations.

41. Susan Sleeper-Smith, *Indian Women and French Men: Rethinking Cultural Encounter in the Western Great Lakes* (Amherst: University of Massachusetts Press, 2001), 50.

42. Dispensations could be purchased for other special privileges attached to marriage. Normally, couples who planned to marry were required to announce/publish their bans (intention to marry) at three masses before the marriage could take place in the church. Persons who wished to skip one or more of these three masses (but never all of them) could purchase dispensations, which would be duly noted in the church register.

43. Maureen Molloy, "Considered Affinity: Kinship, Marriage, and Social Class in New France," *Social Science History* 14, no. 1 (Spring 1990): 9. The French practiced partible inheritance, which meant that all children, whether male or female, were entitled to an equal portion of their parents' estates. This system operated differently than that of Britain, which practiced primogeniture, wherein eldest males ordinarily were the only ones who could expect an inheritance. Molloy reports that local custom in some areas of France, such as Brittany, had never allowed consanguineal marriage at any degree, regardless of what canon law decreed at any given time over the centuries.

44. Raymond J. DeMallie, "Kinship: The Foundation for Native American Society," in *Studying Native America: Problems and Prospects,* ed. Russell Thornton (Madison: University of Wisconsin Press, 1998), 307.

45. DeMallie, "Kinship," 323.

46. Kathryn Labelle, *Dispersed but Not Destroyed: A History of the Seventeenth-Century Wendat Diaspora* (Vancouver: University of British Columbia Press, 2013), 178–180; Karen Anderson, *Chain Her by One Foot: The Subjugation of Native Women in Seventeenth-Century New France* (New York: Routledge, 1991), 110.

47. Molly Turnbull, "Speaking of Family: Constructing Relations in Algonquian English Discourse," in *Papers of the Twenty-Seventh Algonquian Conference,* ed. David H. Pentland (Winnipeg: University of Manitoba, 1996), 277.

48. George Ironstrack, "Walking a Myaamia Trail," April 4, 2011, *Aacimotaatiiyankwi: A Myaamia Community Blog,* https://myaamiahistory.wordpress.com/2011/04/04/

walking-a-myaamia-trail/.

49. For the meaning of the word "Meehtikoošia" to describe the French, see George Ironstrack, "The Myaamia-French Encounter," July 16, 2011, *Aacimotaatiiyankwi: A Myaamia Community Blog,* https://myaamiahistory.wordpress.com/2011/07/16/the-myaamia-and-french-encounter-each-other/.

50. David J. Costa, "The Kinship Terminology of the Miami-Illinois Language," *Anthropological Linguistics* 41, no. 1 (Spring 1999): 37–38. This could remedy any initial disadvantage Euro-American men faced when marrying into Indigenous nations.

51. Bruce White, "'Give Us a Little Milk': The Social and Cultural Meanings of Gift Giving in the Lake Superior Fur Trade," *Minnesota History* 48, no. 2 (Summer 1982): 61–63; Heidi Bohaker, "'Nindoodemag': The Significance of Algonquian Kinship Networks in the Eastern Great Lakes Region, 1600–1701," *William and Mary Quarterly* 63, no. 1 (January 2006): 25–26.

52. Colin Kidd, *British Identities before Nationalism: Ethnicity and Nationhood in the Atlantic World, 1600–1800* (Cambridge: Cambridge University Press, 1999), 12.

53. Julia Adams, "The Rule of the Father: Patriarchy and Patrimonialism in Early Modern Europe," in *Max Weber's Economy and Society: A Critical Companion,* ed. C. Camic, P. S. Gorski, and D. M. Trubek (Stanford, CA: Stanford University Press, 2005), 248.

54. Michael McKeon, *The Secret History of Domesticity: Public, Private, and the Division of Knowledge* (Baltimore: Johns Hopkins University Press, 2005), 116.

55. Richard White, *The Middle Ground: Indians, Empires, and Republics in the Great Lakes Region, 1650–1815* (Cambridge: Cambridge University Press, 1991, 2011), 36.

56. Kenneth J. Banks, *Chasing Empire across the Sea: Communications and the State in the French Atlantic, 1713–1763* (Montreal & Kingston: McGill-Queen's University Press, 2003), 6.

57. For Detroit's status as an entrepôt positioned to benefit from and control trade linking France to the North American continental interior, see Catherine Cangany, *Frontier Seaport: Detroit's Transformation into an Atlantic Entrepôt* (Chicago: University of Chicago Press, 2014).

58. "Mémoire de Lamothe Cadillac à Vaudreuil avec notes," Québec, 31 mars 1706, Série C11A, vol. 24, Folios 273v–274, BAC.

59. "Observations de Vaudreuil sur la lettre de M. de Lamothe du premier octobre 1707," [1707], Série C11A, vol. 26, Folio 104v, BAC.

60. Private sessions seem to have been permitted by a French governor general when his power was strongly rooted at a particular place and time and there was no potential challenge to his ritualized role as Onontio. Before and during official meetings at the

Great Peace of Montreal in 1701, Governor General Callière held "private sessions" in the courtyard of his residence with many of the Indigenous ambassadors. These "secret discussions" usually revolved around issues particular to that nation and their relationship with the French, rather than general discussions of trade and the exchange of prisoners that underlay most of the formal discussions held between all of the participants at the Great Peace (Gilles Havard, *The Great Peace of Montreal of 1701: French-Native Diplomacy in the Seventeenth Century,* trans. Phyllis Aronoff and Howard Scott [Montreal & Kingston: McGill-Queen's University Press, 2001], 140).

61. "Copie de la lettre des directeurs de la Compagnie de la Colonie au ministre Pontchartrain," 4 novembre 1701, Série C11A, vol. 19, Folios 36 and 36v, BAC.

62. "Rapport de Clairambault d'Aigremont au ministre concernant sa mission d'inspection," 14 novembre 1708, Série C11A, vol. 29, BAC.

63. "Paroles aux chefs illinois, ouiatanons et miamis pour leur faire rompre toute liaison avec les Anglais," 1713, Série C11A, vol. 65, Folio 155v, BAC.

64. Bohaker, "Nindoodemag," 47.

65. Patricia Albers and Jeanne Kay, "Sharing the Land: A Study in American Indian Territoriality," in *A Cultural Geography of North American Indians,* ed. Thomas E. Ross and Tyrel G. Moore (Boulder, CO: Westview Press, 1987), 74.

66. Jennifer Spear, "Colonial Intimacies: Legislating Sex in French Louisiana," *William and Mary Quarterly* 60, no. 1 (January 2003): 76.

67. Jean Talon, "Mémoire sur l'état present du Canada," in Louise Dechêne, *Habitants and Merchants in Seventeenth Century Montreal,* trans. Liana Vardi (Montreal & Kingston: McGill-Queen's University Press, 1992), 7.

68. "Lettre du Callière au ministre," 4 octobre 1701, Série C11A, vol. 19, Folio 121v, BAC.

69. "Résume d'une lettre de Vaudreuil date du 6 octobre 1721 et délibération du Conseil de Marine," 23 décembre 1721, Série C11A, vol. 43, Folios 320–323, BAC. Named for a high-ranking seventeenth-century judicial officer, these were civil marriages entered into without the formal blessing of a priest. In 1717, the bishop of Quebec declared against these unions, threatening with excommunication not only those who entered into them, but also those who acted as witnesses or advised parties to take part in these marriages, and the notaries who contracted them (William Kingsford, *The History of Canada,* vol. 2 [London: Trübnar & Co., 1888], 495).

70. "Lettre des sieurs Vaudreuil et Raudot au ministre," 14 novembre 1709, Série C11A, vol. 30, Folio 9v, BAC.

71. *Dictionnaire de l'Académie française,* 1st ed. (1694) and *Dictionnaire de l'Académie française,* 4th ed. (1762), at ARTFL Project, University of Chicago, https://artfl-project.

uchicago.edu/content/dictionnaires-dautrefois.

72. Saliha Belmessous, "Assimilation and Racialism in Seventeenth and Eighteenth-Century French Colonial Policy," *American Historical Review* 110, no. 2 (April 2005): 323.

73. "Lettre de Lamothe Cadillac au Ministre à propos de l'éstablissement du Détroit," Québec, 18 octobre 1700, Série C11E, vol. 14, Folios 58 and 58v, BAC.

74. Leslie Tuttle, *Conceiving the Old Regime: Pronatalism and the Politics of Reproduction in Early Modern France* (New York: Oxford University Press, 2010), 134.

75. Sharon Kettering, "Patronage and Kinship in Early Modern France," *French Historical Studies* 16, no. 2 (Fall 1989): 409.

76. Patricia C. Albers, "Marxism and Historical Materialism in American Indian History," in *Clearing a Path: Theorizing the Past in Native American Studies,* ed. Nancy Shoemaker (New York: Routledge, 2002), 125.

77. Belmessous, "Assimilation and Racialism," 339–340.

78. "The Settlement at Detroit," March 28, 1716, in *Michigan Pioneer and Historical Society Collections,* 33:574–576. Kiihkayonki was often spelled phonetically as Kekionga in eighteenth- and nineteenth-century Euro-American records. For Kiihkayonki as Fort Wayne, see John Bickers and George Ironstrack, "The Many Branches of Tahkamwa's Family Tree," May 29, 2015, *Aacimotaatiiyankwi: A Myaamia Community Blog,* https://myaamiahistory.wordpress.com/2015/05/29/the-many-branches-of-tahkamwas-family-tree/.

79. Guillaume Teasdale, *Fruits of Perseverance: The French Presence in the Detroit River Region, 1701–1815* (Montreal & Kingston: McGill-Queen's University Press, 2019), 19.

CHAPTER 2. CORN MOTHERS, *COMMANDANTES,* AND NURTURING FATHERS: NEGOTIATING PLACE AT DETROIT

1. The journey from the St. Lawrence valley to Detroit would have taken roughly two months, necessitating mostly travel by water, but also the crossing of numerous portages.

2. "Mémoire de Lamothe Cadillac au Ministre donnant la description du Détroit," Quebec, 25 septembre 1702, Série C11E, vol. 14, folio 119, BAC.

3. "Lettre de Vaudreuil et Beauharnois au ministre," Quebec, 17 novembre 1704, Série C11A, vol. 22, Folios 8v–9, BAC.

4. Bob Antone, "Reconstructing Indigenous Masculine Thought," in *Indigenous Men and Masculinities: Legacies, Identities, Regeneration,* ed. Warren Cariou, Daniel Heath Justice, and Gregory Scofield (Winnipeg: University of Manitoba Press, 2015), 16.

5. Cary Miller, *Ogimaag: Anishinaabeg Leadership, 1760–1845* (Lincoln: University of

Nebraska Press, 2010), 135.

6. Brenda Child, *Holding Our World Together: Ojibwe Women and the Survival of Community* (New York: Penguin Books, 2012), 29.

7. *Dictionnaire de l'Académie française,* 1st ed. (1694) and *Dictionnaire de l'Académie française,* 4th ed. (1762), *Dictionnaires d'autrefois,* ARTFL Project, University of Chicago, https://artfl-project.uchicago.edu/content/dictionnaires-dautrefois.

8. Roland Michel, Comte de la Galissoniere, in *Anglo-French Boundary Disputes in the West 1749–1763,* ed. Theodore Calvin Pease, *Collections of the Illinois Historical Library,* vol. 27 (French Series vol. 2) (Springfield: Illinois State Historical Library, 1936), 16–17.

9. Catherine Cangany, *Frontier Seaport: Detroit's Transformation into an Atlantic Entrepôt* (Chicago: University of Chicago Press, 2014), 4.

10. Julia Adams and Chris Shughrue, "Bottlenecks and East Indies Companies: Modeling the Geography of Agency in Mercantilist Enterprises," in *Chartering Capitalism: Organizing Markets, States, and Publics,* ed. Emily Erickson (Bingley, UK: Emerald Group Publishing Ltd., 2015), 207–208.

11. Colonel John Bradstreet, February 1762, in Peter Marshall, "Imperial Policy and the Government of Detroit: Projects and Problems, 1760–1774," *Journal of Imperial and Commonwealth History* 2, no. 2 (January 1974): 157.

12. Richard White, *The Middle Ground: Indians, Empires, and Republics in the Great Lakes Region, 1650–1815* (Cambridge: Cambridge University Press, 1991), 146.

13. Peter Dooyentate Clarke, *Origin and Traditional History of the Wyandotts, and Sketches of Other Indian Tribes of North America* (Toronto: Hunter, Rose and Co., 1870), 37.

14. "Speech of Little Turtle to General Anthony Wayne," Fort Greenville, 1795, *American State Papers: Indian Affairs, 1789–1815,* vol. 1 (Washington, DC: Gales and Seaton, 1832), 570–571.

15. "Indian Speech to Sir John Johnson at Huron Village," August 16, 1790, copied by Joseph Chew from the original speeches in Montreal, September 29, 1796, *Michigan Pioneer and Historical Society Collections,* vol. 20 (Lansing, MI: Robert Smith Printing Co., 1892), 308. Dayenty refers here to River Canard, which is today located in LaSalle, immediately west of Windsor, Ontario. Egouchaway describes Bois Blanc Island, known today as Boblo Island, which is located in the Detroit River and west of Windsor. Bois Blanc Island was the location of the first Jesuit-run mission amongst the Wendat. Dayenty also makes reference to the primary chief Sastereche, more commonly written as Sasteresti. This was an ancient inherited title designating leadership among the Wendat Deer clan recognized by Europeans as king of the nation. Kathryn Magee Labelle, *Dispersed but Not Destroyed: A History of the Seventeenth-Century Wendat People* (Vancouver: University

of British Columbia Press, 2013), 155–156; and Andrew Sturtevant, "'Over the Lake': The Western Wendake in the American Revolution," in *From Huronia to Wendakes: Adversity, Migrations, and Resilience, 1650–1900,* ed. Thomas Peace and Kathryn Magee Labelle (Norman: University of Oklahoma Press, 2016), 71. There were at least two Sasterestis who represented the Wendat at Detroit. One was active in politics from the end of the seventeenth century to the beginning of the eighteenth century. The other Sasteresti, possibly his son, was born at Detroit in 1711 and became a pivotal player in the split between pro-French and pro-English factions of the Wendat in the 1740s.

16. Peter Dooyentate Clarke, *Origin and Traditional History of the Wyandotts, and Sketches of Other Indian Tribes of North America* (Toronto: Hunter, Rose and Co., 1870), iii.

17. William W. Warren, *History of the Ojibway People* (1885; reprint, St. Paul: Minneapolis Historical Society, 2008), 126.

18. Andrew J. Blackbird, *History of the Ottawa and Chippewa Indians of Michigan* (Ypsilanti, MI: Ypsilanti Job Printing House, 1887), 93.

19. Henry Rowe Schoolcraft would describe Great Lakes Indigenous nations' creation of homelands in this manner as operating "irrespective of [Euro-American] political boundaries" and extending "wherever the tribes are actually located." "Extract from the Report of Henry R. Schoolcraft," in T. H. Crawford, *Annual Report of the Commissioner of Indian Affairs,* 25th Congress, 3rd session (Washington: Blair & Rives Printers, 1838), 50.

20. Juliana Barr, "Geographies of Power: Mapping Indian Borders in the 'Borderlands' of the Early Southwest," *William and Mary Quarterly* 68, no. 1 (January 2011): 43; Tyler Boulware, "'It Seems Like Coming into Our Houses': Challenges to Cherokee Hunting Grounds, 1750–1775," in *Before the Volunteer State: New Thoughts on Early Tennessee History, 1690–1800,* ed. Kristofer Ray (Knoxville: University of Tennessee Press, 2014), 70–71; Allan Greer, "Commons and Enclosure in the Colonization of North America," *American Historical Review* 117, no. 2 (April 2012): 371; Neal Ferris, *The Archaeology of Native-Lived Colonialism: Challenging History in the Great Lakes* (Tucson: University of Arizona Press, 2009), 6.

21. William James Newbigging, "The History of the French-Ottawa Alliance, 1613–1763" (PhD diss., University of Toronto, 1995), 226.

22. Ferris, *The Archaeology of Native-Lived Colonialism,* 116.

23. Susan M. Hill, *The Clay We Are Made of: Haudenosaunee Land Tenure on the Grand River* (Winnipeg: University of Manitoba Press, 2017), 43.

24. Gilles Havard, *The Great Peace of Montreal of 1701: French-Native Diplomacy in the Seventeenth Century,* trans. Phyllis Aronoff and Howard Scott (Montreal & Kingston: McGill-Queen's University Press, 2001), 145–149.

25. Allan Greer, *Property and Dispossession: Natives, Empires and Land in Early Modern North America* (Cambridge: Cambridge University Press, 2018), 16.

26. The other location referenced was the area around Fort Frontenac in present-day Kingston, Ontario.

27. *Documents Relative to the Colonial History of the State of New York,* vol. 4, ed. E. B. O'Callaghan (Albany, NY: Weed, Parsons and Co., 1854), 891.

28. *Documents Relative to the Colonial History of the State of New York,* 4:905.

29. "Deed from the Five Nations to the King of Their Beaver Hunting Ground," Albany, July 19, 1701, in *Documents Relative to the Colonial History of the State of New York,* 4:908–910.

30. Daniel Richter, *The Ordeal of the Longhouse: The Peoples of the Iroquois League in the Era of European Colonization* (Chapel Hill: University of North Carolina Press, 1992), 212.

31. *Documents Relative to the Colonial History of the State of New York,* 4:501.

32. *Documents Relative to the Colonial History of the State of New York,* 4:650.

33. "Recensement nominative de Détroit," 1710, Série C11A, vol. 31, folios 160–161v, BAC. Canadians were those men who had lived first in the St. Lawrence valley before taking up residence at Detroit. Frenchmen had come directly from France.

34. LeAnne Howe, "The Story of America: A Tribalography," in *Clearing a Path: Theorizing the Past in Native American Studies,* ed. Nancy Shoemaker (New York: Routledge, 2002), 29.

35. Susan Sleeper-Smith, *Indigenous Prosperity and American Conquest: Indian Women of the Ohio River Valley, 1690–1792* (Chapel Hill: University of North Carolina Press, 2018), 15–16, 29.

36. Lisa Brooks, *The Common Pot: The Recovery of Native Space in the Northeast* (Minneapolis: University of Minnesota Press, 2008), 252.

37. Brooks, *The Common Pot,* 109.

38. Arthur Parker, *Seneca Myths and Folk Tales* (Lincoln: University of Nebraska Press, 1989), 64, quoted in Brooks, *The Common Pot,* 252.

39. Brooks, *The Common Pot,* 253–254. See also Rebecca Kugel and Lucy Murphy, "Introduction: Searching for Cornfields and Sugar Groves," in *Native Women's History in Eastern North America before 1900: A Guide to Research and Writing,* ed. Kugel and Murphy (Lincoln: University of Nebraska Press, 2007), xiv.

40. Vera Palmer, "The Devil in the Details: Controverting an American Indian Conversion Narrative," in *Theorizing Native Studies,* ed. Audra Simpson and Andrea Smith (Durham, NC: Duke University Press, 2014), 271.

41. Brooks, *The Common Pot,* 109.

42. Marian E. White, "Neutral and Wenro," in *Handbook of North American Indians,* vol. 15, *Northeast,* ed. Bruce G. Trigger (Washington, DC: Smithsonian Institution, 1978), 407.

43. Arthur C. Parker, *The Life of General Ely S. Parker* (Buffalo, NY: Buffalo Historical Society, 1919), 45–46.

44. For this description of the role played by Jigonsase in the wars with the French, see Barbara Mann, "Jigonsaseh," in *Encyclopedia of the Haudenosaunee (Iroquois Confederacy)*, ed. Bruce Elliot Johansen and Barbara Alice Mann (Westport, CT: Greenwood Press, 2000), 176–179.

45. Brett Rushforth, *Bonds of Alliance: Indigenous and Atlantic Slaveries in New France* (Chapel Hill: University of North Carolina Press, 2012), 150. Rushforth points out that Denonville also offended the Haudenosaunee by relegating the captives to a life of brutal treatment as slaves on distant seas, rather than designating them to serve in French households.

46. *Myaamiaatawaakani/Myaamia Dictionary,* Miami Tribe of Oklahoma, https://myaamiadictionary.org.

47. Chief Clarence Godfroy (Ka-pah-pwah), *Miami Indian Stories,* ed. Martha Una McClurg (Winona Lake, IN: Light and Life Press, 1961), 24–25.

48. C. C. Trowbridge, *Meearmeear Traditions,* ed. Vernon Kinietz (1823; reprint, Ann Arbor: University of Michigan Press, 1938), 46.

49. Gilles Havard and Cecile Vidal, *Histoire de l'Amérique française* (Paris: Éditions Flammarion, 2003), 178.

50. Heidi Bohaker, "'Nindoodemag': The Significance of Algonquian Kinship Networks in the Eastern Great Lakes Region, 1600–1701," *William and Mary Quarterly* 63, no. 1 (January 2006): 25–26; *nindoodemag* is the plural for *nindoodem.*

51. Child, *Holding Our World Together: Ojibwe Women and the Survival of Community,* 29.

52. Havard and Vidal, *Histoire de l'Amérique française,* 181.

53. Original quote from "Meeting held with the Ottawas," May 18, 1703, as it appears in Gilles Havard, *Empire et métissages: Indiens et Français dans le Pays d'en Haut, 1660–1715* (Sillery, QC: Les Éditions du Septentrion, 2003), 369 and 419.

54. "Paroles adressées à Vaudreuil par des chefs outaouais de Michilimakinac," 1 août 1706, Série C11A, vol. 24, Folio 240, BAC.

55. "Paroles de Jean Leblanc à Vaudreuil," 23 juin 1707, Série C11A, vol. 26, Folio 123, BAC.

56. "Procès-verbaux des conseils tenus à Détroit," Detroit, août 1707, Série C11A, vol. 26, Folio 129, BAC.

57. "Mémoire de LaMothe Cadillac," 14 novembre 1704, Série C11E, vol. 14, folio 189v.

58. Robert Toupin, ed., *Les écrits de Pierre Potier* (Ottawa: Les Presses de l'Université d'Ottawa, 1996), 423.

59. Bruce White, "'Give Us a Little Milk': The Social and Cultural Meanings of Gift Giving

in the Lake Superior Fur Trade," *Minnesota History* 48, no. 2 (Summer 1982): 67. This metaphoric connection between milk and alcohol occurred frequently in French, British, and Spanish imperial records of meetings with Indigenous groups throughout the eighteenth century.

60. French authorities believed that elite men (*gentilshommes*) were particularly prone to abandon polite society and live like and among Indigenous peoples. See "Lettre de Denonville au ministre," Québec, 13 novembre 1685, Série C11A, vol. 7, Folio 90, BAC.

61. Catherine Ferland, "Le nectar et l'ambroisie: La consummation des boissons alcooliques chez l'élite de la Nouvelle-France au XVIIIe siècle," *Revue d'histoire de l'Amérique française* 58, no. 4 (2005): 494.

62. Female drunkenness was also viewed by Europeans as potentially dangerous to the social order (Ferland, "Le nectar et l'ambroisie," 501). The prevailing opinion in New France was that because the bodies of women were in an unstable state, alcohol could upset this balance and take away a woman's femininity. It could also harm any child she might be potentially carrying. For this reason, women were encouraged to abstain, or to drink only with family or members of their immediate social circle who would ensure they did not overindulge.

63. Sara Chapman, "Patronage as Family Economy: The Role of Women in the Patron-Client Network of the Phélypeaux de Pontchartrain Family, 1670–1715," *French Historical Studies* 24, no. 1 (Winter 2001): 13; and Micheline Dumont, Michèle Jean, Marie Lavigne, and Jennifer Stoddart, *L'histoire des femmes au Québec depuis quatre siècles* (Montreal: Les Quinze, 1982), 54–55.

64. Jean Baptiste Campau made the claim that Madame Tonty set the fire; see "Lettre de Jacques et Antoine-Denis Raudot au ministre," Québec, 11 novembre 1707, Série C11A, vol. 26, Folio 214v-215, BAC. Campeau was eventually charged with making erroneous accusations and was fined.

65. For accusation against La Marque, see "Ordonnance de l'intendant Bégon," Québec, 23 octobre 1714, Série C11A, vol. 35, Folios 190–195v, BAC.

66. La Marque stood as godmother on December 4 and twice on December 8 in 1722. On two of these occasions, the record lists her as "commandante," with the final "e" representing the feminine version of "commandant," while on the third occasion, she was designated simply as "commandant." Registre de Ste. Anne Detroit, vol. 1, no. 1252, reel 1, 176–177, Burton Historical Collection, Detroit Public Library [hereafter Registre de Ste. Anne].

67. Catherine Ferland and Benoît Grenier, "Les Procuratrices à Québec au XVIIIe Siècle: Résultats Préliminaires d'une Enquête sur le Pouvoir des Femmes en Nouvelle France" in *Femmes, Culture et Pouvoir: Relectures de l'Histoire au Féminin Xve–XXe Siècles,* eds.

Catherine Ferland and Benoît Grenier (Québec: Les Presses de l'Université Laval, 2010), 131–132. For the legal concept of *procuration* and its use by French merchants and settlers of the continental interior in the mid to late eighteenth century, see Robert Englebert, "The Legacy of New France: Law and Social Cohesion between Quebec and the Illinois Country, 1763–1790," *French Colonial History* 17 (2017).

68. Jan Noel, "'Nagging Wife' Revisited: Women and the Fur Trade in New France," *French Colonial History* 7 (2006): 47. Noel's reference to the "nagging wife" is an allusion to a term used by Canadian historian William J. Eccles in his 1969 book *The Canadian Frontier, 1534–1760.* Eccles believed that excessive nagging by fur-trade wives drove their husbands away and into the mobile lifestyle of the western fur trade (Noel, "'Nagging Wife' Revisited," 45).

69. *Rapport de l'Archiviste de la Province de la Québec pour 1929–1930* (Quebec: Rédempti Paradis, 1930), 269, 270, 278.

70. Patricia Albers and Jeanne Kay, "Sharing the Land: A Study in American Indian Territoriality," in *A Cultural Geography of North American Indians,* ed. Thomas E. Ross and Tyrel G. Moore (Boulder, CO: Westview Press, 1987), 52.

CHAPTER 3. WAR, SLAVERY, AND BAPTISM: THE FORMATION OF THE FRENCH-INDIGENOUS NETWORKS AT DETROIT

1. Marcel Bénéteau, "'Les Mascoutens': Chanson de composition locale," À la table de mes amis: Vieilles chansons du Détroit, vol. 3 (Windsor: Disques Petite Côte Records, 2001).

2. Marcel Bénéteau, "Chansons traditionnelles et identité culturelle chez les Francophones du Détroit," *Ethnologies* 26, no. 2 (2004): 203, 212–213.

3. Marcel Bénéteau, "Aspects de la tradition orale comme marqueurs d'identité culturelle: Le vocabulaire et la chanson traditionelle des francophones du Détroit" (PhD diss., Laval University, 2001), 353, 1062.

4. Bénéteau, "Aspects," 353. Bénéteau cites Frederic Baraga, *A Dictionary of the Otchipwe Language, Explained in English* (Montreal: Beauchemin & Valois, 1878), 70b, for "bata," which carries the meaning described; and Jean-André Cuoq, *Lexique de la langue algonquine* (Montreal: J. Chapleau & fils, 1886), 330a, for "pata." Baraga conducted research among the Ojibwe and Cuoq collected his data from the Nipissing, which means both definitions are part of the general historic Anishinaabowin lexicon.

5. Richard White, *The Middle Ground: Indians, Empires, and Republics in the Great Lakes Region* (Cambridge: Cambridge University Press, 1991), 154–159.

6. Brett Rushforth, "Slavery, the Fox Wars, and the Limits of Alliance," *William and Mary*

Quarterly 63, no. 1 (January 2006), 56–57.

7. Richard Weyhing, "The Straits of Empire: French Colonial Detroit and the Origins of the Fox Wars" (PhD diss., University of Chicago, 2012), 12, 15–16.

8. Indigenous peoples referred to the Recollet as "grey robes" and the Jesuits as "black robes." By the mid-eighteenth century, Father Del Halle was considered a martyr due to the manner in which he had died. Detroit residents ascribed miracles to him, and his remains, regarded as relics, were disinterred and reinterred several times as the community grew and rebuilt its church.

9. François Clairambault d'Aigremont, who had been sent by to inspect all of the forts in the *pays d'en haut* in the summer of 1708, made a detailed report of the disastrous "siege" of the Myaamia fort, describing it as poorly planned and executed. Aigremont and some Indigenous and French informants who related the story of the "attack" were at a loss to explain Cadillac's actions (see "Rapport de Clairambault d'Aigremont au ministre concernant sa mission d'inspection dans les postes avancés," Québec, 14 novembre 1708, vol. 29, Folios 54–58, Série C11A, BAC).

10. "Rapport de Clairambault d'Aigremont au ministre concernant sa mission d'inspection dans les postes avancés," Folios 35v–68.

11. "Lettre du Vaudreuil au ministre," Québec, 8 novembre 1711, Série C11A, vol. 32, Folio 67v, BAC.

12. For Vaudreuil's claim the Fox moved to Detroit to be closer to the English, see "Lettre de Vaudreuil au ministre," 8 novembre 1711, Folios 72v–73.

13. For Cadillac's report on Haudenosaunee, see "Mémoire de Lamothe Cadillac," 14 novembre 1704, Québec, Série C11E, vol. 14, Folio 173, BAC. For Haudenosaunee in church records, see Register of Ste. Anne, April 21, 1707; June 9, 1712; September 21, 1713; August 1, 1718; and August 3, 1718.

14. Register of Ste. Anne, August 1 and 3, 1718.

15. Dubuisson report, *Michigan Pioneer and Historical Society Collections* (Lansing: Michigan Pioneer and Historical Society, 1874–1929), 33:550.

16. "M. de Vaudreuil to M. de Pontchartrain," Quebec, October 31, 1710, *Documents Relative to the Colonial History of the State of New York,* ed. E. B. O'Callaghan (Albany, NY: Weed, Parsons and Co.), 9:847.

17. M. de Vaudreuil, "Reports from the Upper Country," September 6, 1712, *Michigan Pioneer and Historical Society Collections,* 33:560.

18. Cadillac left Detroit in the fall of 1711 and traveled with his family to France rather than proceed directly to Louisiana. The main purpose for the trip to France was to add his voice to that of Minister of the Navy Pontchartrain, who tried to convince Antoine

Crozat, a wealthy investor, to buy Louisiana from the king. Cadillac and Pontchartrain were successful, although the relationship between Cadillac and Crozat would sour in relatively short order.

19. Andrew Sturtevant, "Jealous Neighbors: Rivalry and Alliance among the Native Communities of Detroit, 1701–1766" (PhD diss., College of William and Mary, 2011), 90.

20. For Marguerite as Waapankihkwa, see John Bickers and George Ironstrack, "The Many Branches of Tahkamwa's Family Tree," May 29, 2015, https://myaamiahistory.wordpress.com/2015/05/29/the-many-branches-of-tahkamwas-family-tree/.

21. "Lettre de Vaudreuil au ministre," Québec, 3 novembre 1710, Série C11A, vol. 31, Folios 56–57, BAC. Some of the soldiers were reported to have deserted. Vaudreuil's withdrawal of the garrison would prove a disastrous decision when the conflagration with the Meskwaki occurred two years later. From the time of its establishment, imperial authorities had never been fully committed to maintaining the fort.

22. "Extrait d'une délibération faite entre le Sr de Lamothe et les habitants du Détroit," 7 juin 1710, Série C11E, vol. 15, Folios 38–38v, BAC.

23. "Extrait de la lettre du père Chérubin de Niau, récollect et missionnaire au Détroit," Détroit, 24 août 1711, Série C11E, vol. 15, Folio 75, BAC.

24. In a meeting held between the Onondaga and the French in 1684, the French governor general referred to the Mascouten as brothers to the Myaamia, warning the Haudenosaunee leaders not to strike one or the other of those nations because of this relationship ("Presents of the Onondagas to Onontio at La Famine," September 5, 1684, in O'Callaghan, *Documents Relative to the Colonial History of the State of New York,* 9:237).

25. "Lettre de Dubuisson à Vaudreuil donnant un compte rendu détaillé de la défaite des Renards et des Mascoutens à Detroit," Détroit, 15 juin 1712, Série C11A, vol. 33, Folio 162, BAC.

26. "Note de Dubuisson à propos de munitions appertenant à Lamothe Cadillac," Détroit, 1712, Série C11E, vol. 15, Folio 83, BAC. The large amount of munitions in question (five hundred gun flints, three barrels of powder, five bags of lead, and three bags of shot) had been listed as part of the extensive goods in Cadillac's possession itemized and inventoried when Cadillac was preparing to leave for Louisiana ("Inventory of Cadillac's Detroit Property," August 25, 1711, *Michigan Pioneer and Historical Society Collections,* 33:518–528). Did the goods belong to Cadillac or to the king? Cadillac felt they belonged to him and attempted to sell them before his departure. As incoming commandant, however, Dubuisson believed the goods were the property of the king and therefore now belonged to Dubuisson. He refused to buy the inventoried items from Cadillac and forbade anyone else to make the purchase ("Cadillac tries to sell his personal effects to De

La Forest," July 1, 1711, *Michigan Pioneer and Historical Society Collections,* 33:508).

27. "Extrait de la lettre du père Chérubin de Niau, recollect et missionnaire au Détroit," Détroit, 24 août 1711, Série C11E, vol. 15, Folio 75, BAC.

28. *Thresor de la langue francoyse tant ancienne que moderne,* 1606, ARTFL Project, University of Chicago, https://artfl-project.uchicago.edu/content/dictionnaires-dautrefois.

29. Brett Rushforth, *Bonds of Alliance,* 136, 182, 207.

30. Registre de Ste. Anne, Burton Historical Collection, Detroit Public Library, "Second Livre des baptêmes des sauvages," 113–114.

31. Registre de Ste. Anne, 111–140.

32. The French routinely used both the French "Renard" (Fox) and "Outagami" to refer to this nation. "Outagami" comes from the Ojibwe "otaka-mi-k" which translates as "people of the other shore." The moniker of "Fox" is thought to be an early reference to the Fox moiety of the larger collective, which was then applied to the nation as a whole. Two moieties were known historically by both the French and British—the "red-earth" people and "red-fox" people. The Fox name for themselves is "meškwahki-haki," meaning "Red-Earths." See Meskwaki Nation—Sac & Fox Tribe of the Mississippi in Iowa: https://www.meskwaki.org; and Charles Callender, "Fox" in *Handbook of North American Indians,* vol. 15, *Northeast,* ed. Bruce G. Trigger (Washington, DC: Smithsonian Institution, 1978), 645–646.

33. Susan Sleeper-Smith, *Indian Women and French Men: Rethinking Cultural Encounter in the Western Great Lakes* (Amherst: University of Massachusetts Press, 2001), 43.

34. Registre de Ste. Anne, 141–150.

35. Afua Cooper, *The Hanging of Angélique: The Untold Story of Canadian Slavery and the Burning of Old Montreal* (Toronto: HarperCollins, 2006), 75.

36. Sleeper-Smith, *Indian Women and French Men,* 43.

37. Brett Rushforth points out that "Native women supervised and monitored much of the captive population in the West" (*Bonds of Alliance,* 265).

38. Rushforth, *Bonds of Alliance,* 283; for imperial accusations of private affairs, see "Memorandum from the King," March 22, 1755, *Wisconsin Historical Collections,* vol. 18 (1908): 152, as it appears in Rushforth, *Bonds of Alliance,* 283.

39. Jean-Guy Pelletier, "Coulon de Villiers, Nicolas-Antoine (1683–1733)," in *Dictionary of Canadian Biography,* vol. 2 (Toronto: University of Toronto/Université Laval, 2003–), http://www.biographi.ca/en/bio/coulon_de_villiers_nicolas_antoine_1683_1733_2E.html. For a nineteenth-century view of the Fox, see Walter B. Douglas, "The Sieurs de St. Ange," *Transactions of the Illinois State Historical Society,* vol. 14 (Springfield, IL: State Journal Co.,

1910), 139.

40. French genealogist Cyprien Tanguay (*Dictionnaire généalogique des familles canadiennes depuis la fondation de la colonie jusqu'à nos jours* [Montreal: Eusèbe Senécal & Fils, 1890], 428) lists the multiple last names of Bougoin, Bourguignon (close to Bourdignon), and Didier St. Paul as occurring together in the case of one particular family.

41. For censure of Bourgmond, see "MM. de Vaudreuil et Raudot au ministre," novembre 1706, Série C11G, vol. 3, Folio 61, BAC; Vaudreuil was of the opinion that if Cadillac, Tonty, or La Forest had been present, the Odawa would not have attacked. For a short biography of Bourgmond, see Louise Dechêne, "Véniard De Bourgmond, Étienne De," in *Dictionary of Canadian Biography,* vol. 2 (Toronto: University of Toronto/Université Laval, 2003–), http://www.biographi.ca/en/bio/veniard_de_bourgmond_etienne_de_2E.html. For French imperial opinion of Bourgmond, see particularly "Lettre de Ramezay, gouverneur de Montréal, au ministre," Québec, 18 septembre 1714, Série C11A, vol. 34, Folio 356v, BAC, in which Bourgmond is accused of fomenting division between the Illinois and Myaamia and of wanting to introduce the English of Carolina to the Illinois Indians. See also the biography by Frank Norall, *Bourgmont, Explorer of the Missouri, 1698–1725* (Lincoln: University of Nebraska Press, 1988).

42. Marcel Trudel, *L'esclavage au Canada français: Histoire et conditions de l'esclavage* (Quebec: Les Presses Universitaires Laval, 1960), 159.

CHAPTER 4. *ILS S'EN ALLAIENT TOUS:* ROOTS AND ROUTES OF THE FRENCH-INDIGENOUS FAMILY NETWORKS

1. James Merrell, *Into the American Woods: Negotiators on the Pennsylvania Frontier* (New York: W. W. Norton, 1999), 112.

2. "Lettre de Ramezay gouverneur de Montréal au ministre," 18 septembre 1714, C11a, vol. 34, Folio 356v, BAC.

3. Peter d'Errico turns the European medieval concept of lèse-majesté on its head, suggesting its use by Indigenous nations to extricate themselves from Euro-American legal constructs that continue to lay claim to Indigenous lands and bodies. Lèse-majesté "would manifest the urge to be free of domination, to exercise self-determination in their own territories" (Peter d'Errico, "Indigenous Lèse-majesté: Questioning U.S. Federal Indian Law," *New Diversities* 19, no. 2 (2017): 53.

4. June 30, 1710, Registre de Ste. Anne, Livre des marriages de Fort Pontchartrain de Detroit, 89, Burton Historical Collection, Detroit Public Library.

5. "Recensement nominatif de Détroit," 1710, Série C11A, vol. 31, Folios 160–160v, BAC.

6. "État des contrats donnés, par M. de Lamothe Cadillac aux habitants du Détroit," 1707–1710, Série C11E, vol. 15, Folio 3v, BAC.

7. Louis Fafard dit Longval was related through marriage to the Trottier family.

8. For Fafard as interpreter to La Salle and Du Luth, see René-Robert Cavelier de la Salle, "Description of Wisconsin Rivers; Accusations against Duluth," in *Collections of the State Historical Society of Wisconsin,* ed. Reuben Gold Thwaites, vol. 16, *The French Regime in Wisconsin,* vol. 1, *1634–1727,* 108–109. For Fafard's stint with Enjalran, see "Lettre du jésuite Enjalran à La Barre," Michilimackinac, 1 mai 1684, vol. 6, Série C11A, Folio 525, BAC.

9. "Engagement de Joseph Fafart dit La Fresnaye par Frs. De la Forest," Montreal, May 5, 1690, and "Engagement of the Fafarts, one acting for his brother, to Monsieur de Boisrondel, acting for Monsieur de la Forest," May 8, 1690, in *The French Foundations, 1680–1693,* ed. Theodore Calvin Pease and Raymond C. Werner, *Collections of the Illinois State Historical Library,* vol. 23 (French Series, vol. 1), 195–198 and 202–206. La Forest hired Joseph and Louis Fafard on other occasions to carry furs from Louisiana to Montreal (see "Engagement of Filastreau, Maillou, Cardinal, Fafart, and Morin to Monsieur de la Forest," August 29 and October 1689, in *The French Foundations, 1680–1693,* ed. Pease and Werner, 181–186). For biographical information on La Forest, see Louise Dechêne, "Dauphin de La Forest, François," in *Dictionary of Canadian Biography,* vol. 2 (Toronto: University of Toronto/Université Laval, 2003–), http://www.biographi.ca/en/bio/dauphin_de_la_forest_francois_2E.html.

10. For rarity in the records of cases in the Illinois Country involving adultery, see Margaret Kimball Brown, *History as They Lived It: A Social History of Prairie du Rocher, Illinois* (Carbondale: Southern Illinois University Press, 2014), 47.

11. Margaret Kimball Brown and Lawrie Cena Dean, eds. *The Village of Chartres in Colonial Illinois, 1720–1765* (New Orleans: Polyanthos, 1977), 813–814. It is likely that by "shut away," authorities were allowing Pierre to have Marguerite confined to a convent.

12. Rushforth, *Bonds of Alliance,* 165–173.

13. The communication between the Illinois and Cadillac that was carried by Bizaillon must have taken place prior to the autumn of 1711, when Cadillac left Detroit. Cadillac would not arrive in Louisiana to take up his position as governor until late spring of 1713. At the time of Chachagouesse's speech to Vaudreuil in Montreal, Cadillac was in France.

14. Parolles de Chachagouesse ou autrement Nicanapé chef Illinois, 20 août 1712, Série C11A, vol. 33, Folios 93–93v, BAC. See also Donald J. Horton, "Chachagouesse," in *Dictionary of Canadian Biography,* vol. 2 (Toronto: University of Toronto/Université Laval, 2003–), http://www.biographi.ca/en/bio/chachagouesse_2E.html. Michael McCafferty lists

this Illinois leader's name as šaahšaakweehsiwa, which in the Miami-Illinois language translates as copperhead snake (*Native American Place Names of Indiana* [Urbana: University of Illinois Press, 2008], 24).

15. "Reponse de Vaudreuil aux paroles de Chachagouesse," 1712, Série C11A, vol. 33, Folios 101v–102, BAC. De Liette was a cousin of Alphonse and Henri Tonty. Together with Henri Tonty, he had lived and commanded among the Illinois for several decades by the time of Vaudreuil's speech to Chachagouesse.

16. Jean-Baptiste Bissot de Vincennes was an officer who commanded among the Myaamia and lived near Fort St. Joseph (present-day Niles, Michigan) in 1695.

17. "Lettre de Ramezay, gouverneur de Montreal, au ministre," Québec, 18 septembre 1714.

18. The incident involving the attack on the Jesuit Jacques Gravier by a Peoria man took place in the autumn of 1705. Gravier was shot with several arrows in one of his arms, but because the wound was not well tended, it never properly healed, leading to his death in 1708 (for this biographical information, see Charles E. O'Neill, "Gravier, Jacques," in *Dictionary of Canadian Biography,* vol. 2 (Toronto: University of Toronto/Université Laval, 2003–), http://www.biographi.ca/en/bio/gravier_jacques_2E.html. Other sources describing the attack on Gravier and his retreat to a safe house tell a different story of events, depicting him as being left in the care of "praying women" until Kaskaskia representatives sent by Gravier's "prize convert," the Illinois woman Marie Rouensa, arrived to rescue him (Richard White, *The Middle Ground: Indians, Empires, and Republics in the Great Lakes Region, 1650–1815* [Cambridge: Cambridge University Press, 1991], 75). For Gravier's close spiritual relationship with Rouensa, see Susan Sleeper-Smith, *Indian Women and French Men: Rethinking Cultural Encounter in the Western Great Lakes* [Amherst: University of Massachusetts Press, 2001], 26, 29, 33; and Sophie White, *Wild Frenchmen and Frenchified Indians: Material Culture and Race in Colonial Louisiana* (Philadelphia: University of Pennsylvania Press, 2014), 79–81.

19. Jean Bergier became superior of the Mississippi missions in 1700 and held that position until his death in November 1707 (*Jesuit Relations and Allied Documents,* ed. Reuben Gold Thwaites, vol. 65 [Cleveland: Burrows Brothers Co., 1898], 264).

20. One of his traveling companions was Bourdon—almost certainly the same man who had been accused with Bizaillon of seeking to influence the Illinois to make contact with the English of Carolina.

21. "Justification de Michel Bisaillon," [1716], Série C11A, Folios 99–100v, BAC. Bizaillon's version of events among the Illinois concurs with Chachagouesse's explanation to Vaudreuil of Bizaillon's activities.

22. Registre de Ste. Anne, Second Livre de baptêmes sauvages, 103.

23. David J. Costa, "The St-Jérôme Dictionary of Miami-Illinois," in *Papers of the 36th Algonquian Conference,* ed. H. C. Wolfart (Winnipeg: University of Manitoba, 2005), 114.

24. Two officers attested to Bizaillon's success at gathering the Illinois warriors: Louis, Sieur de Monnoir, eldest son of Claude Ramezay ("Copie d'une lettre de Monnoir à son père Ramezay," Chicagoüe, 28 août 1715, C11A, vol. 35, BAC), and the Sieur Adoucourt, son of Charles Le Moyne de Longueuil ("Copie d'une lettre de d'Adoucourt à son père," 22 août 1715, Le Rocher, Série C11A, vol. 35, BAC). Both Ramezay's and Longueuil's sons would lose their lives during this engagement. According to one account, the two men were making their way to Detroit from the Ouabache when their party was attacked by a Cherokee contingent. The report of the demise of the two officers was communicated along a well-traveled route—the men who managed to escape Cherokee capture traveled to Kaskaskia, where they reported the deaths. From there, the news was taken to Detroit and then to Montreal (see "Lettre de Vaudreuil au Conseil de Marine," Québec, 12 octobre 1717, Série C11A, vol. 38, Folios 101–101v, BAC). An account circulated a year earlier of the deaths of the two officers had more serious implications for Illinois-French relations. According to this rendition of events, the French at Detroit told a group of Seneca warriors that the two officers and four other Frenchmen had been killed by Illinois. Upon hearing this, the Seneca expressed their desire for revenge because they considered one of the dead men, Adoucourt, to be kin (see "Lettre de Vaudreuil au Conseil de Marine avec avis du Conseil," Québec, 14 octobre 1716, Série C11A, vol. 36, Folios 77v–78, BAC).

25. "Lettre de Vaudreuil au Conseil de Marine," Québec, 14 octobre 1716, Série C11A, vol. 36, Folios 71, 72–72v, BAC).

26. "Lettre de Ramezay au ministre," 28 octobre 1715, Québec, Série C11A, vol. 35, Folios 90v–91, BAC. The merchant Desauniers mentioned in Ramezay's letter was Pierre Trottier Desauniers who had also conducted business with Michel's brother Pierre Bizaillon (see "Ordonnance qui décharge Pierre Trotier Desauniers du cautionnement qu'il avait donné en faveur de Pierre Bisaillon," 20 juin 1718, Fonds des Ordonnances des intendants de la Nouvelle-France, BAC).

27. Merrell, *Into the American Woods,* 110.

28. Merrell, *Into the American Woods,* 114.

29. White, *Wild Frenchmen and Frenchified Indians,* 92. See also Sleeper-Smith, *Indian Women and French Men,* 22.

30. Heidi Bohaker, "'Nindoodemag': The Significance of Algonquian Kinship Networks in the Eastern Great Lakes Region, 1600–1701," *William and Mary Quarterly,* 3rd Ser., 63, no. 1 (January 2006): 47.

31. Patricia Albers and Jeanne Kay, "Sharing the Land: A Study in American Indian

Territoriality," in *A Cultural Geography of North American Indians,* ed. Thomas E. Ross and Tyrel G. Moore (Boulder, CO: Westview Press, 1987), 64.

32. Chachagouesse described Bizaillon as having been married "devant l'église" (literally translated "in front of the church"), which is presumably a reference to Bizaillon's 1710 marriage to Marguerite Fafard according to Catholic rites at Detroit.

33. Suzanne Boivin Sommerville, "'But I read it . . .': Who Is the Michel Bisaillon who Married Madeleine Perrier dite Olivier on 11 Jan 1740 in Laprairie? and Did Pierre Bisaillon Father Children Baptized at Kaskaskia?," in *Le Détroit du Lac Érié, 1701–1710,* ed. Gail Moreau-DesHarnais, Diane Wolford Sheppard, and Suzanne Boivin Sommerville, vol. 2 (Royal Oak, MI: French-Canadian Heritage Society of Michigan, 2016), 164.

34. "Reponse de Vaudreuil aux paroles de Chachagouesse," 1712, AN, Série C11A, vol. 33, Folio 102, BAC. Vaudreuil's acknowledgment of the daughters of Indigenous leaders (in this case Chachagouesse's daughter) is somewhat unusual in the record of meetings held between the French governor general and Indigenous nations of the upper country/*pays d'en haut.*

35. At Kaskaskia, marriages or liaisons between French men and Indigenous women were a common occurrence. For the last decade of the seventeenth and first two decades of the eighteenth centuries, the church register records the baptisms of children of these liaisons almost exclusively. This is not the case for the same time period at Detroit, where baptisms of the children of either two Indigenous parents (predominantly although not exclusively Wendat) or of two French parents predominate in church records. Susan Sleeper-Smith has pointed out that Kaskaskia was not a French settlement, but a community where Illinois-Kaskaskia women who were sympathetic to Catholicism were congregated, the most famous of whom was Marie Rouensa (see Sleeper-Smith, *Indian Women and French Men,* 32). The Jesuits reported having more success missionizing among the Kaskaskia than some of the other Illinois tribes, including the Peoria (White, *The Middle Ground,* 74).

36. "Justification de Michel Bisaillon."

37. Coxe and company encouraged settlement by various groups, including the English, Dutch, Swedes, and French (see Albright G. Zimmerman, "Daniel Coxe and the New Mediterranean Sea Company," *Pennsylvania Magazine of History and Biography* 76, no. 1 [January 1952]: 95). At roughly the same time Coxe was attempting to launch his venture, the French were employing voyageurs to reclaim the area of Detroit and the southern end of Lake Erie.

38. For a brief biography of Pierre Bizaillon, upon which this summary is based, see Francis Jennings, "Bisaillon, Peter," in *Dictionary of Canadian Biography,* vol. 3, (University

of Toronto, 2003–), http://www.biographi.ca/en/bio/bisaillon_peter_3E.html. For additional information on the Bizaillons, see also Yves Zoltvany, "New France and the West, 1701–1713," *Canadian Historical Review* 46 (1965): 301–322; Francis Jennings, *The Ambiguous Iroquois Empire: The Covenant Chain Confederation of Indian Tribes with English Colonies* (New York: W. W. Norton, 1990); Michael N. McConnell, *The Upper Ohio Valley and Its Peoples, 1724–1774* (Lincoln: University of Nebraska Press, 1992); and Brett Rushforth, "Slavery, the Fox Wars, and the Limits of Alliance," *William and Mary Quarterly,* 3rd Ser., 63, no. 1 (January 2006): 53–80.

39. Notre Dame de la Conception des Cascaskias, Illinois, U.S.A., Registres Photographie aux Archives d'Ottawa Ont., Reduction 18, Lumiere 4, 2–3. Suzanne Boivin Sommerville hypothesizes that these were children of Michel (see Boivin Sommerville, "But I read it . . .").

40. New York, August 27, 1701. The letter was sold at auction on April 15, 2006. The auction house also sold four other items relating to Pierre/Peter Bisaillon/Besellion ranging in date from 1699 to 1714, all pertaining to licenses and business agreements between Pierre and Pennsylvania merchants; see http://www.worthpoint.com/worthopedia/besallion-peter-1702-child-s-heartbreaking-letter-to

41. José António Brandão, ed. and trans., with K. Janet Ritch, *Nation Iroquoise: A Seventeenth-Century Ethnography of the Iroquois* (Lincoln: University of Nebraska Press, 2003), 102–105; Brandão identified René Cuillerier as the anonymous source of this captivity narrative and believes Cuillerier dictated his experiences.

42. For the biographical outline used here, see Claude Perrault, "Cuillerier, René," in *Dictionary of Canadian Biography,* vol. 2 (Toronto: University of Toronto/Université Laval, 2003–), http://www.biographi.ca/en/bio/cuillerier_rene_2E.html.

43. In 1664, the year after Cuillerier was at Fort Orange, New Netherland was surrendered by the Dutch to the English and the name of the fort was changed to Albany.

44. John Fraser, "La Salle's Homestead at La Chine," *Magazine of American History with Notes and Queries* 24 (July–December 1890): 447–449. The area had also been located near Robert Cavelier de La Salle's proposed extensive seigneury/homestead that he had purchased in 1666.

45. Original speech appears as "Paroles addressées à Frontenac par Teganissorens deputé des Cinq Nations iroquoises," Montréal, 11 septembre 1682, Série C11A, vol. 6, Folio 16, BAC; English translation can be found in "Conference between Count Frontenac and a Deputy from the Five Nations/Speech of the Delegate from the Five Iroquois Nations to Count de Frontenac," September 11, 1682, in *Documents Relative to the Colonial History of the State of New York,* ed. E. B. O'Callaghan (Albany, NY: Weed, Parsons and Co.,

1854–1855), 9:184–185. Cuillerier told Frontenac that the Haudenosaunee planned to attack the Illinois, but Niregouentaron denied the proposed attack, claiming Cuillerier had misunderstood him.

46. "Congé par Robert Cavelier de la Salle au Sieur René Cuillerier," 11 août 1681, Congés et permis enregistrés à Montréal, Bibliothèque et Archives Canada.

47. "Settlement of Partnership Account," Montreal, July 29, 1689, in *The French Foundations 1680–1693,* ed. Pease and Werner, 1:179.

48. "État de la dépense faite en l'année en 1689 au sujet de la guerre en Canada," [1689], Série C11A, vol. 113, Folios 17 and 18, BAC.

49. "Procès-verbal de la saisie de pelleteries provenant du fort Frontenac," Au pied des Cascades, 16 juillet 1700, Série C11A, BAC; "Ordonnance de Champigny," Montréal, 24 août 1700, vol. 18, BAC; "Extrait des informations et autres procedures faites," 1700, vol. 18, Série C11A, BAC; "Procès-verbaux perquisitions faites chez René Cuillerier, Saint-Romain, Couagne, Jean Cuillerier et Fillastreau, pour y chercher Joseph Trottier des Ruisseaux et Lambert Cuillerier," août 1700, vol. 18, Série C11A, BAC. Imperial authorities were still referring to Albany by its Dutch designation of Orange. René and another of his sons, Jean Cuillerier, were questioned in this matter. As a penalty for the illegal trade at Fort Frontenac, Trottier dit DesRuisseaux was ordered to contribute 300 livres to the care of the poor at the Hotel Dieu of Montreal. There was considerable correspondence generated over this illegal trade at Fort Frontenac in 1700, probably because it involved a high-ranking officer, and because the incident occurred in the midst of preparations for the Great Peace of Montreal in 1701. In 1706, Lambert Cuillerier and others would be accused of trading at Fort Orange ("Lettre de Vaudreuil et des intendants Raudot au ministre," 3 novembre 1706, Québec, Série C11A, vol. 24, BAC) and an order sent out to have Lambert imprisoned ("Ordonnance de l'intendant Jacques Raudot pour l'élargissement de Lambert Cuillerier, détenu dans les prisons de Montréal pour avoir trafiqué avec les Anglais au mépris des ordres du Roi," November 10, 1706, Fonds Intendants, Ordonnances, Bibliothèque et Archives Nationales Québec).

50. *Rapport de l'Archiviste de la Province de la Québec pour 1929–1930* (Quebec: Rédempti Paradis, 1930), 206.

51. "Procès contre Joseph Trottier, sieur DesRuisseaux, accusé de traite illégale de fourrures avec les sauvages des lacs Erié et Ontario," August 24, 1702–August 31, 1702, Fonds Juridiction royale de Montréal, Dossiers, Bibliothèque et Archives nationales du Québec.

52. "Lettre du jésuite Joseph-Jacques Marest à Vaudreuil," Michilimakinac, 14 août 1706, Série C11A, vol. 24, Folios 259v–260v, BAC.

53. "Lettre du jésuite Joseph-Jacques Marest à Vaudreuil," Michilimakinac, 14 août 1706, Série

C11A, vol. 24, Folio 260v, BAC.

54. For Lambert Cuillerier's stint as godfather, see Suzanne Boivin Sommerville, "Madame Montour (La Tichenet) and Étienne Veniard, Sieur de Bougmont, according to the 1707 Judgment of Pichon dit La Roze at Détroit: The Perils of Translation and Interpretation," in *Le Détroit du Lac Érié*, vol. 2, ed. Moreau-DesHarnais, Sheppard, and Boivin Sommerville, 106–123.

55. Louis-Thomas Chabert de Joncaire followed a similar course as René Cuillerier in his integration into Haudenosaunee society; after his arrival from France in the 1680s, he was captured by Seneca and adopted by a Seneca woman, who named him Sononchiez (Yves F. Zoltvany, "Chabert de Joncaire, Louis-Thomas, Sononchiez," in *Dictionary of Canadian Biography*, vol. 2 (Toronto: University of Toronto/Université Laval, 2003–), http://www.biographi.ca/en/bio/chabert_de_joncaire_louis_thomas_2E.html.

56. "Lettre des sieurs Vaudreuil et Raudot au ministre," 14 novembre 1709, Série C11A, vol. 30, Folio 9v, BAC.

57. For Cadillac's claims against Joncaire, see "Instructions pour server au Sieur d'Aigremont," Versailles, 30 juin 1707, Série B, vol. 29, BAC; for Vaudreuil's praise of Joncaire, see "MM. de Vaudreuil et Raudot au ministre," novembre 1706, Série C11G, vol. 3, BAC.

58. For genealogical and historical information on Madame Montour and the Couc family, see Boivin Sommerville, "Madame Montour (La Tichenet)," 106–123; for role of Madame Montour and her son in British-Indigenous negotiations, see James Merrell, "'The Cast of His Countenance': Reading Andrew Montour," in *Through a Glass Darkly: Reflections on Personal Identity in Early America*, ed. Ronald Hoffman et al. (Chapel Hill: University of North Carolina Press, 1997), 13–39; Merrell, *Into the American Woods;* Jon Parmenter, "Isabel Montour: Cultural Broker on the Eighteenth-Century Frontiers of New York and Pennsylvania," in *The Human Tradition in Colonial America*, ed. Ian K. Steele and Nancy Rhoden, 141–159 (Wilmington, DE: Scholarly Resources Press, 1999); and Alison Duncan Hirsch, "'The Celebrated Madame Montour': Interpretess across Early American Frontiers," *Explorations in Early American Culture* 4 (2000): 81–112.

59. Pigarouich was named Etienne/Stephen by the Jesuits to commemorate his baptism on December 26, the feast day of St. Stephen. Pigarouich/Etienne figures frequently and prominently in the *Jesuit Relations*, where the nature of his activities as a medicine man in shaking tent and medicinal drumming ceremonies brought him to the attention of the Jesuits. The Jesuits studied the spiritual activities of Pigarouich and other "sorcerers" closely, in order to discredit them and to reduce their influence among their people. After observing several shaking tent ceremonies, the Jesuits were unable to discover how the "sorcerer" was manipulating the tent. Unable to label the practice a charade, they

concluded that it was the work of the devil. Pigarouich became a source of continued frustration to the Jesuits Jean de Brébeuf and Paul LeJeune when he converted to Catholicism on more than one occasion, but continuously reverted to ancient customs of his people, most notably a habit the Jesuits felt was the hardest for Etienne and his kinsmen to relinquish—the taking of more than one wife (see discussion on this matter in *The Jesuit Relations and Allied Documents,* ed. Reuben Gold Thwaites, vol. 25 (Cleveland: Burrows Brothers Co., 1898), 247–249.

60. "Lettre de Bégon au ministre," Québec, 7 novembre 1715, Série C11A, vol. 123, Folios 147v–148, BAC. For discussion of the role of the *panis* slave Joseph, who was interrogated over the matter but was not charged, see Marcel Trudel, *L'esclavage au Canada français: Histoire et conditions de L'esclavage* (Quebec: Les Presses Universitaires Laval, 1960), 214.

61. St. Germain and Sarrazin told Aigremont that while they were hunting north of Detroit at Saginaw Bay, they saw three boatloads of furs diverted in this manner. See "Rapport de Clairambault d'Aigremont au ministre concernant sa mission d'inspection dans les postes avancé," 14 novembre 1708, Folio 60, BAC.

62. Rushforth, *Bonds of Alliance,* 320. Rushforth offers an in-depth discussion of St. Germain's business activities, and possession of and trade in slaves on pp. 309–317.

63. "Lettre de Néret et Gayot au ministre—évacuation du fort Bourbon," Paris, 26 avril 1714, Série C11A, vol. 34, Folio 406, BAC. The original document references only a Sieur Cuillerier who had been operating a long time in the area of Lake Superior and Hudson Bay. It is therefore difficult to ascertain the exact identity of the male member of the family. René Cuillerier Sr. had either died or was ill at this time, leading this author to believe the man referenced here was his son René Hillaire, who would have been twenty-four years old at the time (see "Lettre du Beauharnois au ministre," Québec, 25 septembre 1741, Serie C11A, vol. 75, Folio 185, BAC).

64. Marcel Trudel, *Dictionnaire des esclaves et de leurs propriétaires au Canada français* (LaSalle, QC: Éditions Hurtubise HMH Ltée., 1990), 78. Trudel is sketchy on the timing of this relationship, believing that a marriage eventually took place after René Hillaire had been widowed in 1756. It is much more likely, however, that their daughter was born about 1718 in the Missouri basin, and baptized in Montreal several years later. The considerable gap between the births of René Hillaire's children with his French wife at Cap Santé allows for the possibility that he was moving about the interior of the continent (there is an eleven-year gap between a son born in 1712 and a daughter born in 1723, after which the births of his children resume a pattern of roughly every two years—the standard spacing in New France).

65. Rushforth, *Bonds of Alliance,* 237–243.

66. Registre de Ste. Anne, 149.

67. For Sarah Allen as captive, see Eric Lalonde, "Sarah Allen and the Battle of Deerfield," http://web.uvic.ca/~lalonde/history/history/battle.html.

68. "État des contrats donnés par M. de Lamothe Cadillac aux habitants du Détroit suivant le pouvoir qu'il en avait eu de Sa Majesté en 1704, 1705, et 1706," Série C11E, vol. 15, Folio 8v, BAC.

69. "Ordonnance entre François Pelletier dit Antaya, habitant de Détroit et Julien Trottier des Rivières, marchand à Montréal," 30 juillet 1722, Fonds des Ordonnances des intendants de la Nouvelle-France, BAC.

70. Jan Noel, *Along a River: The First French-Canadian Women* (Toronto: University of Toronto Press, 2013), 95–102.

71. "Copie de l'ordre de La Jonquière adressé aux demoiselles Desauniers," 29 mai 1750, Série C11A, vol. 95, Folio 180, BAC; and "Lettre de La Jonquière au ministre," 1 novembre 1751, Série C11A, vol. 97, Folio 173v, BAC. See also David Lee Preston, *The Texture of Contact: European and Indian Settler Communities on the Frontiers of Iroquoia, 1667–1783* (Lincoln: University of Nebraska Press, 2009), 57–58.

72. In collaboration with Walter S. Dunn Jr., "Chabert de Joncaire de Clausonne, Daniel-Marie," in *Dictionary of Canadian Biography,* vol. 4 (Toronto: University of Toronto/ Université Laval, 2003–), http://www.biographi.ca/en/bio/chabert_de_joncaire_de_clausonne_daniel_marie_4E.html.

73. "Paroles de Teganagouassen et Beauvais, chefs de guerre du Sault-Saint-Louis," 15 mai 1750, Série C11A, vol. 95, Folio 174v, BAC.

74. Beauharnois to Maurepas, Quebec, September 21, 1741, *Documents Relative to the Colonial History of the State of New York,* 9:1071.

75. Nancy Shoemaker, *A Strange Likeness: Becoming Red and White in Eighteenth-Century North America* (New York: Oxford University Press, 2004), 40.

CHAPTER 5. ON SUCH DOES THE FATE OF EMPIRES DEPEND: WOMEN OF THE FRENCH-INDIGENOUS FAMILY NETWORKS

1. Peter Moogk, "Reluctant Exiles: Emigrants from France in Canada before 1760," *William and Mary Quarterly* 46, no. 3 (July 1989): 482.

2. Jan Noel, *Along a River: The First French-Canadian Women* (Toronto: University of Toronto Press, 2013), 80.

3. Bertrand Desjardins, "Family Formation and Infant Mortality in New France," in *Infant and Child Mortality in the Past,* ed. Alain Bideau, Bertrand Desjardins, and Héctor Pérez

Brignoli (Oxford: Oxford University Press, 1997), 17.

4. Allan Greer, *Mohawk Saint: Catherine Tekakwitha and the Jesuits* (New York: Oxford University Press, 2006), 50.

5. For genealogical information on the Roy family, see Cyprien Tanguay, *Dictionnaire généalogique des familles canadiennes depuis la fondation de la colonie jusqu'à nos jours* (Montreal: Eusèbe Senécal & Fils, 1890), 72; Gabriel Drouin, *Dictionnaire national des Canadiens français (1608–1760)*, vol. 2 (Montreal: Institut généalogique, 1965), 1205; and René Jetté, *Dictionnaire généalogique des familles du Québec* (Boucherville, QC: Gaetan Morin Editeur Limitée, 1983), 1018, 1022.

6. For biographical information on Pierre Roy Sr., see Michel Langlois, *Dictionnaire biographique des ancêtres québécois, 1608–1700,* vol. 4 (Siller, QC: Les Éditions du Mitan, 2001), 310–311; and Robert Prévost, *Portraits de familles pionnières,* vol. 4 (Montreal: Éditions Libre Expression, 1996), 251–252. Forty years later, Pierre Sr.'s son François would be working for Jacques Leber as a voyageur ("Obligation de François Roy, voyageur," Montréal, 16 mai 1716, Archives nationales du Québec à Montréal, étude M. Lepailleur de LaFerté).

7. For biography of Cuillerier, see Hélène Bernier, "Cuillerier, Marie-Anne-Véronique," in *Dictionary of Canadian Biography,* vol. 3 (Toronto: University of Toronto/Université Laval, 2003–), http://www.biographi.ca/en/bio/cuillerier_marie_anne_veronique_3F.html. For Cuillerier's annals, see "Relation de Soeur Cuillerier (1725–1747)," in Écrits du Canada français, vol. 42, ed. Ghislaine Legendre (Montreal, 1979), 151–192.

8. Louis Lavallée, *La Prairie en Nouvelle France, 1647–1760: Étude d'histoire sociale* (Montreal & Kingston: McGill-Queen's University Press, 1992), 114.

9. Evan Haefeli and Kevin Sweeney, *Captors and Captives: The 1704 French and Indian Raid on Deerfield* (Amherst: University of Massachusetts Press, 2003), 65.

10. Allan Greer, *The People of New France* (Toronto: University of Toronto Press, 1997), 72–73.

11. Marguerite Bourgeois, in *L'histoire des femmes au Québec depuis quatre siècles,* ed. Micheline Dumont et al. (Montreal: Les Quinze, Éditeur, 1982), 44. La Vierge Marie is French for the Virgin Mary.

12. "Lettre des sieurs Raudot au ministre," Québec, 23 octobre 1708, Série C11A, vol. 28, Folios 259v–260, BAC.

13. This dilemma was exhibited in a letter written by Minister of the Marine Pontchartrain in France to the intendant of New France. Pontchartrain spoke of the benefit of establishing offshoot communities of the Congregation outside of Montreal, but concluded that because the king did not believe members should take vows, such growth of the order was impossible (see "Le ministre à MM Raudot, Versailles, 6 juin 1708, Série B, BAC).

14. For Beauharnois's comment, see "Lettre de Beauharnois et Hocquart au ministre," Québec, 1 octobre 1732, Série C11A, vol. 57, Folios 6–6v, BAC. For the story of the attempt to cloister the sisters of the Congregation, see Hélène Bernier, "Charly Saint-Ange, Marie-Catherine, du Saint-Sacrement," in *Dictionary of Canadian Biography,* vol. 2 (Toronto: University of Toronto/Université Laval, 2003–), http://www.biographi.ca/en/bio/charly_saint_ange_marie_catherine_2E.html.

15. For biographical information on Marguerite Roy, see Andrée Désilets, "Roy, Marguerite, de la Conception," in *Dictionary of Canadian Biography,* vol. 3 (Toronto: University of Toronto/Université Laval, 2003–), http://www.biographi.ca/en/bio/roy_marguerite_3E.html. It is interesting to note that Marguerite Roy's fellow sister and superior of the Congregation, Marguerite Trottier, did not approve of the bishop's plan to establish the offshoot in Louisbourg. Trottier acquiesced in the face of the bishop's greater authority, however, and was eventually forced to travel to Louisbourg herself in 1733 (the same year Roy left Louisbourg) to salvage what was left after Roy's activities. For biographical information on Trottier, see Andrée Désilets, "Trottier, Marguerite, Saint-Joseph," in *Dictionary of Canadian Biography,* vol. 3 (Toronto: University of Toronto/Université Laval, 2003–), http://www.biographi.ca/en/bio/trottier_marguerite_3E.html.

16. Greer, *The People of New France,* 72.

17. Greer, *The People of New France,* 69.

18. Susan C. Boyle, "Did She Generally Decide? Women in Ste. Genevieve, 1750–1805," *William and Mary Quarterly* 3, no. 44 (October 1987): 781. In France, where the Coutume de Paris originated, there were various local legal adjustments made that complicated general mandates of the Coutume (see Janine Lanza, *From Wives to Widows in Early Modern Paris: Gender, Economy, and Law* [New York: Routledge, 2007], 34, 45–47).

19. Greer, *The People of New France,* 69.

20. Peter Moogk, *"Les Petits Sauvages:* The Children of Eighteenth-Century New France," in *Childhood and Family in Canadian History,* ed. Joy Parr (Toronto: McClelland and Stewart, 1982), 21.

21. Amos Stoddard, *Sketches Historical and Descriptive of Louisiana* (Philadelphia, 1812), in Susan C. Boyle, "Did She Generally Decide," 780.

22. Schuyler's son Abraham had himself been a captive of the French in 1687, when he was taken near Detroit. He and a party of traders were making their way from Albany to the French fort at Michilimackinac to conduct trade with the Wendat and Odawa when they were taken.

23. For Pachot meeting with Dellius and Schuyler, see Hugh Hastings, ed., *Ecclesiastical Records State of New York,* vol. 2 (Albany, NY: James B. Lyon, 1901), 1409–1411; and David

Arthur Armour, *The Merchants of Albany, New York: 1686–1760* (New York: Garland, 1986), 54.

24. For discussion of Louis Antoine's ties to the French and Spanish, see Juliana Barr, *Peace Came in the Form of a Woman: Indians and Spaniards in the Texas Borderlands* (Chapel Hill: University of North Carolina Press, 2009), 93, 107–108; and Elizabeth A. H. John, *Storms Brewed in Other Men's Worlds: The Confrontation of Indians, Spanish, and French in the Southwest, 1540–1795* (Norman: University of Oklahoma Press, 1996), 197–205. The Compagnie du Nord was originally chartered by King Louis XIV to encourage trade at Hudson Bay. At the turn of the eighteenth century, it morphed into the Compagnie de la Colonie, which underwrote Cadillac's establishment of the fort at Detroit, among other initiatives. The Compagnie became insolvent a few years later.

25. "Sale Madame de la Forest to Mon. de la Mothe Cadillac," Quebec, January 29, 1706, *Michigan Pioneer and Historical Society Collections and Researches,* 34:229 and 310.

26. For Jean Daniel Marie Viennay Pachot, see "Délibération du Conseil de Marine sur des lettres de Vaudreuil et Louvigny," 28 décembre 1716, Série C11A, vol. 36, Folios 280–280v, BAC; and "Délibération du Conseil de Marine sur une requête du sieur Pachot," 9 avril 1717, Série C11A, BAC. For Pontchartrain's and Raudot's descriptions of Charlotte-Françoise, see Antonio Drolet, "Juchereau de Saint-Denis, Charlotte-Françoise, Comtesse de Saint-Laurent," in *Dictionary of Canadian Biography,* vol. 2 (Toronto: University of Toronto/Université Laval, 2003–), http://www.biographi.ca/en/bio/juchereau_de_saint_denis_charlotte_francoise_2F.html.

27. "Lettre de Tonty à Ramezay," 10 mars 1723, Série C11A, vol. 45, Folios 357–357v, BAC.

28. Yves Quesnel notes that like many of the men who went west, Charles Nolan LaMarque used both his father's and mother's last names (Yves Quesnel, "Nolan Lamarque, Charles," in *Dictionary of Canadian Biography,* vol. 3 [Toronto: University of Toronto/Université Laval, 2003–], http://www.biographi.ca/en/bio/nolan_lamarque_charles_3E.html).

29. For accusation against de la Marque, Quenet, and Leguerrier, see "Ordonnance de l'intendant Bégon," Québec, 23 octobre 1714, Série C11A, vol. 35, Folios 190–195v, BAC.

30. For efforts of French to produce their own version of stroud, see Harold A. Innis, *Fur Trade in Canada* (Toronto: University of Toronto Press, 1999), 79. Stroud or écarlatine was available with either a blue or red tinge. In 1715, the English and French versions of the two colors were both circulating in the colonial marketplace, giving Indigenous customers an opportunity to compare them. Colonial authorities reported that Indigenous buyers preferred the blue of the French-made material to the blue dye used by the English, but conversely, they were more enthusiastic about the tint of the red in the cloth manufactured by the English.

31. "Lettre de Bégon au ministre," Québec, 7 novembre 1715, Série C11A, vol. 35, Folios 130v–131, BAC.

32. Sophie White has conducted extensive research on this New Orleans legal case and I am grateful to her for bringing it to my attention; see Sophie White, *Wild Frenchmen and Frenchified Indians: Material Culture and Race in Colonial Louisiana* (Philadelphia: University of Pennsylvania Press, 2012), 89–90. A transcript and translation of excerpts of Louis Metivier's legal challenge to Louis Turpin and the testimony of the witnesses appears in *Louisiana Historical Quarterly* 6, no. 3 (1923): 506–508.

33. "Extrait d'une lettre de Sabrevois à Vaudreuil," Détroit, 8 avril 1717, Série C11A, vol. 38, Folio 166, BAC.

34. For a summary of Marguerite's life in Pennsylvania and with the Mohawk, see Barbara J. Sivertsen, *Turtles, Wolves, and Bears: A Mohawk Family History* (Westminster, MD: Heritage Books, 1996), 211–212.

35. Louis Turpin owned the largest home in Kaskaskia—a three-story stone house built sometime in the 1740s and at the same time of this series of legal proceedings dealing with his brother's estate. The structure had stone chimneys, a second-floor gallery that ran across two sides, and a shingled roof. Its prominence in the community is attested to by several contemporary documents that used the structure as a point of geographical demarcation (e.g., "the street that leads to Louis Turpin's house") (Natalia Maree Belting, *Kaskaskia under the French Regime* [Urbana: University of Illinois Press, 1948], 37).

36. Belting, *Kaskaskia under the French Regime*, 80. For Dorothée Mechiper8eta's economic status and social connections, see Robert Michael Morrissey, "Kaskaskia Social Network: Kinship and Assimilation in the French-Illinois Borderlands, 1695–1735," *William and Mary Quarterly* 70, no. 1 (January 2013): 130, 138.

37. The son, also called Jean Baptiste, died before his father, possibly in the unsuccessful battle waged by the French and their Indigenous allies against the Chickasaw in 1736. The fighting force against the Chickasaw was composed of Frenchmen from the Illinois Country and Louisiana, along with Indigenous warriors living on the Wabash, including the Illinois and Myaamia. Jean Baptiste Turpin Sr. also had other children—he had conceived a child out of wedlock with a French woman in the St. Lawrence valley before he married Marguerite Fafard in 1710.

38. "Paroles addressées à Frontenac par Teganissorens deputé des Cinq Nations iroquoises," Montréal, 11 septembre 1682, Série C11A, vol. 6–1, Folio 16. English translation can be found in "Conference between Count Frontenac and a Deputy from the Five Nations/ Speech of the Delegate from the Five Iroquois Nations to Count de Frontenac," September 11, 1682, in *Documents Relative to the Colonial History of the State of New*

York, ed. E. B. O'Callaghan (Albany, NY: Weed, Parsons and Co., 1854–1855), 9:184–185. This is the same meeting at which Niregouentaron declared that René Cuillerier had inappropriately translated his words regarding potential attack on the Illinois (see chapter 4).

39. "Réponses de Frontenac aux paroles de Teganissorens," Montréal, 11 septembre 1682, Série C11A, vol. 6–1, Folios 19v–20, BAC. English translation can be found as "Count de Frontenac's Answer to the Speech of the Deputy from the Five Nations," September 12, 1682, in *Documents Relative to the Colonial History of the State of New York,* 9:189.

40. An Onondaga leader by the name of Tenganissorens would become the "leading orator of his generation" who sought to end hostilities between the Haudenosaunee, their Indigenous enemies, and the French and English in the last decade of the seventeenth century (Daniel Richter, *The Ordeal of the Longhouse: The Peoples of the Iroquois League in the Era of European Colonization* [Chapel Hill: University of North Carolina Press, 1992], 180–181).

41. "Parolles de Chachagouesse ou autrement Nicanapé chef Illinois," 20 août, 1712, Série C11A, vol. 33, Folio 92v, BAC.

42. "Lettre du jésuite Joseph-Jacques Marest à Vaudreuil," Michilimackinac, 14 août 1706, Série C11A, vol. 24, Folio 260v, BAC.

43. "Lettre du jésuite Joseph-Jacques Marest à Vaudreuil," Michilimackinac, 21 juin 1712, Série C11A, vol. 33, Folio 72, BAC.

44. "Copie d'une lettre de Lamothe Cadillac à Vaudreuil," Détroit, 27 août 1706, Série C11A, vol. 24, Folios 281v–282, BAC.

45. "Lettre de Vaudreuil au Conseil de Marine," Québec, 14 octobre 1716, Série C11A, vol. 36, Folio 73v, BAC. This figure, if correct, tells us that for every one Meskwaki man there were six Meskwaki women who participated in the battle with the French (a fighting force composed of 86 percent women and 14 percent men). Vaudreuil described the women as having fought "en désespérées," literally "in desperation." The 1904 English translation of this passage that appears in volume 33 of the *Michigan Pioneer and Historical Society Collections and Researches* made a significant alteration in meaning of the original text with this description of the women. The 1904 translation, transforms the adverb "en désespérées" into a noun, with the Meskwaki women depicted as fighting "like furies." This is undoubtedly a reference to the three women of Greek mythology known as the Furies who punished criminals without mercy. The translation adds an extra layer of gender bias by reinstating the exceptional and violent nature of the Meskwaki women.

46. For Pied Froid as *akima,* see John Bickers and George Ironstrack, "The Many Branches

of Tahkamwa's Family Tree," May 29, 2015, https://myaamiahistory.wordpress. com/2015/05/29/the-many-branches-of-tahkamwas-family-tree/.

47. David J. Costa, "The Kinship Terminology of the Miami-Illinois Language," *Anthropological Linguistics* 41, no. 1 (Spring 1999): 36.

48. Costa, "The Kinship Terminology," 37–38. Costa quotes a contemporary account that illustrates this affinial connection. Pierre-Charles de Liette described the relationship between a man and the women to whom his wife is related: "While the [Illinois] women are nursing, their husbands do not ordinarily have commerce with them. As they have several wives, the abstinence is easy for them. It is usually the sisters and the aunts or nieces of their wives whom they marry. These they call *Nirimoua*. When a man is a good hunter, it is a very easy matter for him to marry all who stand within this degree of relationship. The women designate him in the same manner." For de Liette's observations, see *The French Foundations, 1680–1693*, ed. Theodore Calvin Pease and Raymond C. Werner, *Collections of the Illinois State Historical Library*, vol. 23 (French Series 1), 355. Costa adds that sororal polygamy was also permitted within other Algonquian nations.

49. 3 juin 1717, Registre de Ste. Anne, Burton Historical Collection, Detroit Public Library, 63.

50. "Lettre de Vaudreuil au Conseil de Marine avec avis du Conseil," Québec, 28 octobre 1719, Série C11A, vol. 40, Folios 185–186v, BAC.

51. Vaudreuil also ordered the removal of the blacksmith operating among the Myaamia, hoping that depriving the community of a person to repair and maintain their guns would force the nation to relocate. "Extrait du mémoire de Vaudreuil pour server d'instruction à l'enseigne Dumont qui s'en va commander au pays des Ouiatanons et à la rivière des Miamis," Québec, 26 août 1720, Série C11A, vol. 42, Folios 158–160v, BAC.

52. "Contract of François and Pierre Roy to conduct trade at the Miamis," May 12, 1719, Burton Historical Collection, Detroit Public Library. The agreement opened a brisk trade that would last for several years. In 1722, Pierre Roy remained at the Wabash, acting as an interpreter and in possession of an official permit (*congé*) that allowed him to take one boat with four men carrying sixteen pots of brandy for the men and fifteen pots for Pierre's subsistence ("État des permissions accordée par Monsieur le marquis de Vaudreuil aux officiers et voyageurs de la présente année 1722 et la quantité d'eau-de-vie qu'ils ont emportée du envoyée pour leur subsistence," Montréal, 23 septembre 1722, Série C11A, vol. 45, Folio 354v, BAC). See also Ls-A. Proulx, *Rapport de L'Archiviste de la Province de Québec pour 1921–1922* (Quebec: Imprimeur de Sa Majesté le Roi, 1922), 196, 200, 201, 206, for a list of permits granted to the brothers.

53. By the end of 1721, Vaudreuil was no longer trying to compel the Myaamia to relocate to St. Joseph (see "Résumé d'une lettre de Vaudreuil datée du 6 octobre 1721," 23 décembre

1721, Série C11A, vol. 43, Folios 328–328v, BAC).

54. Robert Michael Morrissey, *Empire by Collaboration: Indians, Colonists, and Governments in Colonial Illinois Country* (Philadelphia: University of Pennsylvania Press, 2015), 104–108.

55. Louis Roy had been in Detroit before this date. As early as 1706, he had been hired by the Compagnie de la Colonie to make a trip there (*Rapport de l'Archiviste de la Province de la Québec pour 1929–1930* [Québec: Rédempti Paradis, 1930], 210). On May 28, 1718, he prepared for a trip to Detroit, equipped with a large sum of money (1,220 livres, 9 sols, and 10 deniers) most likely meant to assist his brothers' trading ventures. This was the same day his brother Pierre was hiring men and two days before their brother François was also recorded as bringing a similar substantial sum, all for what was almost certainly the same trip to Detroit (see *Rapport de l'Archiviste de la Province de la Québec pour 1929–1930,* 223).

56. The Neveu/Chauvin and Roy families had a long acquaintance. At the 1695 wedding of Jacques Neveu and Michelle Chauvin in Montreal, Pierre Roy Sr. acted as witness; thirty years later, in 1725, Marguerite Catherine Neveu would marry Etienne Roy.

57. "Census of Natchitoches," May 1, 1722, p. 7; "Census of the Persons Living along the Mississippi River between New Orleans and the German Villages," December 20, 1724, p. 16; and "List of Those Persons Requesting Negroes from the Company," October 1726, p. 77, in *The First Families of Louisiana,* trans. and comp. Glenn R. Conrad, vol. 2 (Baton Rouge: Claitor's Publishing Division, 1970). For Etienne Roy's use of his Indigenous slaves and black day workers, see *New Orleans Architecture,* vol. 7, *Jefferson City,* ed. Dorothy G. Schlesinger, Robert J. Cangelosi Jr., and Sally Kittredge Reeves (Gretna, LA: Pelican Publishing Company, 1989), 12.

58. Original document #2583 from the microfilm copy of the notarial records of Jean-Baptiste Adhémar, Archives nationales du Québec à Montréal. For a detailed description of the trade agreement, see S. Dale Standen, "'Personnes sans caractère': Private Merchants, Post Commanders and the Regulation of the Western Fur Trade, 1720–1745," in *De France en Nouvelle-France: Société fondatrice et société nouvelle,* ed. Hubert Watelet and Cornelius J. Jaenen (Ottawa: Les Presses de l'Université d'Ottawa, 1994), 274. Four years later, Noyelles signed off on a reimbursement from the governor general to François Roy for munitions and foodstuffs Roy had supplied to French and Indigenous men who had participated in two campaigns against the Meskwaki in 1730 ("Etat du fonds à faire pour le paiement des munitions de guerre et de bouche et autres marchandises fournies dans les pays d'en haut," Québec, 15 octobre 1732, Série C11A, vol. 57, Folio 209v, BAC).

59. "Déclaration de François Roy confirmant l'envoi de marchandises à Pierre Chesne," 4 septembre 1728, Fonds Juridiction royale de Montréal, Dossiers, Bibliothèque et Archives nationales du Québec.

CHAPTER 6. UNVEILING THE CONSPIRACY: WOMEN AT THE HEART OF PONTIAC'S WAR

1. Capt. Donald Campbell to Col. Henry Bouquet, Detroit, March 10, 1761, *The Papers of Col. Henry Bouquet,* Series 21646, Northwestern Pennsylvania Historical Series, prepared by Frontier Forts and Trails Survey, Federal Works Agency, Work Projects Administration, ed. Sylvester K. Stevens and Donald H. Kent (Harrisburg: Pennsylvania Historical Commission, 1941), 61–62 (translation by editors of the Bouquet papers).

2. Donald Campbell to Henry Bouquet, Detroit, April 26, 1762, *The Papers of Col. Henry Bouquet,* 9:87–88.

3. Harry Kelsey, "Campbell, Donald," in *Dictionary of Canadian Biography,* vol. 3 (Toronto: University of Toronto/Université Laval, 2003–), http://www.biographi.ca/en/bio/campbell_donald_3E.html.

4. There is over a hundred years of scholarship on the events surrounding collective Indigenous action against the British in the Great Lakes and the Ohio Valley in 1763, beginning with Frances Parkman's 1851 *The Conspiracy of Pontiac and the Indian War after the Conquest of Canada.* More recent monographs include Gregory Dowd, *War under Heaven: Pontiac, the Indian Nations, and the British Empire* (Baltimore: Johns Hopkins University Press, 2004); David Dixon, *Never Come to Peace Again: Pontiac's Uprising and the Fate of the British Empire in North America* (Norman: University of Oklahoma Press, 2005); Richard Middleton, *Pontiac's War: Its Causes, Course, and Consequences* (New York: Routledge, 2007); and Keith Widder, *Beyond Pontiac's Shadow: Michilimackinac and the Anglo-Indian War of 1763* (East Lansing: Michigan State University Press, 2013).

5. Kyle Mays, "Pontiac's Ghost in the Motor City: Indigeneity and the Discursive Constructive of Modern Detroit," *Middle West Review* 2, no. 2 (2016): 116.

6. There seems to be only one exception in a 1934 article written by Helen Humphrey, "The Identity of Gladwin's Informant," *Mississippi Valley Historical Review* 21, no. 2 (September 1934): 147–162.

7. Major William Walters to Colonel Henry Bouquet, Niagara, October 11, 1761, *The Papers of Col. Henry Bouquet,* 8:158.

8. Captain Lewis Ourry to Colonel Henry Bouquet, Fort Bedford, October 25, 1761, *The Papers of Col. Henry Bouquet,* Series 21642, 840–841.

9. Kathleen Wilson, *The Island Race: Englishness, Empire and Gender in the Eighteenth Century* (New York: Routledge, 2003), 41.

10. Kathleen M. Brown, *Good Wives, Nasty Wenches, and Anxious Patriarchs: Gender, Race, and Power in Colonial Virginia* (Chapel Hill: University of North Carolina Press, 1996), 328–329.

11. Andrew Dyrli Hermeling, "Severing Tender Ties: George Croghan's Ironic Policing of Identity and Intimacy during Pontiac's War" (paper delivered at Annual Meeting of the American Society for Ethnohistory, Oaxaca, Mexico, October 11–13, 2018). My thanks to Andrew for providing a copy of his paper.

12. Capt. Donald Campbell to Col. Henry Bouquet, Detroit, April 20, 1763, *The Papers of Col. Henry Bouquet,* 11:103.

13. Lieut. James MacDonald to Col. Henry Bouquet, Detroit, July 29, 1763, *The Papers of Col. Henry Bouquet,* 11:244. The English translation reprinted here appears alongside the original French in Bouquet's transcribed papers and maintains the word "follies" from the original French. I have translated this as "episodes of madness."

14. List of English Prisoners, September 22, 1758, *The Papers of Col. Henry Bouquet,* Series 21643, 180.

15. *The Gladwin Manuscripts,* ed. Charles Moore (Lansing, MI: Robert Smith Printing, 1897), 640.

16. Robert Rogers, "Journal of the Siege of Detroit, taken from the Officers who were then in the Fort, and wrote in their Words in the following Manner, viz.," in *Diary of the Siege of Detroit in the War with Pontiac,* ed. Franklin B. Hough (Albany, NY: J. Munsell, 1860), 126–127. Roger's rendition can be matched virtually word for word with MacDonald's account. Roger's play *Ponteach: Or the Savages of America; A Tragedy* was published in 1766.

17. "Journal of Siege of Detroit by Lt. McDonald," n.d., Baron Jeffrey Amherst, Commander in Chief: Papers, Correspondence between Commander-in-Chief and Officers at Detroit, National Archives of the United Kingdom, Kew, WO 34/49, ff. 1–2. James MacDonald to Henry Bouquet, Detroit, July 12, 1763, *Papers of Col. Henry Bouquet,* 11:220.

18. James MacDonald to George Croghan, Detroit, July 12, 1763, *Papers of Sir William Johnson,* ed. Milton W. Hamilton (1925; Albany: University of the State of New York, 1957), 10:737.

19. Nancy J. Parezo and Angelina R. Jones, "What's in a Name: The 1940s–1950s 'Squaw Dress,'" *American Indian Quarterly* 33, no. 3 (Summer 2009): 376.

20. Rayna Green, "The Pocahontas Perplex: The Image of Indian Women in American Culture," *Massachusetts Review* 16, no. 4 (1975): 711.

21. Hermeling, "Severing Tender Ties: George Croghan's Ironic Policing of Identity and

Intimacy during Pontiac's War."

22. Jeffrey Amherst to William Johnson, New York, May 23, 1763, *Papers of Sir William Johnson,* 10:690.

23. James MacDonald to George Croghan, *Papers of Sir William Johnson,* 10:743. James MacDonald to Henry Bouquet, *Papers of Col. Henry Bouquet,* 11:224.

24. "Journal of Siege of Detroit by Lt. McDonald," Baron Jeffrey Amherst, Commander in Chief: Papers, f. 8.

25. Helen Humphrey researched the various trajectories of the story and their sources in "The Identity of Gladwin's Informant," *Mississippi Valley Historical Review* 21, no. 2 (September 1934): 147–162. Citing Humphrey, Richard Middleton briefly discusses the possible suspects and concludes "there is ample reason to believe that the major [Gladwin] received a number of reports concerning Pontiac's plan to seize the fort" (Middleton, *Never Come to Peace Again: Pontiac's Uprising and the Fate of the British Empire in North America* [Norman: University of Oklahoma Press, 2005], 110).

26. *Ogimawkwe* or "woman leader" is taken from the title of a book by Potawatomi author Simon Pokagon (*Ogimawkwe Mitigwaki [Queen of the Woods]: A Novel* [East Lansing: Michigan State University Press, 2011]).

27. Walter S. Dunn Jr., *Frontier Profit and Loss: The British Army and the Fur Traders, 1760–1764* (Westport, CT: Greenwood Press, 1998), 117–118.

28. "The Pontiac Manuscript: Journal or History of a Conspiracy by the Indians against the English, and of the Siege of the Fort Detroit, by Four Different Nations, Beginning on the 7th of May 1763," trans. Rudolph Worch and F. Krusty, *Report of the Pioneer and Historical Society of the State of Michigan,* vol. 8 (Lansing, MI: Thorp and Godfrey, 1886), 275.

29. "Pontiac Manuscript," 277.

30. John Porteus, *A Short Journal of the Siege of Detroit,* ms, Burton Historical Collection, Detroit Public Library.

31. The testimonials collected by Charles Trowbridge of Mrs. Meloche, Charles Gouin, Gabriel St. Aubin, Jacques Parent, and Mr. Pettier (in all likelihood Peltier) appear in *Report of the Pioneer and Historical Society of the State of Michigan,* 8:340–363.

32. Jonathan Carver, *Travels through the Interior Parts of North America in the Years 1766, 1767, 1768,* 3rd ed. (London, 1781), 154–162.

33. Lewis Cass, *A Discourse: Delivered at the First Meeting of the Historical Society of Michigan* (Detroit: George L. Whitney, 1830), 31.

34. *Francis Parkman Papers,* 1845, Pontiac (Miscellanies), vol. 27d, Massachusetts Historical Society, 178. I am grateful to Catherine Cangany, who uncovered this reference and information pertaining to Parkman's trip to Detroit at the MHS.

35. Francis Parkman, *The Conspiracy of Pontiac and the Indian War after the Conquest of Canada,* 6th ed., vol. 1 (Boston: Little, Brown and Co., 1870), 219. It is interesting to note that Parkman uses almost identical language to describe Pierre LaButte, whose loyalties are similarly in question in Parkman's story. When LaButte reports the capture of Donald Campbell and another British officer by Pontiac, "his [LaButte's] face wore a sad and downcast look . . . La Butte, feeling himself an object of distrust, lingered about the streets, sullen and silent, like the Indians among whom his rough life had been spent" (242).

36. Humphrey, "The Identity of Gladwin's Informant," 152.

37. Henry R. Schoolcraft, *Personal Memoirs of a Residence of Thirty Years with the Indian Tribes on the American Frontiers: With Brief Notices of Passing Events, Facts, and Opinions, A.D. 1812 to A.D. 1842* (Philadelphia: Lippincott, Grambo and Co., 1851), 580.

38. Schoolcraft, *Personal Memoirs,* 580.

39. Lucy Eldersveld Murphy, *Great Lakes Creoles: A French-Indian Community on the Northern Borderlands, Prairie du Chien, 1750–1860* (Cambridge: Cambridge University Press, 2014), 159.

40. Catherine Cangany, *Frontier Seaport: Detroit's Transformation into an Atlantic Entrepôt* (Chicago: University of Chicago Press, 2014), 72.

41. Bradstreet to Campbell, Detroit, September 12, 1764, Gage Papers, American Series, vol. 24, William L. Clements Library, University of Michigan.

42. Rebecca Kugel, "Leadership within the Women's Community: Susie Bonga Wright of the Leech Lake Ojibwe," in *Midwestern Women: Work, Community, and Leadership at the Crossroads,* ed. Lucy Eldersveld Murphy and Wendy Hamand Venet (Bloomington: Indiana University Press, 1997), 27; and Cary Miller, *Ogimaag: Anishinaabeg Leadership, 1760–1845* (Lincoln: University of Nebraska Press, 2010), 231.

43. Mary Catherine Crowley, *The Heroine of the Strait: A Romance of Detroit in the Time of Pontiac* (Boston: Little, Brown and Co., 1902), 169.

44. Crowley, *The Heroine of the Strait,* 268.

45. Middleton, *Pontiac's War,* 66.

46. Pokagon, *Ogimawkwe Mitigwaki (Queen of the Woods),* 156.

47. *Rapport de l'Archiviste de la Province de la Québec pour 1929–1930* (Quebec: Rédempti Paradis, 1930), 269, 270, 278; and Account Book of the Huron Mission, Armand de la Richardie, 1748–1749, in *The Jesuit Relations and Allied Documents,* ed. Reuben Gold Thwaites, vol. 70 (Cleveland: Burrows Brothers Co., 1896–1901), 26–29, 36–37.

48. Clarence M. Burton, "Detroit under British Rule," in Humphrey, "The Identity of Gladwin's Informant," 154; and George B. Catlin, *The Story of Detroit* (Detroit: Detroit

News, 1923), 43.

49. *The Gladwin Manuscripts,* ed. Moore, 641. Gregory Dowd points out that this interaction between Pontiac and Cuillerier was a performance staged to "bring about the return of the French through acts of ritual invocation" (Dowd, *War under Heaven,* 123).

50. As will be discussed further in chapter 7, these clothes are very similar in description to those worn by an Odawa leader on the Wabash who would meet with British officer Thomas Morris a year later in 1764.

51. For population figures of 1707, see Almon Ernest Parkins, *The Historical Geography of Detroit* (Lansing: Michigan Historical Commission, 1918), 55. For 1765 population see Brian Leigh Dunnigan, *Frontier Metropolis: Picturing Early Detroit, 1701–1838* (Detroit: Wayne State University Press, 2001), 50. For comments of Beauharnois, see Parkins, 71. For self-sufficiency of Detroit due to influx of 1749–50 see Dunnigan, 35.

52. *Historical Atlas of Canada: From the Beginning to 1800,* vol. 1, ed. R. Cole Harris (Toronto: University of Toronto Press, 1987), plate 41; for Indigenous population statistics see Andrew Sturtevant, "Jealous Neighbors: Rivalry and Alliance among the Native Communities of Detroit, 1701–1766" (PhD diss., College of William and Mary, 2011), 25.

53. For a discussion of this second state-sponsored wave of immigration to Detroit, see Lina Gouger, "Les convoys de colons de 1749–1750: Impulsion gouvernementale decisive pour le développement de la region de Windsor," in *Le Passage du Détroit: 300 ans de présence Francophone/Passages: Three Centuries of Francophone Presence at Le Détroit,* ed. Marcel Bénéteau, vol. 11 of Working Papers in the Humanities (Windsor, ON: University of Windsor, 2003), 47–57.

54. Gilles Havard and Cécile Vidal, *Histoire de l'Amérique française* (Paris: Éditions Flammarion, 2003), 371.

55. Brett Rushforth, *Bonds of Alliance,* 279.

56. Perhaps the mayor of Detroit's report to Parkman about the daughter of LaButte referenced instead his daughter-in-law, Marie Anne Cuillerier, which still places a woman from the Cuillerier family at the center of the story.

57. For Pierre LaButte Jr. transactions with Langlade and the soldier, see Gail Moreau-DesHarnais and Diane Wolford Sheppard, "Pierre Chesne dit Saint-Onge, #1 Pierre Chesne dit Labutte [1698–1774], #2 Pierre Chesne dit Labutte [1729–1804], #3 Pierre Chesne dit Labutte [1770- 1813], Pierre Labutte of the Detroit River Region [1800–1879], part 3, "Pierre Chesne dit Labutte [1729–1804]," continued from *MHH* 33, no. 3 (July 2012): 160–169; *MHH* 33, no. 4 (October 2012): 215–229," in *Michigan's Habitant Heritage* 34, no. 1 (January 2013): 4 (updated 2015).

58. For LaButte as Onditsouoa, see *Les écrits de Pierre Potier,* ed. Robert Toupin (Ottawa: Les

Presses de l'Université d'Ottawa, 1996), 261. Like the French, the Wendat word translates as "hill or butte." I am grateful to Kathryn Labelle and John Steckley for the translation of LaButte's name from Wendat to English.

59. Johnson kept a diary of his activities at Detroit that was published as an appendix in William L. Stone, *The Life and Times of Sir William Johnson, Bart.,* vol. 2 (Albany, NY: J. Munsell, 1865), 456–464.

60. James Sterling to Mr. James Syme, Detroit, June 8, 1762, James Sterling Letterbook, William L. Clements Library, University of Michigan.

61. Sterling to Syme.

62. For Sterling's request for additional allowance, see Sterling to Captain Walter Rutherford, November 22, 1762, James Sterling Letterbook. For Sterling's comments on local French as cattle, see Sterling to Syme.

63. Michelle A. Hamilton, "In the King's Service: Provisioning and Quartering the British Army in the Old Northwest, 1760–63," in *English Atlantics Revisited: Essays Honoring Ian K. Steele,* ed. Nancy L. Rhoden (Montreal & Kingston: McGill-Queen's University Press, 2007), 328. According to Hamilton, the same situation prevailed at Michilimackinac, where the French also owned the majority of structures that were rented to the British.

64. James Sterling to George Croghan, Esq., January 31, 1762, James Sterling Letterbook.

65. James Sterling to Ensign J. S. Schlosser, June 12, 1762, in Tiya Miles, *The Dawn of Detroit: A Chronicle of Slavery and Freedom in the City of the Straits* (New York: New Press, 2017), 56, 281.

66. James Sterling to John Duncan, February 26, 1765, James Sterling Letterbook.

67. James Sterling to William Johnson, Detroit, April 27, 1765, *The Papers of Sir William Johnson,* ed. Alexander C. Flick, vol. 4 (Albany: University of the State of New York, 1925), 733–734.

68. For gold and silver as popular with Indigenous customers, see "Observations upon the Commerce of Canada; particularly that part, which explains the Indian or Fur Trade," Joseph Hadfield, ca. 1785, Native American Collection, William L. Clements Library, University of Michigan.

69. James Sterling to John Duncan, Detroit, May 31, 1765, James Sterling Letterbook. John Duncan was a Scot and former officer in the British army who became a primary agent of trade at Niagara and joined in a partnership with Sterling in 1761 (see Dunn, *Frontier Profit and Loss,* 111).

70. James Sterling to Colonel John Vaughan, Detroit, July 17, 1765, Sterling Letterbook.

71. Marcel Trudel, *L'esclavage au Canada français: Histoire et conditions de l'esclavage* (Quebec: Les Presses Universitaires Laval, 1960), 159; Rushforth, *Bonds of Alliance,* 343.

72. Miles, *The Dawn of Detroit,* 31.

73. Diane Wolford Sheppard, "Slave Owners in the Detroit River Region through 1762," https://habitantheritage.org/cpage.php?pt=32. Slaves also continued to appear in the church register, a custom begun by French imperial mandate decades earlier that required slaves be baptized. Because the 1762 census only enumerated French individuals, it is difficult to ascertain precisely how many slaves were held by local British peoples or in Indigenous communities, or the number that may have lived temporarily at Detroit before being traded, sold, or gifted, or who died shortly after their arrival.

74. It is possible that the black slave held by Pierre LaButte Jr. was named Jacquot, who Pierre Jr. had purchased for 1,000 livres from his cousin Madame Françoise Hamelin to settle a debt; see Marcel Trudel, *Dictionnaire des esclaves et de leurs propriétaires au Canada français* (LaSalle, QC: Éditions Hurtubise HMH Ltée., 1990), 104. For Pierre Jr.'s relation to Madame Hamelin through the Roy family, see Moreau-DesHarnais and Sheppard, "Pierre Chesne dit Saint-Onge," 5.

75. "Mr. Jacques Parent's Account," in *Report of the Pioneer and Historical Society of the State of Michigan,* vol. 8 (Lansing, MI: Thorp and Godfrey, 1886), 358.

76. Cangany, *Frontier Seaport,* 27. See also Hamilton, "In the King's Service," 329; and Dunn, *Frontier Profit and Loss,* 116.

77. James Sterling to John Porteus, Detroit, September 4, 1765, Sterling Letterbook.

78. Christian Ayne Crouch, "The Black City: African and Indian Exchanges in Pontiac's Upper Country," *Early American Studies* 14, no. 2 (Spring 2016): 302.

79. "Diary of the Siege of Detroit," in *Diary of the Siege of Detroit in the War with Pontiac: Also a Narrative of the Principal Events of the Siege,* ed. Franklin B. Hough (Albany, NY: J. Munsell, 1860), 53.

80. "Major Henry Basset to Gen. Frederick Haldimand," Detroit, August 29, 1773, *Collections and Researches Made by the Michigan Pioneer and Historical Society,* vol. 19 (Lansing, MI: Robert Smith & Co., 1892), 310–311.

CHAPTER 7. BASTARDS AND BASTIONS: DOMESTIC DISORDER AND THE CHANGING STATUS OF THE FRENCH-INDIGENOUS FAMILY NETWORKS

1. Journal of Captain Thomas Morris of His Majesty's 17th Regiment of Infantry, Detroit, September 25, 1764, *Miscellanies in Prose and Verse* (1791; reprint, Cleveland: Arthur C. Clark, 1904), 310.

2. Journal of Captain Thomas Morris, 302. For Morris's interpolation of literary text with the people and places he encountered, see Andrew Newman, *Allegories of Encounter:*

Colonial Literacy and Indian Captivity (Chapel Hill: University of North Carolina Press, 2019), 160–176.

3. For Antony as pawn, see John Rees Moore, "The Enemies of Love: The Example of Antony and Cleopatra," *Kenyon Review* 31, no. 5 (1969): 646–674, 650.

4. Arthur L. Little, *Shakespeare Jungle Fever: National-Imperial Revisions of Race, Rape, and Sacrifice* (Stanford, CA: Stanford University Press, 2000), 144.

5. For a discussion of this incident, upon which the present description is based, see Richard White's *The Middle Ground: Indians, Empires, and Republics in the Great Lakes Region, 1650–1815* (Cambridge: Cambridge University Press, 1991), 298. Harvey Lewis Carter in *The Life and Times of Little Turtle: First Sagamore of the Wabash* (Urbana: University of Illinois Press, 1987), 67–69, provides a more extensive description of the event, including its political implications for the Myaamia and the British and the suggestion that the event was staged and that Tahkamwa was probably present.

6. For a description of this event, see Wallace A. Brice, *A History of Fort Wayne, from the Earliest Known Accounts of this Point, to the Present Period* (Fort Wayne, IN: D. W. Jones & Sons, 1868), 314–315.

7. "Copy of a Council Held at Detroit 18th September 1774 by Pacan Chief of the Miamis Indians with Five Others of the Chiefs and Principal Men of his Nation in the Presence of Richard Berringer Lernoult Esquire Captain in the King's or 8th Regiment Commander of the Detroit and Its Dependencies," Thomas Gage Papers, American Series, vol. 123, William L. Clements Library [hereafter referred to as "Miami Petition"].

8. James Joseph Buss, *Winning the West with Words: Language and Conquest in the Lower Great Lakes* (Norman: University of Oklahoma Press, 2011), 23; Nancy Shoemaker, *A Strange Likeness: Becoming Red and White in Eighteenth-Century North America* (New York: Oxford University Press, 2004), 113; and Gunlög Fur, *A Nation of Women: Gender and Colonial Encounter among the Delaware Indians* (Philadelphia: University of Pennsylvania Press, 2009), 6–8, 178.

9. Heidi Bohaker, "Indigenous Histories and Archival Media in the Early Modern Great Lakes," in *Colonial Mediascapes: Sensory Worlds of the Early Americas,* ed. Matt Cohen and Jeffrey Glover (Lincoln: University of Nebraska Press, 2014), 66.

10. Christian Denissen, *Genealogy of the French Families of the Detroit River Region, 1701–1936,* ed. Harold Frederic Powell and Robert L. Pilon, vol. 2 (Detroit: Burton Historical Collection, 1987), 50.

11. Carter, *The Life and Times of Little Turtle,* 40.

12. T. J. Brasser, "Mahican," in *Handbook of North American Indians,* vol. 15, *Northeast,* ed. Bruce G. Trigger (Washington, DC: Smithsonian Institution, 1978), 205.

13. For André Roy dit Pacane (Pakaana) as French imperial liaison see "Ordre du commandant Raymond à André Roy dit Pacane," Fort des Miamis, 15 mai 1750, Série C11A, vol. 126, Folios 93–93v, BAC. Myaamia historians John Bickers and George Ironstrack point out that the two Pakaanas were not necessarily father and son. Giving the same name to father and son was common among Europeans but was not customary among the Myaamia, and is rarely seen in European-authored records of the Myaamia in the eighteenth century (see Bickers and Ironstrack, "The Many Branches of Tahkamwa's Family Tree," May 29, 2015, *Aacimotaatiiyankwi: A Myaamia Community Blog,* https://myaamiahistory.wordpress.com/2015/05/29/the-many-branches-of-tahkamwas-family-tree/). There is reference made to a Pakane Junr. who along with three other Myaamia leaders met with Wendat diplomats and a French representative in 1773 (see "The Answer of the Miami Indians to Sir William Johnson's Speech, Addressed to Them by the Hurons," Miamis, August 18, 1773, *Collections and Researches made by the Michigan Pioneer and Historical Society* (Lansing, MI: Robert Smith, 1892), 19:308–310). If not a father-son connection, use of the word "junior" suggests uncle-nephew or a familial link of some kind, at least as it would have been perceived by those delivering and translating the proceedings, one of whom, James Sterling, was well acquainted with pivotal members of the Myaamia nation through his marriage to Angelique Cuillerier dit Beaubien.

14. "Paroles adressées à Vaudreuil par le chef outaouais Miscouaky," 26 septembre 1706, Série C11A, vol. 24, Folios 244v–245, BAC.

15. White, *The Middle Ground,* 217.

16. C. C. Trowbridge, *Meearmeear Traditions,* ed. Vernon Kinietz (1823; reprint, Ann Arbor: University of Michigan Press, 1938), 85. Trowbridge was collecting information on the Myaamia at the same time he interviewed French men and women at Detroit about their memories of Pontiac (see chapter 6).

17. Stanley Faye, "Indian Guests at the Spanish Arkansas Post," *Arkansas Historical Quarterly* 4, no. 2 (Summer 1945): 96.

18. The Piankashaw were an allied nation to the Myaamia. They and the Ouiatenon occupied a similar status, considering the Myaamia to be their elder brothers, with whom they traditionally consulted before making important political decisions. For a discussion of the events surrounding La Demoiselle's defection from the French to the British and ramifications for Myaamia politics, see White, *The Middle Ground,* 212–232.

19. "État des fournitures faites par le sieur Cuillerier par ordre de Monsieur Douville, commandant aux Miamis," Détroit, 2 octobre 1747, Série C11A, vol. 117, Folio 37, BAC.

20. "Extraits de lettres et de nouvelles envoyées à La Jonquière par Raymond, commandant

au fort des Miamis," 1749–1750, Série C11A, vol. 95, Folios 375–375v, BAC. Raymond, the commandant at the Miami village, asked Pied Froid to close his ears to Demoiselle's entreaties to join the English. Pied Froid promised to remain loyal to the French.

21. Toby Ditz, "The New Men's History and the Peculiar Absence of Gendered Power: Some Remedies from Early American Gender History," *Gender and History* 16, no. 1 (2004): 12.

22. Honor Sachs, *Home Rule: Households, Manhood and National Expansion on the Eighteenth-Century Kentucky Frontier* (New Haven, CT: Yale University Press, 2015), 7.

23. Elizabeth Elbourne, "Domesticity and Dispossession: The Ideology of 'Home' and the British Construction of the 'Primitive' from the Eighteenth to the Early Nineteenth Century," in *Deep Histories: Gender and Colonialism in Southern Africa,* ed. Wendy Woodward, Patricia Hayes, and Gary Minkley (New York: Editions Rodopi B.V., 2002), 35.

24. Michael McKeon, *The Secret History of Domesticity: Public, Private, and the Division of Knowledge* (Baltimore: Johns Hopkins University Press, 2005), 124.

25. Ditz, "The New Men's History," 12.

26. The portage is at the site of present-day Fort Wayne, Indiana.

27. "Instructions to Maisonville," Sir William Johnson to Alexis Maisonville, Fort Stanwix, October 8, 1771, in *The Papers of Sir William Johnson,* vol. 12, ed. Milton W. Hamilton (1925; Albany: University of the State of New York, 1957).

28. "Miami Petition."

29. White, *The Middle Ground,* 323.

30. For description of the extensive role played by Great Lakes and Ohio Valley Indigenous women in growing Indigenous and European crops and raising domesticated animals, see Susan Sleeper-Smith, "The Agrarian Village World of Indian Women in the Ohio Valley," in *Women in Early America,* ed. Thomas Foster (New York: New York University Press, 2015), 186–209.

31. Susan Sleeper-Smith, "Women, Kin, and Catholicism: New Perspectives on the Fur Trade," *Ethnohistory* 47, no. 2 (2000): 430.

32. Tanis C. Thorne, "For the Good of Her People: Continuity and Change for Native Women of the Midwest, 1650–1850," in *Midwestern Women: Work, Community, and Leadership at the Crossroads,* ed. Lucy Eldersveld Murphy and Wendy Hamand Venet (Bloomington: Indiana University Press, 1997), 100.

33. Trowbridge, *Meearmeear Traditions,* 85–86.

34. White, *The Middle Ground,* 219.

35. Henry Hamilton, *Henry Hamilton and George Rogers Clark in the American Revolution with the Unpublished Journal of Lieutenant Governor Henry Hamilton,* ed. John D. Barnhart (Crawfordsville, IN: R. E. Banta, 1951), 110.

36. "Miami Petition."

37. *Journal of Henry Hamilton,* 135–136.

38. "Miami Petition."

39. *Journal of Henry Hamilton,* 134–135.

40. Thorne, "For the Good of Her People," 114.

41. Pierre Henry Hay provided details of Tahkamwa's activities during his time in Myaamionki in 1789–90 ("A Narrative of Life on the Old Frontier: Henry Hay's Journal," in *Proceedings of the State Historical Society of Wisconsin,* ed. Milo M. Quaife (Madison: State Historical Society of Wisconsin, 1915), 208–261. Pierre Henry Hay was the son of Detroit's British Indian agent Jehu Hay. His mother, Marie Julie Réaume hailed from a family of Detroit traders who operated across the upper country and had a well-established connection with the Myaamia. Pierre Henry grew up with Myaamia leader Le Gris's son and was likely related to a Myaamia man of Eel River referred to as "Old Reaume" by the British. Le Coq Réaume, possibly the same person as Old Reaume, had sought in 1765 to marry Le Gris's niece at the home of Le Petit Fer, a Myaamia war leader (see Charles André Barthe, *Incursion dans Le Détroit: Journaille Commansé le 29 octobre 1765 pour Le voyage que je fais au Mis a Mis,* ed. France Martineau and Marcel Bénéteau [Quebec: Les Presses de l'Université Laval, 2010], 67–73).

42. Trowbridge, *Meearmeear Traditions,* 29.

43. Trowbridge, *Meearmeear Traditions,* 77–78.

44. "Speech in Indian Council at Detroit" was made originally at the Miamis on August 18, 1773, delivered in French in Council at Detroit and translated by James Sterling on August 28, 1773, *Michigan Pioneer and Historical Society Historical Collections,* 19:309 [hereafter referred to as "Speech in Indian Council at Detroit"].

45. Trowbridge, *Meearmeear Traditions,* 29 and 14–15.

46. Carter, *The Life and Times of Little Turtle,* 19.

47. Lieutenant Jehu Hay, Resident at Detroit to Colonel Guy Johnson, August 7, 1774, Thomas Gage Papers, American Series, vol. 123, William L. Clements Library, University of Michigan. Minor changes to spelling and grammatical structure have been made to facilitate understanding of this passage.

48. "Speech in Indian Council at Detroit."

49. "Copy of a Council held by Richard Berringer Lernoult Esquire in His Majesty's 8th Regiment, Commander of the Detroit and Its Dependencies with Sastaresti King of the Hurons and Twenty-Six of the Chiefs and Principal Men of his Nation concerning the Bad Treatment Their Three Chiefs Met With, Who Went with Belts of Peace from Sir William Johnson to the Indian Nations on the Heads of the Wabash," Detroit, September 11, 1774,

Thomas Gage Papers, American Series, vol. 123, William L. Clements Library, University of Michigan. In the Wendat report of the meeting, they identify "Pacanne" as Mascouten. The fact that Pakaana was brother to the Mascouten chief Le Temps Clair and was referred to as Mascouten by the Wendat suggests Pakaana's mother or aunt may have been Mascouten.

50. "Miami Petition."

51. Young Tobacco (son of Old Tobacco, a Piankashaw leader) would call Pakaana grandfather in 1778 at Eel River. The young man sought Pakaana's approval of a Piankashaw/Virginian alliance, for which Pakaana rebuked him, accusing him of opening the road to the long knives (Virginians). See *Detroit to Fort Sackville, 1778–1779: The Journal of Normand MacLeod,* ed. William A. Evans (Detroit: Burton Historical Collection of the Detroit Public Library, 1978), 40–41.

52. "Miami Petition."

53. Kathleen Wilson, *The Island Race: Englishness, Empire and Gender in the Eighteenth Century* (New York: Routledge, 2003), 178.

54. Paul L. Stevens, "The Indian Diplomacy of Capt. Richard B. Lernoult, British Military Commandant of Detroit, 1774–1775, *Michigan Historical Review* 13, no. 1 (Spring 1987): 47–82, 62.

55. *Journal of Henry Hamilton,* 113.

56. Timothy D. Willig, *Restoring the Chain of Friendship: British Policy and the Indians of the Great Lakes, 1783–1815* (Lincoln: University of Nebraska Press, 2008), 23.

57. For a description of La Balme's activities, see Patrick Bottiger, *The Borderlands of Fear: Vincennes, Prophetstown, and the Invasion of the Miami Homeland* (Lincoln: University of Nebraska Press, 2016), 31.

58. "A Narrative of Life on the Old Frontier: Henry Hay's Journal," 230.

59. "A Narrative of Life on the Old Frontier," 223.

60. Ditz, "The New Men's History," 10.

61. George Trumbull to Thomas Gage, April 16, 1767, Thomas Gage Papers, American Series, William L. Clements Library, University of Michigan.

62. Captain James Stevenson to Sir William Johnson, Bart., Detroit, December 18, 1770, Chicago Historical Society.

63. Adriana Greci Green and Karen Marrero, "'Fixing Their Camp in Their Own Manner: The Critical Role of the Miami in British Operations in the Revolutionary Era," *Gateway: Magazine of the Missouri History Museum* 34 (2014): 32–33.

AFTERWORD

1. Joseph Moore, "Journal of a Tour to Detroit in Order to Attend a Treaty, Proposed to Be Held with the Indians at Saundusky," *Collections and Researches Made by the Michigan Pioneer and Historical Society,* vol. 17 (Lansing, MI: Robert Smith & Co., 1892), 643.

2. For a description of the British-Indigenous general council, see Timothy D. Willig, *Restoring the Chain of Friendship: British Policy and the Indians of the Great Lakes, 1783–1815* (Lincoln: University of Nebraska Press, 2008), 38–52.

3. Moore, "Journal of a Tour to Detroit," 645.

4. "Jacob Lindley's Account of a Journey to Attend the Indian Treaty," *Collections and Researches Made by the Michigan Pioneer and Historical Society* 17, 602.

5. Moore, "Journal of a Tour to Detroit," 646.

6. Don Greene and Noel Schutz, *Shawnee Heritage: Shawnee Genealogy and Family History* (Vision ePublications, 2008), 63. For description of Shawnee divisions, see Stephen Warren, *The Worlds the Shawnees Made: Migration and Violence in Early America* (Chapel Hill: University of North Carolina Press, 2014), 77. Shawnee leader Tecumseh was of the Kishpoko/Kispokotha division (Warren, *Worlds,* 22) and a contemporary of Isadore Chesne. There is confusion around the exact identities of the men of the Chesne/Chene/Shane family who had married into Shawnee and Wendat families. The Wyandotte Nation lists an Isadore Chesne as mixed blood and as one of their historic chiefs (see https://www.wyandotte-nation.org/culture/history/general-history/our-great-chiefs/). According to Tecumseh biographer John Sugden, Anthony Shane (probably Anglicized from Antoine Chesne) was a mixed-blood man acting on behalf of Shawnee interests in the last decade of the eighteenth century. He was married to Lameteshe, a relative of Tecumseh (Sugden, *Tecumseh: A Life* [New York: Henry Holt and Co., 1997], 15, 413).

7. Greg Curnoe, Frank Davey, and Neil Ferris, *Deeds, Nations* (London, ON: Ontario Archaeological Society, 1996), 120.

8. Laplant to the Shawnese, River Raisin, October 31, 1794, War of 1812 Papers of the Department of State, 1789–1815, Miscellaneous Intercepted Correspondence, 1789–1814, National Archives Microfilm Publications, Microcopy No. 588, Roll 7. I am grateful to Dennis Au for sharing this resource with me.

9. Charles G. Clarke, "The Roster of the Expedition of Lewis and Clark," *Oregon Historical Quarterly* 45, no. 4 (December 1944): 294.

10. Milo Quaife to Lancaster Pollard, April 5, 1945, George Drouillard Papers, Burton Historical Collection, Detroit Public Library.

11. Betty Houchin Winfield, "The Press Response to the Corps of Discovery: The Making of Heroes in an Egalitarian Age," *Journalism and Mass Communication Quarterly* 80, no. 4

(Winter 2003): 869–871.

12. Meriwether Lewis to Henry Dearborn, January 15, 1807, in James J. Holberg, "A Man of Much Merit," *We Proceeded On* 26, no. 3 (August 2000): 8; and Reuben Gold Thwaites, ed., *Original Journals of the Lewis and Clark Expedition,* vol. 7 (New York: Dodd, Mead and Co., 1905), 359.

13. William R. Swagerty, *The Indianization of Lewis and Clark* (Norman, OK: Arthur C. Clark Co., 2012), 125–126. Lewis did not mention French-Omaha expedition members François Labiche and Pierre Cruzatte.

14. M. O. Skarsten, *George Drouillard: Hunter and Interpreter for Lewis and Clark and Fur Trader, 1807–1810* (Glendale, CA: Arthur H. Clark Co., 1964), 18–20.

15. Robert Englebert, "Colonial Encounters and the Changing Contours of Ethnicity: Pierre-Louis de Lorimier and *Métissage* at the Edges of Empire," *Ohio Valley History* 18, no. 2 (Spring 2018): 57.

16. For Pakaana's time at the Arkansas post in the lower Mississippi River Valley and among the Quapaw, see Kathleen DuVal, *The Native Ground: Indians and Colonists in the Heart of the Continent* (Philadelphia: University of Pennsylvania Press, 2006), 160–161, 167. For murder of Pakaana's father-in-law, see Patrick Bottiger, *The Borderland of Fear: Vincennes, Prophetstown, and the Invasion of the Miami Homeland* (Lincoln: University of Nebraska Press, 2016), 34.

17. Lucy Murphy, *Great Lakes Creoles: A French-Indian Community on the Northern Borderlands, Prairie du Chien, 1750–1860* (Cambridge: Cambridge University Press, 2014).

APPENDIX. CREATING COMMUNITY AT DETROIT: WITNESSING THE MARRIAGE OF MICHEL BIZAILLON AND MARGUERITE FAFARD

1. "Marriage Contract," June 27, 1710, Fort Pontchartrain of Detroit, in *Collections and Researches Made by the Michigan Pioneer and Historical Society,* vol. 34 (Lansing, MI: Wynkoop Hallenbeck Crawford Co., 1905), 260–261.

2. Timothy J. Kent, *Ft. Pontchartrain at Detroit: A Guide to the Daily Lives of Fur Trade and Military Personnel, Settlers, and Missionaries at French Posts,* vol. 1 (Ossineke, MI: Silver Fox Enterprises, 2001), 438. Kent also lists Pierre Gauvreau as a gunsmith who, together with his assistant Guillaume Bonnet, was part of the fifty-two man contingent that first arrived to establish the French fort at Detroit in 1701 (439). Gauvreau seems not to have stayed because his name does not appear in the church register, but we do find him in 1717 in the St. Lawrence valley, his skills in great demand during the Fox Wars, where he attended to the weapons in the king's stores and to those of allied Indigenous nations

("Délibération du Conseil de Marine sur une lettre de Bégon," 3 février 1717, Série C11A, vol. 37, Folios 63v–64v, BAC). For a detailed description of the duties, tools, and wages of metalworkers in New France, see Kent, *Ft. Pontchartrain,* 438–465.

3. Imperial documents make reference to Michel Massé as having been employed temporarily as a blacksmith (*forgeron*) at Detroit. In his 1708 report on the poor state of affairs at Detroit and Cadillac's mismanagement, Aigremont explained that Cadillac had required Massé to pay 150 livres to operate as blacksmith, even though Massé plied this trade for only a short period. Massé was the second husband to Marguerite Couc (sister to Isabelle Couc [Madame Montour]).

4. According to Lina Gouger, this was a rare occurrence for any commandant during the entire French period (1701 to 1765). In all of those years, commandants asked individuals outside their immediate families on only six occasions to godparent (Gouger, "Le peuplement colonisateur de Détroit, 1701–1765" [PhD diss., Laval University, 2002], 299).

5. Marie Anne You Ladecouvert was the daughter of a Myaamia woman named Élisabeth who was the first wife of the French officer and merchant Pierre You de Ladécouverte. Pierre often acted as an imperially sanctioned intermediary between the French and the Myaamia in the early eighteenth century.

6. *Rapport de l'Archiviste de la Province de la Québec pour 1929–1930* (Quebec: Rédempti Paradis, 1930), 205.

7. *Rapport de l'Archiviste,* 214.

8. For Joseph Truteau and Pierre Roy as messengers, see "Copie d'une lettre de d'Adoucourt à son père le baron de Longueuil," Le Rocher (Starved Rock), 22 août 1715, Série C11A, vol. 35, Folio 56, BAC.

9. For further information on François Truteau, see Jay Higginbotham, *Old Mobile: Fort Louis de la Louisiane, 1702–1711* (Tuscaloosa: University of Alabama Press, 1977).

10. "Testament par Jean Baptiste Turpin," 12 octobre 1699, La Rochelle, Notaires, Etude Bonniot: Bagard. Turpin was listed as a native of Quebec in the contract. On the return leg of his journey, Iberville did not land in Montreal, but proceeded to New York, where he sold nine thousand pelts he had purchased from Canadian traders at Louisiana who wanted to avoid making a trip to Montreal. After leaving New York, Iberville sailed for France (Bernard Pothier, "Le Moyne d'Iberville et d'Ardillières, Pierre," in *Dictionary of Canadian Biography,* vol. 2 (Toronto: University of Toronto/Université Laval, 2003–), http://www.biographi.ca/en/bio/le_moyne_d_iberville_et_d_ardillieres_pierre_2E.html.

11. "Mémoire au ministre—compte rendu des négociations avec les chapeliers," [1699], Série C11A, vol. 17, Folio 201, BAC. Iberville's sale of furs to the English and Alexandre's trip to England and Holland to establish ties with manufacturers occurred after the Treaty of

Ryswick of 1697 had restored peace following King William's War.

12. Alexandre had been imprisoned by Governor General Callière for two months in October 1698 (a short time before his departure on the trading mission to England and Holland) when Jean Bochart de Champigny, the intendant of New France, addressed his case. Champigny reported that he was mystified as to why Turpin had been confined, describing him as a "poor bourgeois of Montreal" who "had only had the thought of going to trade in the woods" when he was arrested. Champigny could not understand why Turpin had been incarcerated for merely considering participation in the western trade when others actively engaged conducted their business unchecked ("Lettre de Champigny au ministre," Québec, 27 octobre 1698, Série C11A, vol. 16, Folio 135, BAC).

13. "Requête adressé au gouverneur général Denonville par les cabaretiers de Montréal," 1685, Série C11A, vol. 7, Folios 121–122v, BAC.

14. Morel de la Durantaye recorded having paid L'Orangé (Robert Rivard dit Loranger) and two other men—one of whom was Robert Rivard dit Loranger's brother-in-law Guillet— three bags of wheat for their service (see "Memoir of expenses incurred for the king's service and the execution of the orders of Monsieur the General de la Barre by the Sieur de la Durantaye among the Ottawa in the years 1683 and 1684"/"Memoire de depance faite par Le Sieur dela Durantaye aux outaouaes pour Le service du Roy et Lexecution des ordres de Monsieur Le general delabarre es années 1683 et 1684," in *The French Foundations, 1680–1693,* ed. Theodore Calvin Pease and Raymond C. Werner, *Collections of the Illinois State Historical Library,* vol. 23 (French Series, vol. 1) (Springfield: Illinois State Historical Library, 1934), 65.

15. "Accord et convention," Québec, 22 janvier 1689, Fonds des greffes de notaires du Québec, Bibliothèque et Archives nationales du Québec, Montreal.

16. "Memorandum of M. de la Mothe Cadillac concerning the Establishment of Detroit," Quebec, November 19, 1704, *Michigan Pioneer and Historical Society Collections and Researches* (Lansing: Michigan Pioneer and Historical Society, 1874–1929), 33:224 and 236.

17. Marcel Trudel, *Dictionnaire des esclaves et de leurs propriétaires au Canada français* (LaSalle, QC: Éditions Hurtubise HMH Ltée., 1990), 7. The Lafond dit Mongrain and Rivard families were linked in multiple ways—René-Alexis Rivard's mother-in-law, Marie Madeleine Rivard dit Lavigne, was also his cousin (their fathers were brothers).

18. This trend among French families would continue well into the twentieth century. The image of a "tree" to designate connections of North American French families fails to properly illustrate kinship relations across time. A series of interconnecting circles is a much more apt image.

19. For further information on Antoine Rivard, see Higginbotham, *Old Mobile.* The young French women, most of them Parisian, were carefully selected to serve as wives to wealthy and influential French men. Because the ship that delivered the women to Louisiana was named *Pelican,* historians have often referred to these women as the "Pelican Girls." Their purpose was identical to that of the "Filles du Roy" ("Daughters of the King") who were sent to Canada from France in the mid-seventeenth century to help populate the colony.

Bibliography

Archival Sources

Archives nationales d'outre-mer, Aix-en-Provence, France (ANOM)

Série B, Lettres envoyées

Série C11A, Correspondance générale, Canada

Série C11E, Des limites et des postes

Série C11G, Canada et divers

Bibliothèque et Archives nationales du Québec, Montreal (BAnQ-M)

Fonds Jurisdiction Royale de Montréal

Fonds des Greffes de notaires

Bibliothèque et Archives nationales du Québec, Québec (BAnQ-Q)

Fonds Intendants

Burton Historical Collection, Detroit Public Library

George Drouillard Papers

John Porteus Papers

Registre de Ste. Anne Detroit, No. 1252, Reel 1, Vols. 1–2, 1704–1780

Chicago Historical Society

French Colonial Papers

Library and Archives Canada, Ottawa

Congés et permis enregistrés à Montréal

Fonds des Ordonnances des intendants de la Nouvelle-France

Fonds des Greffes de notaires de France, MG6-A2

Fonds des Greffes de notaires de la Nouvelle-France et du Québec, MG8-A23

Notre Dame de la Conception des Cascaskias, Illinois, U.S.A. Early U.S. French Catholic Church
   Records, Registres Photographie aux Archives d'Ottawa Ontario, Reduction 18, Lumiere 4

National Archives of the United Kingdom, Kew

Baron Jeffrey Amherst, Commander in Chief: Papers, Correspondence between Commander-
   in-Chief and Officers at Detroit

National Archives of the United States

Papers of the Department of State, Miscellaneous Intercepted Correspondence, 1789–1814,
   Microfilm Publications, Microcopy No. 588, Roll 7

William L. Clements Library, University of Michigan

James Sterling Letterbook

Thomas Gage Papers, American Series

Chaussegros de Léry, Joseph Gaspard. *La rivière du Détroit depuis le Lac Sainte Claire jusqu'au
   Lac Érie,* 1764, Map Division

Montrésor, John. *Plan of Detroit with Its Environs,* 1764, Map Division

Map of the Western End of Lake Erie, Lake St. Clair, and the St. Clair River, 1813, Map Division

Published and Secondary Sources

Adams, Julia. "The Rule of the Father: Patriarchy and Patrimonialism in Early Modern Europe."
   In *Max Weber's 'Economy and Society': A Critical Companion,* edited by Charles Camic,
   Philip S. Gorski, and David M. Trubek. Stanford, CA: Stanford University Press, 2005.

Adams, Julia, and Chris Shughrue. "Bottlenecks and East Indies Companies: Modeling the
   Geography of Agency in Mercantilist Enterprises." In *Chartering Capitalism: Organizing
   Markets, States, and Publics,* edited by Emily Erickson. Bingley, UK: Emerald Group
   Publishing Ltd., 2015.

Albers, Patricia C. "Marxism and Historical Materialism in American Indian History."

In *Clearing a Path: Theorizing the Past in Native American Studies,* edited by Nancy Shoemaker. New York: Routledge, 2002.

Albers, Patricia, and Jeanne Kay. "Sharing the Land: A Study in American Indian Territoriality." In *A Cultural Geography of North American Indians,* edited by Thomas E. Ross and Tyrel G. Moore. Boulder, CO: Westview Press, 1987.

Alter, George. "Infant and Child Mortality in the United States and Canada." In *Infant and Child Mortality in the Past,* edited by Alain Bideau, Bertrand Desjardins, and Héctor Pérex Brignoli. Oxford: Oxford University Press, 1997.

American State Papers: Indian Affairs, 1789–1815. Vol. 1. Washington, DC: Gales and Seaton, 1832.

Anderson, Karen. *Chain Her by One Foot: The Subjugation of Native Women in Seventeenth-Century New France.* New York: Routledge, 1991.

Anglo-French Boundary Disputes in the West, 1749–1763. Edited by Theodore Calvin Pease. *Collections of the Illinois State Historical Library,* vol. 27. French Series, vol. 2. Springfield: Illinois State Historical Library, 1936.

Antone, Bob. "Reconstructing Indigenous Masculine Thought." In Warren Cariou, Daniel Heath Justice, and Gregory Scofield, *Indigenous Men and Masculinities: Legacies, Identities, Regeneration.* Winnipeg: University of Manitoba Press, 2015.

Armour, David Arthur. *The Merchants of Albany, New York: 1686–1760.* New York: Garland Publishing Inc., 1986.

Aubert, Guillaume. "The Blood of France: Race and Purity of Blood in the French Atlantic World." *William and Mary Quarterly* 61, no. 3 (July 2004).

Banks, Kenneth J. *Chasing Empire across the Sea: Communications and the State in the French Atlantic, 1713–1763.* Montreal & Kingston: McGill-Queen's University Press, 2003.

Baraga, Frederic. *A Dictionary of the Otchipwe Language, Explained in English.* Montreal: Beauchemin & Valois, 1878.

Barr, Juliana. "Geographies of Power: Mapping Indian Borders in the 'Borderlands' of the Early Southwest." *William and Mary Quarterly* 68, no. 1 (January 2011).

———. *Peace Came in the Form of a Woman: Indians and Spaniards in the Texas Borderlands.* Chapel Hill: University of North Carolina Press, 2009.

Barthe, Charles André. *Incursion dans Le Détroit: Journaille Commansé le 29 octobre 1765 pour Le voyage que je fais au Mis a Mis.* Edited by France Martineau and Marcel Bénéteau. Quebec: Les Presses de l'Université Laval, 2010.

Belmessous, Saliha. "Assimilation and Racialism in Seventeenth and Eighteenth-Century French Colonial Policy." *American Historical Review* 110, no. 2 (April 2005).

Belting, Natalia Maree. *Kaskaskia under the French Regime.* Urbana: University of Illinois Press, 1948.

Bénéteau, Marcel. "Aspects de la tradition orale comme marqueurs d'identité culturelle: Le vocabulaire et la chanson traditionelle des francophones du Détroit." PhD diss., Laval University, 2001.

———. "Chansons traditionnelles et identité culturelle chez les Francophones du Détroit." *Ethnologies* 26, no. 2 (2004).

———. "'Les Mascoutens': Chanson de composition locale." From À la table de mes amis: Vieilles chansons du Détroit, vol. 3. Windsor: Disques Petite Côte Records, 2001. Compact disc.

Bénéteau, Marcel, and Peter Halford. *Mots choisis: Trois cents ans de francophonie au Détroit du Lac Érié.* Ottawa: Presses de l'Université d'Ottawa, 2008.

Bernier, Hélène. "Charly Saint-Ange, Marie-Catherine, du Saint-Sacrement." In *Dictionary of Canadian Biography,* vol. 2. Toronto: University of Toronto/Université Laval, 2003–.

———. "Cuillerier, Marie-Anne-Véronique." In *Dictionary of Canadian Biography,* vol. 3. Toronto: University of Toronto/Université Laval, 2003–.

Blackbird, Andrew J. *History of the Ottawa and Chippewa Indians of Michigan.* Ypsilanti, MI: Ypsilanti Job Printing House, 1887.

Blum, Rony. *Ghost Brothers: Adoption of a French Tribe by Bereaved Native America.* Montreal & Kingston: McGill-Queen's University Press, 2005.

Bohaker, Heidi. "Indigenous Histories and Archival Media in the Early Modern Great Lakes." In *Colonial Mediascapes: Sensory Worlds of the Early Americas,* edited by Matt Cohen and Jeffrey Glover. Lincoln: University of Nebraska Press, 2014.

———. "'Nindoodemag': The Significance of Algonquian Kinship Networks in the Eastern Great Lakes Region, 1600–1701." *William and Mary Quarterly* 63, no. 1 (January 2006).

Bottiger, Patrick. *The Borderland of Fear: Vincennes, Prophetstown, and the Invasion of the Miami Homeland.* Lincoln: University of Nebraska Press, 2016.

Boulware, Tyler. "'It Seems Like Coming into Our Houses': Challenges to Cherokee Hunting Grounds, 1750–1775." In *Before the Volunteer State: New Thoughts on Early Tennessee History, 1690–1800,* edited by Kristofer Ray. Knoxville: University of Tennessee Press, 2014.

"Bourgeois, Marguerite." In *L'histoire des femmes au Québec depuis quatre siècles,* edited by Micheline Dumont et al. Montreal: Les Quinze, Éditeur, 1982.

Boyle, Susan C. "Did She Generally Decide? Women in Ste. Genevieve, 1750–1805." *William and Mary Quarterly* 3, no. 44 (October 1987).

Brandão, José António, ed. and trans., with K. Janet Ritch. *Nation Iroquoise: A Seventeenth-Century Ethnography of the Iroquois.* Lincoln: University of Nebraska Press, 2003.

Brice, Wallace A. *A History of Fort Wayne, from the Earliest Known Accounts of This Point, to the Present Period.* Fort Wayne, IN: D. W. Jones & Sons, 1868.

Brooks, Lisa. *The Common Pot: The Recovery of Native Space in the Northeast* (Minneapolis: University of Minnesota Press, 2008.

Brown, Kathleen M. *Good Wives, Nasty Wenches, and Anxious Patriarchs: Gender, Race, and Power in Colonial Virginia.* Chapel Hill: University of North Carolina Press, 1996.

Brown, Margaret Kimball. *History as They Lived It: A Social History of Prairie du Rocher, Illinois.* Carbondale: Southern Illinois University Press, 2014.

Brown, Margaret Kimball, and Lawrie Cena Dean, eds. *The Village of Chartres in Colonial Illinois, 1720–1765.* New Orleans: Polyanthos, 1977.

Burke, Peter. "History as Social Memory." In *Memory, History, Culture and the Mind,* edited by Thomas Butler. Oxford: Blackwell, 1989.

Buss, James Joseph. *Winning the West with Words: Language and Conquest in the Lower Great Lakes.* Norman: University of Oklahoma Press, 2011.

Byrd, Jodi. *The Transit of Empire: Indigenous Critiques of Colonialism.* Minneapolis: University of Minnesota Press, 2011.

Callender, Charles. "Fox." In *Handbook of North American Indians,* vol. 15, *Northeast,* edited by Bruce G. Trigger. Washington, DC: Smithsonian Institution, 1978.

Cangany, Catherine. *Frontier Seaport: Detroit's Transformation into an Atlantic Entrepôt.* Chicago: University of Chicago Press, 2014.

Carter, Harvey Lewis. *The Life and Times of Little Turtle: First Sagamore of the Wabash.* Urbana: University of Illinois Press, 1987.

Carver, Jonathan. *Travels through the Interior Parts of North America in the Years 1766, 1767, 1768.* 3rd ed. London, 1781.

Cass, Lewis. *A Discourse: Delivered at the First Meeting of the Historical Society of Michigan.* Detroit: George L. Whitney, 1830.

Catlin, George B. *The Story of Detroit.* Detroit: Detroit News, 1923.

Chaplin, Joyce E. *Subject Matter: Technology, the Body, and Science on the Anglo-American Frontier, 1500–1676.* Cambridge, MA: Harvard University Press, 2001.

Chapman, Sarah E. "Détroit to France and Back: Political and Cultural Networks and Colonial Exchanges during Louis XIV's Reign." Paper delivered at the 64th Annual Meeting of the Society for French Historical Studies, Pittsburgh, March 8–10, 2018.

———. "Patronage as Family Economy: The Role of Women in the Patron-Client Network of the Phélypeaux de Pontchartrain Family, 1670–1715." *French Historical Studies* 24, no. 1 (Winter 2001).

———. "Reluctant Expansionists: Louis XIV, the Ministers of Colonies and the Founding of Détroit." In *The Third Reign of Louis XIV c. 1682–1715,* edited by Julia Prest and Guy Rowlands. London: Routledge, 2016.

Child, Brenda. *Holding Our World Together: Ojibwe Women and the Survival of Community.* New York: Penguin Books, 2012.

Clarke, Charles G. "The Roster of the Expedition of Lewis and Clark." *Oregon Historical Quarterly* 45, no. 4 (December 1944).

Clarke, Peter Dooyentate. *Origin and Traditional History of the Wyandotts, and Sketches of Other Indian Tribes of North America.* Toronto: Hunter, Rose and Co., 1870.

Collections and Researches Made by the Michigan Pioneer and Historical Society. Lansing, MI: Robert Smith & Co., State Printers and Binders, 1892.

Collections of the State Historical Society of Wisconsin. Vol. 16. Edited by Reuben Gold Thwaites. Madison: State Historical Society of Wisconsin, 1902.

Cooper, Afua. *The Hanging of Angélique: The Untold Story of Canadian Slavery and the Burning of Old Montreal.* Toronto: HarperCollins Publishers Ltd., 2006.

Cooper, Frederick. *Colonialism in Question: Theory, Knowledge, History.* Berkeley: University of California Press, 2005.

Costa, David J. "The Kinship Terminology of the Miami-Illinois Language." *Anthropological Linguistics* 41, no. 1 (Spring 1999).

———. "The St-Jérôme Dictionary of Miami-Illinois." In *Papers of the 36th Algonquian Conference,* edited by H. C. Wolfart. Winnipeg: University of Manitoba, 2005.

Crawford, T. H. *Annual Report of the Commissioner of Indian Affairs.* 25th Congress, 3rd session. Washington, DC: Blair & Rives Printers, 1838.

Crouch, Christian Ayne. "The Black City: African and Indian Exchanges in Pontiac's Upper Country." *Early American Studies* 14, no. 2 (Spring 2016).

Crowley, Mary Catherine. *The Heroine of the Strait: A Romance of Detroit in the Time of Pontiac.* Boston: Little, Brown and Co., 1902.

Cruikshank, Julie. "Oral History, Narrative Strategies, and Native American Historiography: Perspectives from the Yukon Territory, Canada." In *Clearing a Path: Theorizing the Past in Native American Studies,* edited by Nancy Shoemaker. New York: Routledge, 2002.

Cuoq, Jean-André. *Lexique de la langue algonquine.* Montreal: J. Chapleau & fils, 1886.

Curnoe, Greg, Frank Davey, and Neil Ferris. *Deeds, Nations.* London, ON: Ontario Archaeological Society, 1996.

Dechêne, Louise. "Dauphin de la Forest, François." In *Dictionary of Canadian Biography,* vol. 2. Toronto: University of Toronto/Université Laval, 2003–.

———. *Habitants and Merchants in Seventeenth Century Montreal.* Translated by Liana Vardi. Montreal & Kingston: McGill-Queen's University Press, 1992.

———. "Véniard de Bourgmond, Étienne de." In *Dictionary of Canadian Biography,* vol. 2. Toronto: University of Toronto/Université Laval, 2003–.

d'Errico, Peter. "Indigenous Lèse-majesté: Questioning U.S. Federal Indian Law." *New Diversities* 19, no. 2 (2017).

DeMallie, Raymond J. "Kinship: The Foundation for Native American Society." In *Studying Native America: Problems and Prospects,* edited by Russell Thornton. Madison: University of Wisconsin Press, 1998.

Denissen, Christian. *Genealogy of the French Families of the Detroit River Region, 1701–1936.* Edited by Harold Frederic Powell and Robert L. Pilon. Vol. 2. Detroit: Burton Historical Collection, 1987.

Désilets, Andrée. "Roy, Marguerite, de la Conception." In *Dictionary of Canadian Biography,* vol. 3. Toronto: University of Toronto/Université Laval, 2003–.

———. "Trottier, Marguerite, Saint-Joseph." In *Dictionary of Canadian Biography,* vol. 3. Toronto: University of Toronto/Université Laval, 2003–.

Desjardins, Bertrand. "Family Formation and Infant Mortality in New France." In *Infant and Child Mortality in the Past,* edited by Alain Bideau, Bertrand Desjardins, and Héctor Pérez Brignoli. Oxford: Oxford University Press, 1997.

Detroit to Fort Sackville, 1778–1779: The Journal of Normand MacLeod. Edited by William A. Evans. Detroit: Burton Historical Collection of the Detroit Public Library, 1978.

Devine, Heather. *The People Who Own Themselves: Aboriginal Ethnogenesis in a Canadian Family, 1660–1900.* Calgary: University of Calgary Press, 2004.

Diary of the Siege of Detroit in the War with Pontiac: Also a Narrative of the Principal Events of the Siege. Edited by Franklin B. Hough. Albany, NY: J. Munsell, 1860.

Ditz, Toby. "The New Men's History and the Peculiar Absence of Gendered Power: Some Remedies from Early American Gender History." *Gender and History* 16, no. 1 (2004).

Dixon, David. *Never Come to Peace Again: Pontiac's Uprising and the Fate of the British Empire in North America.* Norman: University of Oklahoma Press, 2005.

Documents Relative to the Colonial History of the State of New York. Vols. 4 and 9. Edited by E. B. O'Callaghan. Albany, NY: Weed, Parsons and Co., Printers, 1854–1855.

Douglas, Walter B. "The Sieurs de St. Ange." In *Transactions of the Illinois State Historical Society,* vol. 14. Springfield, IL: State Journal Co., 1910.

Dowd, Gregory. *War under Heaven: Pontiac, the Indian Nations, and the British Empire.* Baltimore: Johns Hopkins University Press, 2004.

Drolet, Antonio. "Juchereau de Saint-Denis, Charlotte-Françoise, Comtesse de Saint-Laurent." In *Dictionary of Canadian Biography,* vol. 2. Toronto: University of Toronto/Université Laval, 2003–.

Drouin, Gabriel. *Dictionnaire national des Canadiens français (1608–1760),* vol. 2. Montreal: Institut généalogique, 1965.

Dumont, Micheline, Michèle Jean, Marie Lavigne, and Jennifer Stoddart. *L'histoire des femmes au Québec depuis quatre siècles.* Montréal: Les Quinze, 1982.

Dunn, Walter S., Jr. "Chabert de Joncaire de Clausonne, Daniel-Marie." In *Dictionary of Canadian Biography,* vol. 4. Toronto: University of Toronto/Université Laval, 2003–.

———. *Frontier Profit and Loss: The British Army and the Fur Traders, 1760–1764.* Westport, CT: Greenwood Press, 1998.

Dunnigan, Brian Leigh. *Frontier Metropolis: Picturing Early Detroit, 1701–1838.* Detroit: Wayne State University Press, 2001.

DuVal, Kathleen. *The Native Ground: Indians and Colonists in the Heart of the Continent.* Philadelphia: University of Pennsylvania Press, 2006.

Elbourne, Elizabeth. "Domesticity and Dispossession: The Ideology of 'Home' and the British Construction of the 'Primitive' from the Eighteenth to the Early Nineteenth Century." In *Deep Histories: Gender and Colonialism in Southern Africa,* edited by Wendy Woodward, Patricia Hayes, and Gary Minkley. New York: Editions Rodopi B.V., 2002.

Englebert, Robert. "Colonial Encounters and the Changing Contours of Ethnicity: Pierre-Louis de Lorimier and *Métissage* at the Edges of Empire." *Ohio Valley History* 18, no. 2 (Spring 2018).

Englebert, Robert. "The Legacy of New France: Law and Social Cohesion between Quebec and the Illinois Country, 1763–1790." *French Colonial History* 17 (2017).

———. "Merchant Representatives and the French River World, 1763–1803." *Michigan Historical Review* 34, no. 1 (Spring 2008).

Englebert, Robert, and Guillaume Teasdale. "Introduction." In *French and Indians in the Heart of North America, 1630–1815,* edited by Englebert and Teasdale. East Lansing: Michigan State University Press, 2013.

Entrikin, Nicholas J. *The Betweenness of Place: Towards a Geography of Modernity.* Baltimore: Johns Hopkins University Press, 1991.

Faye, Stanley. "Indian Guests at the Spanish Arkansas Post." *Arkansas Historical Quarterly* 4, no. 2 (Summer 1945).

Ferland, Catherine. "Le nectar et l'ambroisie: La consummation des boissons alcooliques chez l'élite de la Nouvelle-France au XVIIIe siècle." *Revue d'histoire de l'Amérique française* 58, no. 4 (2005).

Ferland, Catherine, and Benoît Grenier. "Les Procuratrices à Québec au XVIIIe Siècle: Résultats Préliminaires d'une Enquête sur le Pouvoir des Femmes en Nouvelle France." In *Femmes, Culture et Pouvoir: Relectures de l'Histoire au Féminin Xve–XXe Siècles,* edited by Ferland and Grenier. Québec: Les Presses de l'Université Laval, 2010.

Ferris, Neal. *The Archaeology of Native-Lived Colonialism: Challenging History in the Great*

Lakes. Tucson: University of Arizona Press, 2009.

The First Families of Louisiana. Vol. 2. Translated and compiled by Glenn R. Conrad. Baton Rouge, LA: Claitor's Publishing Division, 1970.

Fraser, John. "La Salle's Homestead at La Chine." *Magazine of American History with Notes and Queries* 24 (July–December 1890).

The French Foundations, 1680–1693. Edited by Theodore Calvin Pease and Raymond C. Werner. *Collections of the Illinois State Historical Library,* vol. 23. French Series, vol. 1. Springfield: Illinois State Historical Library, 1934.

Fur, Gunlög. *A Nation of Women: Gender and Colonial Encounter among the Delaware Indians.* Philadelphia: University of Pennsylvania Press, 2009.

The Gladwin Manuscripts. Edited by Charles Moore. Lansing, MI: Robert Smith Printing, 1897.

Gitlin, Jay. *The Bourgeois Frontier: French Towns, French Traders, and American Expansion.* New Haven, CT: Yale University Press, 2009.

Godfroy, Chief Clarence (Ka-pah-pwah). *Miami Indian Stories.* Edited by Martha Una McClurg. Winona Lake, IN: Light and Life Press, 1961.

Gouger, Lina. "Les convoys de colons de 1749–1750: Impulsion gouvernementale decisive pour le développement de la region de Windsor." In *Le Passage du Détroit: 300 ans de présence Francophone/Passages: Three Centuries of Francophone Presence at Le Détroit,* edited by Marcel Bénéteau. Working Papers in the Humanities, vol. 11. Windsor, ON: University of Windsor, 2003.

———. "Le peuplement colonisateur de Détroit, 1701–1765." PhD diss., Laval University, 2002.

Greci Green, Adriana, and Karen Marrero. "'Fixing Their Camp in Their Own Manner': The Critical Role of the Miami in British Operations in the Revolutionary Era." *Gateway: Magazine of the Missouri History Museum* 34 (2014).

Green, Rayna. "The Pocahontas Perplex: The Image of Indian Women in American Culture." *Massachusetts Review* 16, no. 4 (1975): 698–714.

Greene, Don, and Noel Schutz. *Shawnee Heritage: Shawnee Genealogy and Family History.* Vision ePublications, 2008.

Greer, Allan. "Commons and Enclosure in the Colonization of North America." *American Historical Review* 117, no. 2 (April 2012).

———. *Mohawk Saint: Catherine Tekakwitha and the Jesuits.* New York: Oxford University Press, 2006.

———. *The People of New France.* Toronto: University of Toronto Press, 1997.

———. *Property and Dispossession: Natives, Empires and Land in Early Modern North America.* Cambridge: Cambridge University Press, 2018.

Haefeli, Evan, and Kevin Sweeney. *Captors and Captives: The 1704 French and Indian Raid on*

Deerfield. Amherst: University of Massachusetts Press, 2003.

Halford, Peter W. *Le français des Canadiens à la veille de la Conquête: Témoignage du père Pierre Philippe Potier, S.J.* Ottawa: Les Presses de l'Université d'Ottawa, 1994.

Hamilton, Henry. *Henry Hamilton and George Rogers Clark in the American Revolution with the Unpublished Journal of Lieutenant Governor Henry Hamilton.* Edited by John D. Barnhart. Crawfordsville, IN: R. E. Banta, 1951.

Hamilton, Michelle A. "In the King's Service: Provisioning and Quartering the British Army in the Old Northwest, 1760–63." In *English Atlantics Revisited: Essays Honoring Ian K. Steele,* edited by Nancy L. Rhoden. Montreal & Kingston: McGill-Queen's University Press, 2007.

Hastings, Hugh, ed. *Ecclesiastical Records State of New York.* Vol. 2. Albany, NY: James B. Lyon, 1901.

Havard, Gilles. *Empire et métissages: Indiens et Français dans le Pays d'en Haut, 1660–1715* Sillery, QC: Les Éditions du Septentrion, 2003.

———. *The Great Peace of Montreal of 1701: French-Native Diplomacy in the Seventeenth Century.* Translated by Phyllis Aronoff and Howard Scott. Montreal & Kingston: McGill-Queen's University Press, 2001.

———. *Histoire des coureurs de bois Amérique du Nord, 1600–1840.* Paris: Les Indes Savantes, 2016.

Havard, Gilles, and Cécile Vidal. *Histoire de l'Amérique française.* Paris: Éditions Flammarion, 2003.

Hermeling, Andrew Dyrli. "Severing Tender Ties: George Croghan's Ironic Policing of Identity and Intimacy during Pontiac's War." Paper delivered at Annual Meeting of the American Society for Ethnohistory, October 11–13, 2018, Oaxaca, Mexico.

Higginbotham, Jay. *Old Mobile: Fort Louis de la Louisiane, 1702–1711.* Tuscaloosa: University of Alabama Press, 1977.

Hill, Susan M. *The Clay We Are Made Of: Haudenosaunee Land Tenure on the Grand River* Winnipeg: University of Manitoba Press, 2017.

Hirsch, Alison Duncan. "'The Celebrated Madame Montour': Interpretess across Early American Frontiers." *Explorations in Early American Culture* 4 (2000).

Historical Atlas of Canada: From the Beginning to 1800. Vol. 1. Edited by R. Cole Harris. Toronto: University of Toronto Press, 1987.

Holberg, James J. "A Man of Much Merit." *We Proceeded On* 26, no. 3 (August 2000).

Horguelin, Christophe. "Le XVIIIe siècle des Canadiens: Discours public et identité." In *Mémoires de la Nouvelle France: De France en Nouvelle France,* edited by Philippe Joutard and Thomas Wien. Rennes, France: Presses Universitaires de Rennes, 2005.

Horton, Donald J. "Chachagouesse." In *Dictionary of Canadian Biography,* vol. 2. Toronto:

University of Toronto/Université Laval, 2003–.

Howe, LeAnne. "The Story of America: A Tribalography." In *Clearing a Path: Theorizing the Past in Native American Studies,* edited by Nancy Shoemaker. New York: Routledge, 2002.

Humphrey, Helen. "The Identity of Gladwin's Informant." *Mississippi Valley Historical Review* 21, no. 2 (September 1934).

Innis, Harold A. *Fur Trade in Canada.* Toronto: University of Toronto Press, 1999.

Jacobs, Dean. "Indian Land Surrenders." In *The Western District,* edited by K. G. Pryke and L. L. Kulisek. Windsor, ON: Essex County Historical Society, 1983.

Jacobs, Dean M. "'We have but our hearts and the traditions of our old men': Understanding the Traditions and History of Bkejwanong." In *Gin Das Winan: Documenting Aboriginal History in Ontario,* edited by Dale Standen and David McNab, no. 2, Occasional Papers of the Champlain Society. Toronto: Champlain Society, 1996.

Jennings, Francis. *The Ambiguous Iroquois Empire: The Covenant Chain Confederation of Indian Tribes with English Colonies.* New York: W. W. Norton and Co., 1990.

———. "Bisaillon, Peter." In *Dictionary of Canadian Biography,* vol. 3. Toronto: University of Toronto/Université Laval, 2003–.

The Jesuit Relations and Allied Documents: Travel and Exploration of the Jesuit Missionaries in New France, 1610–1791. Vols. 25, 46, 65, 70. Edited by Reuben Gold Thwaites. Cleveland: Burrows Brothers Co., 1896–1901.

Jetté, René. *Dictionnaire généalogique des familles du Québec.* Boucherville, QC: Gaetan Morin Editeur, 1983.

John, Elizabeth A. H. *Storms Brewed in Other Men's Worlds: The Confrontation of Indians, Spanish, and French in the Southwest, 1540–1795.* Norman: University of Oklahoma Press, 1996.

Kelsey, Harry. "Campbell, Donald." In *Dictionary of Canadian Biography,* vol. 3. Toronto: University of Toronto/Université Laval, 2003–.

Kent, Timothy. *Ft. Pontchartrain at Detroit: A Guide to the Daily Lives of Fur Trade and Military Personnel, Settlers, and Missionaries at French Posts.* Vol. 1. Ossineke, MI: Silver Fox Enterprises, 2001.

Kettering, Sharon. "Patronage and Kinship in Early Modern France." *French Historical Studies* 16, no. 2 (Fall 1989).

Kidd, Colin. *British Identities before Nationalism: Ethnicity and Nationhood in the Atlantic World, 1600–1800.* Cambridge: Cambridge University Press, 1999.

Kingsford, William. *The History of Canada.* Vol. 2. London: Trübnar & Co., 1888.

Kugel, Rebecca. "Leadership within the Women's Community: Susie Bonga Wright of the Leech Lake Ojibwe." In *Midwestern Women: Work, Community, and Leadership at the*

Crossroads, edited by Lucy Eldersveld Murphy and Wendy Hamand Venet. Bloomington: Indiana University Press, 1997.

Kugel, Rebecca, and Lucy Murphy. "Introduction: Searching for Cornfields and Sugar Groves." In *Native Women's History in Eastern North America before 1900: A Guide to Research and Writing*, edited by Kugel and Murphy. Lincoln: University of Nebraska Press, 2007.

Labelle, Kathryn Magee. *Dispersed but Not Destroyed: A History of the Seventeenth-Century Wendat Diaspora*. Vancouver: University of British Columbia Press, 2013.

Lamonde, Yvan. *Trajectoires de l'histoire du Quebec*. Ottawa: Musée de la civilization, 2001.

Langlois, Michel. *Dictionnaire biographique des ancêtres québécois, 1608–1700*. Vol. 4. Siller, QC: Les Éditions du Mitan, 2001.

Lanza, Janine. *From Wives to Widows in Early Modern Paris: Gender, Economy, and Law*. New York: Routledge, 2007.

Lauzon Delorme, Hazel Mary. *Family Tree of Labute, LaBute, Labutte*. Windsor, ON, 1977.

Lavallée, Louis. *La Prairie en Nouvelle France, 1647–1760: Étude d'histoire sociale*. Montreal & Kingston: McGill-Queen's University Press, 1992.

Laxer, Daniel. "A Reservoir of Voices: Franco-Ontarien Folk Songs." *Ontario History* 1, no. 1 (Spring 2009).

Lemieux, Denise. *Les petits innocents: L'enfance en Nouvelle-France*. Quebec: Institut québécois de recherche sur la culture, 1985.

Little, Arthur L. *Shakespeare Jungle Fever: National-Imperial Revisions of Race, Rape, and Sacrifice*. Stanford, CA: Stanford University Press, 2000.

Lytwyn, Victor. "Waterworld: The Aquatic Territory of the Great Lakes First Nations." In *Gin Das Winan: Documenting Aboriginal History in Ontario*, edited by Dale Standen and David McNab, no. 2, Occasional Papers of the Champlain Society. Toronto: Champlain Society, 1996.

Lytwyn, Victor, and Dean Jacobs. "'For Good Will and Affection': The Detroit Indian Deeds and British Land Policy, 1760–1827." *Ontario History* 92, no. 2 (Spring 2000).

McCafferty, Michael. *Native American Place Names of Indiana*. Urbana: University of Illinois Press, 2008.

McClintock, Anne. *Imperial Leather: Race, Gender and Sexuality in the Colonial Conquest*. New York: Routledge, 1995.

McConnell, Michael N. *The Upper Ohio Valley and Its Peoples, 1724–1774*. Lincoln: University of Nebraska Press, 1992.

McDermott, John Francis. *Glossary of Mississippi Valley French, 1673–1850*. St. Louis: Washington State University, 1941.

McDonnell, Michael A. *Masters of Empire: Great Lakes Indians and the Making of America*. New

York: Hill and Wang, 2015.

McGrath, Ann. *Illicit Love: Interracial Sex and Marriage in the United States and Australia.* Lincoln: University of Nebraska Press, 2015.

McKeon, Michael. *The Secret History of Domesticity: Public, Private, and the Division of Knowledge.* Baltimore: Johns Hopkins University Press, 2005.

McLaren, Dorothy. "Fertility, Infant Mortality, and Breast Feeding in the Seventeenth Century." *Medical History* 22, no. 4 (October 1978).

McNab, David T. *Circles of Time: Aboriginal Land Rights and Resistance in Ontario.* Waterloo, ON: Wilfrid Laurier University Press, 1999.

Mann, Barbara. "Jigonsaseh." In *Encyclopedia of the Haudenosaunee (Iroquois Confederacy),* edited by Bruce Elliot Johansen and Barbara Alice Mann. Westport, CT: Greenwood Press, 2000.

Marrero, Karen. "'Fait Chorus': Telling New Histories of Detroit's French Community." *Michigan's Habitant Heritage,* 39, no. 4 (2018).

Marshall, Peter. "Imperial Policy and the Government of Detroit: Projects and Problems, 1760–1774." *Journal of Imperial and Commonwealth History* 2, no. 2 (January 1974).

Mays, Kyle. "Pontiac's Ghost in the Motor City: Indigeneity and the Discursive Constructive of Modern Detroit." *Middle West Review* 2, no. 2 (2016).

Merrell, James. "'The Cast of His Countenance': Reading Andrew Montour." In *Through a Glass Darkly: Reflections on Personal Identity in Early America,* edited by Ronald Hoffman et al. Chapel Hill: University of North Carolina Press, 1997.

———. *Into the American Woods: Negotiators on the Pennsylvania Frontier.* New York: W.W. Norton, 1999.

Michigan Pioneer and Historical Society Collections. Vols. 8, 17, 18, 19, 20, 33, 34. Lansing: Michigan Pioneer and Historical Society, 1874–1929.

Middleton, Richard. *Never Come to Peace Again: Pontiac's Uprising and the Fate of the British Empire in North America.* Norman: University of Oklahoma Press, 2005.

———. *Pontiac's War: Its Causes, Course, and Consequences.* New York: Routledge, 2007.

Miles, Tiya. *The Dawn of Detroit: A Chronicle of Slavery and Freedom in the City of the Straits.* New York: New Press, 2017.

Miller, Cary. *Ogimaag: Anishinaabeg Leadership, 1760–1845.* Lincoln: University of Nebraska Press, 2010.

Molloy, Maureen. "Considered Affinity: Kinship, Marriage, and Social Class in New France." *Social Science History* 14, no. 1 (Spring 1990).

Moogk, Peter. "*Les Petits Sauvages:* The Children of Eighteenth-Century New France." In *Childhood and Family in Canadian History,* edited by Joy Parr. Toronto: McClelland and

Stewart, 1982.

———. "Reluctant Exiles: Emigrants from France in Canada before 1760." *William and Mary Quarterly* 46, no. 3 (July 1989).

Moore, John Rees. "The Enemies of Love: The Example of Antony and Cleopatra." *Kenyon Review* 31, no. 5 (1969).

Moreau-DesHarnais, Gail, and Diane Wolford Sheppard. "Pierre Chesne dit Saint-Onge, #1 Pierre Chesne dit Labutte [1698–1774], #2 Pierre Chesne dit Labutte [1729–1804], #3 Pierre Chesne dit Labutte [1770–1813], Pierre Labutte of the Detroit River Region [1800–1879]." Part 3, "Pierre Chesne dit Labutte [1729–1804]." Continued from *Michigan's Habitant Heritage,* 33, no. 3 (July 2012): 160–169; 33, no. 4 (October 2012): 215–229." In *Michigan's Habitant Heritage* 34, vol. 1 (January 2013)—updated 2015.

Morris, Captain Thomas. *Miscellanies in Prose and Verse.* London, 1791; reprint, Cleveland: Arthur C. Clark Co., 1904.

Morrissey, Robert Michael. *Empire by Collaboration: Indians, Colonists, and Governments in Colonial Illinois Country.* Philadelphia: University of Pennsylvania Press, 2015.

———. "Kaskaskia Social Network: Kinship and Assimilation in the French-Illinois Borderlands, 1695–1735." *William and Mary Quarterly* 70, no. 1 (January 2013).

Murphy, Lucy Eldersveld. *Great Lakes Creoles: A French-Indian Community on the Northern Borderlands, Prairie du Chien, 1750–1860.* Cambridge: Cambridge University Press, 2014.

Newbigging, William James. "The History of the French-Ottawa Alliance, 1613–1763." PhD diss., University of Toronto, 1995.

Newman, Andrew. *Allegories of Encounter: Colonial Literacy and Indian Captivity.* Chapel Hill: University of North Carolina Press, 2019.

Noel, Jan. *Along a River: The First French-Canadian Women.* Toronto: University of Toronto Press, 2013.

———. "'Nagging Wife' Revisited: Women and the Fur Trade in New France." *French Colonial History* 7 (2006).

Norall, Frank. *Bourgmont, Explorer of the Missouri, 1698–1725.* Lincoln: University of Nebraska Press, 1988.

O'Neill, Charles E. "Gravier, Jacques." In *Dictionary of Canadian Biography,* vol. 2. Toronto: University of Toronto/Université Laval, 2003–.

Original Journals of the Lewis and Clark Expedition. Vol. 7. Edited by Reuben Gold Thwaites. New York: Dodd, Mead and Co., 1905.

Palmer, Vera. "The Devil in the Details: Controverting an American Indian Conversion Narrative." In *Theorizing Native Studies,* edited by Audra Simpson and Andrea Smith. Durham, NC: Duke University Press, 2014.

Parezo, Nancy J., and Angelina R. Jones, "What's in a Name: The 1940s-1950s 'Squaw Dress,'" *American Indian Quarterly* 33, no. 3 (Summer 2009).

The Papers of Col. Henry Bouquet. Series 21642, 21643, 21646, 21647, 21648, 21649. Edited by Sylvester K. Stevens and Donald H. Kent. Harrisburg: Pennsylvania Historical Commission, 1941–1942.

The Papers of Sir William Johnson. Vols. 4, 10, 12. Edited by Milton W. Hamilton. Albany: University of the State of New York, 1925, 1951, 1957.

Parker, Arthur C. *The Life of General Ely S. Parker.* Buffalo, NY: Buffalo Historical Society, 1919.

———. *Seneca Myths and Folk Tales.* Lincoln: University of Nebraska Press, 1989.

Parkins, Almon Ernest. *The Historical Geography of Detroit.* Lansing: Michigan Historical Commission, 1918.

Parkman, Francis. *The Conspiracy of Pontiac and the Indian War after the Conquest of Canada.* 6th ed. Vol. 1. Boston: Little, Brown and Co., 1870.

Parmenter, Jon. "Isabel Montour: Cultural Broker on the Eighteenth-Century Frontiers of New York and Pennsylvania." In *The Human Tradition in Colonial America,* edited by Ian K. Steele and Nancy Rhoden. Wilmington, DE: Scholarly Resources Press, 1999.

Pelletier, Jean-Guy. "Coulon de Villiers, Nicolas-Antoine (1683–1733)." In *Dictionary of Canadian Biography,* vol. 2. Toronto: University of Toronto/Université Laval, 2003–.

Perrault, Claude. "Cuillerier, René." In *Dictionary of Canadian Biography,* vol. 2. Toronto: University of Toronto/Université Laval, 2003–.

Perry, Ruth. "Colonizing the Breast: Sexuality and Maternity in Eighteenth-Century England." In *Forbidden History: The State, Society, and the Regulation of Sexuality in Modern Europe,* edited by John C. Fout. Chicago: University of Chicago Press, 1990.

Philips, Lisa, and Allan K. McDougall. "Shifting Boundaries and the Baldoon Mysteries." In *Lines Drawn upon the Water: First Nations and the Great Lakes Borders and Borderlands,* edited by Karl S. Hele. Waterloo, ON: Wilfrid University Press, 2008.

Podruchny, Carolyn. "Werewolves and Windigos: Narratives of Cannibal Monsters in French-Canadian Voyageur Oral Tradition." *Ethnohistory* 51, no. 4 (2004).

Pokagon, Simon. *Ogimawkwe Mitigwaki (Queen of the Woods): A Novel.* East Lansing: Michigan State University Press, 2011.

Pollock, Sheldon. "Cosmopolitan and Vernacular in History." *Public Culture* 12, no. 3 (2000).

Pothier, Bernard. "Le Moyne d'Iberville et d'Ardillières, Pierre." In *Dictionary of Canadian Biography,* vol. 2. Toronto: University of Toronto/Université Laval, 2003–.

Preston, David Lee. *The Texture of Contact: European and Indian Settler Communities on the Frontiers of Iroquoia, 1667–1783.* Lincoln: University of Nebraska Press, 2009.

Prévost, Robert. *Portraits de familles pionnières.* Vol. 4. Montreal: Éditions Libre Expression, 1996.

Proceedings of the State Historical Society of Wisconsin. Edited by Reuben Gold Thwaites. Madison: State Historical Society of Wisconsin, 1915.

Quesnel, Yves. "Nolan Lamarque, Charles." In *Dictionary of Canadian Biography,* vol. 3. Toronto: University of Toronto/Université Laval, 2003–.

Rapport de l'Archiviste de la Province de la Québec pour 1929–1930. Quebec: Rédempti Paradis, 1930.

"Relation de Soeur Cuillerier (1725–1747)." In Écrits du Canada français, vol. 42, edited by Ghislaine Legendre. Montreal, 1979.

Report of the Pioneer and Historical Society of the State of Michigan. Lansing, MI: Thorp and Godfrey, 1886.

Richter, Daniel. *The Ordeal of the Longhouse: The Peoples of the Iroquois League in the Era of European Colonization.* Chapel Hill: University of North Carolina Press, 1992.

Rifkin, Mark. *Manifesting America: The Imperial Construction of U.S. National Space.* New York: Oxford University Press, 2009.

Rollet, Catherine. "The Fight against Infant Mortality in the Past: An International Comparison." In *Infant and Child Mortality in the Past,* edited by Alain Bideau, Bertrand Desjardins, and Héctor Pérez Brignoli. Oxford: Oxford University Press, 1997.

Rushforth, Brett. *Bonds of Alliance: Indigenous and Atlantic Slaveries in New France.* Chapel Hill: University of North Carolina Press, 2012.

———. "Slavery, the Fox Wars, and the Limits of Alliance." *William and Mary Quarterly* 63, no. 1 (January 2006).

Sachs, Honor. *Home Rule: Households, Manhood and National Expansion on the Eighteenth-Century Kentucky Frontier.* New Haven, CT: Yale University Press, 2015.

Schoolcraft, Henry R. *Personal Memoirs of a Residence of Thirty Years with the Indian Tribes on the American Frontiers: With Brief Notices of Passing Events, Facts, and Opinions, A.D. 1812 to A.D. 1842.* Philadelphia: Lippincott, Grambo and Co., 1851.

Scott, James C. *Seeing Like a State: How Certain Schemes to Improve the Human Condition Have Failed.* New Haven, CT: Yale University Press, 1998.

Shoemaker, Nancy. *A Strange Likeness: Becoming Red and White in Eighteenth-Century North America.* New York: Oxford University Press, 2004.

Silvertsen, Barbara J. *Turtles, Wolves, and Bears: A Mohawk Family History.* Westminster, MD: Heritage Books, 1996.

Skarsten, M. O. *George Drouillard: Hunter and Interpreter for Lewis and Clark and Fur Trader, 1807–1810.* Glendale, CA: Arthur H. Clark Co., 1964.

Sleeper-Smith, Susan. "The Agrarian Village World of Indian Women in the Ohio Valley." In *Women in Early America,* edited by Thomas Foster. New York: New York University Press, 2015.

———. *Indian Women and French Men: Rethinking Cultural Encounter in the Western Great Lakes.* Amherst: University of Massachusetts Press, 2001.

———. *Indigenous Prosperity and American Conquest: Indian Women of the Ohio River Valley, 1690–1792.* Chapel Hill: University of North Carolina Press, 2018.

———. "Women, Kin, and Catholicism: New Perspectives on the Fur Trade." *Ethnohistory* 47, no. 2 (2000).

Sommerville, Suzanne Boivin. "'But I read it . . .': Who Is the Michel Bisaillon Who Married Madeleine Perrier dite Olivier on 11 Jan 1740 in Laprairie? and Did Pierre Bisaillon Father Children Baptized at Kaskaskia?" In *Le Détroit du Lac Érié, 1701–1710,* vol. 2, edited by Gail Moreau-DesHarnais, Diane Wolford Sheppard, and Suzanne Boivin Sommerville. Royal Oak, MI: French-Canadian Heritage Society of Michigan, 2016.

———. "Madame Montour (La Tichenet) and Étienne Veniard, Sieur de Bougmont, according to the 1707 Judgment of Pichon dit La Roze at Détroit: The Perils of Translation and Interpretation." In *Le Détroit du Lac Érié,* vol. 2, edited by Gail Moreau-DesHarnais, Diane Wolford Sheppard, and Suzanne Boivin Sommerville, 106–123. Royal Oak, MI: French-Canadian Heritage Society of Michigan, 2016.

———. "Who Was the Anonymous 1702 Wet Nurse for One of Lamothe Cadillac's Children? Additional Documentation for the Birth of a Cadillac Child at Fort Pontchartrain in 1702." *Michigan's Habitant Heritage* 26, no. 1 (2005).

Spear, Jennifer. "Colonial Intimacies: Legislating Sex in French Louisiana." *William and Mary Quarterly* 60, no. 1 (January 2003).

Standen, S. Dale. "'Personnes sans caractère': Private Merchants, Post Commanders and the Regulation of the Western Fur Trade, 1720–1745." In *De France en Nouvelle-France: Société fondatrice et société nouvelle,* edited by Hubert Watelet and Cornelius J. Jaenen. Ottawa: Les Presses de l'Université d'Ottawa, 1994.

Stevens, Paul L. "The Indian Diplomacy of Capt. Richard B. Lernoult, British Military Commandant of Detroit, 1774–1775." *Michigan Historical Review* 13, no. 1 (Spring 1987).

Stoler, Ann. "Tense and Tender Ties: The Politics of Comparison in North American History and (Post) Colonial Studies." *Journal of American History* 88, no. 3 (December 2001).

Stone, William L. *The Life and Times of Sir William Johnson, Bart.* Vol. 2. Albany, NY: J. Munsell, 1865.

Sturtevant, Andrew. "Jealous Neighbors: Rivalry and Alliance among the Native Communities of Detroit, 1701–1766." PhD diss., College of William and Mary, 2011.

———. "'Over the Lake': The Western Wendake in the American Revolution." In *From Huronia to Wendakes: Adversity, Migrations, and Resilience, 1650–1900,* edited by Thomas Peace and Kathryn Magee Labelle. Norman: University of Oklahoma Press, 2016.

Sugden, John. *Tecumseh: A Life.* New York: Henry Holt and Co., 1997.

Swagerty, William R. *The Indianization of Lewis and Clark.* Norman, OK: Arthur C. Clark Co., 2012.

Tanguay, Cyprien. *Dictionnaire généalogique des familles canadiennes depuis la fondation de la colonie jusqu'à nos jours.* Montreal: Eusèbe Senécal & Fils, 1890.

Teasdale, Guillaume. *Fruits of Perseverance: The French Presence in the Detroit River Region, 1701–1815.* Montreal & Kingston: McGill-Queen's University Press, 2019.

Thorne, Tanis C. "For the Good of Her People: Continuity and Change for Native Women of the Midwest, 1650–1850." In *Midwestern Women: Work, Community, and Leadership at the Crossroads,* edited by Lucy Eldersveld Murphy and Wendy Hamand Venet. Bloomington: Indiana University Press, 1997.

Toupin, Robert, ed. *Les écrits de Pierre Potier.* Ottawa: Les Presses de l'Université d'Ottawa, 1996.

Trouillot, Michel-Rolph. *Silencing the Past: Power and the Production of History.* Boston: Beacon Press, 1995.

Trowbridge, C. C. *Meearmeear Traditions.* Edited by Vernon Kinietz. 1823; reprint, Ann Arbor: University of Michigan Press, 1938.

Trudel, Marcel. *Dictionnaire des esclaves et de leurs propriétaires au Canada français.* LaSalle, QC: Éditions Hurtubise HMH Ltée., 1990.

———. *L'esclavage au Canada français: Histoire et conditions de l'esclavage.* Quebec: Les Presses Universitaires Laval, 1960.

Turnbull, Molly. "Speaking of Family: Constructing Relations in Algonquian English Discourse." In *Papers of the Twenty-Seventh Algonquian Conference,* edited by David H. Pentland. Winnipeg: University of Manitoba, 1996.

Tuttle, Leslie. *Conceiving the Old Regime: Pronatalism and the Politics of Reproduction in Early Modern France.* New York: Oxford University Press, 2010.

van Kirk, Sylvia. "From 'Marrying-in' to 'Marrying-out': Changing Patterns of Aboriginal/Non-Aboriginal Marriage in Colonial Canada." *Frontiers: A Journal of Women Studies* 23, no. 3 (2002).

———. *Many Tender Ties: Women in Fur Trade Society in Western Canada, 1670–1870.* Winnipeg: Watson & Dwyer, 1980.

Vidal, Cecile, and Gilles Havard. *Histoire de l'Amérique française.* Paris: Éditions Flammarion, 2003.

Warren, Stephen. *The Worlds the Shawnees Made: Migration and Violence in Early America.* Chapel Hill: University of North Carolina Press, 2014.

Warren, William W. *History of the Ojibway People.* 1885; reprint, St. Paul: Minneapolis Historical Society, 2008.

Weyhing, Richard. "'Gascon Exaggerations': The Rise of Antoine Laumet dit de Lamothe, Sieur de Cadillac, the Foundation of Colonial Detroit, and the Origins of the Fox Wars." In *French and Indians in the Heart of North America, 1630–1815,* edited by Robert Englebert and Guillaume Teasdale. East Lansing: Michigan State University Press, 2013.

———. "The Straits of Empire: French Colonial Detroit and the Origins of the Fox Wars." PhD diss., University of Chicago, 2012.

White, Bruce. "'Give Us a Little Milk': The Social and Cultural Meanings of Gift Giving in the Lake Superior Fur Trade." *Minnesota History* 48, no. 2 (Summer 1982).

White, Marian E. "Neutral and Wenro." In *Handbook of North American Indians,* vol. 15, *Northeast,* edited by Bruce G. Trigger. Washington, DC: Smithsonian Institution, 1978.

White, Richard. *The Middle Ground: Indians, Empires, and Republics in the Great Lakes Region, 1650–1815.* Cambridge: Cambridge University Press, 1991.

White, Sophie. *Wild Frenchmen and Frenchified Indians: Material Culture and Race in Colonial Louisiana.* Philadelphia: University of Pennsylvania Press, 2014.

Widder, Keith. *Beyond Pontiac's Shadow: Michilimackinac and the Anglo-Indian War of 1763.* East Lansing: Michigan State University Press, 2013.

Willig, Timothy D. *Restoring the Chain of Friendship: British Policy and the Indians of the Great Lakes, 1783–1815.* Lincoln: University of Nebraska Press, 2008.

Wilson, Kathleen. *The Island Race: Englishness, Empire and Gender in the Eighteenth Century.* New York: Routledge, 2003.

Winfield, Betty Houchin. "The Press Response to the Corps of Discovery: The Making of Heroes in an Egalitarian Age." *Journalism and Mass Communication Quarterly* 80, no. 4 (Winter 2003).

Witgen, Michael. *An Infinity of Nations: How the Native New World Shaped Early North America.* Philadelphia: University of Pennsylvania Press, 2012.

Zimmerman, Albright G. "Daniel Coxe and the New Mediterranean Sea Company." *Pennsylvania Magazine of History and Biography* 76, no. 1 (January 1952).

Zoltvany, Yves F. "Chabert de Joncaire, Louis-Thomas, Sononchiez." In *Dictionary of Canadian Biography,* vol. 2. Toronto: University of Toronto/Université Laval, 2003–.

———. "New France and the West, 1701–1713." *Canadian Historical Review* 46 (1965).

Index

Hay, Jehu, 157, 160, 230 (n. 41). *See also* Réaume, Marie Julie
Hay, Pierre Henry, 230 (n. 41). *See also* Réaume, Marie Julie
Hiawatha, 33
Hibou (Owl), 160–61, 163
Holmes, Robert (Ensign), 120–21, 143
Hudson Bay, xx, 6, 65, 86, 109; trade to, 51, 181, 211 (n. 63), 215 (n. 24). *See also* Compagnie du Nord; Fort Bourbon
Huron. *See* Wendat

I

Iberville, Pierre Le Moyne d,' 180, 234 (n. 10)
Illinois Country, xix, xxiii; annexation of, 107; British presence in, 141, 159; French presence in, 60–62, 67, 81–82, 86–89; in Pontiac's War, 122; smallpox outbreak, 109; trade links to, xxiii, 5–6, 20, 29, 67–70, 128; war in, 159. *See also* Illinois nations; Kaskaskia; Kiikaapoi; upper country
Illinois nations: alliances with, 60–61; diplomacy with, 14–15, 54, 67–77, 206 (n. 24); French presence among, 5, 133, 142, 203 (n. 41), 205 (n. 15), 205 (n. 20); marriage customs of, 218 (n. 48); trade with English, 72–73; women, 75–77. *See also* Illinois Country; Inoka; Kaskaskia; Kaskaskia (nation); Missouri (nation); Peoria (nation)
Illinois (state), 176
Indigenous nations: agricultural practices of, 31, 35; alliances with, xvii, 18, 30, 49, 60, 99; and the British, 51, 116, 126, 144–45, 153, 162; at Detroit, 26, 52, 56; diplomacy with, 12–13, 15, 38–39, 131, 160, 165–66, 207 (n. 34); and family networks, 20, 42, 48, 57, 74, 82–83, 89–90, 128–30, 134–35, 173–74; and gender, 36, 41, 164; territories of, xviii, 31, 169, 172; trade with, 5–6, 25, 29, 180; women of, 91, 105. *See also* Algonquian nations; Anishinaabe nations; Haudenosaunee; Illinois nations; Myaamia; Odawa; settlement; Shawnee; Wendat
Indigenous women: agency of, 4, 23–24, 75, 102–3, 143–44, 163, 173–74; and agriculture, 31–32; and captives, 202 (n. 37); in diplomacy, 104, 153–55, 163; imperial fears of, xxiii, 15, 39, 80, 115, 118–21; marriage to French men, xxi–xxii, 15–17, 68, 76, 84, 175, 207 (n. 35); and trade, 91, 126–27, 152–53; and war, 103–5. *See also* French-Indigenous family networks; Jigonsase; Wendat; women
Inoka, 10–11
Iowa, 158
Iroquoian nations. *See* Haudenosaunee

J

Jesuit Relations, 81, 210 (n. 59)
Jesuits: at Detroit, 129, 194 (n. 15), 200 (n. 8), 207 (n. 35); in Illinois Country, 71, 76; at Michilimackinac, 49–50, 68; missions, 210 (n. 59). *See also* Brébeuf, Jean de; Charest; Gravier, Jacques; LeJeune, Paul; Marest, Joseph-Jacques; Potier, Pierre; Vaillant
Jigonsase, 33–36, 82. *See also* Haudenosaunee
Johnson, John (Sir), 26

Pierre-Charles; La Marque, Marie-Anne;
Picoté de Belestre family (Marie-Anne)
Tonty, Henri, 5–6, 19, 68, 78, 81, 205 (n. 15).
See also La Forest, François Dauphin de
Toupin dit Dussault, Anne, 178. *See also*
Langlois, Jacques
treaties, xvii, xviii, 50, 68, 170. *See also* Great
Peace of Montreal
Treaty of Ryswick, 234 (n. 11)
Treaty of Utrecht, 86
Trottier dit DesRuisseaux family, 82,
87–88, 93, 133, 204 (n. 7); Alexis, 87, 133;
business of, 87–89; François Marie Picoté
de Belestre, 113; Joseph, 82, 87, 209 (n.
49); Julien, 87–89; Marguerite, Marie-
Anne, and Marie-Madeleine, 87–89;
Marguerite (Congrégation de Notre-
Dame), 93, 214 (n. 15); Marie Catherine,
41, 87, 113; Marie Catherine Godefroy,
133; Paul, 130; Pierre dit Desauniers,
87, 206 (n. 26). *See also* Cuillerier,
René; Cuillerier dit Beaubien family;
Desauniers sisters; Roy, Pierre
Trowbridge, Charles, 123–24, 149, 153, 228
(n. 16)
Trumbull, George, 165
Truteau family, Jean Baptiste, Laurent,
Jacques, Pierre, Joseph, François, 179
Turpin family, 62, 179–80; Alexandre, 180,
234 (n. 11), 235 (n. 12); Jean Baptiste,
100–103, 178, 179–80, 216 (n. 37); Louis,
100, 102, 216 (n. 35). *See also* Fafard
family: Marguerite (La Turpin)
Twichtwicks. *See* Myaamia

U

United States, xiv, xvii, xxiv; borders of, 185
(n. 23); Indigenous relations of, xviii,
62, 164, 169; western expansion of, xx,
167–71, 174. *See also* American Revolution
Upper Canada, 172
upper country, xxiv; alliances in, 18, 49–53,
60, 144, 162; British presence in, 39, 78,
114, 119, 143, 150–51, 160–62, 165; family
networks in, 42–43, 62–63, 74–75, 79–80,
128–29, 138; French presence in, 2–4, 6,
18–19, 21, 30, 98; Indigenous presence in,
26–27, 29, 31, 49, 149–50, 153; settlement
in, 15, 35; trade in, 13–14, 20, 30, 68,
87–89, 99, 172; war in, 28, 47–48, 62, 145,
159. *See also* Detroit; Fox Wars; fur trade;
Illinois Country; Ohio Valley; Pontiac's
War; settlement
Ursulines, 93

V

Vaillant (Jesuit), 74, 76
Vaudreuil, Louis-Philippe de Rigaud de:
authority of, 13–14, 16, 20, 69–70, 84,
90, 104; Detroit policy, 54, 60, 201 (n.
21); diplomacy of, 37–38, 73, 77, 82–83,
104–7, 205 (n. 15), 207 (n. 34); and the
Fox Wars, 50–53; and French-Indigenous
marriage, 17, 76. *See also* French state;
Onontio
Versailles, 4–5, 40. *See also* French state
Viele, Arnout Cornelissen, 29
Vien, Michel, 100–101
Viennay-Pachot, François, 97. *See also*
Juchereau, Charlotte-Françoise
(Isacheran Pachot)